REINVENTING THE WAREHOUSE

REINVENTING
the WAREHOUSE

World Class Distribution Logistics

ROY L. HARMON

Foreword by William C. Copacino

THE FREE PRESS

NEW YORK   LONDON   TORONTO   SYDNEY   TOKYO   SINGAPORE

THE FREE PRESS
A Division of Simon & Schuster Inc.
1230 Avenue of the Americas
New York, N.Y. 10020

Manufactured in the United States of America

2 3 4 5 6 7 8 9 10

Library of Congress Cataloging-in-Publication Data

Harmon, Roy L.
    Reinventing the warehouse: world class distribution logistics /
Roy L. Harmon; foreword by William C. Copacino.
        p.   cm.
    Includes bibliography and index.
    ISBN 0–02–913863–9
    1. Warehouses—Management. 2. Business logistics. I. Title.
HF5485.H33   1993
658.7′85—dc20   92–37644
                                                              CIP

DEDICATED, WITH LOVE, TO MARGARETE, MY WIFE,
WHO IS THE LIGHT OF MY LIFE.

(Even if she does not permit
me to organize closets,
cabinets, and pantry for
utmost space utilization
and productivity.)

Contents

Foreword

Fresh thinking and new, truly innovative ideas are uncommon in most areas of endeavor, particularly in the area of business management. New thinking—which leads to quantum improvements in the performance of a business system—requires two characteristics: *vision* and the *courage* to challenge the status quo. Even singly, each of these characteristics occurs rarely at best; as a set they are far less common. True vision requires the ability to "think out-of-the-box"—to free oneself from the self-imposed constraints that force one to look at a problem from a single perspective. The new, unconstrained view encourages one to conceive solutions that were previously unthinkable and to release an ingenuity and a creativity that have the power to revolutionize a field. This vision, or what I like to call dreams, is beyond strategy. The dreams redefine the possible; strategies outline how to achieve the dreams—the best possible for your business.

Vision in itself, however, is not enough to create quantum improvements in the performance of a business system. It must be accompanied by the courage to challenge the status quo, to suggest that leading thinking in the field might be wrong, and to risk being ridiculed if one's "nontraditional" thinking is not accepted. The world turned out not to be flat, but Christopher Columbus was ridiculed for suggesting it was round; Fulton's Folly, the steamboat, became a dramatically important innovation, obsoleting sailing ships; and Roy Harmon and others challenged traditional manufacturing practices for a decade before their concepts of manufacturing cells, quick changeovers, quality at the source, and worker empowerment became the foundation of accepted world class manufacturing principles.

In *Reinventing the Warehouse*, Roy Harmon again challenges many of the tenets of traditional logistics and warehousing management. As noted in the text, I do not accept all of the principles of "reinvented logistics" suggested in this book.[1] However, I do encourage readers to keep an open mind—to pause before rejecting a concept; to think about how an approach can be made to work rather than why it will fail; and to challenge yourselves to "think out-of-the-box" and envision how Roy Harmon's less traditional thoughts can be applied in your company's operating environment.

The time for new thinking in logistics management is now! In company after company and industry after industry, executives are being pressured to deliver "more for less"—to improve customer service, but at a lower cost. Customers are demanding heightened service performance, that is, shorter lead times, more frequent deliveries, no stock-outs, and delivery within specified time windows, as well as value-added services such as bar-coding of secondary containers, shrink-wrapping of pallets, use of inner packs, display building, drop shipment, and even direct-store delivery. And these customers are expecting this heightened service at the same or even lower cost. The pressure on the logistics manager to improve both cost and service performance is coming not only from our customers but also from our own company's top management. Accustomed to continuously improving logistics cost performance through much of the 1980s and sensitized to the heightened competitive importance of superior delivery performance, top management is demanding more from its logistics function. To meet these new demands, logistics and transportation managers cannot just fine-tune old ways of doing business. They must restructure the basic logistics approach to achieve the quantum leaps of performance being demanded of them.

Companies have already responded to this need to deliver more for less through a number of initiatives:

Fewer Warehouses. Companies are consolidating the number of warehouses they use to serve their markets. In the mid-1980s it was not unusual for a company to have eight to twelve warehouses to serve the United States. Today many companies have consolidated their networks down to three to six warehouses and are using transportation carriers that can provide fast and more reliable service. I anticipate that in the next five years almost all companies will serve their current market areas with still fewer warehouses.

Channel Integration. Leading-edge companies have gone far be-

---

[1] *Author's note:* If *anyone* agreed with *every* new concept in this book it would be a major disappointment. A book containing material so bland that its contents would be universally acceptable would indeed be dull!—RLH.

yond the integrated logistics concept. For many, the quantum improvements in logistics performance are no longer available from fine-tuning their own logistics systems but now must come from integrating them with those of their suppliers and customers. This channel integration has been referred to as "intercorporate logistics," "quick response," and "supply chain management." Call it what you like, the leading firms in the 1990s will be managing inventory, warehousing, and transportation across corporate boundaries. One company's distribution system is another company's supply system. It makes no sense for a manufacturer and a distributor to hold inventory in adjacent warehouses. If they are to be able to manage the inventory jointly, they must first improve the performance of the entire logistics channel. The same lesson applies to coordinating the transportation activities of all companies throughout the channel. Similarly, if a manufacturer knows the real usage or takeaway rate at the retail level and the channel inventories, he will be able to do a better forecasting and production planning job. The challenge in developing integrated channel management depends on building cooperation and trust among channel partners. This is often a substantial challenge, but companies that can find ways to build these channel partnerships will enjoy both operational and strategic advantages.

Third-Party Services. Very slowly, third-party logistics services are gaining ground. Although still only in the embryonic stage, third-party logistics services will expand rapidly in the 1990s. They are gradually becoming a more acceptable option for shippers, and by the close of the decade they are likely to be the option of choice. Also, the range of activities performed by third parties is expanding beyond warehousing and transportation to include broader logistics functions.

Expanded Management Information Systems Role. Logistics is becoming more information-intensive. Companies cannot be leading-edge logistics players without first-class information systems. Clearly this requirement will continue through the 1990s. Information will continue to be substituted for assets (inventory, transportation, warehousing), and the winning companies will be those with source data capture, real-time information access and update, leading-edge applications and capabilities, and advanced decision support systems for logistics planning, transportation management, material management, and warehousing.

Total Quality. Leading companies are bringing a quality philosophy to the logistics function. The concepts of doing it right the first time, understanding the full costs of poor quality in logistics, and striving for continuous improvements are gaining ground and are the hallmarks of the top performers.

Reinventing the Warehouse suggests ways to create additional economic value (for our companies and for our countries) through "new thinking" in logistics. Some parts of the book challenge our prescribed ways of thinking about logistics and suggest fresh concepts for consideration. Other parts encourage faster progress and implementation of what I would describe as traditional logistics concepts. On the whole, the book is provocative and thought-provoking. I imagine it will be regarded as off-base in some regards by many traditionalists. However, I encourage you to think twice before rejecting ideas that challenge your base assumptions. New paradigms are uncomfortable to some but can lead to quantum improvements in performance. Remember, the Swiss watchmakers rejected the electronic timepiece, never en*vision*ing how this innovation would reinvent their market.

This book challenges us to improve and to push ourselves to a new level of performance. It is valuable reading for logisticians, operations managers, and executives concerned with achieving more for less—superior customer service performance at lower cost. I encourage the reader to read and consider carefully the thought-provoking approaches proposed in *Reinventing the Warehouse: World Class Distribution Logistics.*

WILLIAM C. COPACINO
Managing Partner, Strategic
Services-Northeast
Andersen Consulting
New York

Preface

Reader be warned! This book is not for fainthearted, business-as-usual managers and executives. Rather, it is intended for the bold, innovative movers and shakers who are unwilling to delay radical improvements or be bound to past practices. They are ready to break with tradition and join the ranks of leading-edge companies, charging into the braver new world of high-quality, lightning-fast, low-cost customer service. Further, a select few will accept an epochal future vision, enhance it, and begin the titanic struggle to make the future start tomorrow.

The book addresses the design of the new-generation warehouses and transport and logistics systems that raise companies to twenty-first-century world class stature. Farsighted managements will jump at the opportunity to begin not only to envision clusters of small, focused supplier and distribution facilities in regional market areas but also to make the vision a reality for their companies. Modern clusters will virtually eliminate the thousands of miles that products and their components travel from raw material source locations, through production, and into the hands of their customers. Radical changes will lead to drastic reductions in the size and quantity of trucks on highways and will increase the volume of more economical rail and water transport and fast-moving smaller trucks plying local clusters of producers and distributors. Dense, heavyweight shipments of raw materials to distant factories and markets will displace costly, lightweight, low-density component and product shipments previously produced in the vicinity of the raw material source. Perspective readers will discover that the "warehouse of the future" is already largely at hand.

A minority of the author's colleagues have expressed reservations about his often irreverent treatment of "motherhood" issues, preferring to avoid controversial stances on issues that are "generally accepted" and to say nothing that will jar the sensibilities of large numbers of logistics management personnel. They fear that armies of these people will put down the book as soon as they see their beliefs challenged. Nevertheless, the author chooses to take the risk, for he places great value on the intelligence of the reader and expects most to forge ahead, having been challenged to accept or at least consider an alternative viewpoint before discarding it. The author is not alone in his irreverent treatment of some widely praised and practiced palliatives for productivity. For example, Devanna and Tichy (spurred by Peters and Waterman's *In Search of Excellence*),[2] in writing about companies that have documented their set of values, have said:

> They return, as it were, from the mountain and ask those responsible for internal communication to tighten up the language and print a sufficient number of impressive brochures to distribute to all of the employees so they will know what the company's values are. And so ends the "excellence" program. For companies tempted to write their own 10 commandments, it is useful to remember what happened when Moses came down from the mountain with the original tablets of stone. His people were involved in an orgy and were not terribly receptive to the new rules and values.[3]

Unfortunately, the present author, not as polished and humorous as Devanna and Tichy, stands the risk of offending the reader rather than amusing and bemusing him.

Whether or not readers agree or disagree with the author is of less importance than jolting their thoughts into new channels, because only by way of challenging accepted practices will magnificent, revolutionary changes come to be. A few poor souls, unable to discard the notions with which they disagree while accepting those they approve, will undoubtedly reject the author's offerings out of hand. This lost audience is mourned. Fortunately, however, the mover and shakers of the logistics and production worlds are unlikely to fall into this category.

HOW TO USE THE BOOK

Warehousing and distribution logistics are topics that should be of interest not only to those directly involved in logistics management and warehouse operation but also to producers, retail businesses,

---

[2] Thomas J. Peters and Robert H. Waterman, *In Search of Excellence: Lessons from America's Best Run Companies* (New York: Warner Books, 1984).
[3] Mary Anne Devanna and Noel M. Tichy, *The Transformational Leader* (New York: Wiley, 1986), pp. 115–16.

and service organizations. After all, many of the principles of superior warehouse operations and inventory management are common to any storage facility, whether the facility stocks materials and components for production, components for service repair, retail store merchandise products, or office supplies. Therefore, the author has intended the material to be of interest to all the types of businesses as depicted in Exhibit P–1: retail outlets, distributors, factories and vendors that supply distributors and retail outlets, and the vendors that supply the producer factories.

Although many of the concepts and equipment applicable to one type of warehouse or business are universally applicable, some (notably completely automated storage and retrieval systems) are impossible to imagine in all conceivable environments. The first six chapters of the book describe generally applicable (but not universally applicable), superior operations and systems concepts. The author relies on the experience and intelligence of the reader either to sort out the messages that do not apply to his business or to mold some of the ideas to fit his company's needs. Chapter 7 describes superior operations in specific environments, such as retail warehousing and logistics, service parts warehousing, and distribution and production materials and component storage. That chapter overlaps with topics addressed in a more general vein in earlier chapters. The author has viewed this overlap and the early gener-

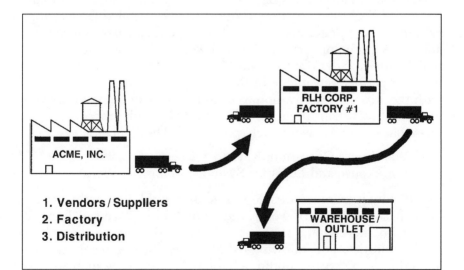

EXHIBIT P–1

Three Logistics Segments

alization as necessary in order to keep the book as compact as possible while still highlighting a few specific business environments. Chapter 8 will have less widespread appeal to those action-oriented executives and managers interested in making things happen *now*. Social, economic, and political issues that may take decades or even centuries to resolve are the main topics of this chapter. However, once these issues are resolved, the benefits to mankind will be enormous! Accordingly, Chapter 8 will be most appreciated by those with vision—movers-shakers who will view the vision as something on which to go to work immediately.

The organization of this book is structured to serve best the purposes of the various individuals in a typical warehouse, distribution organization, or factory storeroom, including those responsible for strategic direction and for improvement projects. The following chapters address topics of primary importance to executive management:

1. Management Perspective: Goldmine of Opportunities
2. A Logistics Network Vision
3. Future Vision: Warehouse and Logistics Master Plan
5. Future Vision: Warehouse and Logistics Systems
9. Conclusion

In addition, executives should read the executive ("zinger") checklists, the first subsections of most chapters. Each zinger list highlights many of the most important messages detailed later in that chapter. The zingers are intended to be management checklists, since they pinpoint some of the vital weapons in the arsenals with which superior distributors, warehouses, and manufacturers can win competitive advantage in the twenty-first century. Executives with the strongest motivation to become superior competitors will want to direct their attention to additional, vitally important subjects that have not been widely published. These include:

4. Warehouse Operation: Keys to Success
6. Warehouse and Logistics Systems: Making It Work

Individuals from various departments should ultimately also review these chapters. However, they may find it more satisfying to start with the chapter(s) that relate most directly to their daily responsibilities. The following list identifies the organizations that should find the corresponding chapter(s) of primary interest. Executives, managers, and supervisors in the organizations indicated should become thoroughly familiar with these subjects. They should also encourage their employees and unions to assimilate the messages and help them get started on improvements. Achieving or continuing superior competitor status depends on making quantum improvements. Thus, everyone needs not only to "buy in" to the new methods but also to march in the new direction.

Chapter	Title	Organization
3.	Future Vision: Warehouse and Logistics Master Plan	Operations
4.	Warehouse Operation: Keys to Success	Operations
5.	Future Vision: Warehouse and Logistics Systems	Systems & Data Processing and Inventory Management
6.	Warehouse and Logistics Systems: Making It Work	Systems & Data Processing and Inventory Management
7.	Industry Applications	Industry Personnel

Finally, many executives and managers want testimony that the techniques described in this and other books have worked in their countries. The author's previous two books included appendixes, "The Achievers" and "The New Achievers," which identify numerous companies, internationally, in which Andersen Consulting—the firm to which he is an exclusive consultant—played a major role in achieving results. Their achievements, expressed in percentages of improvement, are documented in the appendixes. This book includes a similar "Achievers Appendix" that highlights two types of achievers. The first lists warehousing and distribution achievers, and the second, additional manufacturing companies are not listed in the earlier works.

The author's previous books are frequently footnoted in *this* book as sources of definitions and background for subject matter not covered herein. Appendix 2 minimizes the clutter that numerous detailed footnote references to these two sources might cause by centralizing the cross-references. Footnotes referencing *Reinventing the Factory* and *Reinventing the Factory II* will direct the reader to Appendix 2. Readers reading only a few chapters of *this* book may wish first to read related portions of the prior books for important background material. Appendix 2 is organized to facilitate cross-referencing between the books, based on the organization of the chapters in *this* book.

ACKNOWLEDGMENTS

In his nearly four-decade career, the author has been focused primarily on the front end of the logistics network (producers and their vendors), with lesser (although significant) involvement in the tail end (product warehousing and distribution). Accordingly, in line with his belief that writers and consultants need to walk several miles in the shoes of their readers and clients, the author was heavily dependent on his logistics colleagues' contributions to, and review of, the manuscript. Chief among the Andersen Consulting contributors were William C. Copacino, New York; Joseph A. Martha, Cleveland; and Gary C. Garrett, Chicago. Leroy D. Peterson, my longtime colleague and friend, also reviewed the manuscript, contributing substantive commentary and ideas. Other longtime practitioners and pioneers in designing operations and systems of the new, superior ilk, however, are among the most important contributors. Their successful implementation of some of the author's wildest sounding ideas has proved, over and over, that these things work! Among the early pioneers who stand out are William G. Stoddard, New York; Ernesto J. Kuperman, Buenos Aires; François Jaquenoud, Lyon; Raul E. Alvarado, Torrance; Roger E. Dunham, Atlanta; and Edward T. Kennedy, San Francisco. Gregory A. Lee, a graphic artist in Andersen Consulting's Chicago office, coordinated the preparation of the book's exhibits, as he did for its predecessors in the "Reinventing" series, helping the author to demonstrate an important business communication truism—that a picture is worth (at least) a thousand words. Molly Kinnucan of Andersen Consulting's world headquarters marketing staff edited the manuscript. Although the list of contributing colleagues could go on and on, and although some may feel they have been overlooked, this is certainly not the case. Practical space considerations are responsible for limiting the list, but the real list will always live in the author's mind and heart.

The author fervently hopes the reader will find this book entertaining. Far more important, if he has met his objectives, readers will find at least one idea with applicability to their own businesses. Of equal importance is that readers consider alternatives to age-old business practices and operations as a prerequisite for discovering their own visions of the future. Undoubtedly, others will have more exciting visionary contributions, and the author would enjoy hearing (via the Andersen Consulting Chicago office) these ideas.

Good luck on your journey into the world of the twenty-first century!

ROY L. HARMON

CHAPTER 1

Management Perspective

Goldmine of Opportunities

Visionary executives have the power to rationalize costs and lead times in their logistics networks radically. In fact, pursuit of gargantuan improvements in the production pipeline has become a way of life for all major producers. Reduction goals of 90 percent of pipeline inventories and lead times are now relatively common, especially among the most dynamic industry leaders. Nor must customer service, product value, or quality of life be sacrificed on the altar of productivity. In fact, quite the contrary is true! Magnificent strides in adopting the best productivity methods has proved that magnificent strides can be made simultaneously in productivity improvement and in customer and employee benefits, and vice-versa. Goal-setting is a vital milestone on the trip into the twenty-first-century logistics world. Executive management, determined to excel and willing to support every action required to turn goals into self-fulfilling prophecies, must initially set new goals far above those of the past. Recent laudable achievements fall in the range of the following improvement percentages.

- 50% customer service lead time
- 50% space occupied by warehouse and distribution facilities
- 25% personnel costs

- 50% inventory investment in the logistics and production pipelines
- 25% logistics transaction (receipts and issues, for example) processing costs
- 75% better inventory record accuracy
- 75% fewer damaged and defective goods

Unfortunately, hampered by seemingly insurmountable barriers such as demand seasonality, inaccurate forecasts, and vendors convinced that they must have long lead times, progress in *overall* distribution improvement has been less dynamic than in the production operation logistics network. Dogmatic acceptance of the conditions that dictate modes of operation only perpetuates inefficient operations, the costs of which are passed on to the consumer.

Lest North Americans unduly chastise themselves for not having previously seen such mammoth opportunities, they should remember that their distribution and retail operations are still the best in the world, far surpassing those of the Japanese and Europeans, for example, in terms of distribution costs added to consumer prices.[1] Nor should countries lagging behind North America be discouraged that their starting point is behind that of the American model. Their improvement potential is for that reason all the greater.

The keys to success in logistics management are no different from those already found in the production arena. It is vital to understand that no single magic bullets (quality programs or employee empowerment, for example) can transform a logistics network from merely state-of-the-art system to truly superior status. Hard work and attention to myriad details cannot be avoided. In fact, the siren song of employee involvement has led some executives and managers to believe that everyone else in the company will do everything necessary. Nothing could be farther from reality. Mike Budd, President of the Northridge Manufacturing Group of Harman International Industries, Inc., has said that he appreciates the need for employee empowerment but also believes it necessary to find a perfect balance between the consensus of small groups and dictatorial management. The author concurs. It is folly for management to abdicate its responsibility for knowing what is most

---

[1] The Hickmans write: "In much of the world, distribution systems tend to be far more complex than in the United States, due partly to capital restraints and partly to historical factors". Thomas K. Hickman and William M. Hickman, Jr., *Global Purchasing: How to Buy Goods and Services in Foreign Markets* (Homewood, IL: Business One Irwin, 1992), p. 49.

important for the company and leading its march into the future. No army advance should be permitted to become an uncontrolled, undirected, fragmented, multidirectional movement. This, however, would be the consequence of empowering each platoon to decide its own direction! The result would be chaotic. No less is true of a company's assault on progress barriers.

In lieu of magic bullets, there is a finite list of the components of a superior logistics network. The first milestone on the journey to superior status is the successful formulation of a vision of future logistics. The vision will guide preparation of route maps for the sundry activities necessary to achieve it. That there is a crying need for improvement is not in doubt, for, as Duncan wrote, "To a great extent, the very fate of humanity depends on people's ability to effectively manage resources, time and energy—all of which seems in too short supply."[2]

EXECUTIVE SUMMARY: KICKING SACRED COWS

Reader beware! The author delights in kicking everyone's sacred cows. In many cases, the cow-kicking shock treatment is tongue-in-cheek, intended to shock the executive-timber mover-shakers into challenging the dogma of the near and distant past by opening splendid new vistas of opportunity to their fertile minds. The author has no corner on vision or imagination. Most executives will be able to cast apocalyptic predictions of future logistics that are far superior to those of the author. However, to do so requires a mindset in which sacred cows are not permitted to be barriers to progress.

Often the author purposely ignores some logistics environments that occur in less than 100 percent of the various types of logistics businesses. It is easy to do so, in light of the extreme number of products moving through the distribution and production channels. He does not attempt to qualify every strong position with a face-saving statement that the concept might not apply in such-and-such a situation. The purpose here is to avoid the somewhat wishy-washy approach of saying that there are no absolutes, that every single element of distribution operations and systems is subject to a variety of approaches, or that there is always an extremely complex network of circumstances which, considered jointly, determines the "optimum" solution. It is no accident that the author's absolute suggestions are often based on a simplistic view of the

[2] W. Jack Duncan, *Great Ideas in Management* (San Francisco: Jossey-Bass, 1990), p. 244.

world of distribution logistics. Contrary to some authorities on simple and complex problems and environments,[3] the author, like Batten, views anything held to be complex to be simply a large collection of simple elements.[4] The daily challenge at which all superior executives are (and must be) adept is reducing complex issues to their simple components, thus making simple solutions practical.

In many other cases the author strongly believes in seemingly impossible new scenarios that will be completely unrealistic in the eyes of many. Perhaps many have strong, valid reasons for their opposing beliefs, based on unique aspects of their own unique business environments, which the author may not have experienced. The author has great respect for the wisdom of his readers. Based on their own environments, most will be able to apply their own judgments as to which sacred cows are valid and which are not. Others of lesser flexibility might be inclined to toss out the baby with the bath water, rejecting any notion of deviation from existing dogma, and therefore ignoring the entire book's body of work. It is to be hoped that the tide of change will eventually lead those inflexible few to believe in the malleability of our environments. For only through the kind of major metamorphosis that transforms and eliminates environmental restrictions can epic breakthroughs be expected. Thus, the reality of the future vision depends on the executive's commitment to it and his willingness to do his own cow-kicking. True executives (leaders and cow-kickers) are easy to distinguish from managers. As Gardner writes, "Leaders and leader/managers distinguish themselves from the general run of managers—They think longer term—beyond the day's crisis, beyond the quarterly report, *beyond the horizon.*"[5]

Vision is the precursor of business strategy. Attaining the far-reaching limits of opportunity requires that the vision embody fulfillment of seemingly impossible dreams.

---

[3] Kotter, for one, stresses the complexity of today's business environment. He writes: "But simple conditions are not the norm any more. Complexity is the norm." John P. Kotter, *The Leadership Factor* (New York: Free Press, 1988), p. 28.

[4] Joe Batten has some extremely valuable words on the subject of complexity versus simplicity: "We settle for second best, at best, when we settle for the complex answer. The tough-minded leader pulls team members forward in restless search of *simple, tough* answers rather than *complex, easy* answers. Settling for the complex is too easy." Elsewhere he writes: "We must somehow blast the notion that sophistication requires greater intellect and commitment than mastering the basic truths needed to arrive at lean, clean and clear solutions." Joe D. Batten, *Tough-Minded Leadership* (New York: AMACOM, 1989), pp. 89, 164.

[5] John W. Gardner, *On Leadership* (New York: Free Press, 1990), p. 4.

A LOGISTICS VISION

Every business needs a farsighted vision of its operations, facilities, equipment, and products extending decades and even centuries into the future. As Kotter says: "With no vision and strategy to provide constraints around the planning process or to guide it, every eventuality deserves a plan. Under these circumstances, contingency planning can go on forever—without ever providing a clear sense of direction that firms so desperately need today."[6] No company is exempt from the myopia that tends to cast its future vision in terms of the present and past environment and only recent trends. Still, all businesses operate with myriad inefficiencies based on roadblocks that their markets and suppliers, and their own organizations and facilities, place in the way of traffic on the superhighway to superior operations, services, and products. Forming a logistics vision requires a unique frame of mind. Executives must hypothesize numerous seemingly impossible scenarios to be able to begin to see their ideal business emerge from the mists that past experience has placed between them and the utopian situation that will eventually predominate. Here is a sampling of just a few of these impossible scenarios:

1. Suppliers will cut their response time drastically and will deliver perfect quality, precisely on schedule.
2. Customers at all levels of the logistics network will routinely share reasonably accurate short- and intermediate-term projections of their needs (schedule) with their suppliers via electronic data interchange. They will update the information as quickly as changes become necessary. This will radically reduce wild and unexpected demand swings.
3. Seasonal peaks and those within a week or month will be radically reduced since to do so is in the economic interest of everyone in the production, distribution, and consumer supply and demand chain.
4. Rote business practices and government-imposed reporting requirements that drown businesses in a veritable ocean of costly paperwork and systems can and will be replaced by practical, low-cost, fail-safe methods for achieving the same ends.

One factor, more than any other, will radically change the logistics mission for the better. This factor is the blossoming of produc-

[6] John P. Kotter, *A Force for Change: How Leadership Differs From Management* (New York: Free Press, 1990), p. 39.

tion facility clusters in the center of regional market areas. The present outmoded logistics model primarily transports materials, components, and finished products from their production sources to market. Since the sources are often hundreds of miles from their markets, the model demands significant expenditures in transport and logistics facilities. State-of-the-art producers already know that better modes of transportation and warehousing are only temporary patches on a defective industrial infrastructure. They have seen persistent notions of economies of scale lead many companies to build giant single-location production facilities, remote from many suppliers and from large segments of regional, national, and international markets. The best suppliers, however, have seen that the break-even point for production facilities can be far less than dreamed.[7] Therefore, building small, focused production facilities in the midst of market concentrations, thus reducing transportation and warehousing facilities between producers and their markets, is entirely practical. My colleague Leroy Peterson reminded me, at this juncture, to mention again the absurdity of multiplant producers' far-flung networks of production facilities.[8] Many such companies' networks permit materials and components to crisscross continents and oceans, putting thousands of transport miles into final products' costs even before the cost of transportation to market is incurred. Slashing these exorbitant logistics costs in the supply network is every bit as important as in distribution.

Although the exact same economies apply, few producers have expanded their production supply visions and strategies to encompass the scenario of suppliers (vendors *and* each supplier's own factory network) who *also* build new facilities in the vicinity of their regional factories. As these visionary dreams increasingly become reality, vast numbers of trucks will disappear from the highways, and ships in the world's sea lanes will be reduced to those carrying primary raw materials, fuels, and agricultural products, for there is no enduring, economically justifiable rationale for any country or regional groups of countries to import manufactured goods. The author has seen that identical small, focused factories can produce with equal productivity in any two countries of the

[7] Drucker put it this way: "But perhaps equally important, we have learned in the last thirty years how to manage the small and medium-size enterprise—to the point that the advantages of smaller size, for example, ease of communications and nearness to market and customer, increasingly outweigh what has been forbidding management limitations." Peter F. Drucker, *The Frontiers of Management: Where Tomorrow's Decisions Are Being Shaped Today* (New York: Harper & Row, 1986), p. 34.
[8] Multiplant clusters are discussed in much greater detail in the author's previous work. See Appendix 1.

world. The primary difference in their costs is not man-hours worked, but the cost of those hours. Therefore, as fast as living standards of all countries are raised to equivalent levels, people of newly developed nations will be able to afford the products they produce, and the need to export to richer countries will plunge.

New, world class distribution logistics will require management to adopt stringent new twenty-first-century ideals as the basis of their visionary targets for systems, transportation, and warehousing operations. The logistic network ideals to which every company should aspire include the following:

1. Real-time electronic transmission to suppliers of retail customer (or original equipment manufacturer) consumption as it occurs. The purpose of the transmission is to trigger lightning-fast replenishment of the inventory consumed. In ideal circumstances, the supplier will immediately pick the replenishment from stock and load it on a truck for same-day delivery.

2. Electronic transmission of projected customer demand as far into the future as the customer is able to provide. The inventory consumption transmission can only trigger replenishment picking and delivery if an earlier forecast transmission caused the supply network to make the item consumed available at the end of the pipeline of factories and warehouses. The demand-forecast transmission does not trigger immediate delivery. It controls the valves that meter the flow of material and goods through the pipeline. In other words, it must release production at the start of the pipeline, timed to meet actual consumption at the end of the pipeline.

3. In combination, the consumption and demand-forecast transmissions are also used to schedule and control transport from the pipeline head, a basic material producing plant, through all subsequent production stages in both vendor and company factories, through distribution facilities, and into the customer's inventory.

4. The utilization of truck fleets (and their drivers) in every stage of the pipeline will be optimized to the extent practical within the constraints of the end customer's projected demand. Thus, tractors *and* trailers will be virtually in perpetual motion. Delays while awaiting loading and unloading will be slashed to the bare minimum. Not only will outbound trucks be loaded to maximum practical weight

and cubic volume limits, but they will also return as fully loaded as practical. Consequently, the depreciation component of transportation cost and return on capital invested in tractors and trailers will be at near optimum levels.

5. The logistics network calendar of operations will be geared to maximum utilization of the facility and equipment investment, thus minimizing capital requirements. Operation of facilities and equipment seven days a week, twenty-four hours a day will not only reduce capital and operating costs but also will increase the speed of flow through the pipeline, lowering inventories throughout the network. Significant amounts of transport, loading, and unloading should be shifted to hours during which traffic is lightest. This will contribute to the reduction of time in transit.

6. Idle, immobile inventory in any stage of production or distribution wastes the company's available capital. Therefore, inventory not in motion must be reduced ceaselessly until near-continuous movement has been achieved. Supplier factories will deliver production directly to shipping docks where it will immediately be loaded on trucks for delivery to the next point in the production and distribution pipeline. The ultimate goal will be to eliminate the need for warehousing anywhere in the network, including between factories and between factories and customers.

7. Until the need for warehousing is eliminated, the logistics system will support and indeed encourage continuous reduction of warehouse inventories rather than perpetuate current levels. The factors that enable such a continuous reduction are as follows:

   a. Continuous reduction of lead time in the entire pipeline. This permits faster replenishment of consumption as it occurs.

   b. Elimination of setup and ordering costs at both ends of the supplier-customer pipeline.[9] Since these costs usually dictate an "economic" order quantity much greater than immediate needs, the resulting inventory is correspondingly higher than required to satisfy need. In the ideal environment of zero setup and ordering cost, one day's need should be delivered on the day (or even at the hour) required.

---

[9] See Appendix 2 for reference to information on setup cost reduction.

c. Improved transportation logistics. More frequent, smaller truckloads traveling between steps in the logistics network will reduce inventories at each point in the network while achieving a higher level of customer service.

SLS Sears Logistics Services, for one, has one of the most comprehensive visions of future logistics extant. Better still, for SLS the future is now! Its information network, transportation partners, and warehouses operate in a continuum, scheduling and delivering more than a-half-million truckloads through the pipelines that unite manufacturers, warehouses, and retailers in a robust, integrated network of superbly efficient business units. Until recently, SLS services were dedicated to Sears, Roebuck & Co.'s retail and catalog businesses. It has devoted decades and millions in developing logistics facilities and information and action systems, and it recently started a new program to move it into the ranks of the best in the world. State-of-the-art facilities, transportation management, and integrated systems of highest caliber have long been beyond the realm of practicality for businesses smaller than Sears. Recently, however, SLS has made provisions to offer the same advanced logistics services for enterprises outside the Sears family. Thus, the fruits of its massive ongoing investment and previous decades of development and operational experience are available to subscribers to these ultramodern logistics services and systems. For customers of SLS services, the costs of implementing and operating the turnkey package, therefore, are far lower than those of developing and operating their own systems, transport, and facilities. In fact, the cost to any business for developing and operating its own comparable capabilities are prohibitive, precluding all but the largest enterprises from doing so. And, aside from the issues of the initial cost outlay, it takes years, even decades, to achieve the same level of cost-effective performance.

VISIONS: FACTS OR IMPOSSIBLE DREAMS?

Vision formulation is an important, dynamic emerging business trend. Virtually every world class company's executives have brainstormed a vision of their company's, customers' and suppliers' future environment and modes of operations. The vision is the precursor to laying the planning groundwork, which prepares the business to move into the twenty-first century. That companies are taking a longer-term view is the good news. The bad news is that few have been able to divine the difference between a *true* vision and a mere strategy, in terms of the time frame. The author has previously defined the time frame of tactical initiatives as short-term (this year) and of strategies as longer-term (this decade).[10] The time frame of a vision must fall between very long-term and infinitely long-term to enable executives to cast off the imagination-imprisoning shackles of current realities. Strategies are the stuff of today's realities and limitations. Visions are the seemingly impossible dreams of limitless future opportunities. Incidentally, my colleague Bill Copacino provided invaluable insight into the mindset that inhibits many executives when they attempt to create a vision. While discussing one of the author's favorite hard-to-envision visions, Bill pointed out that some would ask where the data were to support (or to project) the likelihood of the vision coming to pass. The author's response was that true visions are not, and cannot be, merely projections of past history and trends.[11] Devanna and Tichy, in describing the reason executives and managers find it difficult to create revolutionary strategic plans (visions) write:

> Managers are not encouraged to fantasize and visualize. They are encouraged to use analytical financial, marketing and production skills—those supported by only left-brain activities. Even the strategic planning process in most organizations is a linear, left-brain activity that does not lead to a vision of a future state but rather results in an extrapolation of current market share, return on investment, or production figures several years into the future.[12]

For example, a few short years ago the Western world's strategy vis-à-vis the Soviet Union was one of containing the dangerous, threatening spread of communism by maintaining a military deterrent to aggression. Massive strategic military investments were therefore devoted to that end, and government investment in any alternative vision was nil. Strategic investment, by industry and government, in anticipation of commercial activity in the Soviet bloc was virtually nonexistent. If only a handful of influential visionaries had had the audacity to dream the impossible dream, that of the lightning-fast fall of the "evil empire," Western governments might have channeled at least some funding into programs for preparing to assist the newly democratized nations in making the

---

[10] See Appendix 2 for reference to information on strategies and tactics.

[11] In this regard the author shares Barker's viewpoint, which is "these rule changes are *not foreshadowed by trends.* These kinds of changes in the rules create new trends or dramatically alter trends already in place. That makes them very special." Joel Arthur Barker, *Future Edge: Discovering the New Paradigms of Success* (New York: William Morrow, 1992), p. 25. Emphasis in original.

[12] Mary Anne Devanna and Noel M. Tichy, *The Transformational Leader* (New York: Wiley, 1986), p. 138.

leap from centrally mismanaged economies to free, capitalistic markets, with a modicum of painful cycles of shortage and inflation. Industry, given the vision of new freedom, could have developed its own strategies for rushing in to participate in the modernization of the new consumer society. They would have researched the opportunities for joint endeavors with existing enterprises, studied the market potentials of the vast expanse of the former U.S.S.R. and its minions, and mastered the knowledge of cities with the transportation, logistics, and utility infrastructure necessary to support the development of new and improved enterprises. Such relatively low-cost preparation, with help from government intelligence agencies, would have prepared industry to unleash profit-motivated investment, benefiting not only the investors but also the enterprises and people of the new nations. The pains of transformation would have been minimized, and the rapid commercialization of new market-oriented production and logistics would have provided earlier profits for all.

The key to developing a true vision is to cast aside all constraints, emphasizing the "impossible" conditions that, once achieved, will permit changes that lead to quantum improvements in the productivity of production and distribution, for the benefit of the populace of the entire world.[13] For one small example of conditions that are "impossible" to change, consider the demand peaks and valleys caused by real and man-made seasonality, and those of day-of-week and time-of-month. Demand valleys put hordes of people in unemployment lines in off-season periods, crowd retail facilities to unbearable levels during peak sales days and seasons, and overflow warehouse capacity as production is amassed for seasonal peaks, while the same warehouses are vast, costly caverns of emptiness in periods following the time of peak demand. Thus, having an "impractical" vision of a world in which radical demand variations are virtually eliminated is a practical way to start to see that the huge benefits warrant initiatives that will eventually produce the changes needed to bulldoze market demand into reasonably level, stable requirements. Once the impenetrable barriers blocking the path to ideal logistics and production are hypothetically deemed to be movable, inventive minds are freed to soar to incredible heights, and solutions to "impossible" blockades begin to cascade forth. Suddenly the "impossible dream" (vision) starts to become reality decades, even centuries, earlier than deemed possible by even the

---

[13] Gardner puts it very aptly: "What is needed is tough-minded optimism. Leaders must instill in their people a hard-bitten morale that mixes our natural American optimism with a measure of realism." *Gardner, On Leadership,* p. 195.

wildest dreamers. The inventors of the world can start to apply today's practical technology and resources to tomorrow's vision and make tomorrow happen today!

Executives who have had the exhilarating experience of developing *real* visions have nevertheless found that not all visions are within the practical realm of any single company, executive, or industry to achieve. In fact, some of the most important, necessary drivers of change will be major new national and international laws to govern world trade in rough balance between nations. Since government bodies move with glacial slowness, often with many moves in directions opposite to those necessary and desirable, the earliest strategies to emerge from the process of developing magnificent visions will be those of the most mundane practicality. Nevertheless, a mind-boggling logistics vision will be the framework of the quantum advances that will occur in the twenty-first century!

VISION-STRATEGY-TACTIC

The logistics vision, spanning decades or even centuries, as shown in Exhibit 1–1, encompasses dreams that go far beyond the practical scope of a business's or government's immediate action agenda. Therefore, strategies that flow from the vision are action-

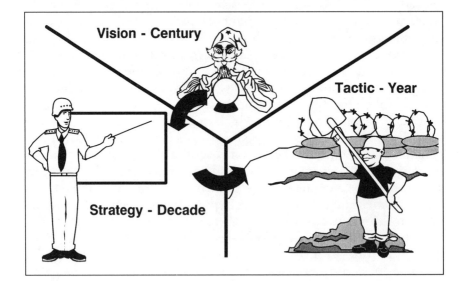

EXHIBIT 1–1

Vision—Strategy—Tactic

able, major initiatives that require several years to come to fruition. For example, a logistics vision would encompass long-term creation of numerous national and international clusters of supplier, production, and distribution facilities in every regional market area. A practical strategy would be to concentrate work in early years on achieving near-ideal clusters in one or two of the largest market regions. However, the troops in the trenches need more specific goals and objectives to drive their tactics in the coming year. Their tactics therefore, would be to locate local supplier/partners in the target region for some important goods and/or components, to work with some distant suppliers to establish production facilities in the region, and to start building the new distribution and production facilities appropriate for the cluster.

This is not to say that some feasible strategies will not come to full fruition beyond the decade time frame. For example, the author's vision is one in which businesses take a much more active role in government and industry associations. The most worthwhile pursuits of industry associations will be those directed at making visions come to pass. Government must create initiatives that will be mutually beneficial to consumers and business. For the common perception of business as an evil entity of a malevolent, wealthy handful of owners is false. We the people, through widespread, direct stock and mutual fund holdings and indirect ownership through our company and private insurance and pension plans, are the majority owners. Our most capable leaders are people in the industries owned by the people. Yet, because they work full-time at their jobs, few have the local, state, national, and international involvement necessary to bring their competence to bear on government operations. Companies *must* have the vision to invest some of their best executives', managers' and employees' time in government activities.

STRATEGIES FOR THE TWENTY-FIRST CENTURY

Most warehouses and storerooms are much larger than they need to be to store the present levels of inventory. This may be hard to understand when one sees pallets stocked in aisles and every other available nook and cranny but will be easier to understand after reading the section in Chapter 4 titled "Maximizing Warehouse Space Utilization." However, the more important issue for strategic planning purposes is to recognize that radical improvements in the supply, manufacturing, and distribution pipeline will revolutionize the amount of warehouse space required to meet significantly improved levels of customer service. Therefore, the challenge to executive management will be to move toward or to stay in front of the leading edge by implementing vendor, factory, and warehouse improvement programs for adopting new technologies that will achieve those ends. Given these improvement programs, management can start to develop strategies for reducing the excess warehouse capacity, and those strategies will evolve continuously as improvement programs progress throughout the distribution and supply network.

TRANSPORT LOGISTICS: KEY TO SLASHING INVENTORY

A long-term vision, from which shorter-term strategies for revising transport logistics will emerge, will be one key to companies' drives to slash inventories in the logistics distribution and supply pipeline radically. Depending on the size of transport vehicles now in use and the frequency of trips between supplier and customer, revised transport logistics has the potential to reduce pipeline inventory by as much as 90 percent. (This despite the recent fantastic reductions of transport costs stemming from the deregulating Motor Carrier and Rail Acts of 1980.) The size and frequency of trucks (and other forms of transport) traveling between links in the logistics chain has a direct impact on the amount of inventory in the pipeline and the speed with which the average item travels. For example, take a hypothesis in which every truckload received contains a supply of every item stocked equal to the demand until the next truckload is received. The average theoretical inventory of both supplier and user can be no less than one-half truckload plus safety stock, for each, in this example. Hence the pipeline inventory for a single user-and-supplier combination would be one truckload plus the average number of truckloads in transit and safety stocks of each. If the frequency of delivery can be changed from weekly to daily, the pipeline inventory would therefore be cut 80 percent. Further, reducing the size of the daily truckload to one-half of its former volume (by using smaller trucks) makes it possible to change deliveries from daily to twice daily, thus increasing inventory reduction to the 90 percent level. Thus, an important part of every company's vision and strategy should be to strive to find ways to increase delivery frequency and reduce the size of loads. Chapter 2 outlines some ways to achieve these goals under the heading "Transport: The Pipe in the Pipeline."

Many readers who are deeply involved in logistics management will note a large gap in transportation modes discussed in this book. Railroad and water transport are not discussed in any depth because they are typically slower than truck transport, so the pipeline inventory is high and responsiveness to demand changes is slow. Rail and water seem to be most suitable for products and materials of great weight, low unit cost, and homogeneity of form, size, and shape. For example, over 80 percent of tonnage hauled by rail consists of coal, minerals and ores, farm products, chemicals, and food.[14]

Further, although contract carrier services have been a fantastically successful component of gains in the 1980s, the author deems the most important new services to be company-owned and company-managed services.[15] Since deregulation has made it possible for company fleets to contract backhaul services, private fleets now have no serious impediment to competing with common carriers or, for that matter, with contract carriers with respect to backhaul. As Bowersox and his colleagues have said, "The flexibility and economy of a private truck operation, customized to the needs of a particular shipper, are difficult for a common carrier to match."[16]

INVENTORY REDUCTION: THE ULTIMATE SOLUTION

The pipeline of supply between producer and consumer would be shortest and least costly and would require the lowest investment if only it were feasible to deliver production directly to consumers, with fewer intervening tiers of warehouses. However, most products are burdened by market and production realities that dictate warehousing. Thus, although most companies will find it impossible to eliminate warehousing, all must realize that through better control and by moderating the circumstances that necessitate distribution inventories, they can drastically reduce the investment while maintaining or improving customer service.

Certain market conditions force companies to stockpile—for example, seasonal peaks and valleys of such great magnitude that producing to demand is impractical. In that case, companies must

[14] William C. Copacino, John F. Magee, and Donald B. Rosenfield. *Modern Logistics Management: Integrating Marketing, Manufacturing and Physical Distribution* (New York: John Wiley & Sons, 1985), pp. 115–17.

[15] Joe Martha puts his finger on the factor most often inhibiting producers from entering the transportation arena—capital investment. He points out that this barrier can be removed by leasing transport equipment and distribution facilities.

[16] Donald J. Bowersox, David J. Closs, and Omar K. Helferich, *Logistical Management: A Systems Integration of Physical Distribution, Manufacturing Support and Materials Procurement* (New York: Macmillan, 1986), p. 168.

produce to inventory (warehouse) in advance of the seasonal sales surge. Products of moderate seasonality are sometimes almost as difficult to produce when demand occurs as are those of radical peak sales. Virtually no product exists for which there is no variation in sales from period to period. Further, the variation in demand from one period to another is virtually impossible to forecast with any reasonable degree of accuracy. Companies meet the uncertainty of forecast demand by providing a cushion of higher-than-needed warehouse inventories. Those cushions are commonly termed "safety stock." Scientifically managed inventories correlate the amount of safety stock and the amount of time between reordering and subsequent receipt. The reason is that the longer the time required to replenish low stock levels, the more severe the deterioration of customer service is likely to be over that period. Equipment and manpower capacity limits and capacity variation are the most common production conditions that force the use of warehousing to meet sales demand as it occurs. For example, worker capacity is also subject to seasonal variation. Absenteeism increases in the winter influenza season and during hunting and fishing seasons, while entire factories and warehouses shut down operations for vacations.

The bad news is that these realities exist and will not completely disappear. The good news is that dynamic managements can plan and execute changes that will cause inventory investment to plummet. One such change would be to reduce sharply inventory replenishment lead time. Because lead time and safety stock quantity should correlate, slashing lead time should be accompanied by drastic reductions in the lead time portion of safety stocks. And, in the event that a company's forecasting and inventory management systems do not provide the data with which to minimize forecast inaccuracy and maximize the accuracy of safety stock calculations, new, improved software may also be a vital ingredient of management's broad array of tools and tactics for improving warehouse operations. A company's factories should rank manufacturing lead time compression close to the top of its priority list. In addition, the company's warehouses and factories should also have an aggressive vendor program with the same emphasis on manufacturing lead time compression.[17] Dramatically increasing the frequency of deliveries from the ware-

---

[17] See Appendix 2 for reference to information on lead time compression. Also, Hout and Stalk have written an entire book on the subject: Thomas M. Hout and George Stalk, Jr., *Competing Against Time: How Time-Based Competition Is Reshaping Global Markets* (New York: Free Press, 1990).

house's own factories and from its vendors, however, usually has the greatest inventory reduction consequences.

DISTRIBUTION AND SUPPLIER NETWORKS: STRATEGY FOR SUCCESS

In this day of space-age computer and communications technology, the painfully slow transfer of demand and inventory replenishment data from point-of-sale back through the distribution channels to the product supplier, and on to the suppliers of components and materials is woefully archaic for all but a handful of leading-edge companies. In many steps of the demand update chain, Exhibit 1–2, companies forward only *order* information to their suppliers. Their suppliers, lacking their customer's forecast and inventory status data must therefore operate in semidarkness, forecasting the customer's demand themselves, or trying to react to it with reorder-point inventory control systems. Further, some links in the chain still operate weekly replenishment systems. When a customer's demand (schedule or order) arrives immediately after a weekly processing cutoff date, transmission of its effect is delayed until the next weekly process. Little wonder that it sometimes takes several weeks to pass demand data from point of sale all the way

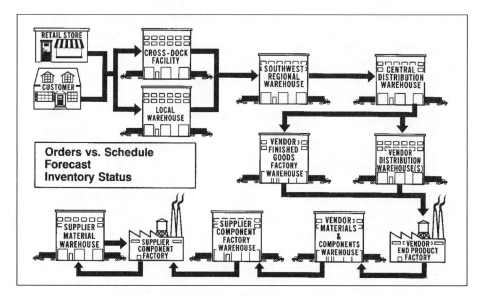

EXHIBIT 1–2

Demand Update Chain

back to the start of the supply chain. The delay in passing data through the chain causes a tremendous information gap. By the time the lowest-tier producers receive data with which to schedule production, they are woefully outdated. Nevertheless, they are the only data available and must be used. As a result, some factories continue to work full blast well into business recessions then lag far behind market recovery, hampering the return to normal production levels. Worse, the delay in turning up production volume causes shortages that in turn trigger price increases and start an inflationary spiral that, short of another business downturn, is almost impossible to check. Even in normal times, the delay causes the lowest tier to be working continuously on the wrong priorities, producing more of items for which demand has fallen and less of those for which demand has risen.

Further, some links in the demand update chain still use old-fashioned media and communication technology. For example, many companies still pass paper orders through the mail or, at best, via facsimile. Conversely, leading-edge companies have already eliminated the labor-intensive order creation process and the need for suppliers to key enter order data. Instead, they use electronic data interchange to pass information in their own distribution or supply network and do so with a system that maintains inventory and demand data for every link in the *company's* chain. In distribution companies this type of system is commonly called a distribution resource planning system.[18] Very few companies have taken the inevitable step of linking *every company and every entity* in the network with a single better demand planning and replenishment system. *Strategy #1*, therefore, is to get to work on the network-wide system. The first step in doing so is for a company to implement the system in its own distribution and production facilities, with linkage to their first-tier vendors a second high priority. Later phases would add additional supply network tiers to the already operational system.

In the author's vision, economic downturns will be moderated as a by-product of the new electronically linked networks. Entire national economies will therefore benefit from the lightning-fast transfer of demand data through all tiers of the network. Early

[18] For more on distribution resource planning, see Andre J. Martin, *DRP Distribution Resource Planning: Management's Most Powerful Tool* (Essex Junction, VT: Oliver Wight, 1990). Incidentally, Leroy Peterson points out that today's distribution resource planning systems are not very popular, because many are too complex and have failed to improve the costs of operations or service levels. Clearly, simpler, more effective systems and operating improvements are what the industry needs!

systemwide awareness of business downturns, on the part of business and government executives, should serve to alert not only business but also governmental economic controllers such as the Federal Reserve Board that remedial action is required. And systemwide visibility of business upturns should also serve to synchronize all businesses in turning up their production volumes, thus helping to avoid the inflationary spirals that so often accompany vigorous recoveries.

Companies with repetitive demand that still use either paper or electronic *orders* should adopt the longer-term strategy of replacing orders with *schedules*, as will be outlined in Chapter 5. However, it is even more urgent that the physical network be simplified and rationalized. *Strategy #2*, therefore, must have minimization of the number of levels in the distribution and supply chains as its goal. (The strategy number used here is not a priority number. Operational improvements are always of highest priority). Astute executives, seeing the lengthy demand update chain Exhibit 1–2, undoubtedly will have questioned the necessity of such a long chain. In fact, the fastest way to achieve the speediest delivery through the network is to eliminate as many stops along the route as possible. Further, numerous links in the chain may be in far-flung corners of the country or world. In these cases, even more time and effort are required to maintain demand information links. Worse, because of the wide transport distances between links, the lowest-tier producers may need to produce several weeks or even months in advance of actual end-of-pipeline sales. The best way to ensure high levels of demand service with minimum inventory and lowest possible transport cost is to eliminate overseas sources by establishing local clusters of distribution facilities and supply factories. *Strategy #3* is to establish local clusters. The supplier program is a vital component of the cluster strategy, because it helps a company and its supply chain establish permanent bonds with strong local vendors and persuades many remote suppliers to establish a small, focused factory in the regional cluster.

Some elements of the logistics vision are so fundamentally advantageous but so contrary to traditional practice and conventional wisdom that accepting them will require mind-boggling imagination. One such example is elimination of middlemen in distribution channels.

ELIMINATE THE MIDDLE-MAN

Why should dealers, distributors, and retail establishments be interjected between producers and customers if they add cost to the price of the product? (And they certainly do add cost!) One reason, traditionally, was to provide a local source from which the customer could obtain instant delivery. A second reason was to provide a convenient place at which the customer could see and touch the products in which he had an interest. Yet another reason was that a local outlet or distributor could be a fast, convenient provider of repair parts and services. The seven-league strides producers and distributors are making are eliminating all these justifications for continuing past practices. These strides include (1) drastic reductions in the supply, production, and distribution pipeline; (2) instantaneous, on-line order entry and same-day order shipment; (3) local clusters of suppliers and company factories; and (4) short, fast, low-cost transport.

The author has long held that dealers and retailers of such big-ticket items as automobiles and appliances are no longer necessary. In fact, if General Motors were to become the first producer to establish factory-to-driver sales and delivery, it would catapult the company to reclamation of its previous predominant market share. It could do so by lowering prices of its automobiles to a point far below it competitors' (at least temporarily, until other suppliers adopted this new away of doing business). Such a move would eliminate billions of dollars that dealers carry in inventory (the cost of carrying this inventory is passed along to the retail customer) and replace it with a much smaller inventory in the assembly plants' yards. Modern systems and transport methods should enable the factory to deliver inventoried automobiles in one to three days. It will be practical to deliver cars produced to customer specifications in five to ten days since large orders for dealer inventories will no longer delay individual customer orders for custom vehicles.

In the short-term, direct-to-customer world, General Motors might operate relatively compact facilities, consisting of a showroom and several interactive consumer-friendly computer terminals for on-line order specification and entry and funds transfer payment processing. The facility might also have a very small yard for unloading delivered, prepaid automobiles. Dealer preparation and its charges would be eliminated since this step would be performed either in production or when preparing the cars for shipment.

Properly handled, present dealers would be overjoyed to become instantly wealthy by selling their prime value real estate (empty sales lots), by eliminating their vastly expensive inventory of automobiles, and by focusing on the profitability of their lucrative service operations. (However, even the service operations will be radically changed, becoming do-it-yourself facilities as defined in Chapter 7. (In fact, in the short term many dealer showrooms and offices may be converted to be the order-taking computer terminal operations and showrooms. From the consumer's standpoint, the disgusting process of price haggling will be eliminated. *Every* customer will be able to take advantage of the standard direct-from-factory prices available to all. No longer will customers worry whether or not they have haggled as successfully, achieving as low a price, as have others.

Down the road, all of this will change as existing and new technologies and their continuing cost reductions bring the showroom into the consumer's home. Interactive big screen, high-fidelity cable television/computer systems with voice recognition and speech synthesizer will permit the consumer to "visit" all the dealer's "showrooms" without leaving his easy chair and, after deciding on the car, conclude financial arrangements and order processing through interaction with bank and factory computer systems. (Obviously, many buyers will continue to want to test drive and otherwise view the products. For these customers, producers will undoubtedly maintain minimal facilities, which will include all of the electronic catalog and order entry facilities. Thus, less advantaged individuals who do not have home systems will have a place at which they can also take advantage of them.) The savings to the consumer will not end with price reductions. Consider, for example, the benefits to the environment. The reduced volume of traffic to and from retailers and dealers will yield additional savings in the world's fuel bills while slashing air pollution and relieving traffic congestion. Further, although armies of jobs will be eliminated, lower prices will enable consumers to buy more of the items they have previously thought of as luxuries. And time saved shopping will generate greater demand for leisure-time products and services. Thus increased demand, new services, and shorter work hours will ultimately offset jobs that would otherwise be lost through abolition of the middleman.

Being the biggest-ticket items, automobiles should lead the way, with such progressive appliance manufacturers as General Electric close behind. Soon after, the momentum of home ordering will expand in ever widening scope. Eventually, the space-age interactive home shopping and ordering systems will extend into the world of the supermarket, department store, and discount operations and, as the lowering of logistics costs progresses, will trigger a rebirth of home delivery service.

Although many will view these visions as outlandish and overly optimistic, belonging to a distant future era, progressive executives will see that the technologies are on the verge of practical application and will begin to develop pilot installations.[19] These pilots might well be focused in small communities, where the small market would minimize the costs of pilot operations. If initial costs exceed benefits, the laboratory-type operation could be funded on the basis of its research and development value. The shining new future is slightly beyond the reach of our outstretched fingertips. It's time for the mover-shakers of the world to reach out and grab it, for the benefit of all!

SUPPLIER PROGRAM: A PARTNERSHIP VISION

Although the customer is or should be, king, the craftsmen (suppliers) are the only ones ultimately capable of servicing the wants and needs of the monarch. It is they who produce the valued products of timely availability that satisfy the desires of the customer at the end of the distribution chain. Too often, however, a seemingly bottomless credibility chasm exists between customers and their vendors. Simply stated, both customer and vendor seem incapable of mutual trust. Customers are wary of vendors putting something over on them, supplying shoddy products and giving other, larger customers preferential treatment in delivery and price. Vendors, accustomed to overnight loss of a valued customer's business to a competitor that lowballs prices, feel that customers have no morals. No matter how hard they work to serve a customer's every need, the customer will desert them at the first chance to save a few dollars.

The stakes of the successful vendor partnership are huge![20] Vendor process improvements in the twenty-first century have the potential for nationwide reduction of pipeline inventories by trillions of dollars, while the value/cost relationship of the products marketed at the end of the logistics pipeline can be doubled and redoubled. Unfortunately, the predominant vendor program is still one of "qualifying" vendors through the use of checklists and "measuring and evaluating vendor performance." Too few companies have realized that the barriers to partnership in profits between customer

---

[19] State-of-the-art models that permit the visitor to see and touch these visionary practices and the hardware and software can be toured at Andersen Consulting's "Smart Store" and "Retail Place."

[20] The author's previous works included extensive discussion of the vendor (supplier) program. Therefore, this book will not duplicate the subject. See Appendix 2 for reference to information on the vendor program in prior works.

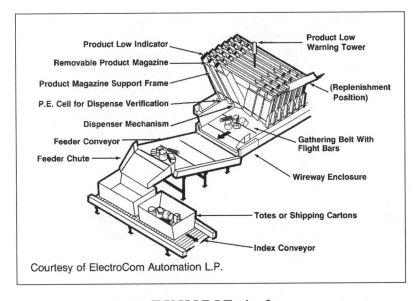

Product Low Indicator

Removable Product Magazine

Product Magazine Support Frame

P.E. Cell for Dispense Verification

Dispenser Mechanism

Feeder Conveyor

Feeder Chute

Product Low
Warning Tower

(Replenishment
Position)

Gathering Belt With
Flight Bars

Wireway Enclosure

Totes or Shipping Cartons

Index Conveyor

Courtesy of ElectroCom Automation L.P.

EXHIBIT 1-3

Automated Order Picking

and vendor require battering down long traditions of adversarial relationships and replacing them with new eternal bonds of a mutually profitable relationship.[21] After all, vendors and their customers must grow to prosper, and the most important key to growth is satisfying their mutual end customer.

WAREHOUSE AUTOMATION: FULL, SEMI-, OR MANUAL?

All of the components of a fully automated, cost-effective warehouse system are already available. However, virtually no one has integrated the components in such a way as to make an economically feasible system for warehouses that stock a virtually infinite variety of item shapes and sizes. Therefore, today's most highly automated systems are found in warehouses that stock items of reasonably homogeneous size and shape. Exhibit 1-3 is an example of an almost fully automated order-picking system suitable for picking relatively small orders of items such as pharmaceutical products, cosmetics, books, video tapes, etc. And although the system is not completely automated (warehousemen must replenish the

[21] Joe Martha, in a note to the author, expresses the need eloquently: "To achieve true supply chain management, companies need to think of quantum improvements across the entire pipeline."

product magazines, for example), it does not take too much imagination to envision a system in which suppliers deliver products in returnable magazines, loaded by the supplier's automated equipment, rather than packaged in cartons. Upon receipt of bar-coded magazines, a conveyor with bar code scanners could rout them to automated storage and retrieval systems, where they could be automatically transferred to the order picker as needed. The reason this type of system is not yet in place is not only that the cost of all required automation components is usually prohibitively high, or that too many companies have too wide a variety of package sizes.[22] Another factor is the complexity of the complete integrated system. Most of today's best automation examples simply integrate numerous automated, semi-automated, and manual systems, in the sense of synchronizing the delivery of items on each order from the many storage areas.[23]

Although it may be impractical to automate warehouse operations fully, every logistics executive should maintain competence in various forms of warehouse automation, including conveyance systems, storage and retrieval systems, computer controllers, handheld and in-transit bar code readers and scanners, conveyance devices, and lift and transport equipment, to name a few. Even better, some small practical portion of the warehouse should be suitable for conversion to a small island of automation. Even if the operation is not cost-effective, the equipment required and the volume handled would be small enough so the investment could be viewed more as an investment for maintaining automation skills (and perhaps as a marketing tool for advertising the company's state-of-the-art automation).

The day will come when the costs of integrated, practical warehouse automation are within the reach of companies both large and small. The necessary disciplines and integration of both customer and supplier operations and systems will force solutions to problems such as damage-in-process and inaccurate inventory records. An automation vision is one important component of the complete vision logistics executives must create for their future operations.

---

[22] The uniformity of package sizes and shapes is the first of seven "order patterns and operating characteristics" that Sims lists as present in successful automated order picking instances. E. Ralph Sims, Jr., *Planning and Managing Industrial Logistics Systems* (Amsterdam: Elsevier, 1992), p. 113

[23] My colleague Joe Martha points out that automated facilities and equipment are too "storage-oriented" rather than "flow-oriented." They are usually ill-suited to new products and businesses. Future automation must focus on movement rather than storage.

MINIMIZE COSTLY TIME AND MOTION

When men and machines are in motion between times when they are actually performing work, unnecessary cost is being added to the process. In such cases, logistics operations are rich in opportunities for improvements. For example, empty and partially loaded trucks, tractors, and trailers are far too often in motion less than full time. Many companies and entire industries have made the mistake of designing and using specialized vehicles and containers that are extremely cost-effective in outbound trips but always return empty.

Exhibit 1–4 depicts examples of two-way transport in the warehouse and on the highway. In the forklift example, any time a trip is made into the warehouse to retrieve an item for issue, a receipt transaction requiring stocking in the same area is carried into the storeroom and stocked. Next, the forklift travels to the nearby item to be issued, retrieves it, and delivers it into the packing and shipping process. Although this example portrays forklift trucks, the objective of making all transport two-way loads is equally applicable to fully and semi-automated storage and retrieval machines and to stockkeepers pushing carts. In the bidirectional conveyance example, docks are multipurpose, used for both shipping and receiv-

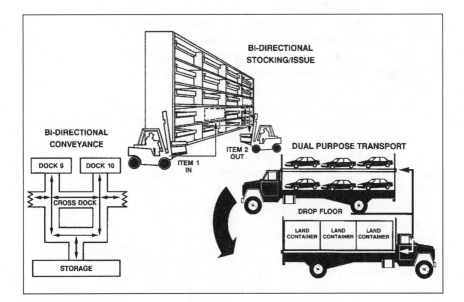

EXHIBIT 1–4

Two-way Transport

ing. Conveyors into and out of the stockroom support the dual function docks and conveyors connecting all docks, thereby supporting cross-dock transfer of receipts to outbound trucks. In the third example, trailers designed to transport automobiles from factory to customer would best be intermodal—suitable for piggyback railroad transport. And, by virtue of a hydraulic lift upper deck that can be lowered, they can accept new standard "land containers" for the backhaul. Although such a design may be less efficient for outbound loads than existing rigs, its overall utilization will be much higher. Existing trailers are a special-purpose design that makes it impractical to use them for backhaul. (New-age "land containers," trailers, trucks, and dock facilities that will help better balance inbound and outbound traffic and slash the time between arrival and departure are discussed in the Chapter 2 section headed "Transport: The Pipe in the Pipeline.")

In warehouses, people, lift trucks, high-rise retrieval equipment, and conveyors travel much farther than necessary and often make virtually every return trip empty (or empty-handed). One of the reasons that automation has seldom proved more cost-effective than manual alternatives is the inclination of many warehouse designers to make lavish use of equipment without making more than minimal effort to ensure that automation designs minimize required investment by avoiding wasted travel time and motion. Even though automated equipment eliminates labor cost, it entails higher depreciation. Therefore, reducing the amount of required wasted time and motion of automated equipment is every bit as important as minimizing wasted labor. Further, a far greater percentage of high-cost logistics equipment sits idle more than it works. Trucks, tractors, trailers, and entire warehouses sit idle more than one-half of the 168-hour week. (The subject of putting capital investment to better use is expanded on in Chapter 2, under the heading "Capital Investment: Use What You Have"). Keeping *all* logistics equipment and facilities in virtually perpetual motion, fully loaded, is one of the most exciting potentials for lowering logistics costs and required investment.

Time and motion study of manpower and equipment, using videotape recording to capture and analyze operations, is a vital ingredient of logistics design methodology. Understanding nonproductive time is the cornerstone of inventing ways to minimize waste. In the warehouse, the techniques that yield high levels of productivity include separate subwarehouses for different package sizes and activity frequency zones within those facilities. (Chapter 3 presents a future vision of the warehouse facility that has these characteristics, while Chapter 4 discusses many key aspects of warehouse management.)

QUESTERS AFTER QUALITY OFTEN OVERLOOK VALUE

For an inordinate number of distribution and production companies the first priority is the quest for quality improvement, or even *total* quality improvement. A dangerous view of many is that poor quality is related primarily to defective products being delivered to the customer. After all, the predominant customer expectation of a product lies in its value (worth *and* quality) in relation to its cost. A company has a real problem if defective products are produced and/or delivered, but too often it misunderstands the corrective action required. Too frequently defects created during production are presumed to be a result of carelessness on the part of machinists or assemblers. In fact, the fault is almost always an imperfect *process*! The same is true of damage that occurs during distribution, a rampant reality, the solution to which offers a great opportunity for ending customer dissatisfaction and lowering distribution costs. However, it is also every bit as important that the products delivered to the customer meet his expectations in that they have satisfactory appearance, function, reliability and inherent *value,* as it is merely be free of defects. There are two clear routes to achieving customer satisfaction in all these categories. One is to focus on the *process,* designing and installing process improvements that virtually eliminate producing or damaging goods in process. The adage "To err is human" is all too true. Therefore, ultimate success depends on designing fail-safe processing systems. In the distribution *process*, reporting errors and order-filling errors have been one of the most pervasive reasons for customer dissatisfaction. Today's bar coding technology, applied in a system designed for fail-safe processing, has almost eliminated this problem, as discussed in Chapter 6 under the heading, "Location Control Systems: Riding the Wave." A second serious distribution concern is damage to containers and their contents during warehousing and transportation operations. Such damage arises from jostling, dropping, or ramming containers or having them jam while traveling by conveyors. These problems can usually be resolved by modifying transport equipment and by addressing the adequacy of the packaging material design.

The second route to solution focuses on *Design improvement.* For logistics personnel, design improvement opportunities are most obvious in the packaging arena. Indeed, if packaging is sadly lacking in terms of providing protection from damage when subjected to minimal jostling, the only economical solution may be to improve the packaging design. However, relatively few logistics organizations employ packaging engineers—those professionally educated, trained, and capable of supplying permanent package protection solutions for eliminating a large percentage of minor logistics damage.[24] Companies with great opportunities for package improvements should include at least one packaging engineer on the vendor program team. Less obvious than packaging problems, but one important reason for customer returns, is displeasure with the product itself. In the case of product rejection, the most natural inclination is to point to defective quality when the real problem may be inferior value. Consider, for instance, the following example.

The difference between a gold and a base metal statue formed in the same mold is value, not quality. Further, when one of two base metal statues is cracked, the most important distinction one makes between them is still a difference of *value* (although the remaining value is likely to be the scrap metal worth). Thus, when we see a shoddy product (or service) or one that fails to perform its intended function or has a short useful life, we are really observing substandard value. We are not necessarily seeing poor quality in the sense of something with defects vis-à-vis perfect conformance to specifications. Incidentally, many surveys have shown that the customer's perception of products and services delivered is often described in terms of poor value (also read poor quality), regardless of the fact that what is delivered meets the customer's specifications.

Another form of quality problem in warehousing and distribution operations is related to poor service quality, primarily out-of-stock conditions that delay shipping customer orders. One popular but usually unwise solution to shortages is to increase inventories. Often this is accomplished by increasing such inventory control factors as safety stock, order quantity, and lead time for all items, regardless of the basic reasons for the often temporary spate of back orders for specific items. As a result, virtually every company the author has seen during his long career has had more than ample room for reduction in its distribution inventories. One way in which the potential for improvement can be quantified is to determine the value of active item inventory in terms of months of

[24] Friedman and Kipnees cite the Packaging Education Foundation, Inc., as being the driving force behind developing packaging engineering programs in eleven universities. Thanks to its efforts, industry can draw upon professionally educated engineers for this specialized function. Walter F. Friedman and Jerome J. Kipnees, *Distribution Packaging* (Malabar, FL: Krieger, 1977), pp. 30–31.

supply. If the inventory is equivalent to a one-month supply, it means that each item, on the average, is received in inventory and sits on the shelf two months before it is used. In fact, fast-moving items just received and on the way to stock often pass the same items just picked from stock and on their way to shipping. When executive management looks at inventory in these terms, it should always be prompted to challenge the logic of existing inventory management practices. All this has led the author to the conclusion that any well-managed company can target substantial, continuous inventory reduction.

THE CUSTOMER IS KING

The 1990s will undoubtedly become known as the decade of the customer. Only in this decade has such a strong cry for attention to the wants and needs of the customer been heard.[25] Indeed, many of us share a belief that we know exactly what our customers want and need. And if the stupid oafs (customers) disagree with us, it's obvious that, because we know best, we merely need to educate those morons to want what they should want. (Please do not take that seriously.) In reality, few of us have (or take) the time really to understand what our customers would value most about our products and services, if only we were to start to pay attention to their wishes and give them what they really want. We are so snowed with the complexities of operating our own businesses that we usually consider issues in the context of what is best for our own companies rather than what would be best in the eyes of our customers. Ultimately, we shall fail in business if our customers fail. Therefore, doing everything possible to make our customers successful is the only way to succeed.

Executives like Carl J. Mungenast, executive vice president of SLS Sears Logistics Services, have recently become acutely aware of the vital importance of placing the customer's wants and needs ahead of their own. If you ask Carl to list his company's priorities in sequence of importance, working to increase customer satisfaction is at the top of his list. However, one should not go entirely overboard in rating the customer's wants and needs above all other considerations. The best marketing and salespeople are those able to mold the customer's wants and needs. They do so by participat-

---

[25] Gunn, for example, highlights the importance of the customer order-to-delivery cycle: "The essential attitude necessary in evaluating this business process is to measure everything in the customer's eyes . . ." Thomas G. Gunn, *21st Century Manufacturing: Creating Winning Business Performance* (New York: Harper Business, 1992), p. 56.

ing in the invention of new products and product features that they know *should* appeal to customers who have not yet had the notion that they want them! When every salesperson and company is pandering to the customer's expressed preferences, customers are quite likely to develop a partiality for the one supplier with enough integrity to help him to understand what he *really should want* in order to lead him to buy the product with the greatest utility and highest value for its cost.

Working with customers to understand (and mold) their wants and needs is usually far easier than one imagines![26] Where there are relatively few customers who account for a large percentage of the business, beginning a *real* ongoing client service dialogue with top customer executives is all that is needed to start the ball rolling.[27] Even for a company daunted by legions of small customers, there is hope. Direct dialogue with *all* of them is not necessary to surface the important issues. Dialogue with a small sampling and surveying the vast majority by mail are usually a completely satisfactory, low-cost substitute for a lengthy dialogue with all. Fortunately, the list of customer wants and needs is not infinitely long. The vast majority, when queried about their top priorities will respond:

1. Timely delivery, short delivery lead time
2. Value for price
3. Performance and conformance

In fact, the best way to describe, in universally applicable terms, what customers want and need is found in *only* two of these answers—delivery and value. As the author has pointed out in his previous work, virtually everyone in the world is confusing value with quality.[28]

---

[26] My colleague Bill Copacino, discussing customer surveys developed for specific companies, says that he has found seven extremely pithy questions are enough to provide the company with earthshaking revelations concerning their misperceptions of the company's image and performance in the eyes of their customers. Such a survey can be one of the lowest-cost, highest-value services, when conducted by an independent, impartial consultant.

[27] The author's previous books discussed the powerful advantage of dealing at the top, between the customer's chief executive officer and/or president and their vendors' counterpart executives. It is only at that level that the players have sufficient experience and wisdom to create the vision of their partnership. It is they who are able to drive their companies to launch the strategic imperatives necessary to forge the permanent relationship so vital to the success of both. See Appendix 2 for reference to more on dealing at the top.

[28] See Appendix 2 for reference to information on quality versus value.

METHODOLOGY: ROADMAP OR INCHSTONES?

Warning! This section on methodology may not be for the typical executive. Rather it is intended for those disgusted with past projects that have delivered less than promised, and far later than imagined. As impossible as it may seem, it is within the realm of possibility that methodology for controlling projects, ensuring successful, timely completion, can be an exciting subject. The subject becomes exciting when the theme is a methodology designed to produce results, to do so on schedule, and to spend a bare minimum of time developing the methodology, detailing the resource requirements for each task, scheduling and rescheduling jobs, and monitoring progress. This can be compared with the less exciting, more current view of project planning and control as a deadly boring process of identifying and estimating the resources required to do thousands of detail tasks, and then rescheduling the same details when it finally becomes apparent that scheduled events are routinely completed much later (occasionally earlier) than planned. In fact, historically progress in complex projects often takes so much longer than planned that it would be reasonable and appropriate to describe major accomplishment-measuring events ("milestones") with a more meaningful, more descriptive word: "inchstones." The primary key to success is full-time project teams with outstanding management backing. Participation by *all* employees is of secondary, albeit highly desirable, importance.

One of the most persistent continuous improvement sacred cows is the notion that all industry needs to leap into the twenty-first century superior performer category is to toss the ball to all of a company's employees (in the form of participative management), and expect this to produce the revolutionary changes that companies need. A few companies have made giant strides as a result of increasing the degree of participation by all employees. Still others that have already practiced widespread involvement have made strides not as a result of the initiation of participative management but, rather, through studying and adopting new practices and developing new visions. The majority of those attempting to attain superiority via this route have had disappointing results. The reasons are that sweeping changes still need management direction and participation, and companywide initiatives of breathtaking scope require substantial, full-time project team efforts to move briskly toward the goal. Part-time efforts, undertaken in times when a lull in ongoing operations permits employees to work on improvement design and implementation, just will not meet the need.

Effective executives must know, at least in general, toward which goals and objectives various teams of employees should be concentrating their efforts, and they must provide the generalship needed to keep project teams and operating units marching together.

Nor are all employees automatically prepared to march to the general's cadence. Fournier and Plunkett have exposed the myth that people "want empowerment, but they have been waiting on management to introduce it in the organization. This myth may be less than a half-truth. It is also a misconception perpetrated by a minority of consultants who have a quick-fix program to sell."[29] They go on to say that "participation in one form or another has been around for years, but it has always been done *to* employees, not *with* them." Thus, if changing a company's culture will require lengthy efforts before participation starts to yield impressive results, management had best not delay getting pilot projects under way! And even when employee participation is working as well as it can, full-time project teams will still be the main tool with which epic advances will be achieved.

The several keys to successful project management include the following factors and considerations.

1. Plan and schedule short phases. What will need to be done and what it will take to do it are virtually impossible to identify accurately, if several weeks or months of study and design work are the start of a project. Study and design, therefore, must be completed to determine accurately what will be done and how much work will be necessary.
2. Schedule very general project activities from the top down. Detailing every possible activity, then summing up the estimated times for each, from the bottom up, will only produce either horrendously large or overly optimistic estimates.
3. Depend on individual resourcefulness and managerial skills to maintain project schedules. Realizing that initial estimates are seldom accurate, the real need is for dynamic reassignment of project personnel from areas ahead of schedule to others falling behind. It may also require dynamic additions of personnel when that is the only way to complete the project on a critically important date such as at the time of annual model changeover. Finally, a project's

[29] Robert Fournier, and Lorne C. Plunkett, *Participative Management: Implementing Empowerment* (New York: Wiley, 1991), p. 26.

scope and objectives may require dynamic reshaping to fit the available resources and time constraints.

4. Projects and/or subprojects should be limited in scope, and hence in their resultant complexity, whenever practical. Redesigning and implementing changes in a single section of a warehouse will keep the tasks of a single design team relatively simple. Or several separate subprojects, each in a single section of a mammoth warehouse, will also be of simple scope for design teams assigned to them, although coordinating several teams will increase the administrative complexity. To bite off an entire, mammoth warehouse all at once may encompass such a complex array of issues that the time required will be humongous.[30] Smaller bites (pilot projects), a step at a time, ensure early realization of improvement. Usually projects of grand scope are implemented all at once, thus delaying the realization of first benefits.

Reinventing the existing methodology used to cast visions, plan strategies, and then design and successfully implement the changed operations and systems makes no more sense than it does to reinvent the wheel. Years of experience in managing various types of projects have been the invaluable basis for developing documented, step-by-step methodologies for every type of project facility, procedure, and systems improvement program. Andersen Consulting's (and others') methodology, suitable for various types of facilities, procedures, and systems, fills numerous books. Therefore, it is not appropriate for inclusion in a book primarily intended as an executive and managerial overview. However, a few of the most important project control success factors warrant coverage. These issues are raised in various chapters under headings that incorporate the term "Step-by-Step Methodology."

When preparing their visions, executives cannot realistically focus only on the description of possible end results of improved logistics, distribution, and warehousing facilities, operations, and systems. Getting from here to there also requires knowing the step-by-step methodology that will provide a roadmap to guide their

---

[30] Claunch and his co-authors put it this way: "Whatever the area, your eye for success should not exceed the capacity of your stomach to digest what you have undertaken. . . . Your goal here is not to turn the company around, but to demonstrate the bottom-line savings possible. The time must be short, but the results dramatic." Jerry W. Claunch, Michael W. Gozzo, and Peter L. Grieco, Jr., *Just-in-Time Purchasing: In Pursuit of Excellence* (Plantsville, CT: PT Publications, 1988), p. 166.

journey into the future. Fast and sizable benefits will accrue to those teams using the simplest, speediest methodology.

SUMMARY

Industry's executives hold the keys to a bright new future. Their most ambitious, imaginative visions will set the pace of advancement into the exciting new world of twenty-first-century logistics. Consumers will be the primary beneficiaries of their efforts, by virtue of the speed with which high-value, low-cost products can be delivered. Transferring the showroom and store into the living room opens new vistas of opportunity for quality leisure time and environmental improvement. Although "fads of the month" abound, only those that fit into the future vision, especially those that accelerate the pace of progress, should be given high priority. Executive and managerial development should be high on the list of prioritized initiatives. As leaders of the pipeline from production to market, logistics executives control massive amounts of gross national product. Accordingly, industry must equip them to be the best conceivable visionaries and managers. Of all the skills an executive brings to a company, vision will ultimately prove to be one of the most important. And the most important ingredient of vision is the ability to jettison old ways. For, as Levitt has written, "Nothing so characterizes the successful organization so much as its willingness to abandon what has been long successful."[31] It's time to break the old molds and march into the world of tomorrow!

---

[31] Theodore Levitt, *Thinking About Management* (New York: Free Press, 1991), p. 67.

CHAPTER 2

A Logistics Network Vision

Long-range visions of logistic networks will be valid only if the predictions on which they are based come to pass. The author's vision is based on prognoses that differ from or go far beyond those of other (perhaps more learned) visionaries. Here are some of them:

1. Transport costs will be reduced by moving source factories to market areas instead of by optimizing long-distance transport methods. Distribution channels will be shortened and simplified and will provide better service with lower inventories.
2. Suppliers will establish factories in close proximity to their customer factories, which in turn will be situated in the market region. Thus, the largest factories will have local clusters of supplier factories. This will greatly simplify logistics and reduce transportation cost.
3. New "land containers" and the open-sided trucks, trailers, and shipping/receiving docks designed to handle the new containers will revolutionize operations at every step in the logistics network.
4. Incredibly successful improvement programs will start to prove that many customer demands can be filled from the

end of production lines.[1] Leading-edge companies will start
to do so, completely eliminating distribution warehousing
for many products.

5. The most important message of continuous improvement
   will be driven home: Not one element of production and
   distribution costs is sacrosanct. All are open targets for
   reduction or virtual elimination. Notions of "balancing opposing costs" will therefore, give way to a drive to reduce
   them to the point of insignificance.

6. Consumers, producers, distributors, and retailers will spark
   a drive to level natural and man-made seasonal demand
   peaks, thus reducing the massive waste that seasonality
   engenders.

7. Government can and will play an important role in moti-
   vating companies to build new facilities to produce the
   products driven out of production by the uneven playing
   field of the 1970s, '80s, and '90s. However, *direct* government interference and involvement in industry would be
   disastrous. Industry needs, and the government will provide, substantial tax credits to provide incentives for companies to rebuild industries destroyed and severely
   damaged by imports.

An executive of superior qualities will welcome the sometimes
revolutionary vision presented in this book, even if the vision is at
variance with his or her own. Such executives understand that the
most important role of industry leaders will always be that of the
revolutionary leader, pushing their companies and industries to
unimagined new heights of innovative service, product, and process improvements. Hickman writes: "The leader, impatient with
small, incremental improvements would far rather *revolutionize*
aspects of an organization. For leaders, refinement presents the
riskier course because it fails to take advantage of the up-side potential of great change. The soul of the leader identifies revolutionary change as the real test of an organization's strength."[2]

---

[1]Bill Copacino points out that less-than-truckload economics and uneven delivery time,
which will not go away, would make it much more likely to cause distribution centers to
be replaced by cross-dock facilities when factories are able to produce to customer
order. The author concurs that this will be the case for the lowest-value products produced in factory clusters not yet located in the center of a regional market (item 1 of the
list) and not yet using some of the new transport methods such as those referred to in
item 3 and in the section of this chapter headed "Transport: The Pipe in the Pipeline."
[2]Craig R. Hickman, *Mind of a Manager: Soul of a Leader* (New York: Wiley, 1990), p. 178.

EXECUTIVE CHECKLIST: SELECTED VISION ZINGERS

Given a vision of the logistics network of the future, executives must start to convert today's operations into methods suitable for the twenty-first century. Some steps into the future world can be taken immediately; others need years to become reality. Still others require action by government, a ponderous body uniquely lacking in visionary business perspective and almost incapable of initiating reasonable legislation capable of benefiting consumer and business alike. Industry's best movers and shakers need to organize to push the legislative and executive branches to enact vitally important laws. However, getting to work on initiatives that can be taken immediately must not be delayed. All of us need to get to work on the initial steps. The following checklist will help us focus on some of the strategic issues.

1. The best companies already have regional clusters of suppliers, company factories, and warehouses that optimize the performance of the entire network. Every other company must begin to develop long-range strategic plans for expanding the number of suppliers, factories, and warehouses in its own nonexistent or limited regional clusters if they are to remain or become competitive. To do so requires a company and its suppliers to cast out outmoded notions of economies of scale and to understand the viability of small, regional focused factories.[3]
2. Capital investment in distribution networks is much higher than required to maintain high levels of service with minimum investment in the goods transported and stored. Large segments of the pipeline operate facilities and equipment that are idle during long weekend and night hours. Many companies will find that investments can be lowered by increasing the hours per day and days per week during which their expensive investment is utilized.
3. Company and supplier truck fleets can provide transport services far superior to traditional common carriers (espe-

---

[3]See Appendix 2 for reference to information on economies of scale and focused factories. Some of the author's esteemed colleagues feel that progress in dispersing supplier factories from huge central facilities into small focused factories in the vicinity of regional markets will be painfully slow and, indeed, may never occur, because such a large and growing percentage of goods and components is imported. The author deems it vital that this trend be reversed in order to rebuild the country's moribund manufacturing industry and restore economic vitality.

cially as customer–supplier clusters of factories and warehouses come into being). For smaller companies and large
ones wishing to take advantage of higher transport volumes, contract carriers are often still the lowest-cost, fastest alternative. Every company should rethink truck fleet
alternatives.

4. Cross-trained warehouse employees are of significantly
greater value to the company and better motivated than are
those assumed to be stupid oafs unable to do more than the
simplest, most menial tasks. Management must undertake
the task of dynamically raising the value of all employees
through better education and training programs.

5. Goods moving through distribution networks and networks
of clustered factories are often damaged by rough handling
and load shifting while in transit. New fail-safe methods of
handling and truck loading must be designed to eliminate
this important element of waste, which not only is costly
but also reduces the quality and timeliness of delivery to
the customer.

6. Dirty, damaged containers and container labels degrade
the supplier's (and delivery service's) quality image in the
eyes of the customer to whom they are delivered. Therefore, the shippers and carriers in the logistics networks
must work together to design the fail-safe devices, methods, packaging, and labels that ensure that undamaged and
unsoiled deliveries arrive at the customer's dock.

DISTRIBUTION NETWORK: ARE FEWER LEVELS BETTER?

Warehousing interjected between a supplier and its customers creates an extra logistics level, complicating the supply network. Exhibit 2–1, an illustration of alternative pipeline paths, serves to
highlight the complexities, the large inventories, and the long lead
times associated with several levels of warehousing in the supply
chain. For example, it is quite common to find component vendors
(and company component factories) and *their suppliers* warehousing their finished products, and still the factories that use the components also stock the components prior to production. In the
longest supply chain path in the exhibit, four warehousing steps are
included in the chain. On the shortest path, where components are
delivered directly from their completion on machines in the component factories to the assembly lines of the end product factories,
a single storage step exists—warehousing of the material at the

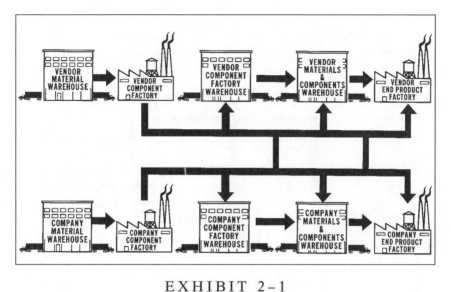

EXHIBIT 2-1

The Supply Pipelines

start of the supply pipeline. And the opportunities for improvement are even better when vendor and company factories have factory warehouses that supply distribution warehouses on demand, as shown in Exhibit 2-2. Incidentally, parts and accessory sales are big business for most assemblers. This makes them one of the major segments of the logistics network.

Since most warehouses store two or more months' supply, the overly long pipeline requires that materials be received (at the beginning of the pipeline) several months before production starts at the end product factories. And since forecasts several months in advance of demand are very inaccurate, factories have been forced to carry high pipeline inventories. Thus, eliminating or drastically slashing warehousing steps at various levels will radically reduce process time and associated inventory, with potentials for long-term reductions of 90 percent or more being entirely feasible.

Unnecessary steps in the distribution process are equally costly in terms of both inventory investment and pipeline lead time. The distribution route with the highest number of steps (levels), Exhibit 2-3, is likely to require several more months of pipeline lead time and massive amounts of inventory. In addition, it increases the price of the service provided, because each distribution step involving people and equipment adds labor and overhead cost to the products distributed. The added steps, in other words, add cost,

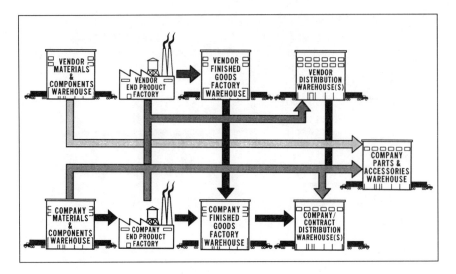

EXHIBIT 2-2

Supply Pipelines to Distribution

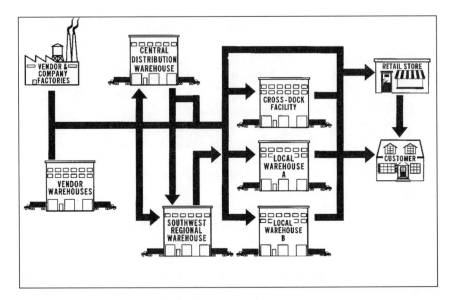

EXHIBIT 2-3

Long Distribution Pipelines

which in turn increases the product price, even though the *intrinsic* value of the distributed product is physically unaltered. To the extent that some of these costs are avoidable or unnecessary, the resulting price to the customer will lower its price/value ratio. Some of the awesome array of avoidable costs added when a warehouse is inserted between a supplier and its customers are truck unloading, counting, inspecting, recording receipts and issues, moving to and from storage, storing, order, picking/issuing, packaging, staging shipments, and truck loading and transport. However, the costs of additional material handling steps are only a portion of the total costs of an additional distribution level. Other less tangible costs include administrative and clerical expenses and higher computer and manual systems expenses attributable to the more complex distribution network.

Consider, for example, the inefficiency that would result if a household were to contract with an independent warehouse operator to stock and supply groceries. In this scenario, the homeowner would order groceries from the grocer for delivery to the third-party warehouse. The warehouse would subsequently deliver the meal-size quantities to the homeowner's kitchen, just-in-time for the homeowner to prepare each meal. The homeowner could eliminate one or two weekly provisioning trips to the grocery store and virtually eliminate a pantry or cabinet inventory. However, it would suddenly be necessary for the homeowner to process receiving reports verifying warehouse receipts and to develop or purchase a system with which to order groceries for delivery from the grocer to the warehouse, a warehouse inventory control system, grocer and warehouse truck scheduling systems, and an accounts payable system for paying for the groceries delivered and reimbursing the third-party warehousing and delivery service fees, to name some of the most basic system needs. Clearly, the added systems and complexity also add another costly array of systems and administrative expenses. Some would argue that the warehouse service might still be less costly than the homeowner's pantry alternative, because the homeowner may be a highly paid, skilled machinist, technician, or executive, in which case the value of his time would be much greater than a warehouseman's. This argument could be invalidated, however, by simply sending a lower-paid household member to the store or by efficiently routing *any* household member (including the executive) to the grocer while he or she travels to and from work (or on other errands), thus making the pickup and delivery essentially free.

The reason the American system purposely accommodates large

home inventories instead of small daily meal-size purchases stems from the historically low cost of cabinets, pantries, freezers, and refrigerators and the economies of large purchases. Small packages and their contents have always been more expensive than the large economy size. In Europe and Asia, living space is outrageously expensive. Thus home and appliance storage space is usually a fraction of that found in homes in the United States. Nor is space in the distribution facilities any cheaper, proportionately, than in the home. Therefore, the entire distribution systems have been geared to smaller packages and smaller inventories throughout the supply chain. In the United States, processed food and beverages must often be transported vast distances from source to market, necessitating giant truckloads and freight carloads to make the most economical deliveries to regional warehouses.

In Europe and Asia, source and customer are much closer together. Thus, smaller trucks shuttling between source and customers in partial truckload deliveries are more common, and transport cost is much less an issue. American companies must understand that large order and delivery quantities, truckload shipments, and regional distribution centers or warehouses with huge pipeline inventories are not necessarily the only way to operate warehousing and delivery logistics. In fact, virtual elimination of supplier lot-size-related costs (setup/changeover and order-related costs) is one of the most significant components of the new industrial revolution that is transforming factories all around the globe.[4]

Some companies have found a contract warehouse/distribution service to be less costly than the company-operated alternative. Often the reason is that the contract warehouse/distribution company has lower costs and thus can offer a lower-price service while still earning a comfortable profit. Solving the problem of excessively high costs by tacking on additional steps is hardly the way to outpace savvy competitors who are likely to know that the ultimate solution is to reduce the company's own costs to a level lower than that of any contract service or competitor.

Some would argue that the household inventory of groceries (hence inventory investment and inventory financing cost) would be lower with delivery from a warehouse being synchronized with meal preparation. While it is true that the household inventory would be lower, the homeowner's warehouse inventory would prob-

---

[4]See Appendix 2 for reference to information on eliminating setup/changeover and ordering costs.

ably be about the same unless the burden of financing the inventory would simply be shifted to the warehouse operator. Some would then contend that the contract warehouse would be willing to absorb the cost of financing the inventory in order to win the business. What utter nonsense! Eventually the third-party warehouse must turn a profit and recoup its costs by charging enough for the service not only to recoup its cost (including the cost of carrying the inventory) but also to turn a reasonable profit.

Like the homeowner's grocery warehouse, any warehouse interposed between supplier and customer also increases the cost of transport. Two separate short delivery trips (the first from supplier to warehouse, the second from warehouse to customer) must cost more than one long one from supplier to customer. This can easily be attributed to the extra time, equipment, and labor required to stop and unload the inbound warehouse delivery and subsequently to load each outbound shipment. Further, it would also be quite unusual to find a warehouse situated directly on the route between supplier and customer. Thus, the milage between supplier and warehouse and warehouse and customer is usually greater than supplier to customer. Hence, if the direct delivery transport cost is higher because of less-than-truckload volume, there are usually major offsetting costs savings compared with the two-level distribution alternative. Therefore greater focus on transportation logistics to lower the costs of frequent less-than-truckload volumes can often be a far better alternative. Cross-dock consolidation facilities are often an important alternative to less-than-truckload shipments.

For example, logistics companies like **SLS Sears Logistics Services** commonly find it advantageous to establish consolidation centers in some regions of the country in which massive volumes of goods are produced that are consumed all over the country (furniture produced in the Southeastern United States, for instance). Exhibit 2–4 illustrates the role of the consolidation center, a collection point, at which shipments from several different factories are unloaded, sorted (moved cross-dock) by regional destination, and combined with shipments from other factories. Were each factory to ship directly to each region, it would need to ship less-than-truckload volumes, incurring much higher transportation costs. Some of the author's clients have found it to be faster and less expensive to shuttle a truck from factory to factory, accumulating a load for each region.[5]

[5]See Appendix 2 for reference to a General Motors case example of "milk route" shuttle.

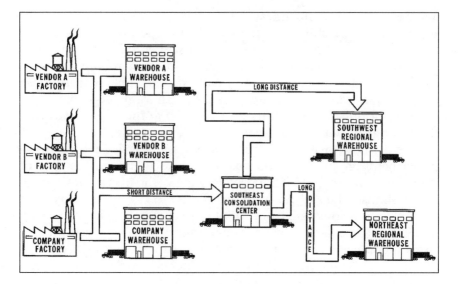

EXHIBIT 2-4

Consolidation Centers

The point of added costs from interposing a warehouse level in the logistics chain brings to mind an example recently used by a graduate course instructor to illustrate a model application of just-in-time delivery coupled with the prerequisite elaborate computer systems. In the example, IBM contracted an express delivery service to warehouse and supply components to IBM's plants. These items were previously warehoused by the plants. The author's daughter Ann, a student well versed in the concepts of superior manufacturing and distribution techniques, argued that moving the warehousing responsibility to a third party was far less than an ideal arrangement. The teacher responded that the third-party warehouse *was* a good solution, because IBM had previously tried to reduce warehousing costs and had failed to do so. Ann's comeback was instantaneous and automatic: "American companies will not be successful international competitors as long as they try something and give up when they first fail to succeed. They must learn not to settle for second best alternatives if they want to be the best and must continue to work on all facets of a problem until achieving the desired, ultimate objective."

The ideal distribution center/warehouse would be no warehouse at all! In this regard, the author disagrees with Smith and Tompkins, who contend that warehousing adds value to products by "having the right product in the right place at the right time."[6] Such service, if feasible only through warehousing, would certainly be of value to customers. But warehousing, in and of itself, adds no greater *inherent* value to the product. Fortunately, in the new era of manufacturing setup/changeover and ordering costs will continuously be reduced, to the point of insignificance. Over time, the feasibility of servicing more and more customer orders without warehousing finished products will therefore also increase continuously. To achieve this objective requires that a manufacturer be capable of shipping customer orders from the end of its manufacturing processes. Hence, both supplier and customer managements must push their organizations to focus on achieving the necessary improvements. If executive management gives half-hearted recognition to the potential for virtually eliminating "opposing costs" and reducing supply pipeline lead time to an insignificant level, or if it is pessimistic about the pace of improvement, its companies will undoubtedly fail to achieve these ends as quickly as other enterprises that *are* dedicated to attaining the ultimate goal. Jim Hall shows a curious mixture of optimism regarding "just-in-time" improvements and pessimism about the possibility of completely eliminating warehouses. "Two fundamental axioms show us why the warehouse is here to stay," he writes. They are (1) "Production efficiencies will always drive some level of investment in inventory" and (2) "forecasting consumer demand will forever be an inexact science, and as a result, inventory will always be needed to ensure that customer needs are met."[7] While the author agrees that *some* percentage of warehousing *may* always be necessary, this is no reason for companies not to target warehouse elimination as their ultimate goal. For disbelievers he recommends visiting a Finnish computer company that operates very successfully although it has completely eliminated warehousing/stores for materials, components, *and* finished goods.

The obvious goal of every company distributing products must be to move as rapidly as possible to shorten the distribution pipeline for as many products as feasible. Exhibit 2–5 illustrates some of the shortest possible pipeline paths, even including direct factory-to-retail-customer delivery.

[6]Jerry D. Smith and James A. Tompkins, *How to Plan and Manage Warehouse Operations* (Watertown, MA: American Management Association, 1982), pp. 2–3.
[7]Jim Hall, "The Warehouse of the Future Is Still a Warehouse," *Industrial Engineering,* January 1992.

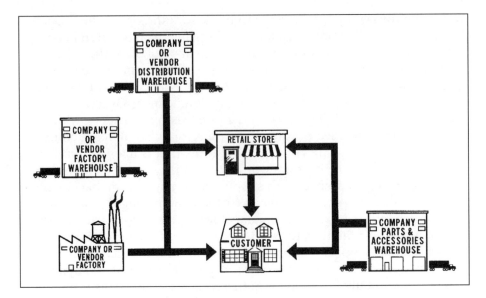

EXHIBIT 2–5

Short Distribution Pipelines

TRANSPORT: THE PIPE IN THE PIPELINE

American consumers have been unnecessarily paying incredible billions of dollars to give products, materials, and components costly tours of the country and of the world. Companies can avoid this unnecessary trucking and voyaging in the network by adopting the major strategies of superior companies. As described in *Reinventing the Factory II*, the first strategy is to develop local clusters of suppliers (whether they are the company's own factories or those of its vendors).[8] In order to achieve this goal, companies need to destroy the myths of economies of scale and learn the lessons provided by numerous companies that have more than proved that new small, focused factories can drastically slash their break-even point. At Bill Copacino's suggestion, the author notes that many continue to believe economy-of-scale arguments have been proved erroneous for job shops and assemblers, but not for some process industries. While the author agrees that there may be some differences in process industries, he doubts there would ever be a single, massive paper machine in the United States, spewing out paper in 5-mile-wide rolls with output approaching the speed of light. The country will continue to operate thousands of paper machines but

[8]See Appendix 2 for reference to information on clusters.

will discover that it is not necessary for one giant paper mill to operate tens of machines. Several smaller mills of one or two machines will prove to be the best model. (Note: whether we are talking about thousands of paper machines or dozens of petroleum refineries, the same logic is applicable). In addition to gaining productivity by dispersing production from single, massive factory sites to several smaller regional focused factories that are close to customers, companies can dramatically slash total transport and distribution logistics costs (capital equipment and inventory investment included). For example, the United States' Southeastern region is the focal point of a high percentage of upholstered furniture manufacturing. The underlying historical reason for this heavy concentration was proximity to two of the most important furniture raw material sources, textiles and wood. However, the economies of distributing finished furniture, which is relatively light weight per cubic foot, is much less favorable than those of dense, heavyweight shipments of fabric and lumber. Thus, furniture sold in various regions can and should be produced in those regions and sold at lower total cost and delivered faster than from the Southeastern industry colossus.

Bill Copacino also felt it important to mention that, in some instances, the initial raw material conversion factory might logically continue to be located near the basic raw material source. For example, many believe that it will continue to be logical to locate lumber mills and paper factories close to the forest. However, evidence that such thinking may also be passé is provided by the economic success of the Koreans and Japanese, who import *logs* from forests thousands of miles away, in North America, the South Pacific, and Southeast Asia. His second point is that when the first processor of a raw material reduces the *bulk* of the product (as in the case of iron ore), transportation costs will be lower if the producer is near the source. This is also a valuable point for contemplation. Taconite factories in the Mesabi Range of Minnesota were developed in the 1960s to improve the economies of transport between the mines and the steel mills in Chicago, Detroit, and Pittsburgh. Taconite is a highly condensed, processed form of iron ore. Now far fewer Japanese vessels ply the Great Lakes and pass through the Panama Canal on their way to Japan, laden with taconite, than when they transported only iron ore. The author finds his colleague's comment to be highly valuable but, in light of the contradictions in these examples, suggests that rethinking these issues will ultimately be of greater value than clinging to the conventional wisdom of centuries past.

Existing visionary views of future logistics networks are credible in most respects but incredibly naïve in many other prediction-based assumptions. For example, few should fail to see that one of the factors that multiplies the costs of bringing products to their ultimate customers is the distance separating raw material sources, production factories, and ultimate customers. In the logical world of the future, manufacturers, their customers, and even elected government officials will see that it just does not make sense to give materials, components, subassemblies, or products rides around the globe in search of cheap labor[9]—at the cost of maintaining global inventory investment and paying exorbitant transportation costs. In this regard, the author respectfully disagrees with such leading experts as Grabner, LaLonde, and Robeson, who have written: "Increasingly, the distribution function of these companies can be expected to have to deal with omnidirectional moves among plants producing subassemblies in various countries moving toward a final assembly operation in other countries with finished products being exported to yet other countries."[10] Instead, they will gravitate toward moving production facilities and clusters of supplier factories to the remote market area (a one-time move) rather than perpetually moving products.

During the early 1980s one of the author's client companies decided to move component and subassembly operations from the northern Midwestern United States to Mexican border plants. These new border operations feed their output to assembly plants in northern Midwest locations. The assembly plants supply finished products to the entire country. The purpose of the moves was to escape the high labor and operating costs of highly industrialized areas. Today, this company's total transportation costs are higher than total labor costs. While such short-term tactics as moving production to low-cost labor areas offshore have been necessary for individual companies' survival, the resultant elimination of more than 2 million manufacturing jobs in the United States has inexorably led to lowering the national standard of living. Some espouse the theory that the public benefits from cheap imports, and the cheap imports should force domestic producers to be more productive. It would be sheer nonsense to claim that the only way to

[9]Blind pursuit of cheap labor can be perilous, as Cahill and Gopals emphasize with their list of offshore production dangers. Gerry Cahill, *Logistics in Manufacturing* (Homewood, IL: Business One Irwin, 1992), pp. 60–62.

[10]John R. Grabner, Jr., Bernard J. La Londe, and James F. Robson, "Integrated Distribution Systems: Past, Present and Future," in James F. Robeson and William C. Copacino, eds, *Logistics Handbook* (New York, Free Press, 1992), ch. 2.

raise the living standard in undeveloped countries is to lower the standard in those that fought hard to develop the industry that is the basic source of wealth in any nation. In reality, cheaper imports have mainly eradicated entire industries. A company in a nation with high standards of living, no matter how productive, cannot compete with countries in which dollars-a-day wages are the norm. Even the Japanese would find it difficult to compete with producers in the United States and Europe, if its workers were paid enough to enjoy the high standard of living and quality of life of those industrialized nations. When Japanese workers' benefits rise to Western levels, the international trade playing field will tilt in favor of others. Japanese companies will find it almost impossible to overcome the costly burden of transporting products and virtually all materials and energy across the wide oceans separating them from their customers and sources. Superb businessmen with accurate visions of the future, the Japanese are now rapidly building production facilities all around the globe. When the inevitable day arrives in which "fair trade" practices make them unable to compete with local companies, those local companies will be theirs. Thus, at least the profits of these companies will be Japanese.

In the true spirit of vision creation, the author deems the ultimate pipe in the logistics pipeline indeed to be some form of pipe, or tube. A network of high-speed delivery tubes, to and from production sites to suppliers and customers, would have several business, public, economic, and ecological benefits. The author was pleased to note that he is not the only one to whom such a seemingly ridiculous vision has occurred. McKinnon reports that J. G. James wrote about this possibility as early as 1980.[11] Among the benefits would be the reduction of vast truck fleets plying the roads, consuming oceans of fuel and spewing tons of pollutants into the air. By contrast, the ideal tube, occupying existing overhead space on streets and highways, would make optimum use of energy and minimize pollution. The costs of continuous highway repairs would be slashed by reducing the pavement punishment caused by the billions of tons of truckloads that traverse the roads every day. In fact, for almost the first time in history, streets and highways throughout the country, freed of truck traffic, would have excess capacity. Costs of drivers or train crews accompanying shipments would also be eliminated by tube traffic. The reader will probably find the vision of tube transport inconceivable in any foreseeable time frame. Some people will even label such a vision "impossible."

---

[11]Alan C. McKinnon, *Physical Distribution Systems* (London: Routledge, 1989), p. 1274.

In fact, even the author deems such a vision to be beyond the limits of practicality in the short term (as in his youth he and the rest of the world both viewed space travel as beyond the realm of practical reality).

However, some of the elements of the dream already exist. Railroad systems, for example, are as close to being tubes as the world has to offer. The only problems with railroads is that they have not yet learned the simple modifications necessary to making the networks work like tubes. For example, the ultra-large trains, consisting of one hundred-plus cars, complicate and delay the train composition. Smaller trains with smaller, faster, lower-cost locomotives could speed up the composition of trains and put them into almost perpetual motion. Modern technology can and should virtually eliminate train crews. By better marriage of piggyback and new "land containers" (described below) with frequent small, fast-moving trains, many of the features and benefits of the delivery tube could be achieved, and are achievable in the coming generation.

An additional major transport-related strategy of the future will borrow from the invaluable lessons gained from the invention and use of the standard intercontinental shipping containers. Before the introduction of large shipping containers, considerably smaller containers required swarms of longshoremen to load and unload vessels. Small containers were loaded into cargo nets, hoisted into the hold of the boat, individually unloaded, and carried to and placed in their storage locations. The handling of small containers kept ships worth tens and hundreds of millions of dollars tied up in port much longer than ultimately necessary. It was extremely labor-intensive and added days and weeks to the time required to deliver materials and products to overseas locations. It also swelled the inventory investment in the logistics pipeline.

Today the process of handling truckloads is still essentially the same as that for the old-fashioned loading and unloading of ships. When the components of a shipment are extremely variable in size and shape and defy the use of slip sheets or shrink-wrapped unit loads, people carry (manually or by forklift) one small package or stack of packages into or out of the back of the truck or trailer (especially less-than-truckload shipments), making innumerable trips into the confined space. Even when packages are of reasonably homogeneous size and shape and can be unitized, it takes about forty-six minutes for a forklift truck, moving at high speed, to unload and reload a trailer. Even when a company's high volumes and uniform package sizes justify installing telescoping conveyor

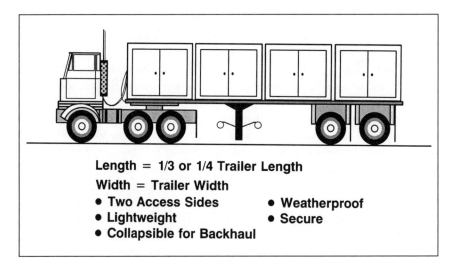

Length = 1/3 or 1/4 Trailer Length
Width = Trailer Width
● Two Access Sides   ● Weatherproof
● Lightweight   ● Secure
● Collapsible for Backhaul

EXHIBIT 2–6

Land Container Specifications

systems (often costing $50,000 per dock, or more), to carry pack-ages into or out of the front of the truck or trailer, the process may still tie up the dock and trailer or truck for several hours. This stone-age methodology will continue to be used until companies adopt a solution to the basic problem of enclosed trailers and trucks. For example, open-sided, roofless trucks and trailers (widely used in Japan and Germany) enable shippers to take advantage of the power of large shipping containers by opening access to loads from all the vehicle's sides.[12] Exhibit 2–6 spells out some of the critical "land container" specifications for the new large containers, which will increase the percentage of time that trucks and trailers will spend in transit, thus improving their overall utilization, low-ering the size of the truck fleet required, and speeding products to market. The new container sizes will be fractions of the overall trailer length and will be the same width as the trailer. For maxi-mum flexibility, the new containers will have access doors on both sides. (Some truckloads are loaded and, in fact, some items are even manufactured in the required unloading sequence. Consider, for example, the automotive industry's major subassemblies such as seats. They are loaded on trucks in the reverse sequence of sched-uled assembly. This enables the assembly plant to unload them in assembly sequence, directly onto the assembly line. With accessi-

[12]See Appendix 2 for reference to information on side-loading trucks.

bility on both land container sides, scheduling, production, and loading will be simpler since reversing the sequence of subassemblies will no longer be necessary.)

Today's trailer and truck cargo bodies are often made of aluminum to minimize their weight. (Excess weight adds fuel cost and cuts load capacity). New containers must also minimize weight. Further, to make back-hauling of containers most practical, they must be easily collapsible. The new enclosed containers will also protect contents from the weather and will be designed to provide protection against theft while in transit. The open trailers, custom-manufactured for handling new "land containers" (Exhibit 2–7), will have built-in hydraulic or electric clamps for locking the containers on the trailer and highly efficient beds of conveyance balls that will make pushing containers onto and off of the trailer an easy one-man task. The ball system permits loading and unloading from the sides of the vehicle as easily as from the rear. Dividers between containers, on the floor of the trailer, will help guide them effortlessly into position.

The advantages of the new "land container" and its trucks and trailers are enhanced when teamed with new corresponding docks designed to accommodate them. Exhibit 2–8 is an example of one such dock design. In this exhibit, ball conveyors in the docks, on each side of the trailers, enable a four-container trailer to be unloaded or loaded in a few minutes. One-man conveyance design

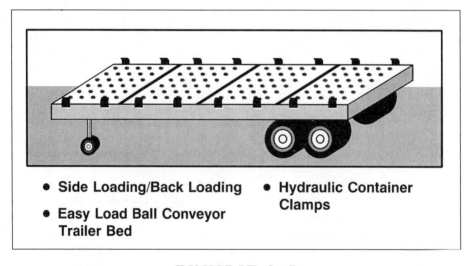

- **Side Loading/Back Loading**
- **Easy Load Ball Conveyor Trailer Bed**
- **Hydraulic Container Clamps**

EXHIBIT 2–7

Trailer Specifications

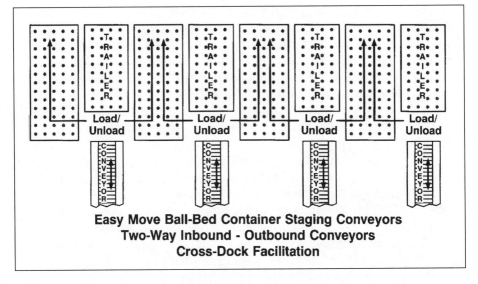

Easy Move Ball-Bed Container Staging Conveyors
Two-Way Inbound - Outbound Conveyors
Cross-Dock Facilitation

EXHIBIT 2-8

Container Dock Specifications

will make it easy to push each container off of or onto the trailer. These docks are designed to facilitate either inbound or outbound loads. In fact, the most efficient use of a facility will be purposeful turnaround of inbound vehicles with outbound loads. For this reason, the design includes conveyance facilities on both sides of the trailers.[13] In this example, each dock, on average, has only one and one-half conveyors. In fact, in many factory and warehouse facilities, two per dock would be unnecessary. In the factory, inbound materials and components are much denser than outbound products, so less unloading conveyor space is required than for loading outbound products. And in the best warehouse facilities, a high percentage of inbound loads will be cross-docked to an adjacent dock. In these cases the inbound and outbound conveyor is shared by two docks. The best of the new "land container" docks, manned by a highly efficient crew, would be able to unload and load a trailer in under five minutes, a reduction of almost 90 percent from the time required to load and unload unit load packages.

Small containers, loaded and unloaded into and out of "land

[13]The author has included virtually no material on conveyance equipment in this book. Those interested in reading more about conveyors will find that other authors have described various equipment types. For example, E. Ralph Sims, Jr., *Planning and Managing Industrial Logistics Systems* (Amsterdam: Elsevier, 1992), pp. 208–15.

containers" at the back of the trailer, are handled by one or two conveyor systems that move receipts into stock and shipments from stock or from the end of production lines. (The most cost-effective facilities will utilize two-way conveyors to minimize capital requirements.) The distance from conveyor end into the most remote corner of the new "land container" is a mere fraction of the distance from the conveyor to the front end of a closed trailer. This reduces the time spent in loading and unloading to approximately the same fraction.

The savings from "land containers" and their correspondingly designed trailers and dock facilities extend out into the network of supplier and customer factories and through the distribution channels. As Exhibit 2–9 indicates, the large semitruck and trailer rig that leaves the product factory with three "land containers" would be used when its deliveries and backhauls are not short, local trips. However, it delivers its three containers to a regional cross-dock facility, where its containers are transferred almost directly to much smaller trucks suitable for short delivery hauls. In the case of such services as UPS, the "land container" contents may have been loaded in the local delivery route sequence, eliminating the need to take the contents through an unloading, sorting, and reloading process. In other cases the container contents may all be delivered to

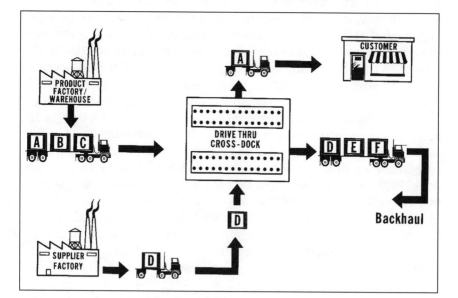

EXHIBIT 2–9

Container Distribution Networks

one customer, such as a retail store. While at the cross-dock facility, the product factory semi picks up cross-dock materials from local suppliers, delivered to the facility by suitably smaller trucks. The customers and suppliers in this future scenario must also be equipped to handle inbound "land containers." This will require a nominal investment in a dock (or docks) equipped with one-man ball-conveyance facilities.

The fact is, "land containers" of a sort are already creeping into use, given impetus by the railroad industry to provide intermodal transportation among ship, rail, and highway carriers. TTX Company's 37,000 intermodal flatcars already make up almost 40 percent of its flatcar rolling stock. Unfortunately, however, many of the containers it handles are special-purpose, such as car carriers. These special containers are not suited for backhaul. Thus their real utilization is less than 50 percent.

Incidentally, the author's use of the word "backhaul" is anachronistic. It is easier and better to strive for "circulating density," whereby it is not important for a tractor-trailer to return to its starting point with a return load, but rather that it pick up something quite close to the destination and take it to any other point. Thus, equipment is continuously *circulating*, and the *density* of average load is very high. For example, today's state-of-the-art transportation businesses are managing their truck fleets with high-tech information systems that keep track of every unit's location by means of in-cab computer communications that relay location and route information back and forth between central logistics management systems and the driver. Customers are given the utmost in rapid response service, and near-perfect equipment utilization is achieved by maintaining instantaneous location and status information on the entire fleet. Available and soon to become available tractors and trailers can be assigned to customers with a minimal delay. The power of the computer is used to reexamine work assignments continuously, optimizing the idle time and empty travel of all vehicles in the fleet. In the future, transport companies might do well to take a page from the railroad's book and found a separate corporation in which all major trucking companies own an interest.[14] Such a company would own and control every tractor, trailer, and "land container" in the system, thus the utilization could be much higher than for any single company, and the total number of units required would be lower. Since financing a fleet of vehicles

---

[14]TTX, founded by several railroad companies, is the owner and operator of all the rolling stock and containers they use. It has lowered the cost of transport per ton quite dramatically.

involves large investments in equipment and maintenance facilities, the better utilization of both would lower the logistics cost, and the size of the single equipment company would give it superior financing leverage.

Another transport strategy might be to increase the amount of transport performed by truck fleets operated by the company and its suppliers. Truck fleet operations of Outboard Marine Corporation of Waukegan, Illinois, and The Leather Center of Carrollton, Texas, to name two, exemplify highly productive, rapid transportation. Although recent deregulation of the trucking industry in the United States has opened sizable opportunities for lowering the transport bill, the resulting lower common carrier freight cost is not the light at the end of the tunnel. An even better alternative to lower-cost common carrier or even contract trucking is greatly increased reliance on company and supplier trucking. Bill Copacino thinks it unlikely that producer-owned or -operated truck fleets will be able to displace the contract carriers, whose recent emphasis on keeping rigs in perpetual motion has permitted them to lower costs drastically. However, the author believes it defies logic to imagine billion-dollar, deep-pocket producers would be incapable of forming their own "contract carrier companies" (many, such as Caterpillar, have had them for decades). Further, as more and more regional clusters of factories and their suppliers are developed, more and more transport will be very short-haul movement in smaller trucks shuttling between factories in a production network and customer facilities. It is hard to see these potentials unless one opens one's perspective to encompass the *entire* range of new operations. Were the author inclined to believe that all current practices would continue, without radical change, he would concur that contract carriage would continue to be dominant. At any rate, it is the best short-term solution for companies with shallow pockets.

In his previous works, the author has neglected to discuss one vital issue central to the overall truck fleet strategy: whether it should use company fleets or persuade suppliers to operate fleets and use them to deliver their focused factories' output. An established fact of business life in most companies of the world is that labor and overhead costs of big companies are higher than those of small companies. Therefore it is tempting to leap to the conclusion that the size of the company vis-à-vis that of its suppliers would be the main criterion for deciding the issue of whether customer or supplier should own the transport. This is, however, only one of two important criteria. The additional factor concerns the distance from the supplier's to the customer's warehouse (or factory) and the number of truckloads that travel between the customer and supplier locations. In most cases of items supplied by smaller local sources, it should be feasible for the supplier's fleet to have lower operating costs than the user's. Smaller companies usually have lower pay rates and less costly bureaucracy. Further, the most economical vehicle size and travel frequency between the two would be those required to shuttle continuously between them throughout the day.[15] For most small local suppliers, this would dictate the use of small, inexpensive trucks, rather than the monsters that make up most fleets. It is no accident that the familiar United Parcel Service local delivery trucks are relatively small. Long experience has proved time and again that these smaller trucks are the most economical for fast local delivery. The advantages of small vehicles are low capital investment (trucks), high utilization, fast delivery, and low inventory in the pipeline. Utilization of small trucks for local delivery is high because the mileage traveled per day is normally much higher than for large tractor-trailer rigs, owing to the greater mobility of smaller vehicles in urban traffic and the shorter time required to load and unload them. New containers also contribute to the overall cost-effectiveness of the local logistics network cluster.[16] Since the best containers (other than distribution-ready packaging) are reusable, trucks that travel between local suppliers and users are always very nearly full, further ensuring that truck utilization will be maximized. Small trucks help to minimize the inventory investment at each end of the pipeline, since the total inventory is at least inversely (often exponentially) proportionate to the frequency of shipments.[17] The decision as to whether to use supplier or company trucks for nearby sources will therefore depend on how many trucks each could shuttle between the two points. For example, the supplier might have total local outbound and inbound traffic requiring only one truck trip per day, not only for the one user's volume but also including all other local customers. By contrast, the user could keep a small truck fleet busy making several "milk route" stops a day at various local vendor and customer facilities. In that case the goal should be for the company to establish its own fleet. When the supplier is

[15]Hewlett Packard's Analytical Instruments Plant in Avondale, Pennsylvania, for example, operates a dedicated truck on a dedicated route. The daily shuttle operates between the factory and eight suppliers, all of them located within an 8-mile radius. Michael Mackey, "Achieving Inventory Reduction Through the Use of Partner-Shipping," *Industrial Engineering*, May 1992, pp. 36–37.

[16]See Appendix 2 for reference to information about containers.

[17]See Appendix 2 for reference to information on total supplier and user inventory phenomena.

smaller and the number of small trucks he would require locally is somewhat smaller than that of the customer, the supplier, not the user, could more logically be the trucking fleet's owner-operator. This would simplify the traffic operations of the customer and minimize the inherent dangers of bureaucratic bloat arising from larger, more complex operations.

When user and supplier are far apart, the use of smaller trucks is more difficult to justify, even though the frequency of shipments would have a major impact on inventory levels. However, although it may be more difficult to justify, it is not impossible. For example, the latest, fastest rail freight moving techniques, such as "piggy-backing" trucks or using tandem trailers, like those in Exhibit 2–10, could make smaller vehicle and trailer sizes somewhat more economically advantageous. Nor is this the sole advantage of using tandem trailers for long-distance transport. For example, a company might have five customers in close proximity, each needing one truckload every five days. The conventional view would be that one complete truckload should be shipped to each customer once every five days, to save less-than-truckload shipping charges. However, when local laws permit using tandem trailers, dropping one at each destination, it usually becomes cost-effective to deliver the somewhat smaller tandem loads daily. In switching from weekly to

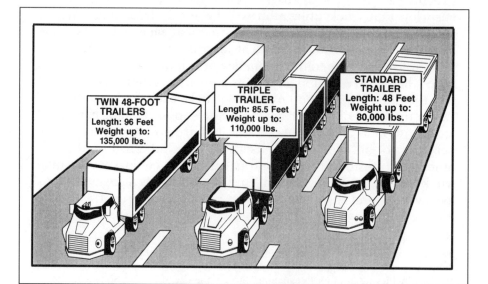

EXHIBIT 2–10

Tandem Trailers

daily deliveries the inventory resulting from delivery frequency can be reduced by as much as 80 percent.

When distances between customer and supplier grow, it becomes more and more unlikely that outbound shipments of products to a single region will be in balance with inbound materials and components. Thus, contract carriers and logistics companies such as SLS Sears Logistics Services are often a more cost-effective option than either customer or supplier fleets. They usually have higher volumes of traffic in both directions and hence a higher utilization of backhaul capacity. Even so, manufacturers and distributors needing relatively little additional backhaul volume to balance volumes in both directions might be able to make mutually rewarding arrangements with other companies needing to ship out of the region in question. The company-owned truck fleet that makes such an arrangement would be, in a very limited sense, providing a contract trucking service. Executives of the entrepreneurial bent are those most likely to engage in these practices and will be those whose companies are most likely to outstrip their competitors. In the largest manufacturing and distribution companies, the volume of traffic from their region to their suppliers' region is often higher for their products, materials, and components than the volume of shipments from the suppliers' region to their own. The author would expect the customer company to have much more total long-distance inbound and outbound freight traffic than most of its suppliers. Thus it would seem to make sense for the customer to be the truck fleet owner and operator for large amounts of long-distance traffic. However, any supplier, even if smaller, can be expected to have higher traffic in some regions. That being the case, the supplier should be the fleet owner-operator.

CAPITAL INVESTMENT: USE WHAT YOU HAVE!

Living in the Chicago area, the author has had years of opportunity to drive past billions of dollars' worth of idle warehouse and transport equipment during second- and third-shift hours and on weekends. That they are idle is easy to see in the case of parking lots full of tractors, trailers, and smaller trucks. Warehouse idleness can be deduced from the percentage of the employee parking lot occupied in off-hours versus the occupancy during daytime, weekday use. The fact that the warehouse is idle for a great percentage of the time is prima facie evidence that capital investment is greater than would be required if the facility were operated around the clock, seven days a week, or as much of the time as is practical. This can easily be understood in terms of the number of receiving and shipping docks required. If trucks were scheduled to arrive and depart around the clock, not on a single shift, loading and unloading activities could be focused in an area that would be one-third the size otherwise required. High-cost automated order sorting equipment used in the most modern warehouse facilities then could be downsized to facilitate sorting of lesser complexity and volume. Further, the lengths of travel between storage locations, order sorters, and docks would be substantially reduced, lowering the cost of conveyors, driverless vehicles, and lift trucks.

Further, as customers move closer and closer to the ideal of just-in-time replenishment from world class producers, the size of the warehouse itself might be drastically smaller. For example, many superb warehouses that operate on a single shift receive and hold a day's worth of goods for the next day's order picking. When operating three shifts, the goods scheduled for receipt each shift could be those destined for shipment on the next. The average inventory in this case would be one-third that of the single-shift operation. (In one of the author's earliest conversations with Ken Clark, general manager of the Manteno, Illinois, Retail Replenishment Center of SLS Sears Logistics Services, Ken's quick estimate of the impact of increasing the hours of operation was that it might lower the inventory of goods by about 30 percent.) Better still, warehouse space requirements will be lower, mainly as a result of increasing the percentage of receipts that are "cross-docked" or, in other words, moved from an inbound to an outbound truck.

The main argument against multiple-shift operations has always been that the prime shift has the best supervision and instant access to support staff. Customarily, support staff work only the daytime shift and are available to other shifts only when called in under exceptional circumstances. As a result, it is customary to see lower productivity and lower-quality performance on the other shifts. Further, conflicts often result from failure to communicate adequately between shifts. In some instances a supervisor or manager on one shift might countermand the instructions of a counterpart on an earlier shift. In one such example, the priority of customer order picking or truck loading might be changed. Although an adequate rationale for the change may support the need to do so, the difficulty of adequate communications most often leads to animosity between shifts.

Fortunately, resolving these problems is a relatively simple, logical process. Exhibit 2–11 is a schematic of shifts illustrating how supervision and staff support people can be scheduled so that they

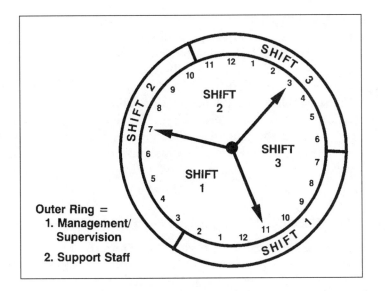

EXHIBIT 2–11

Three-Shift Operation

routinely work hours spanning two shifts, thus making their expertise equitably available for at least a portion of two shifts. Incidentally, the unusual shift schedules on the twenty-four-hour clock are no accident. They are examples of near-ideal work hours, at least to the author. Recently the author had occasion to make a working visit to Los Angeles and to be driven in morning rush-hour traffic to the firm's office. As the odds dictate, a fender bender transformed the freeway into a massive parking lot. As a result, like most typical California days, the trip took several times longer than in non-rush-hour traffic, wasting untold millions in fuel. All this because we tend to be slaves to the clock, bound to traditional work hours, regardless of their inhumanity.

The shifts on Exhibit 2–11 start and end at times in which there is no rush-hour traffic. Further, the hours of each shift are much less brutal to the biological clock, permitting each shift to have some sleep hours in natural darkness. Further, these hours can be an employee benefit boon, as they would permit one of two working parents with different shifts to be home during hours critical to their children, before and after school. Single parents could elect to work a shift during prime sleeping hours, making it easier to find friends, relatives, and even paid sitters to be with the children at night, since the sitters could work on their own full-time jobs during the day. Additionally, every shift would have hours free during periods of lowest activity in supermarkets, department and discount stores, banks, barber shops, and so on. This leveling of peak traffic in *all* businesses has the potential for a major impact on the efficiency of their operations, thus the cost to the consuming public. The author believes that innovative work hours, being a potential employee benefit of major proportion, is an issue in which the entire participatory workforce should be involved. Initial education sessions to explore the practical alternatives, followed by formal surveys of worker preferences, are just one course of action for involving everyone in a decision critical to improving the quality of life.

WAREHOUSE LOCATIONS: FAST, LOGICAL DECISIONS

The author ranks his vision of regional clusters of production and distribution facilities as the single most important logistics issue. Understanding (not necessarily agreeing with) the cluster hypothesis, therefore, is extremely important as a reference point from which to track with the author's viewpoint concerning the question of locating distribution network facilities (including not only warehouses but also consolidation and cross-dock installations). When regional clusters become a widespread reality, distances between network points and customers will be relatively nominal, when compared with today's distances. In fact, much larger percentages of production will flow directly from producer to customer. In this environment route analysis, not network analysis, is likely to have the most valuable applications. The author therefore considers the use of network facility location analysis to be a temporary issue, pending the realization of the matter of much greater importance, a strategy for establishing regional producer-distributor clusters.

Regional warehouses may help a company to provide superior, speedy, and convenient customer service. Further, using regional warehouses disperses distribution operations from mammoth central warehouses to smaller, easier-to-operate locations in close proximity to the customers served. Therefore, many companies would not need to weigh a single, central warehouse location versus regional alternatives. Instead, the logical questions to be answered are (1) how many warehouse facilities should there be, (2) what type of facility should they be, and (3) where should they be located? As Bill Copacino points out, alternatives to warehouses include cross-docking and pool distribution. Bill's note to me says:

> Expanded transportation service offerings (like cross-dock and pool distribution) increase the options available to a company and make

a careful network analysis essential to building a service-sensitive *and* cost-sensitive logistics capability. You should *not* locate a warehouse in a service area for "marketing purposes" if you can achieve the same service performance *and* low cost through pool distribution. A careful analysis can tell you if this option (pool distribution) is preferred for *your* company. It may or may not be. There is no pat answer.

The author would add that customer perceptions also enter the equation. A customer located a block or two from a distribution warehouse who feels the need to make frequent emergency pickups might not be inclined to give his business to a competitor a few hours distant. Marketing is not simply a numbers game. It involves people and their emotions and perceptions.

The issue of how many distribution facilities to operate is treated extensively in literature as a subject of economic evaluation[18] as well it should be. However, in the author's experience the logistical issues of warehouse location are far less important than marketing considerations. If warehousing in locations near the market is a determinant in governing market share, the business volume gain or loss attributable to warehousing locally may cause sales volume to fall below a break-even point (if there is no warehouse). Alternatively, a new local warehouse might increase profitability by faster absorption of fixed costs by increasing sales to customers preferring to deal with a local source. Thus, simply calculating opposing costs of the warehouse alternatives is seldom the sole criterion on which executives should base their decisions. (Leroy Peterson has suggested that a word of caution is in order when discussing the importance of marketing considerations when determining warehouse locations. He has seen marketing vice presidents who have caused an unjustifiable proliferation of warehouses in their haste to expand. Moderation and careful logic must prevail in order to balance the market's potential with cost-effective measures).

My logistics colleagues strongly believe that detailed analysis and simulation of alternative distribution modes and facilities are necessary when considering the very complex pros and cons of the distribution network design. They cite hundreds of studies in which the locations selected for distribution facilities were substantially

[18]For example, see William C. Copacino, John F. Magee, and Donald B. Rosenfield, *Modern Logistics Management: Integrating Marketing, Manufacturing, and Physical Distribution* (New York: John Wiley & Sons, 1985), pp. 311–15; and Donald J. Bowersox, David J. Closs, and Omar K. Helferich, *Logistical Management: A Systems Integration of Physical Distribution, Manufacturing Support, and Materials Procurement* (New York: Macmillan, 1986), p. 281.

different from the hundreds of facilities located in the vicinity of the six most common locations in Exhibit 2–13 or ten additional locations in Exhibit 2–14 (see pp. 68–70). The author has no doubt that his colleagues have performed some of the best possible analyses and have given their clients very valuable advice, considering the data on which their analyses were based at that time. Undoubtedly, *every* logistics professional, having spent an entire career in performing economic and network service analysis (simulation) of logistics operations, will disagree with the author, as do the author's logistics colleagues. They argue that their hundreds of experiences have proved the simulation approach to be right in that the simulations identify the widely varying higher costs associated with warehouse locations other than the ones selected. The author's "scientific inventory management" colleagues, however, specializing in manufacturing, are more inclined to understand that the author wasted years following the mathematical approach, only to conclude that he can obtain widely varying results by changing the assumptions used in the model (for example, establishing regional supplier clusters rather than accepting the suppliers' current locations). Further, the author has never seen a model that proves that the factors and forecast used will be the same in the real world as they are in the model. The only thing that the model proves is that it performs the mathematical and logical functions at high speed and accuracy, producing whatever the results should be, based on the assumptions adopted. More important, the most substantial benefits come not from accepting the parameters of simulation but from changing them in the real world. Nevertheless, the author believes that he would call on his colleagues to perform their numbers magic as one of several important ingredients in the decision-making process. However, he would expect to look to other factors at least as important, if not more so, before making a decision.

The author, once an avid advocate of "scientific management" by simulation, now believes that in fact the picture of the future world as forecast or aggregated from past experience is quite inaccurate in terms of what subsequently comes to pass. Users of simulation tend to have a critical blindness when viewing the results of their numbers. They invariably fall into the trap of believing that their numbers are reality, and they are not. The single most important numbers in the distribution network model are those of the forecast, and the forecast, viewed realistically, is rarely accurate when projected over long periods of time. As Copacino and his co-authors wrote when discussing the mix and level of forecast demand, "Unfortunately, the facts of business life do not match these requirements. It is often difficult for a company to estimate its mix of demand and level of throughput with *any* degree of accuracy even a few years in advance."[19] (The author believes that a more accurate statement for most companies would be even a few *months* (not years) in advance). Bill, however, maintains that the network analysis model compensates for the gamble with demand uncertainty. Bill's note to me says:

> We are certainly gambling with demand uncertainty. A proper network analysis allows you to choose a better solution for the range of demand profiles you may face. This sensitivity analysis must be part of a network analysis. Which solution set provides the best answer for a company across the range of likely or possible demand profiles/ cost factors we face? Again, there is no pat answer. You must do the analysis to find out.

The author concludes from this that the analysis is only as precise as the *prediction* of the person(s) "choosing a better solution." (Chapter 5 contains a lengthier explanation of the problems and opportunities related to distribution forecasting, under the headings "Forecasting, Formulae for Failure," "Business Demand Patterns: Profiles of the Past and Future," "The Seamless Forecast: Continuous Revision," and "Distribution Network Forecasting.")

During the recent Gulf War, much to-do was made of video pictures of modern weapons' pinpoint accuracy. In such examples, whether the missile went through a building's open doors or down its smokestack would have had no effect on the results, unlike a hit in the corner of the building (as evidenced by video pictures of the missiles that penetrated bunker walls up to 30 meters thick). Either hit would have demolished the building's contents. In reality, later analysis proved that the extremely precise hits were the exception rather than the rule. In some instances detailed simulation for identifying the "best" location for a distribution facility might be comparable to weapons systems designed to pinpoint a target. Sometimes the site selected would be right on target; at others it might be in the vicinity. In still more instances the target might have moved by the time the facility is put into operation. (Actual demand deviated from the forecast.) The point is, after considerable simulation to control the path with great precision, the actual results, in real life, are not as often precisely on target as they are near-target or off-target. Part of the reason would be events that occur after the simulation is completed (a change in wind speed or

[19]Copacino, Magee, and Rosenfield, *Modern Logistics Management*, p. 169. Emphasis added.

direction). Another important part is the incredible complexity. The logistics network simulation, as a computer problem, can be infinitely more complex than weapons trajectory, making it very difficult for executives to understand the results. Koontz and Weihrich have written, in describing the limitations of operations research: "The number of variables and interrelationships in many managerial problems, plus the complexities of human relationships and reactions, calls for a higher order of mathematics than nuclear physics does."[20]

Finally, in response to the argument one could not possibly come to a conclusion on warehouse locations without ever having performed (lengthy, costly, detailed) analysis, the author is reminded of thousands of people who once said essentially the same thing when he contended that he could reduce setup costs on almost any machine by at least 75 percent, even before he had ever done so. Since then, he and his colleagues have achieved at least that much on more than 10,000 machines. This time his confidence in his position is equally strong, although he lacks historical proofs as much as he did then.

It is the author's contention that companies know, or can quickly learn, the geographic dispersion of customers and/or sales volume and can record it on a pictorial representation that helps make it easy to determine a roughly feasible location for a regional distribution facility. Exhibit 2–12 is one such depiction, showing the five Northeastern states that are home to more than 20 percent of the country's population. If a company's sales are consumer-oriented, population demographics may be one of the most important criteria for a location decision.

Thousands of companies have asked where to locate their distribution facilities and have tended to come to the same conclusions. Exhibit 2–13, for example, shows six of the most popular distribution facility areas in the United States. A similar pattern of highly popular warehouse areas is present in the United Kingdom, as reported by McKinnon.[21] These locations and surrounding areas

---

[20]Harold Koontz and Heinz Weihrich, *Essentials of Management* (New York: McGraw-Hill, 1990), pp. 450–51.

[21]The author is especially heartened by McKinnon's study results, which included the following important points. First: "The results of these surveys confirm the view frequently expressed in the literature—that there are several well recognized locations around the country to which distribution depots gravitate. Sussams contends . . . that most traders have, over the years, arrived at good, if not optimum, solutions by a process of trial and error." Second: "Approximately two-thirds of the depots [warehouses] used by the sample of manufacturers were located in accordance with the generalized se-

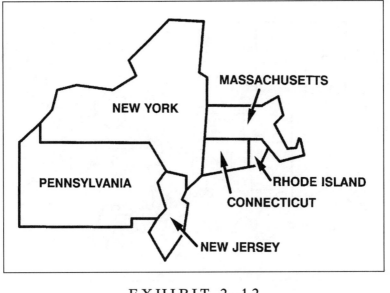

EXHIBIT 2-12

Population: Twenty Percent

have become widely popular because each is roughly central to the population it serves. A company planning to establish its first regional warehouses or cross-dock consolidation centers would be well advised to consider the selection of one or more of these areas, taking into account the following additional basic factors.

1. The central warehouse should normally be located near the largest production facility to facilitate communications and cooperation between it and the supplying factory. The existing central warehouse may already be situated in a location suited to servicing one of the six regions. Therefore, the first new distribution centers (warehouses) would be located near the other five alternatives. Incidentally, Bowersox and his colleagues label the warehouse near the manufacturing facility as a "production-positioned" warehouse and that located near the market as "market-positioned."[22]

---

quence. The deviation of the remaining depots may, in part, be attributable to variations in the spacial distribution of firms' sales and to geographic variations in their relative dependence on different distribution channels. Plant locations can also distort the pattern of depot location. Approximately 13 percent of all the depots surveyed were located at a factory site." Alan C. McKinnon, *Physical Distribution Systems* (London: Routledge, 1989), pp. 140–50.

[22]Bowersox, Closs, and Helferich, *Logistical Management*, pp. 278–79.

EXHIBIT 2–13

Six Regional Warehouses

2. The business strategy alternatives for new regional facilities should be either to serve an established base of customers better or to win customers in a new, unpenetrated region. Although the author's preference would usually be the latter (to increase sales and, thus, profitability), some companies need to consider warehousing in an area of high market penetration to protect their market share in that region.

3. If a company's overall strategy is to protect existing market share, facility locations should be selected in the regions of highest sales volumes. If, alternatively, the main strategy is to penetrate new customers in regions of little or no sales volume, the new locations should be prioritized according to the population of the regions. (However, in some instances, such as products produced for use in customer's factories, it will be of primary importance to locate in the vicinity of the highest concentrations of customer facilities.)

The cubic volume of the existing or potential market is also an important criterion to use in locating warehouses. If the products warehoused are small and lightweight, warehouses could be located almost anywhere with little cost penalty for less-than-truckload shipments. Conversely, the primary decision criterion would be to establish warehouses in regions in which the *practical, achievable* market share would be equal to or greater than one truckload (or economical shipment)[23] per day. This rule of thumb would help to maximize customer service (a daily opportunity to replenish an out-of-stock item would be available). It would also help to minimize safety stocks and total inventories. A second rule of thumb would be to limit warehouse locations based on a projected need for a warehouse staff of no less than three or four. To have a warehouse employing only one or two could be quite wasteful since workload would be highly unlikely to equal *exactly* one or two persons, especially when the warehouse is expected routinely to have large demand peaks and valleys. Further, absenteeism and turnover in such a small workforce could have disastrous effects on customer service. With a larger workforce, comprising a logical mix of part-time and full-time warehousemen, it is simpler to cope with these problems.

Incidentally, aggressive, fast-growing companies will soon outgrow the original six regional warehouses and will therefore need longer-term strategic plans for additional locations. As in the case of the first six regional warehouse locations, companies might find it relatively simple to prioritize the next ten areas, since the most popular demographic concentrations of the next tier are also well known, as shown in Exhibit 2–14.

In summary, the author hopes that ways will be found to simplify the location selection process. As a realist, however, he expects complex, detailed analysis to be the primary decision support tool for some years to come. It is his hope that discussion of simplification of this critical business aspect will serve to spur mover-shakers, smarter than the author, to devise the simpler means through which the process can be streamlined. Ultimately, however, the problem will be simplified most through the creation of regional production clusters.

INDEPENDENT DISTRIBUTORS: SIPHONERS OF POTENTIAL PROFIT

Alternatives for the ownership of the distribution pipeline components is one of the key issues marketing and top management ex-

---

[23]Truckload shipments are not necessarily the only economical shipment volume. For example, when the company has a fleet of trucks, each of which makes daily runs to suppliers and/or customers in the region, a truckload consists of goods for multiple stops. Thus, the truck loaded for multiple stops is better utilized than one that is partially loaded for a single stop. When the truck is able to make additional stops along the way to pick up return loads, its utilization can be even better.

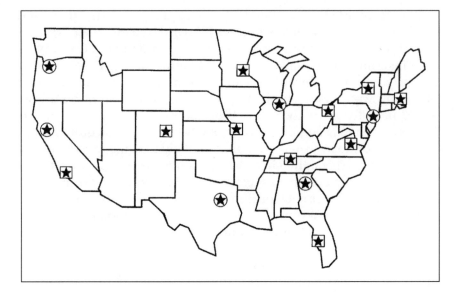

EXHIBIT 2–14

Ten Additional Warehouses

ecutives should weigh. They must then come to conclusions that will lead them to alter the strategic direction in which the business is headed. The author holds that the "best" alternative should never be in doubt. Only the timing of its achievement and the action plan for getting there are topical. What, then, is the "best" alternative? It is the author's opinion that the ultimate objective of every producer should be some day to own the distribution channel components. (Similarly, it should be the goal of independent distributors to acquire or merge with producers). The primary reason for this opinion is that no independent distributor can possibly have as great an interest in marketing, selling, and servicing a product as its manufacturer. And as long as the distributor makes a profit, why should it go to anyone but the manufacturer? In fact, when a company owns its own distributors, whereas competitors do not, it would do well to forgo some of the profits of distribution. By treating distribution facilities as cost rather than profit centers, producers can lower their product's price to the end customer to gain a competitive price advantage. Further, in most instances producers can more easily integrate the management of network operations and systems when the distributor and supplier are units of the same company. Incidentally, McKinnon has noted that the British have already been experiencing a continuous trend away from wholesalers and into direct distribution from producer to retail outlet.[24] At the time of his writing, almost two-thirds of all distribution bypassed wholesalers.

The author views every link in the distribution chain between producer and ultimate customer as a temporary expedient until all problems blocking direct supply from production to customer have been resolved. It is against the best interests of independent distributors to eliminate themselves from the chain, so they never will. In fact, when faced with increasing pressure to improve delivery timeliness and to reduce pipeline inventories, the independent can be expected to put innovative systems to work to schedule direct producer-to-customer delivery but will continue to rake off its normal profit although it never touches the product. Some of the most visionary independents, however, may see the ultimate solution to be the integration of both the production and the distribution chain. Their strategies will be to start a program of acquisition and merger to ensure their future existence and to be one of the first to offer the best in fast, low-cost product delivery.

Not that all or even a majority of the author's colleagues agree. Some feel this position to be completely erroneous and without factual basis. Bill Copacino, one of the foremost authorities on logistics operations and systems, has been invaluable in helping the author to recognize the difficulty of convincing logistics practitioners to believe in the vision that virtually eliminates the independent distributor from the picture. Bill suggested the medical products industry was an example with which to illustrate the impracticality of breaking the stranglehold that some types of independent distributors have on entire industries.[25] In this industry, independent distributors, by virtue of their lock on their relationship with hospitals and other customers, have forced major suppliers into bankruptcy when they have had the audacity to try to establish their own distribution systems. The distributors (in concert nationwide) have done so by shifting their purchases from the offending companies' products to those of their competitors.

[24]McKinnon, *Physical Distribution Systems*, p. 51.
[25]Copacino points out that two logical reasons for a producer (or ultimate customer) to elect to use a distributor are the distributor's ability to provide faster and more frequent delivery, and the ability of the distributor's sales force to be in constant contact with the ultimate customer. The author sees little reason for disbelieving that these services can be provided by producers from their new regional market clusters and reorganized operations. However, it will be hardest for small producers of low-cost products delivered to customers in small quantities to develop to the point of not needing distributors. The author agrees that this may perpetuate the existence of at least some independent distributors.

The author agrees with his valued colleague that any single supplier would probably face business suicide if it tried to defy the unique form of collective monopolistic presence represented by the independent medical products distributors. Nevertheless, rather than accept the independent stranglehold to be an invincible, eternal evil, the author finds exceptional reason for optimism in this scenario. In a recent battle with cancer, the author had occasion to buy his first supply of a drug (taken in conjunction with chemotherapy for one full year) at the hospital. The hospital's charge was $60 for a day's supply. Hospital personnel were of the opinion that drugstore costs must be the same. In fact, the author has since bought his supply (of the identical drug) for $16 a day from a drugstore chain that happens to be its own distributor. Many, upon hearing that example, will know that the exorbitant difference is in large measure the fault of the hospital, but many will also understand the distribution middleman's role in adding his cost and profit to the overall cost to the ultimate consumer. In an era in which medical costs have continuously spiraled ever higher, at a rate faster than any other industry segment, Congress is finally being forced to investigate the astronomical costs. It might eventually stumble upon the fact that one important cost component of the supply chain—with no value added—is that of the independent middleman. Further, industry giants will sooner or later wake up to the fact that the suppliers, as a group, have every bit as much power as the independents and will organize the producers to force the independents to adhere to fair competitive practices. Better still, far-seeing independents and producers will see the writing on the wall and will start a merger, acquisition, and equity-sharing process that will ultimately result in making producers and their distributors single entities. Medium-to-large companies (either distributor *or* manufacturer) especially may find it entirely feasible to become more competitive and profitable by vertically integrating the manufacturing and distribution pipeline. Doing so may be as simple as acquiring complete or partial ownership of a distribution (or manufacturing) company. As the author discussed in his previous book,[26] trading even a small portion of stock in one company for that of its supplier (or distributor) often serves to forge an important bond—a mutuality of business interest—that puts each company's priorities ahead of other suppliers or customers. As an alternative to acquisition, opening a new producer-distribution business may have the greatest potential for

[26]See Appendix 2 for reference to information on equity ownership of suppliers.

success if it operates as a full-line distributor, offering more than just its own products.

The foregoing vision of a world in which independent distributors virtually disappear will be accepted by some but rejected by many who do not recognize that visions are not factually based on the harsh realities of today. True epic visions depend on turning today's rules upside down, based on the systemic benefits for all mankind. Thank God for the movers and shakers who convert dreamers' visions into the plans and actions that ensure achievement of the shining new world of the future. Thank God, also, for the legions of nonvisionary realists who keep business operations running at top efficiency in today's world.

In the practical world of today, there are often compelling reasons for selling through distributors, especially when a company is small. An established distributor may often have an established base of customers and a business volume great enough to support a large investment in marketing its wares in the region in which it operates. Since many distributors (automotive component and beer and spirits distributors, for example) carry many different manufacturers' products, they provide their customers with a convenient service that is hard (but not impossible) for any single manufacturer to duplicate. Such distributors can offer their customers a single source of supply for a wide variety of products from several competing manufacturers. Therefore, the total range of products the distributor stocks is likely to be much greater than those produced by any single company whose products they sell. It would be a great nuisance for customers to have to reduce the number of products they order from a single distributor, only to have to order the remainder from a different distributor. In fact, the only likely reason for doing so would be if the new distributor were to offer significantly better prices. However, this will no longer be true as soon as customers (1) have computer systems that enable ordering from multiple producers as easily, and at the same order processing cost, as from a single distributor, and (2) receive the same fast, reliable service from multiple producers as they do from the single distributor.[27]

---

[27]Bill Copacino has pointed out that it would appear to many (especially those reluctant to accept an alternative to eternal use of distributors) that the logistics cost of ten shipments from ten suppliers could be ten times higher than the cost from one distributor. The author counters that the fallacy in this argument is that it ignores the costs ten suppliers incur in shipping to one distributor and the added costs of operating the independent distribution service. After all, the distributor adds his own costs and profits to the price paid.

SMART WAREHOUSEMEN: VALUABLE ASSETS

Too many executives and managers accept the image and work role of the warehouseman to be that of an individual on the bottom rung of society's and the company's ladder. Those best informed know better. They understand that warehousemen, like any group, are a cross-section of individuals, some more capable than others. Most are able to master higher levels of achievement when they receive the necessary training. As their skills increase, they become more valuable to their companies. Employee turnover rates in warehouse operations have always been among industry's highest as a result of the low pay scales that are deemed necessary because of the low skill requirement. As employees gain value through improved company-administered education and training programs, their enhanced value and productivity will logically be rewarded with improved earnings, which will be one of the new ways to encourage warehousemen to plan long-term careers in the field.

Empowerment of employees with the authority to contribute improvement ideas and to implement them quickly in their operations must be part and parcel of every company's strategic direction toward employee value enhancement. According to Carl J. Mungenast, executive vice president of SLS Sears Logistics Services, process review by empowered warehouse, distribution, and logistics employees is one of the key cornerstones of the strategy for achieving world class performance. Atkinson has written:

> Many people who attend work are imaginative and display enthusiasm when working on projects they enjoy—probably outside work! They will throw themselves into activities which interest them and give them a level of satisfaction. On the whole, the vast majority of people are imaginative, keen to contribute, creative, flexible and enthusiastic. However, the important question is why, in many instances, are these behaviors more common outside the work environment than inside?[28]

Unleashing the capabilities of *all* employees to contribute to the improvement of operations has the potential for tapping a vast reservoir of talent and manpower. However, as powerful a force for improvement as they are, the empowered employees' ideas will be limited by their experience, education, and training. Thus, optimum results will depend on upgrading employee skills.

[28]Philip E. Atkinson, *Creating Culture Change: The Key to Successful Quality Management* (San Diego: Pfeiffer, 1990), p. 64.

ASSOCIATE VALUE RECOGNITION AND BENEFITS

A bold new vision would be incomplete without provision for enriching the life-styles of all society's people, including every stratum of public and private working people, especially associates.[29] Business and government have incredible opportunities to enrich the lives of everyone in society by valuing people and giving them valuable jobs. In this way every working person can be challenged to grasp the opportunity for rich, full lifetime employment and personal value improvement. For example, the scourge of the working man, unemployment, is an anachronism that should have no place in the world of rational thinkers! Every nation and every industrial business has mountains of work that cry out to be performed. The infrastructure of not only developing countries but also the most developed are never ideally maintained or developed, thus infrastructure public works are *always* a vast source of jobs. Unfortunately, most politicians seem to be incapable of managing and eliminating unemployment through the simple expedient of efficiently diverting surplus labor, temporarily, into meaningful public works projects during periods of private employment downturn. It is easy to see that to do so would eliminate the ludicrous waste of nonproductive unemployment and welfare benefits, which drain the public coffers to pay people to be idle. Further, virtually any public works project involves construction, which in turn generates increased demand for materials and products of the companies that supply them. Thus, efficient use of otherwise idle people will not only give them gainful employment but also stimulate the economy by creating demand in industry.

Industry and labor unions have the potential for making great strides toward reducing unemployment far earlier than it is reasonable to expect the rascals in government to do so. It is truly incredible that neither management nor labor has seen the inhumanity and inefficiency of a system that has three work alternatives: full-time employment, full-blast overtime work, and unemployment. Why, if unions are truly brotherhoods, should siblings condone brethren being thrown out of work when business slack-

[29]While working with Sears, the author was first exposed to the term "associate" used by Sears (and other companies) to identify those working people who cannot be described as executives, managers, or supervisors. The author has long sought a term that would impart the proper degree of respect and dignity for working people other than those considered to be "management." Employee, worker, bottom-rung person, subordinate, and many other terms do not adequately reflect the value of people who, after all, are potentially a businesses's most valuable asset. "Associate" is a term that seems to fit best.

ens? One logical, humane way to adjust would be to share equally in the work available, by cutting all workers' hours (and pay and benefits), each day, to the level of the work available. Unfortunately, human greed and potential financial disaster stand in the way of equal sharing of available work. Thus, even though most business slowdowns raise unemployment rates from a seemingly irreducible 2 percent, workers with seniority resist seeing their own paychecks reduced by the nationwide average of 8 percent necessary to keep all people employed.[30] In the United States, where saving and credit purchase habits are abominable, cutbacks in pay would severely jeopardize the personal assets of large numbers of workers who commit every penny of earnings to credit payments and to routine living expenses. However, the burden now falls most heavily on the associate least able to weather the downturn—the youngest employee likely to have the least amount of savings and assets and the highest degree of debt. Hence, to apportion available work fairly to all associates will require solving this dilemma.[31]

Another logical way to eradicate unemployment, long practiced in logistics companies, is to employ "part-time" people. Part-time does not need to mean either temporary or intermittent work. At SLS Sears, it means that the part-time worker is guaranteed a minimum of four hours a day and can expect to work full days and even overtime when workload peaks occur. When part-time workers enjoy circumstances in which the part-time work is preferable to full-time (high school and college students, farm operators, one of two earner-parents of small children, for example), they may be most able to absorb reductions of work hours during downturn periods. The author believes there are far fewer part-time jobs offered than there are potential part-time employees, hence progressive companies will be more readily able to adopt the use of part-timers than might be suspected.

Nor should there be great gulfs between the wages of the highest and lowest paid workers in a society that logically recognizes the

[30]The Japanese manage unemployment as well as anyone but so far have been unable to reduce it much below the 2 percent level.
[31]It is helpful to keep the nationwide benefits of eliminating unemployment in mind. One such benefit would be the drastic reduction of unemployment taxes and welfare payments. Even if tax money were used to compensate associates for the cost of reduced private industry job hours, the costs to society would be less, since every person would continue to earn roughly the same amount and pay taxes on the combined total earnings. Workers on unemployment and welfare, by contrast, have little income and thus pay no taxes. Better still, since the workforce would continue to earn as much as always, it would have money to spend. Recessions would not feed on themselves by reducing the disposable income of the population.

almost universal value of every type of labor regardless of the task performed. The rationale for paying different wages for different types of work, after all, stems from the fact that some jobs are more complex than others and require longer periods of education and on-the-job training. Job simplification and cross-training for several simple jobs has the potential for virtually eliminating huge differences in skills people need to be of great, uniform value to their companies.

SEASONS COME, SEASONALITY SHOULD GO!

The industries and peoples of every nation of the world pay a heavy penalty for the natural and manmade seasons of the year! In terms of logistics costs, peak seasonal sales necessitate vast numbers of warehouses to store goods produced in the off-season. Alternatively, producer, distributor, and retailer capital investments are geared to handling peak loads during their seasons, rather than average demand plus a small allowance for variation. In societies like that of the Japanese, the nonexport-oriented workforce capacity (i.e., department stores) is maintained at an even level throughout the year, making their (nonexport-oriented) workers some of the *least* productive in the industrialized world (in sharp contrast to workers in export-oriented production networks). In industrial societies the burden of seasonality is partially borne by all consumers. (Industry inefficiencies are passed on to the consumers.) Unfortunately, too much of the burden is borne by society's poorest members, those who find work during seasonal peaks but are unemployed for much of the rest of the year. Recognition of the potential for lowering demand peaks and mounting national efforts to implement all of the seasonality-leveling devices that mankind's fertile imagination can create is long overdue. The time to begin is now!

Christmas is celebrated with gifts in many countries. Other countries celebrate New Year's instead of Christmas. These holidays are examples of one of the most pronounced man-made seasonal peaks, especially for retail products. Most retail shops and department stores in the United States sell 50 to 70 percent of their annual volume in the two months preceding Christmas! It behooves industry and consumers to pursue various avenues for spreading Christmas cheer throughout the year. One imaginative way would be to give greater emphasis to ceremonial exchange of *healthy* gifts during such holidays as Valentine's Day, Easter, the Fourth of July, Halloween, Thanksgiving, and others. At present, children are the main recipients of the *unhealthy* gifts (candy and big meals that emphasize desserts) that characterize those holidays. By creating a new tradition, broadening the ritual mystique of family gift exchange on non-Christmas occasions and reducing the munificence of Christmas to the same gift-giving level, Christmas joys could be spread more evenly across the calendar.[32] This would have tremendous benefits for industry! And, when industry benefits, consumer prices drop!

The conventional way that retailers, distributors, and producers level seasonal peaks has been to give customers monetary incentives to purchase more than required in the slack season. However, in recent years the cutthroat competition (in the form of lowered prices) for Christmas sales has trained consumers and their distributors to delay purchasing even longer—until the Christmas season, at which time prices are at an annual low. In these circumstances, people are fools to make purchases at higher prices during the rest of the year. The Christmas lowest-price strategy works against the best interests of all. A much better (temporary) strategy would be for all industry to launch a campaign to price higher in the Christmas season and lower in the other holiday periods. Eventually, when buying patterns are leveled across the calendar, prices during the Christmas holiday period should be no different from those during any other holiday period.

Realistically, it is hard to imagine organizing business and citizen groups with the power to drive industry and government to take the required demand-leveling steps. However, to start the ball rolling only needs a few powerful mover-shaker chief executive officers in a few of the largest production and retail businesses to dedicate their organizations to pursuing these goals. In fact, some industries would benefit from pacts with their chief competitors to eliminate traditional annual or semiannual weeks and months during which all offer exceptional sales prices, thus creating manmade seasonality in demand. Concerns regarding charges of price-fixing would need careful skirting. The objective would be not to fix prices but to stabilize them throughout the year, at each companies' own average price.

In the short term, while seasonality is still a fact of life, companies should seek better solutions for minimizing the costs, market

---

[32]A pragmatic realist, my colleague Leroy Peterson would have preferred this passage to be deleted, as it is a prime example of something with little value in the foreseeable future. Although the author agrees that he is unlikely to see global change in his lifetime, he hopes that mover-shakers in some industries will start the ball rolling in limited areas. The author views the potential benefit as too great to omit comment.

responsiveness difficulties, and workforce problems springing from spiky demand. Peak seasonal demand can be and is being addressed by various companies in different ways. Many companies, for example, simply produce or procure the required products according to an artificially leveled forecast. Then they warehouse the inventory until the season in which it is required. The penalties of this approach are as follows:

1. Forecasts prepared long in advance of a peak sales season are rarely accurate with respect to individual stock-keeping units. They are even less accurate when the items forecast are fashion or fad items. The popularity, or lack thereof, of such items first starts to emerge too late to react—during the sales season.
2. Inaccurate forecasts cause both shortages and surpluses during the sales season. Shortages reduce the amount of potential sales while surpluses must often be sold at distress-sale prices.
3. Warehouse space is grossly underutilized most of the year and barely adequate as the sales season approaches. This, of course, adds to distribution cost.
4. Average and peak inventory investment ties up a substantial portion of a company's assets.

Many companies have shifted most of the burden of carrying peak season inventory to the next customer in the distribution chain. They have done so by any of several means, each of which entails some cost. Some examples:

1. Shipping early and delaying customer payment into or near the sales season (This practice, of course, merely shifts the investment from the inventory asset account into receivables. It does reduce or eliminate the company's warehousing costs.)
2. Shipping early and billing at substantial price discount (Although the costs of carrying inventory and warehousing are reduced or even eliminated, this method lowers the marginal profit contribution of the sales.)
3. Consigning inventory to the customer
4. Shipping early, guaranteeing the customer and its bank that unsold inventory will be returnable at the original billed value

All of the above merely shift costs to customers, causing them to increase their prices to *their* customers in order to maintain their profit margins. Although these approaches do not solve the inaccuracy of forecasts and related shortages and surpluses, inventory in the hands of retail outlet customers tends to generate more sales in the off-season. This occurs, in part, for two reasons: (1) When the outlet inventory on the sales floor is higher, customers tend to buy more, and (2) the retailer will be more likely to advertise and discount in order to reduce his inventory investment.

Large retail chains were once amenable to receiving and stocking in advance of seasonal sales, based on delayed billing or special prices. This practice is rarer today, since they have learned that their added costs are seldom less than the savings from the supplier's discount or delayed billing. Perhaps they believe that shifting inventory back to their supplier will lower the warehousing cost or that the supplier will be willing to eat the added cost, at the expense of his bottom line. However, if a supplier has lower warehousing costs, the customer's goal must be to lower its cost even more. Moreover, no supplier will permanently eat costs for its customers. Savvy customers know that when the supplier offers short-term price concessions, today's reductions will be the basis for next year's increases.

Where practical, maintaining flexible capacity capable of meeting demand during the peak season is a far superior method for producing seasonal demand than price concessions or producing to stock in advance of the peak. When capacity can be varied to match demand, elimination of seasonal warehousing and inventory investment costs is the obvious result. If the primary capacity constraint of a company and its suppliers is unskilled people, flexing capacity to equal period demand may be comparatively easy. Even when employment is at near-record levels, people are always available and willing to work temporary jobs, especially if a company structures working hours and duration to fit the schedules of those willing to work part time: homemaker mothers of small children, recent retirees, and students, to name a few.

Where capital equipment limits capacity, producing peak season demand in the sales season is often extremely difficult but not utterly impossible. The obvious solution to the dilemma is to find products with complementary demand peaks and valleys that require the same processes. This, however, is much easier said than done. In fact, in the author's experience, not more than 5 percent of companies that have conducted a search have actually found such products. A more fruitful avenue to pursue would be to hunt for companies that have the highest number of the same critical machines. For example, consider a company with extremely high seasonal peaks that produces molded plastic or rubber parts. This company would find that some of the larger kitchenware manufacturers have hundreds of molding machines. The additional seasonal need of the company searching for molding capacity might be a very small portion of the kitchenware producer's capacity. Therefore, it might be quite receptive to selling the *capacity of specific molding machines* during the brief seasonal period. When the real need is for equipment capacity in the peak season, the author would expect to be able to find a match in about 10 percent of the companies with which he has had experience.

Chapters 4 and 5 cover the seasonality issue in more detail.

LOGISTICS: EMPIRE OR SERVICE?

Creeping bureaucracy is one of the worst business viruses. For example, such global-sounding catch phrases as "Total Quality Management" are all too often appealing to the manager or executive with responsibility for quality control. Suddenly he can see his empire expanding dramatically, from the limited parameters of product, components, and materials quality into quality tentacles reaching into every corner of an organization. Similarly, logistics executives and managers, viewing the panoramic scope of the logistics network, see their influence starting with material and component suppliers, spreading through product manufacturing, into distribution channels, and finally through retail outlets into the hands of consumers. They understand that the time and inventory in this pipeline can be controlled only by the people and systems that determine the quantity and timing of transport and stock levels throughout the network. Thus, no matter how well the logistics function executes its own *logical* responsibilities of transport between facilities in the network (and, possibly, the operations of warehouses in the distribution network), the total performance, in terms of network inventory and lead time, will be a combination of transportation efficiencies and the skills of the procurement, inventory management, and manufacturing organizations. In fact, sales and marketing also play an important role, since it is these organizations that must provide accurate forecasts and sell the finished products as quickly as they become available.

Grandiose schemes to give the authority and responsibility for the entire logistics network to a super logistics organization are undoubtedly as doomed to failure as was the predecessor materials management organization.[33] Moving partial responsibility and authority from operating organizations into centralized functions merely shifted the responsibility from organizations that could control the total performance within their physical jurisdictions into ivory tower offices in which products, components, and materials became abstractions, merely lines on computer displays. There is no way that an ivory tower analyst can match the performance of an active operations person who manages by virtue of being able to *see* the size, status, and value of the items currently in stock and in process. Therefore, the author, for one, strongly advocates limiting the centralized logistic role to the functions of transportation and, in some instances, product distribution facility operations.[34] The logistics organization should therefore be primarily a service organization, not a largely independent empire within a company.

THE STEP-BY-STEP VISION METHODOLOGY

The basic steps for creating a company's vision of the future are relatively simple, as seen in the planning chart for vision methodology, Exhibit 2–15. The steps are simple, but the execution of the steps demands the utmost perceptiveness, creativity, and imagination. The first step of any project should be its organization.[35] Subsequently, the project requires administration throughout its life. The first actual (nonadministrative) step of vision formulation requires the management team to identify every major barrier to improving operations. For example, the market for the products distributed by a company may be highly seasonal, thus prohibiting level employment or forcing the company to build inventory during the off-season. Another barrier might be vendor reluctance to give

[33]Since the materials management organization became popular in the late 1950s, it has failed to make any significant contribution to lowering national (or international) manufacturing and distribution inventories. Isolated instances of improvement, more often than not, came not from the organization form but, rather, from operating and systems improvements. The driving force has often been simply a forceful individual who bulldozes obstacles to improvement though sheer dint of his personal dynamism.

[34]Although Bill Copacino may disagree with the author's view that the logistics professional should *not* be the executive responsible for the entire production and distribution network (he cites ICI Chemical as one company in which it works very well), he makes the important point that the entire company and its network must be taught to think in terms of the entire pipeline. They must, cooperatively, prevent one organization from operating in a fashion that optimizes its own costs or quality while causing higher costs or lower service in the total process.

[35]One of the author's previous books dealt extensively with the detail tasks within the organization and administrative project step. The tasks in this step are applicable to any well-organized project, including those of logistics facility, operation, and systems design. Appendix 2 references the appropriate book pages.

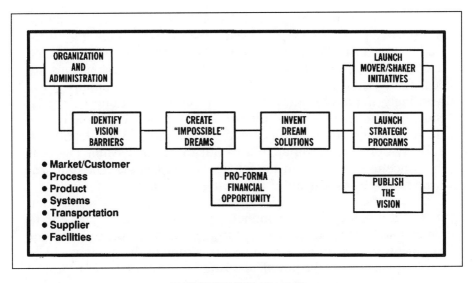

EXHIBIT 2-15

Vision Methodology

wholehearted support to programs designed to ensure total on-time delivery. The barriers, in other words, are conditions that have predominated for countless ages and seem impossible to remove.

The next methodical step is the key to true vision creation. It entails creating an "impossible dream" scenario in which the barriers magically disappear.[36] Dreaming "impossible dreams" is a vital element in creating true visions, for as Kotter has written, "Although visions and strategies are sometimes brilliantly innovative, in a sort of magical sense, most of the time they are not."[37] And although his point was that exciting visions should not be expected in the vision development process, the author disagrees, believing that visions *must* consist of several new exciting scenarios, if quantum improvements are to be achieved. The dream scenario enables the executive team to open two important new vistas. The first is the financial benefits achievable when the barriers are removed, and the second is the emergence of new scenarios in which prac-

[36]Barker suggests the following self-question as a starting point for developing radically new visions. "What is impossible to do in your business (field, discipline, department, division, technology, etc.—just pick one) but, if it could be done, would fundamentally change it?" Joel Arthur Barker, *Future Edge: Discovering the New Paradigms of Success* (New York: William Morrow, 1992), p. 147.
[37]John P. Kotter, *A Force for Change: How Leadership Differs from Management* (New York: Free Press, 1990), p. 44.

tical ways for demolishing barriers start to develop. The next methodology step, invention of dream solutions, entails the most challenging task: inventing solutions to remove the barriers, no matter how impractical or unachievable some of the solutions appear to be initially. As the creative juices start to flow, many of the seemingly impossible hurdles start to come tumbling down. Of course, some barriers defy solution in any reasonable time frame. However, even some of the dreams requiring the greatest, most unlikely upheavals ultimately turn out to be conceivable (witness the peaceful revolution in the former Soviet Union). The only *real* issue in these cases is not *if* the changes will occur but *when*.

During the dream creation and solution steps, the project team should develop pro-forma financial statements quantifying the financial advantages of achieving those dreams. In this way dreams can begin to take on aspects of reality. Some of the dreams will be found to be beyond the practical resources of the company and will remain in the company's misty vision of the far distant future. For that reason, vision creation is not a one-time process. Visions and strategies should be updated whenever the mists between today and the future start to part, permitting a visionary glimpse of tomorrow. The third-type visions should be viewed as within the purview of top executives, since it is they who must work to establish industry programs, political initiatives, and societal habit-molding efforts that might take decades to come to fruition. Given the long time frames of these initiatives, executives must conclude that launching strategic programs for immediate achievement of the visionary objectives would be less than practical. Therefore, the executive approach would be to launch the preliminary, executive-level actions that will eventually enable the company to make its initial advances in its march into the future.

SUMMARY

Logistics networks are incredibly complex, and that is where a good deal of opportunity lies. Many companies' intertwined distribution and supply networks span oceans and continents. Other than raw materials not available domestically, chasing low-cost labor is the primary impetus for overseas procurement of components and goods. These labor costs are often so low that they give the exporter a price advantage even after incurring the added costs of higher pipeline inventories and transport costs. Even the surge in Japanese exports would never have occurred had there not originally been a tilted playing field vis-à-vis Japanese wages as compared to the rest of the industrialized world. Local clusters of suppliers (and *their* suppliers) will ultimately replace the nonsense of farflung sources. Ever increasing improvements by producers will steadily swell the volume of goods shipped to customers directly from the end of production lines, bypassing the need for warehousing and other distribution facilities, especially those of independent distributors. Big-ticket producers will learn to sell from factory to customer, using fantastic new technologies that will move the showroom and ordering into the living room. Production pipelines will be shortened, except for basic raw materials, and new intermodal "land containers" will speed manufactured components and finished products to their destinations at a fraction of present time and cost. Heavy concentration on process and product improvement will bring better products to market at substantially less cost. The stream of materials, components, and products through the supply and distribution channels will tend to flow more evenly during all seasons of the year, and periodic economic peaks and valleys will be moderated. And mankind will learn to master the skills required to manage national economies in the most business-like manner consistent with the well-being of all the populace. The citizens of the twenty-first century have the prospect of seeing unparalleled prosperity and peace.

CHAPTER 3

Future Vision

Warehouse and Logistics Master Plan

Businesses interested in maintaining or, better yet, improving market share must continuously strive to reduce operating costs and investment. To fail to do so runs the risk of losing ground to fierce competitors who should be working every bit as hard to achieve the same ends. The most important costs and investments of a warehouse are not an infinite array. Among costs of greatest importance are transport to and from the warehouse; the building, equipment, people, and inventory investment; and the operating expense. Of these, controlling building and equipment design stands out as a vital key to success because of the designs' impact on other operating costs. The distribution center-warehouse-storeroom with the lowest cost per unit of space occupied will have the best potential for reducing all other costs and investments. For example, in buildings that are larger than necessary, people and automatons spend more time in motion. The result? Higher payroll and equipment expenses and capital investment than would be necessary in a smaller building in which better space utilization makes it possible to store and process the same business volume.[1] Mundane expenses

[1]At least one colleague argues that, in his experience, as storage density increases, productivity decreases. The author concurs that excessive clutter, as a result of storing more than the warehouse is designed to manage, may decrease productivity as it causes

such as utilities are also often proportionate to the degree of warehouse space utilization.

Outboard Marine Corporation's SysteMatched Parts and Accessories Division eliminates central warehousing *per se* for many large, high-demand accessories and service parts by transferring (cross-docking) central warehouse receipts directly from trucks inbound from suppliers to outbound trucks or truck staging areas destined for branches and high-volume customers. In fact, Outboard Marine goes even further by taking advantage of drop shipment services offered by suppliers like A/R Packaging Corporation, Milwaukee. Orders for direct shipment to the division's distribution branch warehouses and for certain major customers are faxed to A/R Packaging. Items supplied by A/R are then shipped directly to the order destination, completely bypassing receipt, storage, and shipment at the central distribution warehouse. Incidentally, the majority of the volume shipped is moved by Outboard's own truck fleet rather than common carrier or contract carrier. In this respect, it resembles many of the world's most successful producers, including almost every major Japanese company.

Although the ideal warehouse is no warehouse at all, even the most visionary seer has difficulty foreseeing complete elimination of distribution warehousing of slow-moving, inexpensive, and small parts or products. However, this should not deter superior companies from pursuing continuous reduction of warehousing through vendor programs designed to upgrade their supplier's ability to fill customer orders directly from the end of the production process. In the long transition period during which distribution inventories are continuously being reduced and warehouses are still a practical reality, it will behoove companies to reorganize their facilities to yield superior results. The following zinger list will help guide the executive through the basics of superior warehouse design concepts.

EXECUTIVE CHECKLIST: WAREHOUSING ZINGERS

Following is a short list of some of the key ingredients of the new warehouse environment. The author hopes that this zinger list, together with lists from other chapters, represents a fundamental

warehousemen to travel around pallets blocking access to an area and makes finding required items difficult. However, in the main the author holds the high storage density–high productivity relationship to be factual and of utmost importance.

framework for most companies' vision of the principles and goals for future operations.

1. New warehouses must be designed in improved modular form to allow for future growth of products and product lines if it is reasonable to anticipate increases. However, provision of "just-in-case" extra space would be foolhardy in the new era in which drastic inventory reductions will finally become practical for most superior companies. Preplanned future warehouse modules should be added only when needed and with minimal disruption to the logic and flow of the previously constructed modules.

2. Most warehouses operate best with a blend of high-tech automation, semi-automation, low-cost automation, and manual storage for the range of high-, medium- and low-demand items and their various container sizes and shapes. Therefore, the best warehouse master plans will be based on the most logical match of families of stocked items to various storage, transport, and conveyance equipment alternatives. The typical warehouse will have more than one family of items of like characteristics and, thus, a variety of equipment types.

3. Wise, thorough utilization of the warehouse's cubic space is vital to maximizing the use of the capital while minimizing operating expenses and payroll. Storage spaces that precisely match the size of *full* containers destined to be stored in them slash wasted space by 50 percent, as compared with container sizes that are one-half of the size of the space or containers that are one-half full. Both situations are found in a fairly high percentage of all warehouses, thus most warehouses have huge potential for improvement.

4. Virtually every warehouse that the author visits can benefit from physically reorganizing and shrinking the space it occupies. One reorganization target should be to establish or improve the zones of activity frequency. By locating the fastest-moving items in one area and equipping them for high-volume processing, a warehouse can greatly increase the productivity of stocking and shipping/issuing the relatively few items that account for the largest volume of activity.

5. Wherever practical, long-range plans should include slashing warehouse inventories to the bone while maintaining or improving customer service.[2] (Most distribution facilities the author has visited have huge potential for further reductions.) This will be accomplished by continuous improvement, over time, through company and vendor programs that will dramatically reduce resupply lead time and increase the frequency of smaller warehouse deliveries. A vendor program to achieve that end can reduce the supply lead time, through the entire production and distribution pipeline, by as much as 90 percent. In addition, many companies can and should achieve immediate large reductions by simply reexamining safety stocks and delivery quantity policies and judiciously lowering them.

6. Warehouses that are designed to receive, ship, and pick orders twenty-four hours a day will best utilize the investment in building and equipment. In contrast to these facilities, warehouses designed for and operating only one shift are at a great competitive disadvantage. Their investment in building and equipment must be significantly greater than competitors' facilities that operate around the clock, seven days a week.

7. Extra warehouse space, provided for just-in-case, long-term future growth, and seasonal peaks, often causes the warehouse to have capacity far in excess of its usual need, especially in the early years. Modular warehousing designs that incorporate features for fast, nondisruptive building additions as growth actually occurs and temporary leasing arrangements during peak storage seasons are two valuable key options for minimizing this type of waste.

8. Queues of trucks awaiting loading and unloading increase transport cost. Therefore, new equipment, practices, and

[2]The caveat "wherever practical" was added in response to one colleague's avid opposition to the statement that all companies should cut distribution inventories. His valid position is that many sales organizations have decided to increase distribution inventories and, as a result, have been able to increase sales. Thus, it is politic to recognize past and (sadly) existing realities. However, the author believes that "wherever practical" applies to companies unable to envision the new ilk of production facilities. Another argument the author has heard has been that "all distribution companies" have approximately four inventory turns per year, so where is the evidence that they should do better? The author holds this argument to be compelling evidence of the need for reform. Four inventory turns is roughly equivalent to the average item's being received six months before being used!

procedures for slashing these delays are integral elements of the new distribution pipeline.[3]

9. Straight-line flow through a warehouse is almost always a poor layout alternative.[4] The best layout usually would have entrance and exit at the same docks, with high-volume items closest to the point of receipt and shipment.

10. Drastically reduced aisle sizes are one method for reducing movement and increasing the storage density.[5]

11. Many warehouses have a wealth of unoccupied space in receiving, packing, and shipping areas. Some even waste overhead space in storage areas. The best warehouses will use every cubic inch of space for either vertical storage or overhead offices. The reduction of space occupied pays large dividends in terms of reducing overhead costs and improving the productivity of warehousemen.

LONG-RANGE WAREHOUSE FACILITY PLANNING

After the warehouse (distribution center, storeroom) design team completes the selection and design of containers, racks, and shelving (covered later in this chapter), it is a logical next step to determine the quantity of each type to install in the revised (or new) warehouse layout. In the past, the first—and unwarranted—preoccupation of warehouse layout planning was forecasting the long-term *growth* in storage needs for individual items and determining new and expanded product line's storage requirements. The purpose of these space-inflating exercises was to forecast "accurately" future cubic storage capacity needs. This approach presents at least three severe problems. First and foremost, the science or art of long-term forecasting is very imprecise, and the likelihood of ac-

[3]Often warehouse executives are less than enthusiastic about the potential savings on the receiving-and-shipping docks. In the first place, if trailers can already be loaded in less than one hour, the potential savings of personnel loading and unloading time seem trivial measured against the transportation costs in the logistics network. Often they fail to see that the theoretical truck turnaround time is considerably less than actual turnaround time. They often also fail to see that the biggest benefit comes from keeping transport equipment in even better near-perpetual motion. And those who contract transport often overlook the potential for negotiating more favorable rates as a logical reward for slashing turnaround time.
[4]This is a point of disagreement for the author and others. As of this writing the author has not yet seen convincing arguments for straight-through (or L-shaped) processing, except in factories as explained later in this chapter.
[5]Not everyone agrees with the author on this point. However, the author contends that, if narrower aisles halve their size of the warehouse, the distances traveled when going to and returning from stock locations will usually decrease in correlation with the reduced aisle sizes.

curacy over the warehouse's long life is quite low. Second, most companies have little inkling as to the product line changes that will occur beyond the immediate future. Third, most companies will be able to reduce pipeline inventories radically, especially in warehouses that store items for long periods. Credence can now be given to the idea that although demand might increase, the amount planned to be stored nevertheless can and must decrease over time. Therefore, companies must shift the emphasis of their space planning strategy away from inventory growth to methods for its reduction. Thus, internal company and external vendor programs are imperative needs for beginning the march toward radically lower twenty-first-century inventories.

Even if companies address the realities of impractical, inaccurate long-range forecasts by making compensation for inaccuracy, it is not enough. If they base storage planning on each item's current demand and replenishment order sizes and tack on a flat percentage to provide for future growth in sales volumes and product line expansion, results can be dismal, for many of the reasons discussed previously. The add-on provision for future growth has been one of the factors contributing most to the surplus space in warehouses, especially in the early years of their useful life. Conversely, some warehouses suffer from inadequate space due to faster-than-anticipated growth, inaccurate forecasts, and the typically limited horizon of future expansion plans. Regardless of the outcome of warehouse space planning (excess or inadequacy), many (like the author) who have been through the planning process come to realize that the precision and detail that go into the process are too costly in light of the actual needs that emerge after the warehouse has been constructed and in operation for some time. For, as Copacino and his colleagues write, "the effort to build the ultimate . . . warehouse has led designers to insist on firm specifications for the mix of product and level of throughput. Unfortunately, the facts of business life do not match these requirements."[6]

In the waning days of the twentieth century and the early years of the twenty-first, the planning of warehouse space needs to be based on an entirely new perspective. In the new environment, the best strategies will be continuously to reduce the number of items previously stocked (even as other new items are added) and to decrease the average stock level of each item. Here are some of the reasons for reduced storage space requirements:

[6]William C. Copacino, John F. Magee, and Donald B. Rosenfield, *Modern Logistics Management: Integrating Marketing, Manufacturing, and Physical Distribution* (New York: John Wiley & Sons, 1985), p. 169.

1. Drastic reduction of the vendor's setup and changeover costs and both company and supplier order-related costs, in combination with improvements in transport costs, will make it practical to reduce delivery lot sizes and increase the delivery frequency of each item continuously.
2. Suppliers will be able to respond much more rapidly to new and changed demands since their manufacturing and procurement lead times will be slashed. Therefore, supplier deliveries will be much closer to actual demand than in the past.
3. With faster supplier response time and more frequent deliveries, the warehouse's need for safety stock should drop sharply.
4. Strategies for increasing production flexibility to match factory and supplier output more closely with seasonal sales peaks will eliminate warehouse space that is used to accumulate stock in advance of peaks.
5. Product line rationalization and product simplification and standardization should reduce or stabilize the number of *existing* products and sharply reduce the number of components and materials.[7]
6. Responsibility for shipments to customers should be increasingly shifted from warehouse to supplier factories as quickly as this becomes practical. Alternatively, systems and procedures to transfer receipts on inbound trucks to outbound trucks (cross-docking) should be expanded.

In light of the drastic changes that can be anticipated and those that no one can possibly predict or forecast, a logical question arises: What strategies should a company pursue to best match warehouse capacity to unpredictable but significantly lower future requirements? Following is a checklist of some of the strategies that should be considered.

1. As space requirements shrink, the warehouse area occupied should be continuously compressed, freeing large areas over time. This can be made to yield continuous improvement in warehouse efficiency by reducing travel time and can free up one or more areas of the warehouse for other uses.
2. The new layout should be designed to accommodate new lower levels of inventory. Allow for a temporary overflow

[7]See Appendix 2 for reference to information on product line simplification and product design standardization.

area in which to store existing inventory that exceeds the new target levels. Replenish new stock locations from the temporary transition stocks, avoiding placing new orders (or supplier schedules)[8] with vendors until the overflow stocks have been depleted.

3. A modular design should be developed when a company decides there is a potential for significant future growth in storage needs. Such a design is an important solution to the uncertainty of future need and helps avoid the cost of partially empty facilities while waiting for the increased demand to occur. When planning a new modular warehouse, the company should construct the initial module to meet immediate needs and erect additional modules as growth actually occurs. Excessive beginning inventory can be accommodated until it is used up by using the temporary overflow storage in *leased* facilities (point 2 above). The recourse to temporary leased facilities is also useful when rapid growth unexpectedly outstrips the pace of constructing new modular additions.

4. Warehouse planners must be especially careful in controlling costs when high-rise storage and retrieval systems are applicable. The modular design is an extremely important way in which the high cost of automation can be paced to match, as closely as practical, the actual growing need.

The logical starting point of warehouse design is determination of the types, sizes, and volumes of containers to be stored and the equipment to be used to transport and store them. Accordingly, it might have been logical to start this chapter by addressing those issues. However, the author deems it more important to discuss first (in the following section) how to put it all together in a facility layout, thus providing a framework into which to place the detail components.

WAREHOUSE LAYOUT: ROAD MAP TO EFFICIENCY

Smith and Tompkins have sagely identified the ideal shape of a warehouse (from an efficiency standpoint) as circular![9] However, they envisioned shipping and receiving docks all around its perim-

---

[8]See Appendix 2 and the index for references to information on supplier schedules replacing purchase orders.
[9]Jerry D. Smith and James A. Tompkins, *How to Plan and Manage Warehouse Operations* (Watertown, MA: American Management Association, 1982), pp. 97–98.

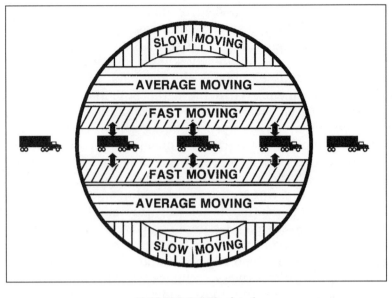

EXHIBIT 3–1
Warehouse Ideals

eter, a design that would be highly inefficient. A round warehouse alone would not take full advantage of the fact that a few items have very high demand, while a very large percentage of items have very low demand. The even more ideal round warehouse in Exhibit 3–1 solves this shortcoming with a drive-through lane. As the exhibit indicates, the average distance from the combination drive-through receiving and shipping lane to the storage location is shorter than in square or rectangular alternatives. Fast-moving items are stocked closest to the truck lane, so inbound trucks can be rapidly unloaded and reloaded with outbound shipments with a minimal amount of travel (which assumes a superb traffic system that uses the same trucks for both receipts and shipment). Slower-moving items are stocked farther from the truck lane, and the slowest-moving in the most remote warehouse locations.

If all trucks were open-sided, as the author discussed in a previous book,[10] a warehouse team could speedily load and unload from both sides of the truck (given the logical dock design), greatly reducing the time required as against the use of trucks from which loads can be accessed only through the rear doors. Each truck could then move rapidly from one "dock" to another, unloading

[10]See Appendix 2 for reference to information on open-sided trucks.

and reloading the items stocked in that area of the warehouse. Moving the truck from point to point can be considerably more economical than using a lift truck to move individual items from all over the warehouse to any single loading dock. (An elaborate conveyance system that eliminates the need for lift trucks would change this argument). To achieve the potential economies of movement, however, the systems for coordinating order picking in different warehouse areas must be under superb control. Neither Smith and Tompkins nor the author mean to imply that the circular structure is necessarily a practical option. Rather, the example points out some basic objectives of warehouse design and the importance of coordinating transport scheduling and design in order to obtain the best results achievable only through the combination. Further, Exhibit 3–1 is an oversimplified warehouse, omitting several real-world logistics requirements such as packaging, truck staging, and offices. Incidentally, the author has left further discussion of dock design to Bruce Ketchpaw, who has provided an excellent description of the most widely recognized traditional options: flush, enclosed, staggered, and angled "finger" docks.[11]

Many still harbor erroneous notions about the advantages of straight-through versus **U**-form warehousing. Copacino, for one, recognizes that the straight-through design was well suited to a factory's storage facility, where the storage dock is on one side of the storage area and factory operations on the other, while the **U**-form is best suited for distribution warehouses.[12] Endorsing the straight-through warehouse form as applicable for factories is not intended to be an endorsement for factories of the past, which were designed with giant central storerooms. As discussed in *Reinventing the Factory,* the factory of the future will have docks and storage all around its perimeter.[13] As Exhibit 3–2 indicates, each such dock and storage area will be located as close as possible to the subplant point at which the items received are used. The author has found that in most factories in which such docks have been designed for just-in-time delivery (or earlier), the required storage depth, adjacent to the dock, is so shallow and small that the question of storage shape becomes largely academic.

Practical warehouse designs will, in reality, be rectangular in shape, as are the two examples in Exhibit 3–3. This illustration addresses the issue of where to locate receiving and shipping docks.

[11]Bruce Ketchpaw, "Dock Design," in Jerry D. Smith and James A. Tompkins, eds., *The Warehouse Management Handbook* (New York: McGraw-Hill, 1988), ch. 11, pp. 211–35.
[12]Copacino, Magee, and Rosenfield, *Modern Logistics Management,* p. 161.
[13]See Appendix 2 for reference to information on perimeter docks.

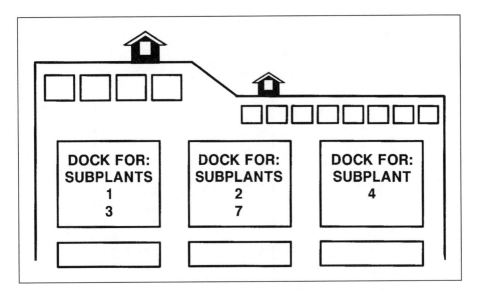

EXHIBIT 3-2

Multiple Subplant Docks

The options shown are on opposite sides or both on the same side of the building. Although Exhibit 3–3 shows two warehouses of the same size, combining receiving and shipping on a common end of the building normally reduces the overall space required. For example, when receiving and shipping are located at separate ends of the building, each needs sufficient space and docks to handle peak loads. In the combined facility, where peaks in receiving can often be offset by valleys in shipping, the total space and dock requirement can be less. It is of even greater importance to see that travel in the straight-through warehouse will be substantially higher! Trips from either receiving or shipping to a storage location will average 50 meters in the warehouse in Exhibit 3–3, with one-half of all trips transporting nothing. Further, the straight-through layout makes it virtually impossible to reduce the transport travel average by organizing zones of storage on the basis of customer demand volume. In the **U**-form warehouse, the logistics of inbound and outbound transport to and from storage can be designed and managed so that almost every trip into storage will first transport products received into storage and then pick up products to be shipped. (In light of their high cost, automated storage and retrieval systems *must* be designed and computer-controlled to achieve this objective.) With the highest-volume products closest to the docks, the

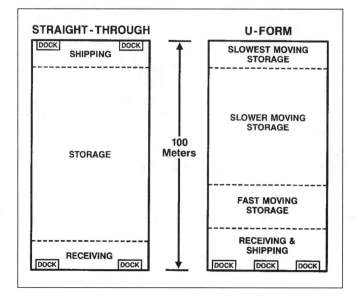

EXHIBIT 3–3

Dock Location Alternatives

majority of trips (in the Exhibit 3–3 warehouse on the right), to and from storage are much shorter than 50 meters.

Most large warehouses are designed to operate as one huge business, with several different specialists operating within separate departments, such as receiving, shipping, storage, and packing. The sheer size of the entire warehouse requires unreasonable management involvement if the responsible executive is expected to play an active participating role in controlling its overall performance. As in the case of the reinvented factory, the author advocates reorganizing the large warehouse into several smaller warehouses, each with a manager and team completely responsible for the products received, stored, picked, sorted, packed, and shipped. The advantages of the smaller, focused business-within-a-business are discussed extensively in the author's prior works.[14]

With its several different types of storage racks and shelving for the different sizes of containers, the warehouse in Exhibit 3–4 begins to get closer to a realistic layout for a "reinvented warehouse." Storage, conveyance, and transport equipment that match the size of items stored and the volume of demand is of the utmost impor-

[14]See Appendix 2 for reference to information on small, focused factories-within-a-factory.

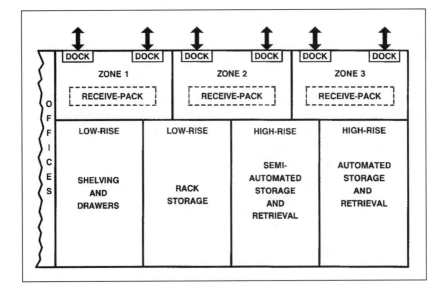

EXHIBIT 3–4

Storage Racks and Shelving

tance in minimizing labor and investment costs. There are usually five basic forms of storage. In addition to the various types of racks and shelving illustrated here, some products require no racks or shelves, because they are packed in a manner suitable for storage in stacks. The completely automated storage and retrieval option is most applicable to items that are stored and retrieved in full-container multiples. Since the several types of storage–retrieval machines described by Jerry Fuchs are critical limiting resources in the expensive automated system,[15] the automated system will be best utilized when *only* full containers are stored and retrieved. In this way, every trip into and out of the facility can be used for storing one newly received container when the machine goes into the storage rack, and can return with a different container of an item needed for shipment or issue.

If a warehouse system permits partial containers, it may be necessary for the storage–retrieval machine to retrieve a container and to return it to storage after the warehouseman has removed (picked) part of its contents. When order picking *must* be characterized by picking part of a container's contents, it is almost always best to con-

---

[15]Jerome H. Fuchs, *The Prentice Hall Illustrated Handbook of Advanced Manufacturing Methods* (Englewood Cliffs, NJ: Prentice Hall, 1988), pp. 430–64.

sider a semi-automated storage and retrieval system or even manual storage and retrieval (rather than one that is fully automated). In the semi-automatic system, the storage and retrieval machine, Exhibit 3–5, is designed to carry the warehouseman to the storage location, rather than to bring products to him automatically.

The Yamaha Motor Company service parts warehouse in Japan, designed by my friend Mr. M. Takayanagi, now president of the TTW Corporation, has an extensive semi-automated storage and retrieval system. Mr. Takayanagi's decision to use semi-automation was consistent with the relatively low-volume demand for thousands of high-reliability parts. Whether the travel path of the machine is manually or computer controlled, this type of machine has certain advantages. It can carry a load of receipts and the warehouseman to storage, where he can stock the new receipt, then proceed to pick and count partial container quantities and return the partial container to stock before transporting the item(s) picked out of the storage area. Thus, most trips into and out of storage can be productive, loaded trips. And although the machine usually moves much slower than the completely automated system, its effective speed will be much higher in terms of the number of receipts and picks processed.

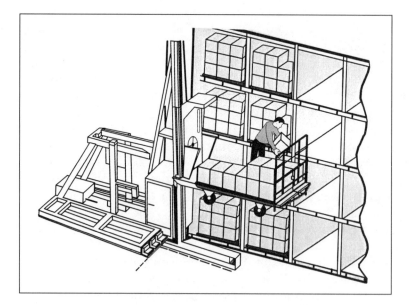

EXHIBIT 3–5

Semi-automated Storage/Retrieval

The carousel automated storage–retrieval system, an example of which is shown in Exhibit 3–6, is sometimes useful for small items of relatively low consumption. Ken Clark, manager of SLS Sears Logistics Services' Manteno, Illinois, Retail Replenishment Center, has some valuable insight into this and other forms of automated systems. Of the carousel newly installed in his operation for small, slow-moving items, Ken said, "There was no way to justify the very high cost of the carousel in terms of picking the items stored in it. The justification came from taking these items out of the area in which they were previously stocked, reducing order picking travel time in that area by compressing its size." Ken's observations about the lack of other automated systems in his warehouse were equally insightful. When asked why his huge warehouse contained mainly conventional low-rise and high-rise equipment, and after pondering over the question, we came to a logical consensus. The extremely diverse number of sizes and shapes of the 13,000 items stocked (stock keeping units, or SKUs) is such that systems expecting to find uniform container or pallet sizes in uniform-size stock locations just would not work without wasting lots of space to accommodate a large range of container sizes.

Courtesy of
White Storage &
Retrieval Systems, Inc.

EXHIBIT 3–6

Carousel

The layout in Exhibit 3–4 has the automated and semi-automated storage side by side because the heights of both are typically much greater than through the rest of the warehouse. Rack storage, which is supplied in several different varieties from innumerable vendors, is usually used to store pallet-size loads. Rack storage might be used for surplus (bulk storage of items normally stored in the shelving area), for very large and/or irregular-shaped items (the most difficult to store in automated systems) or for items that have such extremely high-volume turnover. Achieving high space utilization of a large variety of items with irregular sizes and shapes is usually difficult, to say the least. (Ken Clark coined the term "uglies" for these types of items. Indeed, they are a warehouse-man's nightmare when it comes to mastering the application of conventional techniques and equipment for storing and retrieving them.)

Equipment for shelving and drawer storage (especially applicable to service parts) is available in an almost infinite array of configurations, including modular equipment, which permits the warehouseman to create a custom storage facility. The facility can be tailored to match the size of every storage slot to the containers or loose pieces stored. Shelving and drawers are usually most applicable to small and/or low-volume demand items. The rack storage and shelving and drawer areas are adjacent, because both have relatively low ceiling height requirements.

Every dock in the warehouse should be a combination receiving and shipping dock, as indicated by the arrows pointing into and out of shipping docks in Exhibit 3–4. Further, inbound trucks should be routed to the dock zone in which the majority of the items on the truck will be stored (or the closest available alternative dock when the docks in the designated zone are full). Thus, the trucks directed to Zone 3, automated and semi-automated storage, should usually arrive with truckloads of large, pallet- or skid-size containers. At the opposite extreme, the trucks arriving at and departing from Zone 1 (shelving and drawer storage), would normally contain less-than-truckload volumes and/or be small package delivery services (parcel post, UPS, etc.). Signs over each dock entrance should indicate the storage zone. Where necessary, the gate guard or dock traffic controller should be equipped with systems to direct inbound trucks to the appropriate docks.[16] The *widths* of the four

---

[16]As one of my colleagues, Bob Mann, has pointed out, many warehouses in the United States and Europe have docks directly on the street. Warehousemen in these facilities will find the concept of a gate guard quite foreign. However, in factory complexes and in

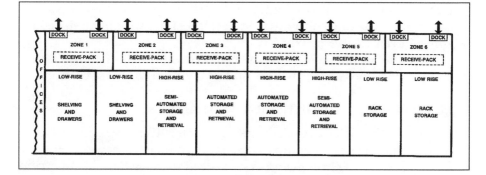

EXHIBIT 3-7

Modular Warehouse Addition

storage types will never be as uniform as illustrated in Exhibit 3–4. However, it would be desirable to design the facility with a uniform *depth* and to vary the *width* of each storage type according to its need. The objective of the standard depth would be to achieve a regular, rectangular building perimeter, because such a shape would best fit rectangular building sites and would help to minimize construction cost.

Dock zoning helps to reduce further the distance between the dock and stock. Exhibit 3–4 indicates that each zone has areas where receipts and shipments (or issues) are processed. The same areas are used to prepare and package products for shipment. These areas are surrounded by space available for staging both inbound and outbound truckloads. It is no accident that offices in the layout are on the left, the low-rise, lower-volume end of the warehouse. The warehouse office, after constructing an add-on module, should not be in the center of two warehouses, interfering with flow between them. Therefore, a modular addition should be easily added to the right (nonoffice) end of the building. This also keeps together the high-volume, high-rise sections of the original building and the addition. These sections are the most critical in terms of efficiency, since they contain the items with highest revenues.

In the event that a company outgrows the first module of warehouse storage, illustrated, a modular addition, Exhibit 3–7, could double the warehouse size while maintaining most of the logic of the original layout and minimizing the need to reorganize the warehouse completely. In this example the building addition is a virtual

many developing nations where security is a serious concern, gate guards or traffic directors are of vital importance.

mirror image of the original warehouse. Only the low-rise rack equipment was moved in order to keep most of the similar storage zones in reasonable proximity.

After the overall concept of the warehouse layout is determined, specific decisions about the size and layout of aisles must be made.

PUTTING IT ALL TOGETHER—WITH AISLES

In *Reinventing the Factory* the author wrote: "Every structure—no matter what its size or complexity—is based on a framework. For a factory layout, the framework is its aisle system—whose symmetry often indicates the quality of the factory layout itself."[17] The warehouse aisle system is no less important. In many of today's warehouses, aisles (other than those in automated storage and retrieval systems) are broad avenues, regardless of the fact that such magnificent boulevards alone occupy as much as 40 percent of the warehouse. Aisles need to be only wide enough to accommodate the minimum practical size of the equipment that moves in them. Otherwise warehouse productivity can be adversely affected by travel paths that are much longer than necessary. Therefore, considerable attention to minimizing aisle size is warranted.

In one small warehouse that previously used only rack storage, containers, regardless of size, were placed in any available rack location. Further, skid-size loads might be stored in any aisle when empty racks spaces were hard to find. Therefore, every aisle had to be wide enough to accommodate lift trucks. When the warehouse changed to the use of both rack storage and variable shelving to match container sizes, it was able to reduce all aisle sizes, as illustrated in Exhibit 3–8. To handle the new containers in the aisle applicable to the racks and shelving used, the warehouse used new transport equipment: manual carts for medium-size containers (and aisles) and narrow-aisle lift equipment for skid-size containers. No transport equipment was required for the very smallest, lowest-usage-volume items, which were retrieved so infrequently that they could be hand-carried. Thus the aisles needed to be only wide enough to accommodate the single person infrequently working in them (the work assignments were by zone, and the level of activity low, thus the potential for two people needing to be in an aisle at the same time was virtually nil.

Lanker points out that conventional lift trucks need space enough to make a 90-degree turn, necessitating aisle widths of 10 to

---

[17]See Appendix 2 for reference to more information on aisles as the framework for design.

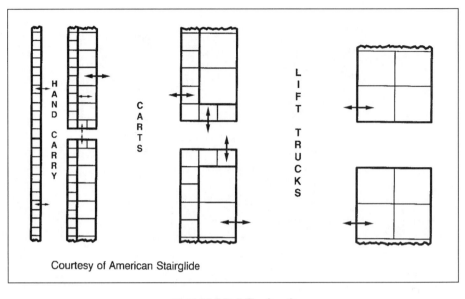

Courtesy of American Stairglide

EXHIBIT 3–8

Aisle Size

15 feet,[18] a veritable boulevard that greatly increases the overall
size of the entire facility. Specialized equipment that can move
stock into and out of storage without turning can slash required
aisle sizes. For example, Lanker points out that narrow-aisle trucks
need 7 to 9 feet, while very-narrow-aisle equipment needs only 4 to
6 feet. He describes several examples of this type of powered equipment (see Exhibit 3–9 for just two examples) as well as lower-cost,
manually operated alternatives and various typical performance
specifications. Professional warehousemen should maintain routine contact with lift equipment suppliers to stay up to date with the
most recent price and performance characteristics of all practical
alternatives.

RECEIVING: BOTTLENECK OR FUNNEL?

Receiving (and shipping) operations in many warehouses are critical bottleneck areas (Exhibit 3–10) that substantially hinder the
company's ability to provide satisfactory customer service and to
eliminate the just-in-case time provided for routinely performing

[18]Karl E. Lanker, "Lift Trucks," in Jerry D. Smith and James A. Tompkins, eds., *The
Warehouse Management Handbook* (New York: McGraw-Hill, 1988), ch. 15, pp. 321–71.

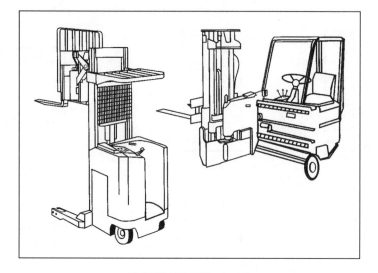

EXHIBIT 3–9

Narrow Aisle Equipment

receiving, stocking, picking, and shipping activities. There are several basic reasons for problems in these operations. Chief among these are:

First, trucks tend to arrive and depart in peak periods during a month, a week, and each day. Therefore, the total time required to process receipts and shipments into, through, and out of the warehouse is variable. It has always been (and probably always will be) impractical to vary planning lead time factors according to the

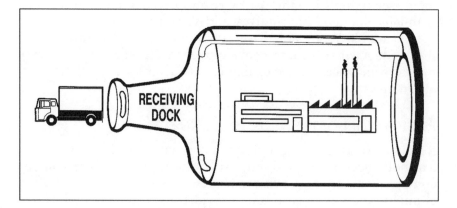

EXHIBIT 3–10

Critical Bottleneck

precise hour, day, or week of anticipated workloads. Therefore, the optimal solution is one designed not to accommodate peaks and valleys but rather to develop methods for eliminating them, or at least drastically reducing the difference between peak and valley.

Second, most warehouses operate with relatively fixed work-forces despite the peaks and valleys of activity. When a warehouse processes every receipt and shipment in the day of its actual receipt or target shipment, it might do so by having a larger-than-necessary workforce or one that works overtime to meet the peaks. Again, the best solution is to strive to minimize the peaks. However, in reality it will never be possible to eliminate them completely. Thus, another important business objective must be the development of a more flexible workforce to make a better match of warehouse activity level with the manpower capacity to handle it.

Third, the process and flow through the receiving process is often unnecessarily complex and longer than necessary, largely because of supplier and freight carrier inadequacies and poor facility layout. The primary supplier and carrier inadequacies are their inability to deliver perfect, undamaged products and to do so precisely on schedule and free of count discrepancies. These inadequacies force the warehouse to inspect and count most receipts, which requires more space. Some of this wasteful space, in the vicinity of receiving, is used for storing receipts that are queued up for counting and inspection, while more space is needed to perform the actual counting and inspection operations. Because of the wasteful count and inspection operations, warehouse executives should find it critically important to learn how to work systematically with vendors and carriers to develop permanent solutions to these problems at their source. The goal must be to eliminate counting and inspection completely! The author's previous book explained approaches with which vendors can design low-cost tooling and machine design modifications to achieve fail-safe processes incapable of producing imperfect quality and a program for working with vendors to develop permanent solutions to both quality and quantity problems.[19]

Intermittent receiving workload peaks and valleys during a day, week, or month are often self-inflicted burdens. For example, many computer systems are not yet designed to schedule receipts uniformly throughout a month, based on the best possible up-to-date, accurate projection of a runout date. Usually the main deterrent is that the systems operate on weekly or monthly cycles, calculating requirements no more precisely than the week or month of pro-

---

[19]See Appendix 2 for reference to information on fail-safe process design.

jected need. The end result is that most deliveries are scheduled in clusters during a certain day of the week or week of the month. Some would argue that producing a more precise schedule is made impossible by the unreasonably long time required to put the more accurate, up-to-date purchase order reschedule into the hands of suppliers and to have it approved by them. They argue further that forecasts of future demands are too inaccurate, and, in the end, the vendor and/or carrier will not deliver on schedule with any reasonable degree of precision. However, it is no longer necessary to continue to live with any of these restricting situations, and the vendor program is the key to improvement.

Some additional reasons for peaks and valleys stem from the way we, our suppliers, and our carriers operate. For example, our warehouses most often work a single day shift. Many long-distance truck drivers, meanwhile, prefer driving at night (when other highway traffic is lightest), and many drive during the weekend. Overnight driving causes long lines of trucks to arrive during the night and in the early morning hours. And weekend driving often causes long lines of inbound trucks on Monday morning. Further, like the warehouse, most suppliers tend to have shipping peaks in the late afternoon, because most of the day is spent in preparing the day's shipments. Finally, receipts from local suppliers, prepared for shipment during the previous work day, also tend to be received either late in the afternoon or in the early morning.

Delays in unloading and loading trucks cause the costs of receiving and shipping operations to be much higher than necessary. When tractor-trailers, trucks, docks, work teams, and traffic and logistics systems are all of superior design and performance, time spent in unloading and reloading a truck should take no more than a few minutes. In the entire national transportation network, the percentage of tractors and trailers in motion determines the size of the capital investment and is therefore an important component of the cost of operations. A very significant percentage of equipment is idle at any point of time; therefore, major improvements are in order. Further, idle tractors and trailers usually mean nonproductive time for their drivers. Nationally and globally, lines of waiting trucks and those at docks partially loaded or unloaded tie up hundreds of billions of dollars in inventories of products, components, and materials waiting for inefficient loading and unloading functions to be completed.

Receiving delays can be minimized in three ways. One is to eliminate peaks as much as possible. First, if the warehouse were to operate around the clock and schedule all inbound traffic accordingly, peaks caused by short (daytime) hours of operation could be leveled. Carefully scheduling easiest-to-control, around-the-clock arrivals from local vendors is therefore an important peak-leveling method for warehouses with clusters of local suppliers. The second way to eliminate variable peak queuing is to develop workforce flexibility, scheduling temporary workers to meet seasonal demand and permanent employees with flexible hours to match unavoidable (as yet) peaks within days and weeks. The best results from workforce flexibility, however, depend on companies' systems for planning and scheduling both inbound and outbound traffic. The third overall way to reduce or minimize peaks is to level customers' demands. For example, a company can work with its customer on pricing and payment deals that reduce or shift peaks. They can even undertake to mold the market's buying habits, thus decreasing peaks. Years ago, one leisure products client had a huge summer sales peak that it tried to cover by producing to forecast months in advance of the season. The practice required a huge warehouse to store products. Often forecast errors caused large surpluses of some products at the time of the model year changeover and shortages and lost sales of other products during the peak season. Today the company has zero stored product inventory. Instead, it offers dealers substantial discount and delayed payment terms to take delivery over a period of several months prior to the big sales season. This practice has merely shifted assets on the balance sheet from inventory to receivables, while price reductions have largely offset the discounts previously offered to clear the end-of-season surplus product inventory. The big advantage was clearly the elimination of the company's giant finished goods warehouses and the associated labor costs and operating expenses.

THE STEP-BY-STEP PHYSICAL WAREHOUSE APPROACH

Reinventing the wheel is the epitome of foolishness. Yet many companies are inventing their own methodology instead of acquiring and adapting one to their unique needs. The best tried and proven methodology provides a methodical step-by-step procedure for designing and implementing superior physical warehouse/storeroom layouts, equipment, and methods. Despite the importance of methodology to the improvement process, the author finds it extremely difficult to convey its essence in a terse yet interesting way, despite being accustomed to following Andersen Consulting's methodology, developed in the course of completing more than a thousand warehouse and storeroom projects. To design and implement new or revised warehouse layouts and operations requires careful attention to tens of thousands of details, all of which must be integrated into a single superb, operational organization. Small wonder, then, that the methodology fills several volumes. Clearly, to include more than a modicum of methodology in a management-oriented book like this would be impossible. Besides, such a detailed methodology is a good sleep-inducing opiate, regardless of its exciting future prospects. Fortunately, however, the methodology is anchored in a hierarchy of "planning charts" that starts with a one-page overview (Exhibit 3–11) for each of three major phases and then descends into succeeding degrees of detail.

The author has always subdivided projects into the standard phases listed below, using a warehouse reorganization project as an example.

1. *Initial design.* A very narrow segment of an entire organization is studied in great depth, and a very in-depth design of proposed changes is sketched. For example, a team studies one warehouse bin/bay and all of the items stored in it in great detail. The results are used to design and illustrate improved storage methods based on using better equipment, containers, and layout and low-cost semi-automation

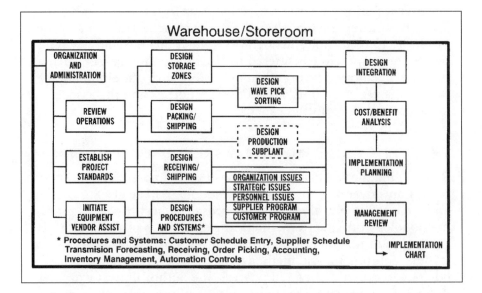

EXHIBIT 3–11

Overview Planning Chart

and full automation and computer support. The detail results would then be projected into order-of-magnitude
costs and benefits for the entire warehouse. The in-depth
design sketches make it easy for all management and employees to know precisely what changes will be made,
their cost, and how long it will take to pay for improvements before committing to starting the next phase.

2. *Design.* The *breadth* of the work performed is expanded.
Detailed design, in this phase, encompasses many more
bin/bay locations, perhaps even an entire warehouse. Operating personnel are heavily involved in this phase.

3. *Implementation.* The detailed conversion and operating
procedures are finalized, and training is conducted. New
equipment is ordered, constructed, and installed; the physical reorganization is performed.

4. *Follow-up.* After successful implementation, the team mon-
itors the results, not only to tweak the design as much as
necessary to achieve the desired results but also to ensure
the perpetuation of benefits and to outline additional
changes for the next improvement project.

One purpose of the above project segmentation is to divide the
overall program into small, manageable phases. Company executives then have the opportunity to alter the program's course at the
end of each of the first two phases, and a planned review during the
followup phase ensures that the planned benefits have been
achieved. This is not to say that management should view the end
of each phase as an opportunity either to approve or to cancel
continuation. Management commitment to a program means *full*
support of an initiative that all agreed *will have the desired benefits,
at reasonable cost.* It may be necessary for management to break a
program into multiple projects, the starting points of which are
spread over time, in order to schedule payout and payback into
more manageable bites. Or else, management may need to direct
the project team to pursue lower-cost methods. However, management would have been at fault if it were to abandon the program
after initially supporting it.

Lower-level charts expand each overview segment into tasks (the
"Design Storage Zones" segment of Exhibit 3–11 is expanded into
the tasks in Exhibit 3–12). Tasks, in turn, are broken into detail
steps.

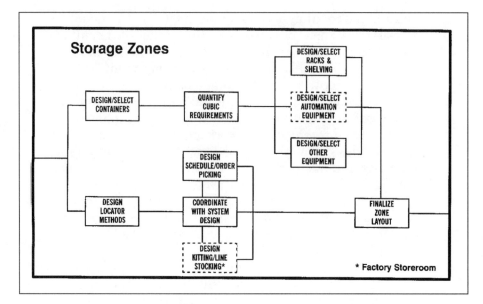

EXHIBIT 3–12

Design Planning Chart

This form of documentation is analogous to a series of road maps starting with the country, dropping to the state level, and finally descending to the street map for a single community. At each level, the shape and characteristics of the entire geography are visually defined in sufficient detail to see the starting point of a trip, the route to be taken, and the destination. The importance of the visual presentation of the simple level-by-level planning chart cannot be overstated. In this case a picture is truly worth a thousand words. As contrasted with volumes of detail work programs and massive critical path network diagrams, the simple, uncluttered planning charts help all involved in the process to find the level of detail they need quickly and efficiently. The charts then help to understand the interrelationships of that segment, task, or step in the overall scheme of all other activities.

For several years the author scheduled all Phase I projects to be completed in four months. Most projects comprised several sub-projects, the scope of which was set by the author based on his experience in what a two-to-four-man, full-time subproject team could reasonably accomplish in a four-month period. The "final" management review meetings of the author's Phase I projects were always scheduled (at the start of project) for the last day of the four

1	2	3	4
Typical:			
Organization/Detail Review		Design	Wrapup
Project 1:			
Project 2:			
Project 3:			

EXHIBIT 3–13

Four-Month Schedule Typical Distribution

months and were always conducted on schedule.[20] Further, every subproject was given the same schedule (Exhibit 3–13) for the milestone completion of review, design, and wrap-up activities.

The advantages of the top-to-bottom technique (with only consecutive activities) is best illustrated through comparison with an alternative typical project schedule built by totaling bottom-up estimates of the steps within the activities, as seen in Exhibit 3–14. In the example, the various activities of different subprojects have different start and completion schedules. Scheduling and monitoring these subprojects are more complex. However, this simple example may not adequately depict the degree of complexity of a project with dozens of subprojects. Cooperative subproject teams can much more easily lend or borrow people and modify the scope of their work to equalize workload among teams and guarantee that every activity is completed on schedule. Further, work on various activities tends to overlap. For example, a good team member reviewing shelving equipment currently being used would, almost surely, instantly see inefficiencies in the present method of storage and have ideas for improvement. Thus, while performing his re-

[20]Leroy Peterson prefers to schedule the management meeting in the final *week*, not day. He finds this flexibility sometimes provides time to incorporate changes in direction in the next phase. The author, by contrast, makes such changes during the first week of the next phase.

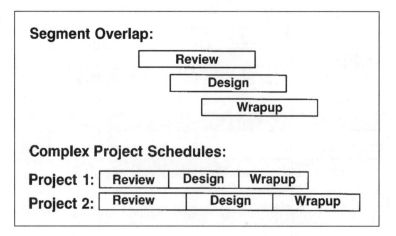

EXHIBIT 3-14

Bottom-up Schedule Characteristics

view activity he would sketch or make a picture (videotape or still photograph) of the existing equipment and an improved version. These products (sketches, photos, and films) would fulfill some of the planning chart *design* activity requirements and some of the wrap-up needs (prepare management review presentation). Further, after the review activity has been considered complete, the team inevitably discovers (during the design activity) that something was missed, and a little additional review work would be necessary. Carried to the extreme, if every activity were permitted to overlap with another, none would be completed until an entire project was completed. All too often this happens, and as the project nears the scheduled completion date it finally comes to light that each and every activity is really far from complete. By forcing teams to complete activities on schedule, they must face up to the *real* degree of completion much earlier than with stretched-out, overlapped activities. Thus they and project management have an opportunity to redistribute personnel or to redefine subproject scopes much earlier.

The author has previously written at some length on a few key segments of the overview planning chart that are common to any project and recommends that the reader review the earlier, universally applicable comments.[21] Following is a synopsis of the most important points:

---

[21]See Appendix 2 for reference to information on project planning charts.

1. There are no magic shortcuts (quality circles, for example) to superior warehouse operations. Thus, management cannot shirk its responsibility to be actively involved in the design and implementation process. Achievement requires thousands of hours of hard work.
2. Drastic revision of the warehouse cannot be a "hobby" activity, accomplished by the same people responsible for ongoing operations. If they have the spare time to do so, they probably should be fired for having wasted time in the past. After all, effective managers should fill their days with necessary activities and devote their few spare moments to short-term improvements on existing operations.
3. Full-time project teams—comprising the company's best people—are the keys that unlock the door to rapid, fruitful progress. Weak executives often permit second- or third-rate individuals to be assigned to such projects because they seem to be the easiest to cut loose from current operations. The best individuals are often assumed to be irreplaceable, which, in reality, is rarely the case. Placing the future of the business in the hands of any but the best, most creative individuals is folly.
4. Full, long-term executive commitment is a vital prerequisite to success. The author has seen far too many projects abandoned because of changes in the executive suite. The new executive often has his own pet priorities and prefers quick fixes to long-term improvements. Thus, he uses all available personnel (including those assigned to projects started before his arrival) to help execute his own program. However, in companies where superior performance is deemed important enough for oversight by the board of directors, executive turnover rarely interferes with board-approved projects.
5. The starting point of all projects should be the adoption of a successful, tried and proven methodology. As previously mentioned, it is pure folly for any team to invent its own methodology. The team would be hard-pressed to improve upon one developed in the crucible of hundreds of successful projects.

SUMMARY

The science of warehousing, like the science of manufacturing, has not reached its zenith. Nor is it ever likely to do so. Continuous challenges to every aspect of the physical warehouse, its methods and procedures, and its management organization and policies have proved that there is always room for improvement. And it is not necessary to settle for small increments of improvement, spread over years or even decades. Establishing bold new goals can force the organization and its internal and external consultants to stretch their capabilities to the utmost. Aggressive goals have been proved to provide the extra incentive necessary to motivate an organization to excel.

Further, opportunities for improvement are not restricted to only the biggest warehouses or those suitable for costly automation. In fact, it has been the author's experience that the fast payoff and small effort required to implement changes in small warehouses, because of their usual lack of complexity and bureaucracy, make them ideal targets for improvement projects. Regardless of how large or small the potential opportunities for improvement are, capitalizing on them is overwhelmingly important to every company, regardless of size. This time to get your program into high gear is now!

CHAPTER 4

Warehouse Operation

Keys to Success

Efficient warehouses, characterized by superior manpower and equipment productivity and economical asset cost and utilization, simply are not being designed, constructed, and operated. Part of the reason is antiquated perceptions of how warehouses need to be run, as discussed in Chapter 2. Boards of directors must not be satisfied with only a strategy dependent on the monumental changes that will someday evolve from the continuously emerging vision of the warehouse of the future. In reality, earthshaking innovation is far from what is required to do much better temporarily with the facilities, equipment, and personnel currently available. Giant immediate strides can be made merely by paying more attention to detail, with emphasis on the highest practical utilization of cubic space and least wasteful movement of manpower, equipment, and goods in the processes of receiving, stocking, retrieving, and shipping. Much of this chapter addresses existing opportunities, long recognized and covered in exquisite detail in numerous handbooks—basic truths that every professional warehouseman knows and understands. Nevertheless, in tens of thousands of warehouses and storerooms the job is not getting done.

Although there are no magic bullets for transforming ordinary operations into exciting, superior organizations, the secrets of success are clear. No less than continuous improvement is required to overcome the past complacency that has been responsible for the minuscule headway. Shifting the gears of continuous improvement into overdrive demands perpetual, hard-working dedication to the designing, implementing, operating, and constant improvement of new, near-perfect operations and elimination of unnecessary waste. Nor is dedication and hard work something that can be assigned solely to others. Executives and managers in the position to approve, sponsor, and participate must be the drivers, pushing the throttle to the floor. The driver, more than anyone, must understand the route to follow. He or she must understand the journey's starting point—present logistics operations—as well as the ultimate destination, the future logistics world, and must instill in his or her organization a widespread passion for progress.

The purpose of this chapter is to highlight, not detail, some of the relatively mundane operating practices that distinguish the leaders from the pack. Not surprisingly, the near-ideal achievement of these mundane aspects of warehouse operations should be part of every warehouseman's vision of the future. The author's hope that this simple, management-oriented presentation of these basic methods will heighten executive understanding and will lay the groundwork for serious self-evaluation in their own facilities. The executive checklist of the fundamental issues should be a helpful tool for self-assessment.

EXECUTIVE CHECKLIST: WAREHOUSE OPERATION ZINGERS

1. Orders (purchase and customer) are extremely costly in terms of both money and delay in transmitting requirements to suppliers. Use of orders for repetitive demands is an obsolete practice that should be replaced by supplier schedules throughout the distribution network as soon as practical.[1]
2. Supplier schedules can and should be used immediately —at least for items of highest repeat-use value. There is little excuse for not starting as early as today.
3. Flexible new work schedules and workday calendars, managed dynamically, will help to align manpower better with

[1]An explanation of supplier schedules versus orders can be found in this book through the index. Additional information can be found through Appendix 2 references to prior books.

workload peaks and valleys. This will bring to an end the common reality of yearlong overstaffing or overtime to meet periodic peak loads.

4. Drivers of inbound and outbound trucks often stand idly by, watching while receiving–shipping personnel (using lift trucks) unload and load their vehicles. Companies that successfully utilize drivers to perform or participate in loading and unloading have the potential for reducing significant amounts of payroll cost in the receiving–shipping operation.

5. Wave picking, while not a new methodology, will be improved and will be the wave of the future warehouse for those not yet employing it. Those warehouses not yet wave picking have the potential to increase order picking productivity by up to 500 percent.[2]

6. Multifunctional warehouse teams that have complete responsibility for an area of the warehouse, including receiving, stocking, packing, and shipping, will replace the individual working alone in one specialty. The typical warehouse operating environment, in which each worker is an island and no one individual is responsible for the receipt, storage, and shipment cycle, must be converted to one in which each team takes great pride in performance in its zone of responsibility and its members' mastery of the entire process.

7. Warehousemen must be educated and cross-trained as multifunctional individuals rather than specialists in a single warehouse function. Their improved efficiency will increase the value of their contribution to the warehouse's success, which will lead to greater remuneration. Further, companies will benefit from lower employee turnover by offering a better paid and more prestigious, satisfying career path.

8. Repackaging after receiving at the warehouse or after picking from stock is costly and often unnecessary. Companies should work with suppliers to adopt the use of containers that can be received, stocked, and picked from

[2]The author's definition of wave picking may differ from that of some warehousing technicians. To the author, batch order picking and wave picking are the same. Scheduled wave picking, in the author's terminology, closely synchronizes truck loading, wave picking, and order sorting and usually eliminates the necessity to stage several truckloads in advance of loading. The index will guide the reader to more information on these terms.

stock without repackaging (for as many stocked items as is practical).

9. The causes of inaccurate inventory records are identifiable and therefore can and should be addressed by new fail-safe inventory transaction design, procedures, and systems that eliminate the potential for human error.

10. New low-cost and free cycle count transactions and better cycle count procedures and systems have the potential for eliminating complete annual physical inventory taking, slashing the labor required to perform cycle counts and increasing the customer service levels by reducing the number of shortages stemming from inaccurate records.

11. Queues of trucks awaiting loading and unloading increase transport cost. Therefore, new equipment, practices, and procedures for slashing these delays are integral elements of the new distribution pipeline.

12. Simple, easy-to-implement, semi-macro-level standards (as against detailed operation standards) can be rapidly developed and put into use to give an immediate powerful boost to short-term warehouse productivity in warehouses not using standards. However, simpler, macro performance measures are more applicable to the twenty-first-century warehouses-within-a-warehouse. Thus the discontinuance of detailed warehouse standards must be part of the long-term strategic plan.[3]

13. Inspection of incoming goods is the epitome of waste. The supplier program must teach suppliers how to modify production processes to produce perfect quality, thus eliminating all need for inspection at either the supplier or the customer site.

WORKFORCE FLEXIBILITY VERSUS BULLDOZING PEAK LOADS LEVEL

Leveling inbound receiving and stocking workloads and developing workforce flexibility in the receiving department are not the only areas of opportunity. Superior companies are already establishing flexible workforces throughout the distribution logistics network

---

[3]The author's position that the use of *detailed* standards must be eliminated is bound to be one of the most controversial issues in this book. He has written more extensively on the subject in prior books, as referenced in Appendix 2. Only time will tell how dynamically companies will adopt viewpoints radically different from those which are now almost universally accepted in the United States and heartily rejected by most Japanese companies.

and working with their customers to find ways to bulldoze peak demand into periods of lower demand, thus reducing mountainous peaks to manageable molehills. Trucking terminals, for example, have long been geared to operating with most of their workforce functioning on flexible schedules. They must do so to be competitive, since the entire trucking industry is subject to all of the same hour-of-day, day-of-week, and month-of-year variability that warehouses and manufacturers experience, and every trucking company works on flexible schedules. The flexible schedule can be equally beneficial to producers and distributors; it is high time they get on the move!

Most companies around the world are fortunate that they encounter a common peak season—summer vacation—in which a maximum number of temporary workers is available. In many countries, tens of thousands of students would almost kill to get a summer job. However, many companies are hesitant to employ seasonal workers because of their common unsatisfactory experience with skyrocketing errors and inefficiencies that result from using untrained people for short periods. Two important factors are key to increasing the efficiency of the temporary seasonal workforce while lowering errors. The first is elimination of the painful time and effort required to bring new temporary workers on board and train them. Work and process simplification, superior training material and programs, and improved on-the-job training techniques are all elements that help in this arena. However, the greatest pain of on-the-job training is that warehouse supervisors and lead people are often erroneously viewed as sole limiting resources for training new workers. Conventional wisdom is that one supervisor can effectively train only a few new employees at one time. The result is that major warehouse workforce increases must often be spread over a lengthy time span, regardless of the urgency involved.

Therefore, the second key to workforce flexibility is to recognize that every experienced warehouse team member is a potential on-the-job trainer. In the warehouse of the future, teams must be trained and educated to train new employees. Since warehousing jobs can be simplified to the point that each routine team job (except those involving powered light and heavy transport equipment) will require only minutes to learn, large numbers of temporary workers can be added in peak seasons with relative ease. Although each warehouse team member's routine job can be simplified to the point of requiring only minutes to learn, temporary workers will still require months to master all of the team's routine jobs, those of lesser frequency, such as preventive maintenance, and those involving equipment operation that require special, longer training because safety is of the utmost importance. Every team's most experienced members, therefore, should be cross-trained and given experience in both manual and equipment operations. Then, when seasonal peak manning requires temporary infusion of large numbers of seasonal workers, a large cadre of people qualified to operate equipment can move to those jobs, leaving the simpler, less critical manual jobs to the seasonal workers.

Some would say that manning during the peak (summer) season would be too late, because the distribution pipelines must be filled months in advance of the season. However, twenty-first-century superior companies and their customers will reduce inventories in the pipeline by as much as 90 percent, thereby moving the peak in the distribution network much closer to the retail peak. Doing so can help to reduce both inventory surpluses and shortages stemming from forecasts errors, since the pipeline will be geared to rapid response to seasonal demand as it occurs.

Up to this point the author has stressed time and again the importance of maximizing storage space utilization. Before proceeding further into the details of warehouse/storage design, the reader should find it helpful to explore further the reasons why space utilization is so important to efficiency and cost control.

MAXIMIZING SPACE UTILIZATION

Paying to warehouse air sounds foolish, but that is exactly what many companies do! The wasteful use of space is foolish in terms of the capital investment in the building surrounding it. Further, larger-than-necessary facilities cause personnel and equipment costs to be much higher than in more compact warehouses. The main reason is that larger facilities require more movement by people, transport equipment, and conveyors than smaller facilities, despite having equal storage and throughput capacity. Therefore, careful attention to maximizing warehouse space utilization pays handsome dividends in the form of lower total operating costs and capital investment per unit of goods received, stored, picked, sorted, packaged, and shipped (or issued). Even the most sophisticated, automated warehouses often utilize the available cubic space far less effectively than they should. Warehouse managers usually have overlooked simple but important reasons for wasted space. The first reason is that container and storage space sizes for various items have been inconsistent with the minimum cubic volume needs of individual items to be stored, considering their various sizes, shapes, and demand levels. The second reason has been deliberate provision of space in excess of average need, to meet either future growth or periodic fluctuations of demand, or both. The author routinely glances at and attempts to assimilate three factors whenever taking a first fast tour of a storeroom or warehouse: (1) the percentage of the face of storage racks occupied by inventory; (2) the average percentage of space on the racks (and inside containers) used for storage; (3) the ratio of aisle space to storage space versus the minimum feasible aisle space. Rapid analysis, done on the fly during warehouse tours, usually gives the author a sufficient basis to advise executive management that they should target space utilization improvements of 50 percent or more!

It is easy to fall into the trap of believing that inefficient space utilization can be found only in small or poorly managed companies. That is far from the reality. The author finds huge opportunities for improvement in companies both large and small, successful and teetering on the brink of bankruptcy. Thus it is vitally important for every warehouse executive to be able to make a rapid assessment of his own facility, analyzing the same factors that the author uses. He can then advise his company's top management of the approximate space saving potential of its warehouses.

Exhibit 4–1 illustrates what the author so often sees on warehouse tours. In this typical example of one storage space, close examination reveals that as much as 50 percent of the cubic volume of the storage location is wasted. Further, if the containers in the location were found to be one-half full, it would mean that the real space utilization would be only 25 percent. In this example, part numbers are stored in approximate part number sequence, but more than one part number can be stocked in one storage slot (bin). Thus, cubic space utilization is much better than it would be if one space were to be allocated to each part number stocked. However, one penalty of such a storage method is that order filling of part number 12 requires extra labor (part number 11's container must be moved to get to part number 12). A second drawback is that some containers may be shuffled to the back of the bin, making them hard to find. This often causes the order filler to conclude that the item is out of stock. When that happens, he unnecessarily creates backorders, delaying shipment and thus lowering customer service.

In older storerooms and warehouses the author often sees stor-

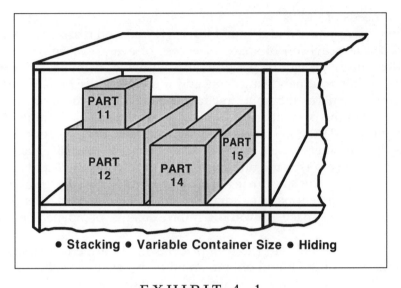

• **Stacking** • **Variable Container Size** • **Hiding**

EXHIBIT 4–1

Storage Waste

age like that illustrated in Exhibit 4–2. In this example, storage bins for plastic caps of various sizes (used to protect the threads on the ends of pipes) were designed and constructed to store loose, unpackaged caps. Caps received in containers would be emptied into the open front bins. While this eliminated opening and closing containers each time an order was filled, the open-face construction made it impossible to fill the bin space to its cubic capacity since caps would spill out of the open face. In fact, the amount of caps stored averaged well under one-half of the space occupied by the rack. Further, the bin design was responsible for several inefficiencies. First, parts received in inbound containers could not be simply poured out but had to be laboriously emptied into the bins by handfuls since the inbound containers were too large to pour into the bin opening. Second, because the bins were somewhat difficult to get into, picking parts entailed a large amount of time and motion to reach into the bin's far corners. All of this contributed to much higher than necessary labor costs.

A new storage rack with smaller drawers enabled the company to reduce the floor space occupied to less than one-half the previous area and cubic space utilization to one-quarter of the old bins. The smaller area cut the walking time, and it became easy to place standard-size containers in the drawers of the same size, further

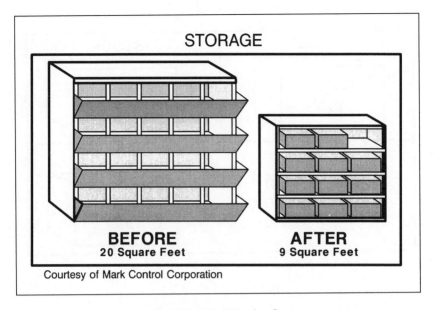

EXHIBIT 4-2

Pipe End Protectors

reducing waste labor. (Much less effort is required to stock any item when storage facilities are designed to enable the stockkeeper to place intact inbound containers on racks, stacks, or shelving). In Brazil, the author worked with one of the country's largest producers and distributors of plastic plumbing. The company's central distribution center had several thousand square feet of bins similar to those in Exhibit 4–1. Thus, the storage space savings was of major importance in improving total storage costs and stocking and order filling efficiency. Hence, even with ridiculously inexpensive Brazilian labor, savings were great enough to justify new storage containers and racks.

Now that the framework of the facility and some vital strategic issues have been addressed, it is time to look into some of the detail components of warehouse design. The efficient model requires matching containers with bins, racks, and shelves in which they will be stored, the subject of the next section.

MATCH CONTAINERS AND BINS TO ISSUE NEEDS

Far too many storerooms and warehouses operate with too few different storage device types and far too many types and sizes of

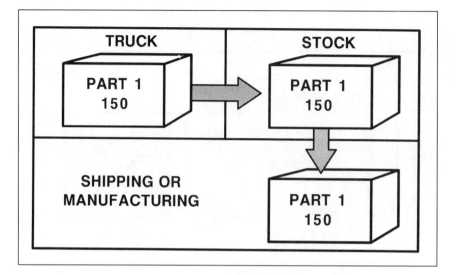

EXHIBIT 4–3

Eliminate Counting/Packaging

containers. It is rare to find businesses that produce, buy, and store items in containers that are *all* the same size and usage quantity. Nevertheless, these same businesses have warehouses with only one or two different sizes of racks, shelving, or automated storage and retrieval systems. Nor do all companies aggressively standardize the types and sizes of containers in which they require suppliers to ship goods. As a result of storing containers smaller than storage slots, many warehouses utilize space far less efficiently than possible. Therefore, superior warehouse design must start by determining the types and sizes of containers in which each item will be stocked and issued.

Exhibit 4–3 illustrates one ideal container design and usage objective. In this example, a truck delivers part number 1 in containers that hold 150. The containers stored are the same ones received, so repackaging and count verification are no longer part of the receiving process. (The author describes a vendor program to achieve perfect quality and quantity from suppliers in his prior book.)[4] Since the container quantity specified is the same as, or in multiples of, picking/issue requirements, full containers or multiples of containers can be picked from stock and sent to shipping (or to manufacturing operations) without counting or repackaging (to

[4]See Appendix 2 for reference to information on the vendor program.

do this requires customers or production to order in these multiples). When a company finds the long-term goal of eliminating counting and repackaging to be a practical objective, prodigious amounts of warehousing labor and packaging material costs can be slashed.

After storage container sizes have been determined for each item, storage racks, shelving, and bins can be modified or obtained to match the containers selected, as illustrated in Exhibit 4–4. The costs of modification or procurement are usually far less than expected, because the quantity of storage equipment needed is drastically reduced. Further, a large number of existing racks and shelving can continue to be reused, with modifications. Avoiding investments for new equipment is often vitally important for maximizing return on investment. Some cash-strapped companies have too readily decided that the requirement for *different* equipment makes changing impossible. Savvy professionals will strive to avoid purchasing new equipment until every lower-cost possibility has been explored. For example, as illustrated in Exhibit 4–5, many low-cost modifications can be made to existing equipment by adding shelves, dividers, or even bin inserts.

Of course, designing new containers is simply not enough. Businesses need to adopt and put into operation a systematic action

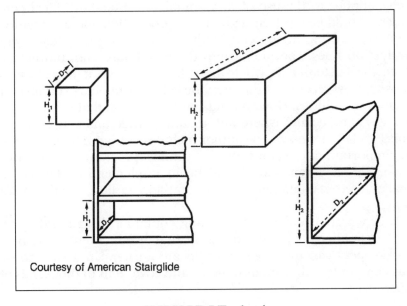

Courtesy of American Stairglide

EXHIBIT 4–4

Container Bin Size

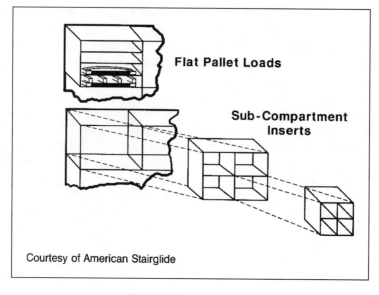

Flat Pallet Loads

Sub-Compartment
Inserts

Courtesy of American Stairglide

EXHIBIT 4-5

Bin Inserts

plan for converting its own factories and those of its vendors and their supplier to the use of new containers. Standard, ideal containers should be used throughout the production and distribution network, starting at the end of their suppliers' (and their own) production lines, continuing into the warehouse and, ultimately, on to the customer. It would be ridiculous were it necessary to transfer most receipts at the warehouse into containers suitable for its storage facilities. However, it is quite common that repacking *is* necessary, especially where automated storage and retrieval systems (AS/RS) are used. The author includes new containers among the important ingredients of the vendor program in his prior books.[5] Most companies should begin implementing the use of smaller, better containers as one of their earliest improvement steps.

After warehouse design (including container design and selection) is finalized, the next question that needs attention is how stockkeepers can most efficiently locate an item in a warehouse that may contain thousands of items and cover tens of thousands of square feet.

---

[5]See Appendix 2 for reference to information on container design.

LOCATION CONTROL: COMPLEXITY OR SIMPLIFICATION?

The evolution of warehousing and distribution in companies that have grown from small, entrepreneurial businesses to large national or international enterprises have been accompanied by changes in their warehouse methods, logistics, and distribution networks. Simple, easy-to-manage warehouse businesses have grown to the point where they involve multiple giant facilities and complex networks of national and international distribution stock locations. At the same time, methods for finding stocked items have evolved from the simplest level to one of greater complexity, as follows:

1. Personal knowledge (one or two warehousemen know where everything is)
2. Logical sequences of storage (like items are stored together or in part number or product code sequence)
3. Random sequence, requiring that a stock location information system be developed
4. National and international sites, with or without location control, and centralized or local systems of location control

Most warehousing authorities give too little credit to the effectiveness of personal knowledge and logical sequences of storage as valid, efficient, and effective methods for small, focused warehouses that are still small or simple enough for "personal responsibility" management of stock location to be a practical option. "Personal responsibility" is also suitable in mammoth facilities reorganized into small, focused warehouses-within-the warehouse as described in Chapter 1. For example, when Ward wrote that "an informal system implies that no records are kept, which only works (*although seldom well*) when everything about the environment in which it is operating is small,"[6] he stated an experience (or opinion) that is quite different from that of the author. The author has seen numerous such systems that work extremely well. However, he has also seen many with serious problems, because the operation was permitted to grow beyond the limits of control by individual responsibility. In fact, the author has seen numerous companies in which changing to random storage control has caused the system to go out of control.

The fact is, storage location methods should be designed to

[6]Richard E. Ward, "Stock Location and Inventory Control," in Jerry D. Smith and James A. Tompkins, eds., *The Warehouse Management Handbook* (New York: McGraw-Hill, 1988), p. 626.

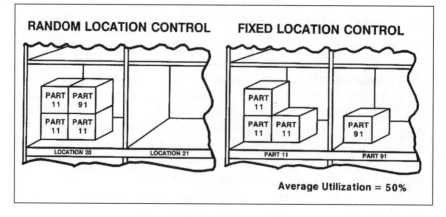

EXHIBIT 4-6

Location Control

match the equipment used and the complexity of the storage problem. For example, the author cannot imagine a completely automated storage system that would function without a computer location control system. However, in the rack and shelving environment of a focused warehouse-in-a-warehouse, manual or computer locator systems add an often unnecessary layer of complexity to management. For example, in the relatively small warehouses in retail and dealer environments, simple personal knowledge and logical (family) groupings of stocked items are usually the most suitable methods and can operate problem-free for years. Further, the strongest argument in favor of random storage systems may lose most of its logic in the twenty-first century, when deliveries into and out of the warehouse should be "just-in-time." Exhibit 4–6 highlights some differences between the two alternatives.

In the random location example on the left, receipts can be placed in any available location. Thus, any item can be stocked in any partially occupied location. In the example, location 20, containing item numbers 11 and 91, represents the near-100-percent utilization of space that can be achieved when demand is relatively constant and random storage location control is used.[7] In the fixed location example, part numbers 11 and 91 are assigned permanent locations and, as a result, the average stock location utilization is only 50 percent (not considering safety stock). The point is that

---

[7]For realistic random stock location code schemes, see Andrew J. Briggs, *Warehouse Operations Planning and Management* (Malabar, FL: Krieger Publishing, 1978), pp. 198–208.

when deliveries to stock are equal to days, weeks, and even months of demand, the difference between an item's maximum and minimum stock levels is extreme. In the future world of superior factories and vendors, where each day's needs of every item are delivered daily, the difference can be expected to shrink continuously. Although this will not change the need for location control in the automated and semi-automated storage subwarehouse, it should be considered when selecting the techniques for low-rise rack, shelving, and drawer storage.

Low-rise storage areas are almost automatically subdivided for smaller groups of items. For example, when a warehouse-in-a-warehouse is of considerable size, it most often makes sense to have the main warehouse organization focus on stocked items' frequency of receipts and issues. Other possible groupings and subgroupings include the size of the containers/items stocked and the commodities stored (e.g., motors, belts, fans).

The informal stock locating scheme and sequence within the logical groupings is often *approximate* item number sequence, an alternative that combines the advantages of random and fixed location methods. For example, the storage bin in Exhibit 4–7 shows how part numbers 1, 2, 3 and 4 would initially be organized within one storage bay. At this point the part numbers are in actual item/part number sequence. As shown in the exhibit, the storage bay contains some planned empty space, a provision that acknowledges that stock levels do vary over time. Soon after the initial organization, the perfect part number sequence starts to deteriorate as items are received and issued. In the example, two containers of part

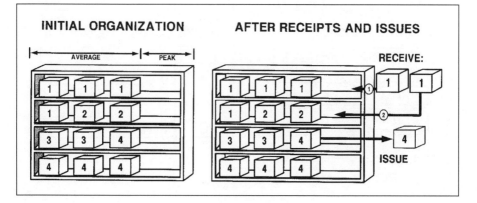

EXHIBIT 4–7

Item Number Sequence

number one are received. One container fits into the part number sequence, but since there was no room for the second container it would be necessary to put it into the empty space on the second shelf. Issue of a container of part number four from the third shelf makes it likely that this shelf will be used for the next receipt, regardless of item number. The resulting organization of the storage sequence deteriorates over time to the *approximate item number sequence* on the left side of Exhibit 4–8.

The preceding example was oversimplified. It overstated the potential for deterioration of strictly sequential organization in order to make it easier to understand. In superior companies, teams of warehousemen are actually trained to take pride in "their" warehouse-in-a-warehouse and find it requires relatively little effort to slide containers around to maintain perfect sequence when stocking or issuing items. However, storage in item number sequence can be more complex in the real world, as shown on the right side of the Exhibit 4–8. Nevertheless, as long as the item numbers are easily visible, the order picker will need only a second or two to locate the item. The height of the shelving and racks must be low enough, and the lettering of the container identification label, tags, or cards bold enough, for the warehouseman to be able to see the item number easily when standing in an aisle or sitting on a lift truck. Even newly hired warehousemen should find it easy to locate the storage bays in which to find specific part numbers, because overhead signs and signs on each bay identify the zone (storage group code) and the range of part numbers stored in the bay.

At one 3M factory the kanban card in Exhibit 4–9 was used in the

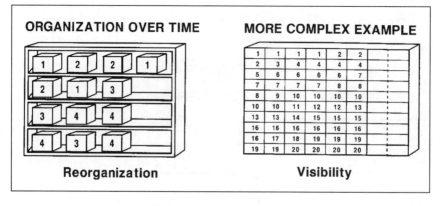

EXHIBIT 4–8

Location Management Problems

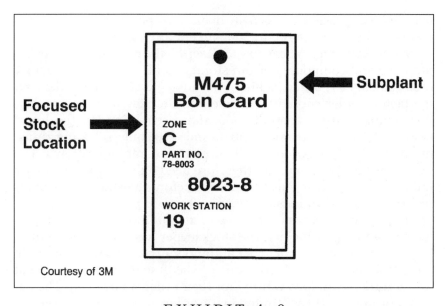

Courtesy of 3M

EXHIBIT 4–9

American Kanban Card

focused warehouse to label containers of components used on one product's (M475) assembly line. Part number 78-80038023-8 was stored in storage group C (zone C). Spotting the item needed was made easy, despite the long and complex part number. The last five digits of the part number, 8023-8, were enlarged and highlighted. The five digits highlighted were the only digits of importance to locate the item for which the rest of the part number was the same for *all* items stocked in the bay. Hence, part number scanning was simplified, and the label was easy to see, even on containers on the highest warehouse shelves.

Now that items in the warehouse can be found, highly productive new methods for picking orders (issues) from stock should be considered.

ORDER PICKING: MAKING WAVES

Rearranging warehouses not previously organized into logical activity zones based on the volume and frequency of usage; compressing them into highly utilized space; and operating with wave (order batch) picking methods are steps that have the potential for dramatically improving the efficiency of retrieving products and parts from storage to fill customer (or factory) orders. If none of these features has previously been in operation, productivity improvements in the range of 100 to 500 percent are not unreasonable. (It is a paradox that it is necessary to describe the process of retrieving products and components from storage to fill customer or factory requirements as "order picking," because the customer order and the factory order should be obsolete in the new world of twenty-first-century *repetitive* production and distribution. In the brave new world, the electronic kanban and electronic schedule transmission will replace orders as they are now commonly known. The warehouse of the future will therefore need only the internal order number. However, it may be decades before the state of the art is this far advanced in most companies.)

In the service parts storage area of an automotive dealer's maintenance and repair facility, the stockkeeper has little option but to fill each service parts order (per automobile) one at a time. After all, mechanics are nonproductive during the time they stand in line at the storeroom window, waiting for their orders to be filled. Thus, it is important to fill each individual's order, first-come-first-served, in order to get them back to work. Many garages charge standard rates for each type of repair (regardless of how long it takes), so the garage can ill afford idle mechanics. Nevertheless, occasionally and coincidentally every stockkeeper has picked two mechanics' orders simultaneously. Further, they have seen that they are able to fill two orders thus picked in less total time than it would have taken to pick the two orders separately (although slightly more time than to pick parts for just one order). Obviously, picking two orders takes much less time, since the stockkeeper walks only *once* through the storeroom to gather all the parts required for both orders, rather than twice. The term the author and a few others use for simultaneously picking multiple customer orders is "wave picking" (others prefer to call it batch order picking).[8]

A closer look at the elements of wave picking methodology should be helpful in understanding how the typical system operates. The process starts with the entry of customer orders either conventionally (in paper form) or electronically. As Exhibit 4–10 illustrates, in a highly simplified example, a batch of customer orders is "exploded" into picking lists for each storeroom zone. The number of orders in one batch might range from all orders for one day's demand down to as little as a batch equivalent to one or two hours of order picking activity. When customer orders require pick-

[8]*"Scheduled* wave picking" is the author's terminology for extremely well-coordinated wave picking and truck scheduling. "Batch order picking" is another term often used in place of "wave picking."

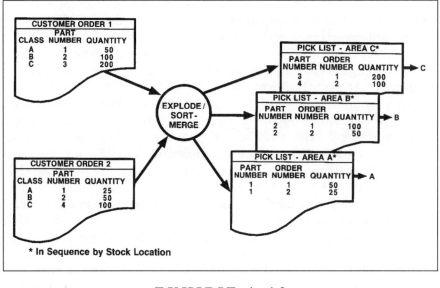

EXHIBIT 4-10

Order to Pick Lists

ing to be completed in a few hours, or even minutes, batch sizes must be quite small. When customers are content with receiving their shipments within one or two days after order entry and the number of outbound truckloads per day is very low, a daily batch could be used for optimum order picking productivity. (If the number of daily outbound truckloads is high, large batch sizes would delay completing the load of any truck. An alternative, truckload staging, would minimize the time between truck arrival and departure, but with other, often exorbitant, costs. Staging truckloads is a costly, space-consuming practice that also entails double handling (move to staging and later onto the truck) as opposed to loading trucks directly upon receipt of goods from order picking and sorting.

The example shows three order picking zones: A, containing the fastest-moving items; B, medium movers, and C, slowest-moving items. Each zone's pick list is sorted into stock location sequence. If items are stocked in exact or approximate part number sequence, sorting into part number order is the same as sorting by location number. In some of the best order picking operations, the computer system uses each item's weight and size among other data to calculate approximate picking time and to divide the pick list into roughly equal workloads for each order picking team member. Further, most systems provide labels for marking (e.g., bar code) each container picked with the order sorting number used in the subsequent order sorting processing phase.

Stockkeeper teams in all zones simultaneously pick the same order batch, traveling through their assigned stock area in location sequence. At each location they pick stock for all orders for the same item. In Exhibit 4–11, for example, the stockkeeper in Zone A picks two quantities of part number 1: fifty for order 1 and twenty-five for order 2. The stockkeeper attaches labels containing the sorting order number to each container, as illustrated. (In warehouses that use or plan to use automation, the container labels, generated by the computer, are bar-coded with an order sorting code. The bar-coded label can subsequently be used in a fully automated order sorter.)

Next, all zone picking teams deliver the containers they have picked to an order sorting area. In storerooms where the cubic volume of parts or products shipped is high, stockkeepers may need to make several trips, using carts or lift trucks, to the order sorting facility, where one or more additional team members work full-time sorting orders. At a Siemens distribution warehouse in Amberg, Germany, the cubic volume of orders was high enough to justify designing the conveyorized order picking facility illustrated

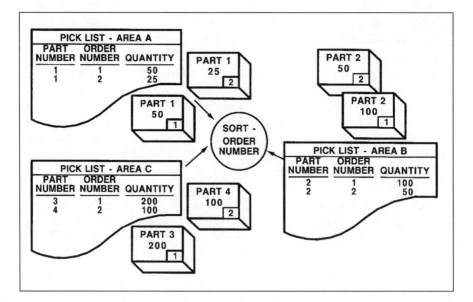

EXHIBIT 4–11

Pick to Sort

in Exhibit 4–12. In this example, order pickers in the fastest-moving zone operate on both sides of a conveyor running between the stock racks. For each order batch, the stockkeepers make a single trip from one end of the conveyor to the other, picking enough of each item to fill all orders for that item. Forklift trucks replenish the racks from the rear, from a separate storage facility behind the order picking racks.

Simultaneously, order pickers in medium-speed and slow-moving zones (each of which has numerous rows of racks) pick the same order batch, using carts to transport the picked items to the conveyor at the end of the rows of racks. Since the typical trip from any row to the conveyor, per batch, is less than one trip per row, conveyors were not warranted in these areas. The conveyors feed an initial sorting station where single item orders (with a distinctive colored label) are diverted directly to packing and shipping. In this warehouse, 50 percent of all orders were single-item orders. All remaining items continue down the conveyor to the order sorting facility.

ORDER SORTING: PUTTING THE PIGEON IN ITS HOLE

Siemens's order sorters place items for each order into a flow-through "pigeonhole" order sorter, Exhibit 4–13. When any order is

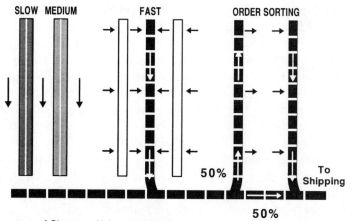

Courtesy of Siemens Aktiengesellshaft

EXHIBIT 4–12

Activity Zones

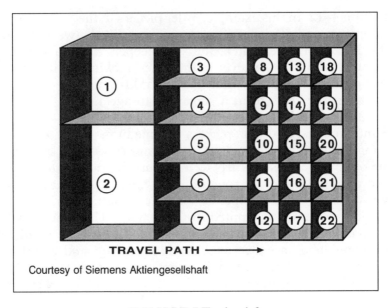

TRAVEL PATH ⟶

Courtesy of Siemens Aktiengesellshaft

EXHIBIT 4–13

Order Sorter

completely accumulated, all items on the order are pulled from the back side of the order sorter and sent by conveyor through packing to shipping. (The shipment volume of five truckloads per day required a less than full-time order sorter, thus expensive automation of the order sorting function was not seriously considered.)

The packing list, Exhibit 4–14, is another routine output of most customer order processing systems. In this case, however, it includes the internal order sorting code used to label the containers with the code that corresponds to the number on the order sorter bins. The packing lists for each wave picking batch are normally delivered directly to the order sorter and hung on the sorter bins. It is used as a checklist to verify the subsequent receipt of all the required items and to flag completed orders. Flagged orders are then forwarded from the order sorter to packing and shipping. Note two interesting points: (1) The order sorter has large bins for the orders with the highest cubic volume; and (2) the sequence of bins (highest to lowest volume in relation to the flow along the conveyor) permits the order sorting warehouseman to empty most of the conveyor rapidly without moving back and forth excessively. The other end of the sorter works similarly, except that the warehouseman–sorter can walk from the conveyor to the order

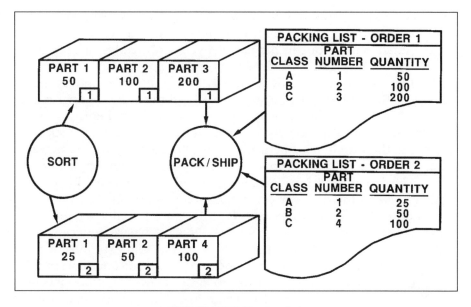

EXHIBIT 4–14

Sort to Pack and Ship

sorter bins with several (typically small) order items for the set of bins in that area. The computer system is invaluable for supporting this operation, because it calculates the cubic volume of each order and uses the result to assign the order sorting bin number that corresponds to the size needed to handle the order's cubic volume. Where volumes of orders are extremely high, as they are in SLS Sears Logistics Services Catalog Merchandise Centers, automation of order sorting is much more feasible than automation of storage and retrieval. SLS's state-of-the-art order sorter systems, most of which comprise hundreds of feet of conveyors, are very expensive, costing more than $5 million each. Still, small armies of people attend the manual stations in the automated sorter and at the packaging end of the process. Indeed, low-cost conveyance in the order sorting, packing, and shipping areas is often the most feasible area of the warehouse in which low-cost automation can have high returns in increased productivity. As in factories, the trick is to design these systems to be as short as possible, avoiding the mistake of cavalierly linking two widely separated areas, wasting money on unnecessary conveyance (a much better solution would be a layout with virtually no distance between any two areas in the flow into and out of the warehouse). Even the low cost of conveyors can quickly mount to millions of dollars—money that could be saved by rearranging the layout to minimize the conveyor length.

As Fuchs points out in his list of twenty principles of material handling, it is wise to use gravity-powered conveyance whenever possible.[9] It is still the least costly, most reliable conveyance method. Recently, while the author was looking at the 1920 gravity (corkscrew) conveyors that link floors in SLS Sears Logistics Services' nine-story Kansas City Catalog Merchandise Center, Jack De Simone, the warehouse operation manager, pointed out that newer warehouses would have powered conveyors for this application. What he left unsaid but correctly implied was that, in this case, gravity is still the best, lowest-cost conveyance method.

In almost every set of extremely different alternatives there are one or more additional approaches lying somewhere between and even beyond the two presumed extremes. The two extremes of order picking methods are picking one order at a time and picking all of a day's orders simultaneously. In production situations where components are picked for electronic assemblies, such as printed circuit boards, the author has often found it feasible to pick a batch consisting of several different assemblies in a single pass through the storeroom. As each component is picked, the warehouseman places each assembly's required quantity into its own "kit" containers on the order picker's cart. This eliminates a separate step to count and sort the components into kits when completing order picking of all components of every assembly. Order picking carts designed and constructed with enough shelf capacity for a fixed number of assembly kits have made this batch order picking practical. In distribution warehouses in which the quantity and cubic volume of customer orders is extremely high, the author has often found it necessary to "wave pick" smaller batches of orders several times a day. Doing so provides a method for maintaining a smooth, uniform flow of orders from order picking through order sorting and onto outbound trucks. It also permits a high percentage of orders to be picked and shipped on the same day they are entered.

Roger Wolfe, manager of the branch operations of Outboard Marine Corporation's SysteMatched Parts and Accessories Division, invented another ingenious order picking system suitable for branch operations. Order picking of one day's shipments is performed in about one hour by picking all orders simultaneously and

[9]Jerome H. Fuchs, *The Prentice Hall Illustrated Handbook of Advanced Manufacturing Methods* (Englewood Cliffs, NJ: Prentice Hall, 1988), pp. 428–29.

placing the items picked in one of nine sorting groups of fifty to sixty orders. Subsequently the items in each order group are sorted into individual orders, packaged, and shipped. A second order picking wave of emergency orders is made later in the day. This highly productive methodology has made it possible for small branch warehouses, employing as few as ten people, to receive, stock, pick, and ship more than $20 million worth of parts and accessories annually from a stock of more than 20,000 items. One magic key to Outboard Marine's success was an order picker's cart with the capacity for nine sets of presorted order items. If the order volumes were to grow to the point where they greatly exceeded the cart capacity, it might force the order picker to make several trips back and forth between the bin storage area and the place where the nine sort groups are temporarily stored prior to sorting. If this happens, Outboard Marine might find it necessary to increase the number of waves per day.

In the previous example of an order sorter facility, Exhibit 4–12, a two-level sorter would have facilitated larger wave picking batches. This may well have appreciably improved the productivity of the order picking operation without causing deterioration of response time or disrupting the uniform flow of material from picking through shipping. In many larger warehouse operations, picking a single wave per day would be infeasible because of the sheer volume. For example, SLS Sears Logistics Services' Catalog Merchandise Center warehouse in Kansas City was processing more than 60,000 order items ("tickets") a day when the author first visited it. Those tickets filled forty truckloads on the average day. Today, by processing ten separate picking waves a day and conveying shipments directly to the trailer at the dock, SLS requires no truck staging areas and avoids double handling into staging and on to truck loading.

In summary, somewhere between the extremes of individual order picking—wave picking once a day and wave picking several times a day—there is a point best suited to each individual warehouse, based on the best balance of order picking efficiency, space utilization, truck loading efficiency, and timely service. The best combination is usually found by fine-tuning during actual operation.

The order picking and sorting operations described above rely on the support of a modern computer system. The system that drives warehouse operations is severely crippled when the data it depends on are inaccurate. Thus, fail-safe accuracy techniques for inventory records are critical to success.

INVENTORY RECORD ACCURACY

Despite technological advances in computer hardware and software, too little progress has been made in solving one of the most persistent problems to plague companies—inventory record inaccuracy. When faulty inventory balance information is combined with high-speed computers, the result is erroneous replenishment orders that are spewed out faster than clerical staffs can process them, let alone detect and correct errors. More than a few chief financial officers, chief executive officers, and presidents have lost their jobs when annual audited physical inventories have caused anticipated profits to vanish overnight. They can verify that inaccurate inventory records can be extremely costly indeed! However, the surprise inventory shrinkage problem is but one of an avalanche of headaches (Exhibit 4–15) that will bury Mr. Pres I. Dent when his organization operates on the shaky foundation of inaccurate inventory balances. Others include poor customer service, disruptions stemming from shortages, costly cycle counting, and annual or semiannual physical inventory taking, as well as higher-than-necessary obsolete and surplus inventory. These latter excess

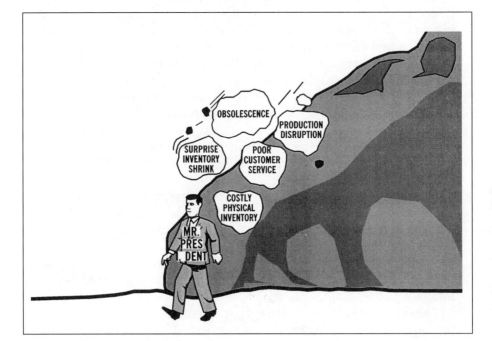

EXHIBIT 4–15

Results of Inaccuracy

inventories arise from high levels of safety stock, provided to cushion the effects of stockout stemming from inaccurate inventory balances. Yet when the causal source problems are finally identified, they are almost always basic and simple. Therefore, simple, fail-safe solutions can be developed to eliminate the possibility of error permanently.

Common accuracy source problems originate when storage locations and/or item numbers are improperly written or simply not reported at all. When random storage location systems are used in warehouses that employ conventional racks and shelves, lost receipts might never be found were it not for the taking of a complete annual physical inventory. Modern technology has contributed tools that can be used to attack accuracy problems. For example, a computer-controlled automated storage and retrieval system (AS/RS) eliminates the possibility of these error sources. The computer does this by keeping track of where things are stocked and when they are retrieved. Bar-coding, another technological tool, can also help by eliminating the possibility of errors in writing down such data as stock item and location numbers. For example, the Kansas City Catalog Merchandise Center of SLS Sears Logistics Services has bar-coded every stock location and will soon require all suppliers to bar-code their packages and package labels according to Sears's code standards. Incoming receipts are scanned to record the receipt and to route it to the appropriate warehouse storage areas. The responsible warehousemen take the receipt to an empty location and wand both the label on the item received and the bar-coded label at the location to record both the location and the quantity of the item stored there. Since customer order "tickets," prepared by the computer, identify the location from which each order item is to be picked, the procedure is somewhat similar. The warehousemen go to the specified location, wand the "ticket," and then wand the merchandise located there and the location bar code label. All of these steps in combination are used to record the issue. Small wonder that the warehouse rarely loses any of the 170,000 items stocked there!

Not all companies have volume high enough to warrant fully automated equipment and other technological tools to handle all types of products and components stocked. (In fact, they cannot afford it for *any* type, regardless of volume). Such businesses can sharply reduce mistakes by using low-cost equipment and procedures designed to minimize the possibility for human error. Exhibit 4–16 illustrates a few points of systems the author uses to achieve those ends. In the example, all receipt and issue transac-

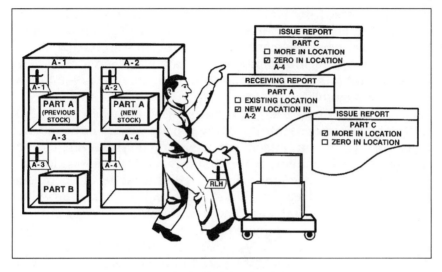

EXHIBIT 4–16

Rubber Stamps

tions require the stockkeeper to enter his personal identification. Therefore, each stockkeeper is issued a stamp with his initials (RLH in the example). Further, both issue and receipt transactions are designed for and require positive reporting of the stock location from which items are withdrawn or into which they are placed. Warehouses that equip each location with another stamp with its location code virtually eliminate human errors in reporting the code. The individual's stamp is not used to punish the stockkeeper in the event of an error but rather to identify the need for more or improved training and to pinpoint opportunities for better fail-safe methods. The exhibit shows that issue transactions have a data block for reporting when a stock location for an item is emptied or low. This enables the stockkeeper to make frequent low-cost or virtually free cycle counts as part of the standard routine for issuing stock. In the age of portable data entry devices and bar-coding, a less-than-fully-automated approach should use bar-coding wherever practical to achieve the same ends. For example, bar-coding at the stock location, on the employee badge, and on issue and receipt transactions are all usually practical applications.

Fully automated storage and retrieval systems can also eliminate many other human errors. The most common error of all is mathematic miscalculation. For example, a stockkeeper might issue a partial quantity from a container and make a counting or arithmetic error in calculating or counting the balance in the container. He perpetuates and compounds the error by writing the wrong quantity remaining on the outside of a container. When such mistakes occur, the quantities marked on the container are likely to be used, without verification, the next time an issue or cycle count is made. From that point forward, the inventory record balance would be wrong. In fully automated storage and retrieval systems, only full containers are stocked and issued, each container holding the same standard quantity for a given item. This completely eliminates the incidence of arithmetic errors stemming from partial issues.

Businesses with semi-automated and completely manual storage systems can also benefit from adopting standard containers and standard quantities for each item and by stocking and issuing only in full multiples of the standard container. At times the fully automated approach and full container receipt, storage, and issue options are not practical. In these cases the accuracy of mathematical calculations can be improved by changing the transactions and permitting the computer to do the required calculations. For example, the stockkeeper is often required to calculate and record the total quantity received in cases in which multiple cartons make up one item's receipt and not all cartons contain the same quantity. The stockkeeper (using any available scrap of paper for his calculations) has the opportunity to make errors in multiplication (number of containers times quantity per container) and errors in addition (adding the different quantities in various containers, when several different container sizes and quantities are received).

However, when receipt transactions are designed to require detailed information pertaining to the number of containers and quantities per container, as in Exhibit 4–17, the power of the computer to make fast, error-free calculations can be exploited. As an interim measure (or as a permanent procedure in small storerooms or warehouses with manual records), a clerical person equipped with a personal calculator can perform the calculations two times, virtually eliminating the potential for mathematical mistakes.

Regardless of how many safeguards are provided, something will still happen to cause inventory balances to be wrong. Therefore, every warehouse or storeroom should process cycle counts as frequently as possible and at the lowest possible cost.

FREE AND LOW-COST CYCLE COUNTING

Obtaining and maintaining accurate inventory records is vital to companies that plan to capitalize on the capabilities of their mod-

NUMBER OF CONTAINERS	COUNT PER CONTAINER	TOTAL QUANTITY*
(A)	(B)	(C)=(A)x(B)
2	2,525	5,050
1	1,217	1,217
1	314	314
STOCKKEEPER TOTAL		(D)
CALCULATOR TOTAL**		(E) 6,581

* Computer Calculated When Using Fully Automated Storage/Retrieval System
** Calculated by Second Clerical Person Using Calculator When Computer Is Not Used

EXHIBIT 4-17

Mathematical Mistake Minimization

ern computer hardware and software. This is not to say that it is any less important for storerooms and warehouses so small that they do not warrant having a computer inventory management system to maintain record accuracy. (Incidentally, the author finds it increasingly difficult to think of a situation in which it is inappropriate to use a computer, in light of the continuous cost/performance improvement ratio in recent years. Nevertheless, manual procedure examples continue to be of value since the computer should be used to automate the best possible noncomputer procedures and enhance them by applying the dazzling computational speed and storage capacity of a suitably sized computer.)

Early, crude cycle counting procedures and systems were based on the premise that the preferred way to cycle count was to count every item stocked at least once a year and to vary the number of cycle counts per item according to the item's usage value (ABC classification). High-usage-value items (class A) might be counted every quarter, medium-value items semiannually, and low-value items annually. Such a procedure has numerous shortcomings, from the standpoint of both continued inaccuracy and labor inefficiency. Many companies that have switched from the annual physical inventory to traditional cycle counting have been disappointed to learn that the accuracy achieved was not sufficient to persuade either internal or independent auditors to permit them to eliminate the annual physical inventory. Traditional cycle counting *plus* an annual physical adds counting costs instead of reducing them. This is not the case for superior companies that practice low-cost and free cycle counting techniques. For example, Warren Daley, inventory manager of Outboard Marine Corporation's SysteMatched Parts and Accessories Division, has said: "Free and low-cost cycle counts and improved systems have enabled us to convince Arthur Andersen & Co. auditors that annual physical inventory taking could be eliminated." *Effective* cycle count systems can and should drastically cut the total cost of counting.

The first key to low-cost and free cycle counts is that the stock-keeper should capture an easy count whenever he has the opportunity to do so during the normal course of stocking or issuing an item. When he picks all of an item's bin contents, bringing the stock level to zero, or picks all except one or two containers, he can perform the equivalent of a virtually free cycle count by merely entering information in the cycle count data block on the issue transaction document, as Exhibit 4–18 illustrates. In the example, after picking the required customer order quantity of 145, the stock-keeper notices only two containers of part number 344320 left in bin location A199. He therefore decides to complete the "Automatic Cycle Count" block on the transaction, thereby recording an almost

---

CUSTOMER ORDER PICK TICKET

ITEM LOCATION A 199	ITEM NUMBER 344320	CUSTOMER ORDER 0901
PICK QUANTITY 145	OTHER	

AUTOMATIC CYCLE COUNT ☐ OUT OF STOCK	
QUANTITY OF CONTAINERS	QUANTITY PER CONTAINER
1	55
1	200

EXHIBIT 4–18

Free Cycle Counts

free count. Since he had one partial container of 55 after picking 145 from a container of 200 and another full container of 200, he entered the data illustrated.

A second key to efficient cycle counting is purposely to count only those items that are at their lowest planned stock levels (but only when no low-cost or free cycle counts have been received recently, and only if the item's target cycle count date is near). Every company *should* establish target times between cycle counts for each inventory classification, exactly like those used in the early crude cycle count systems. However, instead of blindly scheduling counts according to these count frequency criteria (thus always counting the *average* quantity stocked rather than the *minimum* level), the system should trigger cycle counts only when free and low-cost updates have not occurred recently. Further, it would be folly to expect to be able to perform an unlimited number of cycle counts. Thus, the system should limit the number of daily counts to the minimal number for which stockkeepers *should* have time available. This will usually mean that conventional cycle counts will be zero in peak periods of order picking activity. However, the system should be continuously fine-tuned to achieve the ultimate objective, completely replacing conventional counts with cycle counts that are low-cost or free.

WAREHOUSE PERFORMANCE MEASUREMENT

Business is in a sorry state when incentive pay, based on the amount of work individuals perform each day, is the only way to motivate people to do the work they were hired to do. The best business executives and managers should master the art and science of motivation so that incentive pay is not required to receive a full day's honest effort for a full day's pay. Unfortunately, this is not reality. In every case of direct incentive pay that the author has seen, average output surges when its use is adopted. Even when warehouse performance standards are employed only as a basis for measuring and discussing warehousemen's performance, average individual output rises, albeit less than with incentive pay. Therefore, the author finds it easy to condone the use of warehouse standards for either incentive pay or for measuring performance *if the warehouse is operating in outmoded fashion* and if the administration of the system is less costly than its benefits.

Fortunately, it is a relatively simple matter to develop semi-macro-level standards for various types of warehouse activities (e.g., order picking, receiving, stocking, cycle counting). It is then quite practical for the supervisor or manager to parcel out work assignments in small batches and to record the expected and actual time taken to complete a batch.[10] Simple systems of this sort can be developed in a very short time and require only a fraction of the manager's or supervisor's work day. However, much the same results can be obtained by simply batching work fairly and creating an atmosphere in which it is fun for warehousemen to race to outperform their peers. Such short-term performance upgrading techniques are temporary tools for training warehouse management in the basics of applied motivation. However, in the long term management must champion and oversee rearrangement and reorganization of the physical warehouse and form cooperative work teams that are empowered with the responsibility and authority for managing the performance of their focused warehouse-within-a-warehouse.

Completely reorganizing a warehouse for superior performance is not a short-term project. Although some major overhauls may be accomplished in one or two years, even then the process of continuous improvement should proceed not only in the warehouse but also in the operations of the rest of the network, including supplier factories. Thus, achieving near-optimum results will usually require years. This does not mean, however, that radical improvements cannot be started tomorrow or even today! Every warehouse needs a short-term improvement strategy.

FAST, LOW-COST IMPROVEMENT SUMMARY

What are the short-term, fast issues that could be addressed? The author sees different opportunities in every warehouse or storeroom he sees. Thus, he has provided a "zinger" list at the beginning of each chapter. Not every zinger applies to *all* companies. Some are already in operation; others do not fit certain businesses. For these reasons, readers should modify the list by determining on which "zingers" to concentrate improvement efforts, based on the applicability to the business and the speed with which improvements can be achieved. The company can use the shortened list to evaluate its priorities and to set short-term and longer-term plans and objectives. Then management must determine the persons in operations and on full-time teams to be assigned responsibility for various design and implementation steps.

---

[10]For more discussion of this technique (short interval scheduling), see Alexander Keeney, "Personnel Planning," in Smith and Tompkins, *Warehouse Management Handbook*, p. 127.

In the majority of warehouses, the process of reviewing operations vis-à-vis the "zinger" checklist identifies a handful of extremely important problems and opportunities for relatively easy,
low-cost improvement. Chief among them are the following:

1. Warehouse space utilization is typically about 50 percent.
2. Warehouse/storeroom organization does not include zones
   based on volume of activity.
3. Inventory management policies and system factors are so
   liberal that inventories of most items are irrationally
   greater than necessary.
4. Items of the highest annual usage value are not really any
   better managed than those of low usage value.
5. Despite large time-of-week and time-of-month peaks and
   valleys in receipt and shipment activity, the workforce is
   maintained at relatively static levels.
6. Employee turnover is high, primarily because specialized
   warehouse tasks pay little, are simple, and require little
   skill.
7. Smooth operation is impossible because rampant inventory record inaccuracy is so disruptive.

Although this chapter has extensively covered subjects relating
to the improvement of warehouse operations, the methods that
often lend themselves to fast implementation, as opposed to those
that might require complete reorganization of warehouse facilities,
may not be completely clear. Therefore, a few common short-term
improvement areas and approaches are outlined below.

The overall improvement of warehouse efficiency should start
with obtaining ABC analysis reports of the volume, value, and/or
usage frequency of stocked items. Since any improvement effort
involving reorganization of the physical warehouse might take
weeks or months, the logical attack would start with the items of
greatest importance and would work down to those of least importance. Since minimizing wasted travel within the warehouse and
increasing space utilization both raise efficiency, one early objective should be to relocate the highest-usage-volume items to the
location closest to receiving–shipping. This can be accomplished,
over time, with nominal extra effort by simply designating the area
for high-volume movers and subsequently placing new receipts of
high-volume movers in that zone. Eventually the zone will contain
only high-volume items, as stocks of medium- and slow-moving
items originally stored in the area will be used up.

Early evacuation of medium and slow movers from the new fast-moving zone would obviously be a more aggressive, faster approach. This might involve one or more weekend overtime efforts since stockkeepers are busy during normal work hours. In preparation for the actual move, it is often necessary to create space into which to move the medium- and slow-moving items by compressing space in some other zone in which space utilization is especially poor.

The irrationally large inventory investment of most warehouses can serve as a bank. Withdrawals (inventory reductions) from the bank can be used to finance both low-cost and high-technology warehouse automation as well as longer-term systems improvement and integration projects. Capitalizing on the opportunities merely requires tightening up existing safety stock, order quantity, and lead time factors. Further, as quickly as possible routine use of (manual) supplier schedules should be adopted for at least the high-usage-value items and extended to other classes as fast as resources permit.

Few warehouses manage their staffing in such a way as to vary the number of people, shifts, or work hours with workload peaks and valleys. Although some companies will find that necessary changes require lengthy union negotiations, new flexible work week hours, annual calendars, part-time (permanent) workers, and additional shifts can have such a dramatic favorable impact on operations that the process of negotiation should be put into high gear as quickly as possible. Simultaneously, consideration should be given to increasing the value of warehousemen. Thus, as productivity increases, it will be practical to raise their compensation consistent with their new level of professionalism and increased output. This will benefit the rank and file of the union and the company alike.

It is not always necessary to wait for the conclusion of union negotiations to start a process of educating and training the workforce. For example, purposeful rotation of employees through various warehouse specialties (receiving, storage, order picking, packaging, shipping) will prepare them to become cross-trained members of new warehouse teams responsible for all operations within their zones. Simply beginning or accelerating the pace of cross-training enhances the workforce's flexibility, making it easier to shift personnel as workloads shift. Further, warehouse textbooks and handbooks should be made available for off-duty reading assignments and supplemented by coordinated education and training. These steps should begin a career-spanning program of individual value enhancement. Such personnel programs, in conjunction with a management–labor commitment to make wages consistent with the value of employees' contributions, will do wonders for the employee turnover problem.

Finally, inventory record inaccuracy can easily be improved though adoption of the low-cost techniques described in the sections of this chapter titled "Inventory Record Accuracy" and "Free and Low-cost Cycle Counting."

As the author has so often said, the best warehouse improvements require systemwide reorganization in both the distribution and the supply networks. Such tremendous change of such a grand scope demands a full-time team, devoted to achieving the company's long-term vision. It would be a mistake to unduly burden the full-time team with responsibility for shorter-term improvements. To do so would diminish the time and effort they have to spend on achieving longer-term goals, delaying the realization of the company vision. To be as successful as possible, operating managers and new empowered warehouse teams must operate using the new methods. They should also be given primary authority and responsibility for short-term improvements. Not only is this logical from the standpoint of delegation of responsibility and authority, but it is also the best way to achieve enthusiastic participation of all operations personnel. Nor do those in operations need to restrict the scope of their improvements for fear that they will implement something either inferior to or better than the full-time, long-term design team. Continuous coordination between operations and the full-time team is necessary to avoid duplication or heading in diametrically different directions. Combined efforts always produce the best results.

THE STEP-BY-STEP WAREHOUSE OPERATIONS APPROACH

Most of the issues covered in this chapter call for the warehouse operations personnel to perform new, improved warehousing procedures. Although these procedures are usually supported by new and improved computer systems and hardware, the core of warehousing procedures is still physical work—receiving and putting products on the shelf and retrieving, sorting, packing, and shipping them. The methodology used to develop functional specifications for manual systems and procedures is quite similar to methodology applicable to that used for computer systems. In fact, both are components of the design phase of any logistics, distribution, or warehouse project. Exhibit 4–19, a planning chart for the design phase, highlights the step of designing functional specifications for manual procedures.

The specific tasks of the manual procedure development step are detailed on the next-lower-level planning chart, Exhibit 4–20. This step includes designing required inputs and outputs and outlining manual processing functions. Later, during the implementation phase of the program, the actual procedure will be developed from the outline. The author advocates videotaping the new manual procedures as the fastest, clearest medium for initial and long-term training. Writing words to describe procedures simply and clearly is mind-bogglingly difficult. Thus, most warehouses have inadequate, if any, formal procedures with which to train all employees in the best methods for performing their jobs. As a result, different people do the same type of job differently. When the new processes require rearranging old equipment and installation of new, people will need procedures for the conversion process as the planning chart also indicates. Since other tasks in this phase are less critically important, they are not explained here.

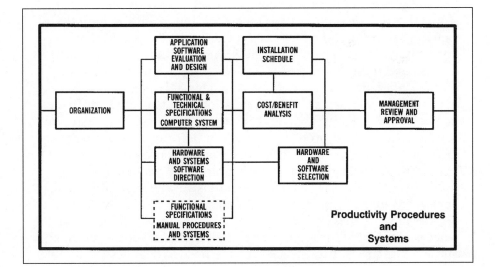

EXHIBIT 4-19

Preliminary System Design

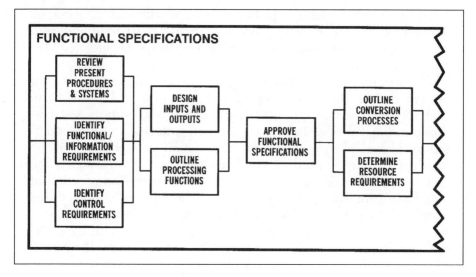

EXHIBIT 4-20

Manual Procedures and Systems

SUMMARY

The building blocks of the warehouse of the future are the contain-ers in which goods are received, stocked, issued, sorted and shipped. For near-optimum performance and quality, container de-sign is important enough to warrant using packaging design engi-neers. With containers able to flow into, through, and out of the warehouse without requiring repackaging, a common source of wasted labor cost will have been avoided. Misplaced goods and inaccurate inventory status information are two chief problems facing warehouse and logistics management. Therefore, vastly im-proved systems and procedures are required to control inventory locations and to maintain inventory status accurately. Order pick-ing, sorting, packaging, and truck unloading and loading opera-tions are some of the most labor-intensive and capital-intensive operations in the logistics network. The typical productivity of peo-ple working in these functional areas is quite low in contrast to what is achievable through improved design of layout, equipment, and manual procedures. Several of the needed changes are simple improvements that can and should be put into operation in the next few hours, days, or weeks. It's time to make it all happen, starting today!

CHAPTER 5

Future Vision

Warehouse and Logistics Systems

Business executives responsible for companies that warehouse and store products, materials, and components must put their managers and operating teams on the road to radically improved operations. While giant improvements stem from revised physical warehouse and distribution operations, executives must not overlook the fact that superior logistics rely heavily on new-generation systems and procedures for achieving the best results. Indeed, many warehouses need to improve systems even more than physical operations. The author believes strongly that business needs executives who believe they have to immerse themselves in the details of their organization's most important projects.[1] This belief clashes with the view of many who perceive the ideal executive's time to be too valuable to allow any more than passing involvement

---

[1] The author previously described the need of the executive suite as follows: "Industry leaders are smarter today. They understand that they alone are the champions who must breed additional champions throughout their organization. Further, they cannot be lofty generals, directing the battle from remote command centers, but must be in the thick of the fray, continuously urging the troops to ever greater heights of accomplishments." Roy L. Harmon, *Reinventing the Factory II: Managing the World Class Factory* (New York: Free Press, 1992), p. 358.

in either operations or improvement activities.[2] This (presumably) ideal executive parcels out scant increments of time to keep minimally abreast of vital operations and projects. Thus, with delphic wisdom, this omnipotent person is capable of passing judgment on the most profound issues after the shortest possible briefings on matters that have required his organization to study and analyze the pros and cons for many man-months or man-years.

Chapters 5 and 6 are organized to be helpful to both types of executives—those who skim the surface and those who are involved in essential details. Chapter 5, with relatively little in-depth description of the system details, covers the most vital principles of the systems, policies, and operating practices that lead a company to superior performance. Thus, the executive who spends relatively little time on detailed understanding of issues will find the chapter better suited to his management style than Chapter 6, which delves deeper into the particulars. As for the executive who feels a need to manage at a level of even less detail, the author recommends restricting his reading to no less than the "Executive Checklist" zingers in both chapters.

EXECUTIVE CHECKLIST: SELECTED ZINGERS

The purpose of this executive checklist, like the checklists in other chapters, is to provide executives, managers, and their associates with a basis for comparing their operations and systems to the author's perceptions concerning the characteristics of both the state of the art (current technology) and his vision of the future. Some will find it difficult, if not impossible, to accept all the checklist points as valid. For those who disagree with some points, the author earnestly suggests reading more on the subject here and in other publications. The point of doing so is not necessarily to come to agreement but rather to help the reader ensure that full, open-minded consideration has been given to alternative viewpoints before he selects the path most suitable for his own unique business. For indeed, the viewpoints and visions of many readers will be better suited to their operations than those of the author. Even though some may find the list less than perfect, the author hopes

[2] Blanchard and Johnson's "one-minute manager" seems to be an example of an executive who is perhaps less involved in details than the author feels is desirable. However, this impression may be misleading, as one of the one-minute manager's objectives is to train subordinates to think through and solve problems. The most important role of an executive is to develop his people in preparation for increased responsibility. Kenneth Blanchard and Spencer Johnson, *The One Minute Manager* (New York: William Morrow, 1982).

that many will find his checklists to be of immediate value, as did Tom Gelb, Vice President, Continuous Improvement, Harley-Davidson Inc.[3]

1. Electronic data interchange of projected demand (customer schedules) and vendor requirements (supplier schedules) will be "broadcast" throughout the distribution network. This will keep the network's production and deliveries in nearly real-time synchronization with the latest network inventory, forecast, and actual demand information.

2. Purchase, customer, and factory orders will become obsolete for use with repetitive demand items and will be replaced by electronic interchange of *schedules* between customer and supplier. Thus, all suppliers in the distribution network will have a time-phased schedule of their customers' actual orders and future forecasts. Hence they will be better able to plan future operations based on the most timely and accurate information available.

3. Economic order calculation, never widely used, will be phased out. It will be replaced by shipments totaling "N" periods of actual or projected customer requirements. The trick to being able to do so will be to reduce all of the formula's (actual) cost factors to nearly zero. The long-term winners of the competitive race will be companies that receive all shipments as close to just-in-time (daily or multiple times per day) as possible.

4. On-line entry of customer orders, temporarily, and automatic electronic transfer of customer schedules, ultimately, will eliminate armies of clerks in purchasing, order entry, and accounting roles. Order and schedule pricing will be an automatic system function as computer-generated customer schedules are fed directly from customers' computers to those of their suppliers.

5. Small companies will not be able to afford the cost of developing or purchasing the best possible software applicable to the distribution network. Nor can they expect to be the driving force behind putting such software into use between themselves and their larger customers and suppliers. Big companies, by contrast, need these modern

[3] Tom commented—as printed on the jacket of *Reinventing the Factory II*—"The list of 'Zingers' for each chapter challenges the reader to quickly examine his operations and provide a list of items for next Monday morning action."

systems and can afford the necessary investment. Once they have superior system software they will be able to offer it to their *customers* as an extraordinary customer service. And they should impose (diplomatically and co-operatively) its use on their smaller *suppliers* to help support slashing network inventories and operating costs of both customer and supplier.

6. Reorder point logic, including provisions for replenishment lead time, is a concept long outdated by the power of the modern computer and the virtual elimination of significant lead time in the new distribution network. The system should no longer launch replenishment orders. Rather, it should maintain a supplier schedule out to and beyond the network's replenishment time.

7. User and data entry productivity improvement will be one mandatory objective of all system projects. It will no longer be acceptable to implement systems that merely hold the line on personnel costs (or, worse, permit them to increase). Modern, simplified systems inherently lower the amount of clerical work-seconds required per business transaction—with the ultimate, achievable objective being zero seconds.

8. Statistical forecasting systems rarely accommodate customer-originated schedules of future needs. Yet customer schedules are the best tool for projecting future needs as accurately as possible. (There is no such thing as a completely accurate forecast.) Most existing forecasting systems must be revised or replaced by software that routinely captures and uses customer schedules.

9. Twenty-first-century forecasting systems and procedures will not be constrained to monthly or even weekly processing. All new and revised customer orders, schedules, forecasts, and internal planner data changes will be processed every day. These "seamless" forecast systems will contribute mightily to slashing weeks out of the time required to react to new and changed customer requirements in the distribution and manufacturing pipeline.

10. Many companies will learn that recording shipments as historical demand is a simpler and more accurate way than recording them at the time of order entry. In the long term, most customers with repetitive demand will "order" by electronically transmitted time-phased schedules. Shipments made just-in-time will be in accord with the

most current daily computer output, ignoring all earlier schedules. Thus, shipments (sales) will become the only realistic demand history.

11. New business calendars will make operation requirements (workload) much easier to analyze and understand. They will dispense with the illogic of the Gregorian calendar and will fit the business's specific needs. New work schedules and marketing methods will virtually eliminate peaks and valleys, thus leveling the business workload.

12. Ever greater emphasis will be placed on the application of the long-established principles and practices of Pareto analysis (ABC classification). These tools channel the majority of business control efforts to the vital few (products, customers, suppliers, etc.) that are most important to profitable operations.

13. Many current measures of customer service that are based on one or more of thousands of complex gauges are utter nonsense. A simple, logical way to judge service in superior operations of the future will be to keep track of the percentage of out-of-stock items as a percentage of the total number of items in the same inventory classification.

It is impossible to begin to visualize the twenty-first-century business world realistically without electronic data interchange as the pivotal element of its systems. It is perhaps the most important of the above zingers and the subject of the following section.

ELECTRONIC DATA INTERCHANGE: AN ELECTRIFYING PROSPECT

Superior executives, laying the groundwork for the systems of the twenty-first century, already recognize the senselessness of handwriting data that must subsequently be key-entered into computer systems, converted to computer output in paper or display form for manual review and approval, and subsequently keyed into the same or another computer system. Human intervention between computers that should "talk to each other" wastes computer capacity and is a dreadfully nonproductive use of human resources and strengths. For instance, *Reinventing the Factory II* gives a vivid pictorial presentation of twenty-first-century accounting.[4] It depicts the elimination of both accounts receivable and accounts payable

---

[4] See Appendix 2 for reference to information on accounting in the future.

through the adoption of an automatic funds transfer from customer to vendor bank account. The transfer is triggered by the electronic scanning of the kanban card (or electronic kanban) accompanying every receipt.[5]

In a move in the opposite direction to that of eliminating payables, Sears, Roebuck & Co. in 1991 advised its vendors that it would immediately add thirty days to the time lag between receiving goods and paying for them. This practice is in sharp contrast to that of Japan's best manufacturers, who have already used daily automatic funds transfer for at least two decades, eliminating the need to maintain payables computer systems and personnel operations. Sears's presumed advantage was a massive conversion from costly bank funding of inventory to free (?) supplier funding. However, as my friend Alan Baumann, President of A/R Packaging Corporation, Milwaukee, says, "Nothing is free." Al agrees that Sears's suppliers will not be able to support an investment in Sears inventory without eventually adding the inventory carrying cost (inventory in the form of increased accounts receivable balances) to their product prices. To do otherwise would seriously erode their profitability. In addition, both Sears and its suppliers will find that their costs of maintaining millions of additional invoice line items will strain their computer systems to the limits and will vastly complicate the manual control of those systems. A more honest, direct, and imaginative approach would perhaps have involved adopting automatic funds transfer and therefore simultaneously *reducing* payables by thirty days. This arrangement could have been based on the supplier's agreement to purchase a specified amount of a new Sears stock issue equivalent to the otherwise increased payables (sixty days) amount. Had this approach been used, both Sears and its suppliers would have benefited tremendously. Sears would have profited from the massive infusion of capital provided by the new stock offering and the elimination of all costs of old-fashioned accounting and aging of payables. The suppliers would have gained by being able to use the stock as collateral for its purchase. They also would have reduced the systems, people, and financing costs associated with receivables accounting and, finally, would have been able to pay interest charges from new and perpetual income in the form of Sears dividends.

Electronic data interchange will characterize the nature of business data transmission in the twenty-first century, obsoleting vir-

---

[5] See Appendix 2 for reference to material describing kanban and electronic kanban.

tually every form of paperwork transaction.[6] In the process, armies of clerical paperwork processors will be freed to work on activities that add value, not cost, to the process and product. Order entry systems will be one of the most important applications to which the latest in electronic communications hardware and software should be employed.

DEALER–CUSTOMER ELECTRONIC ORDER ENTRY COMMUNICATION SYSTEMS

One of the most exciting prospects in the vision of the twenty-first-century distribution system is the electronic linking of every major supply and distribution network, including the connections of a company with its customers and its supplier chain. Everyone in the pipeline knows that far too much time passes between the end customer's determination that an item needs to be replenished and the day it is actually received into stock. Currently, this process typically requires producing and mailing or transmitting a purchase order to the supplier, key entry of the order in the supplier's customer order processing department, and order picking, shipment, and, eventually, receipt and stocking by the customer. The portion of the process between the determination of need and completed entry into the supplier's production and shipping systems can now be reduced to an almost instantaneous event, thanks to modern computer systems and state-of-the-art communications hardware and software. Consequently, customers will view electronic linkage as an important tool with which to lower the number of shortages dramatically while at the same time slashing inventories (throughout the pipeline) that are intended to compensate for the long replenishment cycle time. Further, electronic data interchange will drastically reduce the potential for data entry errors. As Palmer has noted, rekeying information introduces an opportunity for error.[7] He cited one motor producer that had key entry errors in 50 percent of the incoming invoices processed.

Marketing and sales organizations quite readily recognize the huge competitive advantage of being the first among competitors to

---

[6] Cahill and Gopal schematically depict the electronic data interchange network as encompassing the entire production and distribution pipelines, a majestic vision with which the author concurs. Gerry Cahill, *Logistics in Manufacturing* (Homewood, IL: Business One Irwin, 1992), pp. 262–65.

[7] D. M. Palmer, "An Introduction to Electronic Data Interchange" in L. F. Gelders, and R. H. Hollier, eds., *Automation in Warehousing: Proceedings of the 9th International Conference* (New York: Springer-Verlag, 1988), p. 60.

work with customers on establishing an electronic link between their purchase orders (or, preferably, schedules) with the supplier's order entry process. In such a perfect, paperless environment, customers would be able to deliver their orders (or schedules), untouched by human hands, to the supplier. Such a system, triggered by actual usage, will operate in a black box mode on items ordered from the linked supplier. Because customers would find it faster and easier to order from the company that offered the free, directly linked system and service, the newly linked supplier would suddenly experience a surge in orders for items previously placed with other, nonlinked suppliers.

When customers are smaller than a given supplying company, and not yet in possession of sophisticated replenishment software, the supplier that can offer such systems, free of charge, will have a stupendous promotional tool—but only if the software meets certain important criteria. For example, customers should be wary of adopting a system that can manage replenishment ordering from only one supplier. This would not only tend to restrict purchases to that single supplier (to the exclusion of competitors) but would also force the customer to have one system for the supplier offering electronic linkage and another for all other suppliers. However, this need not be the case. The replenishment system can be designed to handle all suppliers, electronically in the case of the linked supplier and in conventional paper formats for all other suppliers. Next, the system should accommodate both replenishment orders and schedules. Schedule features, which permit the customer to transmit routinely a string of future time-phased requirements, work well to help ensure future availability to the customer. In addition, they provide a better basis for the supplier's future forecast and production plans and fit well with special promotions that require scheduling of time-phased requirements. This last benefit is familiar to producers of products with extreme seasonality, such as toy makers. These producers often offer better prices to customers willing to schedule receipts over several months during the slow season. Other advantages of using schedules instead of orders are another topic to be treated later. In addition to features for generating electronic and paper schedules and orders, the system of greatest appeal to customers would include inventory management and forecasting capabilities, also discussed in a later section.

The electronically linked system can and should have certain features that will give the supplier a large competitive advantage over other suppliers. For example, the customer can have on-line access to the latest prices and price breaks and current and pro-jected availability, including current replenishment lead time. The most sophisticated systems might even offer access to the current production status of items being produced to the customer's or-der specifications. In addition, on-line ordering screens could be designed to display catalogs from which items could be ordered by filling in quantity blanks. This feature would be especially useful to customers who provide repair service and thus routinely need to order spare parts. Chapter 7, "Industry Applications: Service Parts Warehousing and Distribution," contains a section describing such a dealer–customer catalog and order entry system.

Customers who are larger than the supplier may be reluctant to use the supplier's software, unless it is available for not only small but also large computers and has features superior to those of the customer's existing systems. For this reason, the most advanced suppliers should consider offering customers a shell system that, when customized, can serve as the electronic data transmission interface between the customer's existing system and that of the leading-edge supplier. When fully operational, this system would permit the customer to transfer time-phased delivery schedules and/or orders automatically into the supplier's system. The lightning-fast data transfer will be the near-ultimate in reducing reaction time between the customer's initiation of new or changed requirements and putting those changes into effect in the supplier's systems and operations (only near-ultimate because the state of perfection at which additional improvement is not possible will never be reached).

Systems for electronically transferring schedules and orders are only half of the potential package that canny suppliers should be able to offer to their customers. Inventory management systems, including forecasting modules, are the other half.

DEALER–CUSTOMER INVENTORY MANAGEMENT SYSTEMS

Based on the experience of the author and his colleagues, today's state-of-the-art inventory management systems in distribution and manufacturing companies in every corner of the globe are primi-tive at best, when measured against a vision of future systems. Few companies (especially small and medium ones) can afford the ma-jor investment and man-years required to pioneer their own vision-ary systems. Large companies most often take the leadership role in inventing and incorporating the system features necessary to achieve near-optimum benefits, in terms of operational costs and customer service. Therefore, larger companies are essential to pro- liferating the use of visionary systems in the distribution and man- ufacturing pipeline. They need to work with their customers and suppliers toward cooperative use of systems that they develop and make available gratis or at a nominal cost. For example, such com- panies as Baxter's Healthcare Corporation have demonstrated that their inventory management systems and service capabilities are superior to those of its customers. Baxter recently signed a five-year "just-in-time" agreement with the Methodist Hospital in Arcadia, California. Under the agreement, Baxter will manage the hospital's inventory and make daily deliveries of ready-to-use medical and surgical supplies.[8] (The author believes customers will eventually manage their own systems rather than allow their suppliers to do so. Undoubtedly, the new arrangement with Baxter is more cost- effective than the old system, but in the long run there should be no logical reason to believe that Baxter's inventory management per- sonnel *should* entail less cost than the hospital's, given the avail- ability of the same system.)

The twenty-first-century pipeline inventory management system will differ substantially from the Manufacturing Resource Planning II (MRP II) and Distribution Resource Planning (DRP) models that most gurus describe in today's literature.[9] For example, most cur- rent literature is still fixated on "economic order quantities" and "economic transfer quantities." But these calculations will become largely irrelevant in the new world, where setup, personnel, and all other indirect costs are slashed to the point of insignificance and where clustering of suppliers and users and improved transporta- tion practices make less-than-truckload shipments competitive with full loads. The point is this: Eliminating costs is far better than accepting them as necessary and encouraging their use by devising formulae that balance, and thus optimize, the opposing (although unnecessary) costs.

Further, although the author believes accurate forecasting to be

[8] "Baxter Signs Supply Pact with California Hospital," *Chicago Tribune*, June 10, 1990, section 3, p. 2.

[9] Andre Martin's book is a valuable resource for understanding distribution resource planning. Andre J. Martin, *DRP Distribution Resource Planning: Management's Most Powerful Tool* (Essex Junction, VT: Oliver Wight, 1990). Berry, Vollman, and Whybark's book is one of the most comprehensive in describing all aspects of manufacturing resource planning. William Lee Berry, Thomas E. Vollmann, and D. Clay Whybark. *Manufacturing Planning and Control Systems* (Homewood, IL: Business One Irwin, 1988).

impossible, every business needs a forecast. The better the forecast, the better the results of business operations.[10] Consequently, superb forecasting system features, already in use in the largest companies, need to be pushed out into the pipelines of supply and distribution to help our industries retain and regain international competitiveness. Later sections of this chapter delve deeply into the difficulties of, and opportunities derived from, improved forecasting techniques.

Future systems designers cannot ignore the lessons of the past. One such lesson, a critical component of the best twentieth-century inventory management systems, is based on the universal reality of the important few versus the insignificant many. This characteristic of the populations of all groups of business entities (customers, suppliers, and products, for example) calls for an ABC analysis to identify the vital few. It should come as no surprise that this life phenomenon will persist, making ABC analysis (discussed later in this chapter) an even more important component of twenty-first-century business systems.

In summary, companies that capture more and higher-quality data concerning customer forecasts, safety stock, and stock levels on a more timely basis will vastly improve the quality of their forecasts and production plans. Both customer and supplier will benefit, since sharing forecast and plan information will enable both to operate with much leaner investment in just-in-case inventories, shorter replenishment lead time, and fewer instances of poor customer service. Of course, the loop will not be completely closed until inventory management data (electronically shared and communicated) have been integrated in all entities of the supply and distribution pipeline.

DELIVERY QUANTITY: LESS IS BEST

In the Americas and Europe, customer order quantities requested from suppliers' warehouses and warehouse orders to their suppliers average approximately a one-month supply. In theory (which

---

[10] It is important to remember that no sales forecasting system has ever been developed (and none probably ever will be) that is capable of accurately forecasting a major economic downturn or recovery. Thus, the most important aspect of forecasting is not to foresee these changes but to react rapidly as they start to occur. One of the costliest failures of production and distribution industries' heads has been the failure to recognize and accept the indicators of major economic changes. As a result, inventories grow unreasonably during downturns, and production gears up too slowly when recovery is under way.

presumes an accurate demand forecast), this would mean that the average inventory resulting from the one-month order would be one-half a month for both end customer and warehouse, or one month total. When supplier and warehouse find practical means to cut the order quantity, thereby increasing the frequency of delivery, astounding inventory reductions and customer service improvements occur. For example, changing from monthly to weekly delivery quantities will slash the portion of inventory attributable to delivery quantity by 75 percent. Further, since weekly deliveries are always in the pipeline, reaction to higher-than-expected demand is faster, decreasing the frequency and duration of stockouts. And by implementing *all* the practical methods necessary to increase receipt frequency further from weekly to daily, companies will find that they can reduce the remaining inventory by an additional 80 percent! Logically reducing order (delivery) sizes requires solving several practical problems that will arise as a result of increasing the number of receipts to be processed. One such potential problem (if not addressed) would be increased workloads in receiving, receiving inspection, and the warehouse. Further, the order (delivery) quantity may in some way affect the economics of the supplier's setup and order processing costs. Sharp reductions in these costs are a necessary prerequisite in the logical process of increasing the frequency of receipts. Fortunately, it is entirely practical to expect suppliers to reduce setup costs. And both customer and supplier can virtually eliminate ordering, shipping, and receiving costs (including those related to payables and receivables accounting, eliminated by electronic funds transfer, as previously described). Through drastic revisions in receiving and stocking practices, daily receipts can become reality without ever increasing the warehouse workload and budget.

The inventory of an item stocked in a warehouse is generally replenished by orders. The authorized order quantity is usually either formally calculated as an "economic order quantity" or less scientifically set at "N" periods of demand, based on annual sales value. Unfortunately, many warehouse replenishment order quantities are still controlled by inventory analysts who operate without *any* formal rules or policies. In the case of no formal rules or policies, a company really has no way to predict or project future inventory levels systematically except to hope that past levels will continue in the future. In short, none of the three common methods is suitable for achieving the fastest pipeline delivery lead time and minimum inventory levels. Supplier schedules, not orders, are the tide of the future![11]

The most economical delivery to the warehouse and its customers—and the one that will yield the highest level of customer service—is delivery "just-in-time," which means at least daily delivery of each item stocked. However, if a purchase order were to be processed for each delivery, the avalanche of orders would bury customers, warehouses, and vendors and would paralyze their operations. Nor is it a reasonable alternative to place monthly orders that specify daily deliveries. Since forecasts are always inaccurate, these orders could never schedule deliveries accurately enough to match actual needs. They would therefore spawn frequent purchase order change notices, a burden even greater than purchase orders for each delivery. A supplier schedule, by contrast, can be transmitted daily or weekly by electronic means or on paper. Wherever possible, an electronic *kanban* should be used to trigger shipments from suppliers, while the supplier schedule should be used to schedule manpower and equipment capacity.

DISTRIBUTION AND WAREHOUSE ABC INVENTORY CLASSIFICATIONS

Pareto analysis has been and always will be one of the most important tools in the tool kit of superior executives and managers.[12] The basis for Pareto analysis is simple: in almost every population of any entity type, a few entities are extremely important while the vast majority are individually and collectively of lesser importance. Unfortunately, too few companies consider every way in which this fact can be translated into computer analysis to support improved operating practices. Therefore, many executives and managers may find rapid, low-cost improvement opportunities by merely identifying the entities involved in their businesses, obtaining analyses, and putting new operating practices into effect, based on the analysis results. In a warehouse or storeroom, the few inventory items with the highest annual cubic volume of demand are typically of the greatest importance when organizing the layout for maximum space utilization. For example, in previous chapters the ideally or-

[11] See Appendix 2 for reference to information on supplier schedules.
[12] Juran notes that the "Pareto Principle" has become deeply rooted in managerial literature. J. M. Juran, *Juran on Leadership for Quality: An Executive Handbook* (New York, Free Press, 1989), p. 136.

ganized warehouse was shown to be one in which the items stocked and used in the highest cubic volume are located closest to the point of receipt and/or shipment. Therefore, one standard and very important warehouse ABC classification report is the cubic volume analysis, Exhibit 5–1. The first line of the analysis is the inventory item with the highest annual usage, in terms of cubic volume, while the last is the item with lowest requirements. In other words, the analysis report lists inventory items in descending sequence of annual cubic volume usage. The last line gives the best perspective regarding the overall inventory population. It shows that the warehouse stocks 10,000 items with a total annual usage of 900,000 cubic units.

Too many analysis systems end at the real starting point, making decisions based on the data and executing the changes indicated. All too often, these vital steps are performed manually, without the powerful assistance of the computer. An example of improved use of the analysis to set usage volume classifications follows. The warehouse manager, based on the Exhibit 5–1 analysis, might decide to split the inventory into three classes as shown in the accompanying table. The most modern computer system would provide the man-

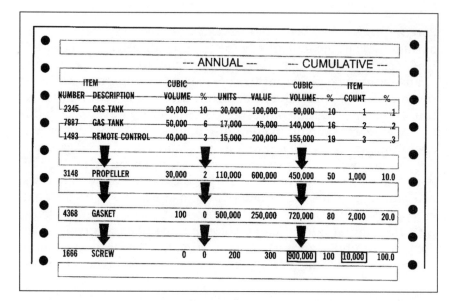

ITEM NUMBER	DESCRIPTION	--- ANNUAL --- CUBIC VOLUME	%	UNITS	VALUE	--- CUMULATIVE --- CUBIC VOLUME	%	ITEM COUNT	%
2345	GAS TANK	90,000	10	30,000	100,000	90,000	10	1	.1
7987	GAS TANK	50,000	6	17,000	45,000	140,000	16	2	.2
1493	REMOTE CONTROL	40,000	3	15,000	200,000	155,000	19	3	.3
3148	PROPELLER	30,000	2	110,000	600,000	450,000	50	1,000	10.0
4368	GASKET	100	0	500,000	250,000	720,000	80	2,000	20.0
1666	SCREW	0	0	200	300	900,000	100	10,000	100.0

EXHIBIT 5–1

Cubic Volume Analysis

Class	Quantity of Items	Percentage of Items	Cubic Annual Usage	
			Volume	Percent
A	1,000	10	450,000	50
B	1,000	10	270,000	30
C	8,000	80	180,000	20
Total	10,000	100	900,000	100

ager with a display of the analysis, through which the manager could page rapidly to set the classifications shown above. The system should then automatically update the cubic volume classification of each item, providing computer-prepared instructions for moving items for which the classification has changed from old to new storage zones. The system should also provide a cubic volume storage space requirement analysis for each inventory value classification. The average storage space requirements of all items of the same classification should be calculated and totaled. The analysis report, summarizing the cubic volume and storage area required for each ABC classification, should be used for storeroom layout planning. Incidentally, average cubic volume of stocked items can coincidentally (albeit rarely) parallel the annual usage in monetary value, but usually it does not. Therefore, at least two ABC classifications per item are usually needed: one for planning warehouse or storeroom space organization and a second for managing inventory investment.

Exhibit 5–2 is an example of the type of ABC classification analysis often applicable to setting inventory management targets based on annual usage value. This example is similar to but different from Exhibit 5–1, in that the sequence is based on annual usage value rather than the cubic volume. (Annual usage would preferably be the same as the forecast for the year but could also be based on past usage.) In the example, the last line again gives the best perspective on the overall annual usage. In the example, the 10,000 items stocked have annual usage value of $60 million. (The usage value should normally be based on an item's *cost* but could also be based on sales price if cost is less readily available.)

The warehouse manager might decide, on the basis of the annual value analysis, to split the inventory into the following three classifications:

Class	Quantity of Items	Percentage of Items	Annual Usage Value	
			Volume	Percent
A	500	5	15,000,000	25
B	1,000	10	44,000,000	73
C	8,500	85	1,000,000	2
Total	10,000	100	60,000,000	100

It may appear that the break points in the ABC analysis are arbitrary and judgmental. They are. The author has no magic formula for making the necessary decisions. However, for most warehouses and storerooms he typically concludes that the following six classifications are applicable.

S-The annual usage value of a very few items is super-high. Often 1 to 5 percent of all items stocked.

A-The annual usage value of a few more items is quite high. Often 4 to 10 percent of all items stocked.

B-The annual usage value of a fairly large number of items is moderate. Often 20 to 25 percent of all items stocked.

C-The annual usage value of a large number of items is low. Often 50 to 80 percent of all items stocked.

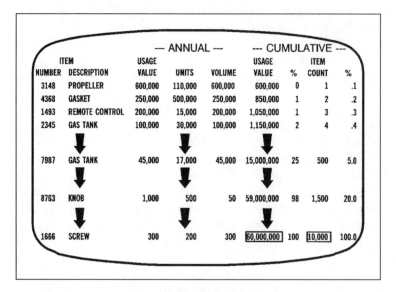

EXHIBIT 5-2

Annual Usage Value

D-The annual usage value of a few items is ultra-low. Often 1 to 10 percent of all items stocked.

Z-The annual usage value of a few items is zero. Often 1 to 4 percent of all items stocked.

THE CURSE OF THE CALENDAR

Just because some idiots, centuries ago, invented a totally illogical (Gregorian) calendar, most businesses have perpetually lived with the confusion resulting from the same absurd chronology. Exhibit 5–3 may be helpful in understanding the complexity that the conventional calendar imposes on every aspect of business management. The exhibit's jagged chart of monthly sales disguises the fact that in reality the sales pattern is the epitome of market demand for which every business yearns. In reality, the sales chart shows a uniform, level market demand pattern, as can be seen by a calendar that equalizes the number of business days in each business period.

Exhibit 5–4 converts sales into average daily sales by dividing sales by the number of business days in the month. It now becomes easy to see the real significance of sales in the period. Sales have neither risen nor declined. This contrasts starkly to the distorted sales trend information that the conventional calendar imposes on analysis of monthly operating statements. Incidentally, the number of business days per month varies from year to year as a function

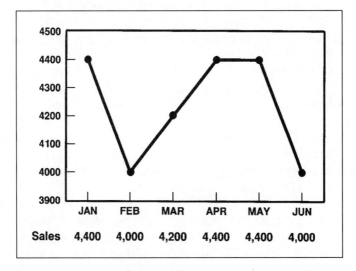

Sales	4,400	4,000	4,200	4,400	4,400	4,000
	JAN	FEB	MAR	APR	MAY	JUN

EXHIBIT 5–3

Conventional Calendar Sales

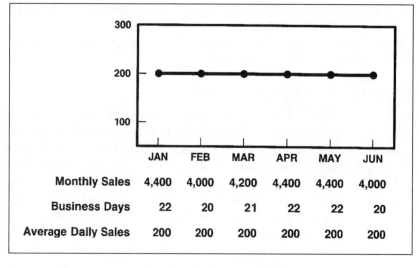

	JAN	FEB	MAR	APR	MAY	JUN
Monthly Sales	4,400	4,000	4,200	4,400	4,400	4,000
Business Days	22	20	21	22	22	20
Average Daily Sales	200	200	200	200	200	200

EXHIBIT 5-4

Average Daily Sales

of when weekends fall. As a result, the accuracy of the seasonality calculation can be degraded when using sales history by month.

The author has long advocated the use of separate business calendars for business operations. Exhibit 5–5 is an example of a business calendar in which each business period consists of five business days. At Yamaha Motor Company in Iwata, Japan, the author and his colleagues used a calendar of ten-day periods and reported operating information either by day or by five- or ten-day periods. (Superior manufacturers will soon be recapping information no less frequently than every five business days, with additional recaps each twenty business days, for purposes of reporting financial status.) Some systems require that user personnel understand and use B-days or M-days (business days and manufacturing days) when using computer-prepared displays and reports. At Yamaha a "black box" computer table of Gregorian calendar dates, by period number, translates people's calendar dates into business and manufacturing dates and vice-versa. It has thus been unnecessary to complicate the working universe of all Yamaha people (whose natural calendar is the Gregorian) by forcing them to learn to use new calendars. All date information in any system should appear in the user's natural calendar language to avoid unnecessarily complicating the business environment.

The complexity of business calendars may be unavoidable in

PERIOD NUMBER	GREGORIAN CALENDAR DATES				
1	JAN 2	JAN 3	JAN 4	JAN 7	JAN 8
2	JAN 9	JAN 10	JAN 11	JAN 14	JAN 15
3	JAN 16	JAN 17	JAN 18	JAN 22	JAN 23
4	JAN 24	JAN 25	JAN 28	JAN 29	JAN 30
5	JAN 31	FEB 1	FEB 4	FEB 9	FEB 6
6	FEB 7	FEB 8	FEB 11	FEB 13	FEB 14

EXHIBIT 5–5

Business Calendar

some instances because a single company might require more than one business calendar. For example, different warehouses, factories, and divisions of the same company often have a need for separate business schedules because their facilities are located in different countries, states, and cities that have different holiday and vacation schedules. Also, the office or service division of a company may have no annual or semiannual shutdown periods for vacations or physical inventory taking as distribution and manufacturing often do, thus have more "normal" business days. Further, sales at the retail level may occur seven days a week, whereas the distribution/warehouse organization may operate only five days. Such differences routinely force automotive executives and security analysts to qualify the significance of sales reports by identifying the number of sales days in the reporting period.

Careful scrutiny of Yamaha's pocket calendar, one month of which is shown in Exhibit 5–6, reveals an unusually strange work schedule. All Yamaha employees and most of their suppliers refer to this calendar to plan their work days. (Days that are *not* circled are work days). National uniformity has eliminated different holiday schedules for different prefectures, and suppliers and Yamaha cooperate in synchronizing production by working on the same days. Since many items are delivered several times a day, synchronized work days for Yamaha and its suppliers are necessary to avoid big inventory pools (one day's usage) between the suppliers'

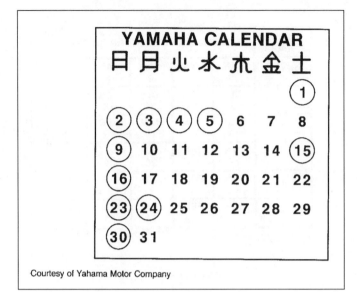

Courtesy of Yahama Motor Company

EXHIBIT 5–6

Work Day Calendar

factories and Yamaha. At Yamaha, normal weekends include Sunday and *Monday.* This unusual employee benefit gives Yamaha employees a big advantage over others, who swell crowds on their primary shopping day off, Saturday. Such businesses as banks, stores, and recreational facilities are not jammed with people on Monday, so Yamaha employees are able to use them without fighting the Saturday crush of people and traffic. Only a person who has lived in Japan can fully appreciate this benefit's immense value.

Further, Yamaha's work weeks are not always five days (in nonholiday weeks). In fact, the number of work days (scheduled a year in advance) is designed to match seasonal peaks and valleys closely, giving Yamaha tremendous flexibility to vary capacity to conform with traditional demand patterns. Cooperation among company, government, and union enables Yamaha and its employees to benefit from an annual work schedule of a fixed number of days per year with work weeks varying from three to seven days. This eliminates overtime payments except for days worked in addition to those in the year's preplanned calendar. Not many Western businesses are working aggressively to adopt such bold, imaginative practices, which break away from conventional custom. But the benefits may be enormous! Our best mover-shaker executives need to focus on innovations of this type. Others may be too dogmatic, viewing radical changes from past practice as inconceivably difficult to achieve. Eventually, they too will adopt the new calendars and work schedules—after their best competitors have already done so.

FORECASTING: FORMULAE FOR FAILURE

During the author's nearly four-decade career he has heard many business misconceptions. One of the most common has been that all of the company's woes would disappear if only the dolts in the marketing and sales organizations could be convinced that they should either produce an accurate forecast or else freeze a demand plan over the distribution, production, and procurement lead time. However, attainment of an accurate forecast is as improbable as capturing a rainbow or finding the pot of gold.[13] And freezing a demand plan while actual market requirements shift daily is akin to resolutely manning the Maginot Line while the enemy is adroitly bypassing it and attacking from the rear. The fact is, it is impossible to produce a completely accurate forecast. Further, companies that accept long replenishment lead times are putting the shoe on the wrong foot. Instead of operating systems to manage inventory despite long lead time, they should be systematically working to reduce it. Long lead times can be slashed to the minimum! Even companies with mature, sophisticated systems able to produce demand projections of near optimum accuracy see that these systems are still not able to eliminate unanticipated surpluses and shortages of supply at the individual item level.

Future demand may be forecastable (albeit with acceptable inaccuracy), but it cannot be predicted! Why? There are at least six important reasons. First, seasons come and seasons go with regularity, but unseasonable weather disrupts the plans of millions with irregular regularity. Second, economic peaks and valleys occur with startling frequency within generally regular periodicity. However, the range of peak and valley deviation from the average is wide and randomly dispersed. Industries and entire nations have the potential for drastically reducing the severity of seasonal peaks and valleys, thus improving the accuracy of their forecasts. Third, demand levels are unpredictable because competitors refuse to cooperate. They have the audacity to develop unexpectedly new, improved products or novel marketing approaches that erode a company's

---

[13] Smith writes, "All forecasts are wrong. The percentage errors are usually much more extraordinary than people would want to believe." Bernard T. Smith, *Focus Forecasting and DRP: Logistics Tools of the 21st Century* (New York: Vantage Press, 1991), p. 53.

market share. Fourth, technology would need to come to a standstill to allow the computers and electronic gadgetry of yesterday to remain the mainstay of tomorrow's demand. This would provide stability in one of the most dynamic reasons for demand uncertainty. Unfortunately, those crazy inventors are continuously designing better products and improving those already in production. Fifth, the buying public should learn to be less fickle and decline to plunge zestfully into the latest fads and fashions, instead sticking to the garments, furnishings, food, tools, and playthings of the past. But it hasn't yet. Sixth, economically underdeveloped countries insist on massive shifts of industrial prowess, starting from dependency on inexpensive labor and the newest imported factory technology and proceeding to international market dominance in the mass production fields in which they choose to specialize. This erodes the market share of competing companies, invalidating their history-based forecasts.

Those future supply and demand imponderables, and myriad other factors that make exact forecasting and predicting impossible dreams, might seem to dictate abandoning the pursuit of more accurate forecasting. Nothing could be farther from the truth! As faulty as any methodical forecast might be, operating a business without one would be disastrous. Especially when one understands that poor customer service stemming from forecast errors can be minimized by providing safety stocks consistent with typical error experience. By calculating the mathematical probability of forecast error a company can establish safety stocks to meet reasonable demand peaks. Safety stocks, however, are not the ideal solution. Carrying inventory in excess of actual sales carries a penalty by tying up funds that might otherwise be used for better investment opportunities. Nor is freezing the early weeks or months of a forecast an ideal approach. Even as forecasts are being finalized, market and supply trends are changing by item, region, and country, and even worldwide. Thus, every attempt to freeze production and inventory plans results in an overall surplus or shortage of inventory even though some individual items are in short supply while others have excessive inventory balances.

Unfortunately, the fact is that the dolts in marketing and sales are not really nuts. They know, through long experience, that when stock is available, they are able to sell more. When a retail customer calls in an order, it would be unusual if he were not to go to a competitor if an item he requires is out of stock. The retailer knows that *his* customers can *also* find a competitor down the street with stock on the shelf, so he cannot afford to wait until stock becomes available from his usual source. Thus, as much as production and warehousing management would like to reduce inventories to the bone to minimize operating cost and inventory investment, doing so without some way of guaranteeing equal or better service levels could have a disastrous effect on sales volume.

A far better solution than carrying excess inventory (large safety stocks) would be to produce to sales as they occur rather than in anticipation of sales. The inaccuracy of forecasts is not the real problem. The real problem is that the distribution pipeline, including the entire manufacturing chain, is too slow to respond to today's (or even recent) market demand. Therefore, every forecasting system must project demand over the pipeline lead time, in a futile attempt to keep the first producer in the pipeline producing each day the items that are expected to be sold one day weeks, or even months, later. Unfortunately, the input at the start of the pipeline is never quite right, and what eventually comes out of the pipeline is too much of one item and too little of another. When the pipeline is several months long and a massive market shift occurs, it may take that many months to get the output up or down to the new level of demand. And by that time another major market shift is likely to have occurred. How much simpler the problem becomes with the time through the pipeline is reduced to days rather than months. It becomes even simpler to respond rapidly when the flow through the pipeline is continuous, enabling every pumping station to increase or decrease the rate of flow simultaneously.

A plethora of experts and forecasting system software alternatives are available to help companies produce forecasts of relative accuracy. If a company's gap between forecast and actual demand is wide enough to make it obvious that improvement is necessary, better systems should be developed. However, if the replenishment lead time is still overly long, reduction of the lead time will be of much greater long-term benefit regardless of the forecast system's accuracy.

The popular forecast formulae are designed to fit the numerous market patterns that various items' sales repeat over time. These formulae range from sublimely simple to supremely challenging for even the professional mathematician. To the author's knowledge, no statistical forecast system has yet been devised that completely eliminates the need for human intervention in the event of wild, uncharacteristic swings in demand. Yet some have come close, routinely casting and automatically using forecasts for thousands of items in near "black box" processing while the computer channels a relative handful of items to humans for review and action. Human intervention almost always involves setting and resetting the factors and manual overrides on which a forecast is based, and many of these have complex names and functions. Merely mentioning the complexity of forecasting factors invokes the most basic and important design principle: complex operations automatically indicate that a procedure or system needs to be *simplified.* The best procedure is the one that is simplest to operate. If a system is so complex that only a limited number of specialists can be expected to master the extensive knowledge and expertise demanded, its design is bound to be more complex than necessary.

Outboard Marine Corporation's SysteMatched Parts and Accessories Division has a system that may well represent the epitome of all the features necessary to be do the best possible forecasting job with the least amount of personnel effort (in nearly "black box" fashion). Only seven people are needed to maintain, monitor, and modify the computer forecast factors and results. This is especially impressive when one considers that the seven are responsible for well over 400,000 forecasts in the company's international network of central and regional branch warehouses. The list of the forecasting system features that enables Outboard's forecasting effort to be virtually automatic, once the controlling factors are entered by the responsible analysts, reads much like a table of contents from Brown's textbook.[14]

When any individual looks at a graphic display of past demand and an extension projecting future demand, it is relatively easy for him to assess whether the future demand projection is reasonable based on the past. He can easily plot a different projection should it appear to be warranted. (However, it *would* be unreasonable to expect him to predict accurately a radical change in the economy's future, a condition not forecastable based on past demand). It would be much harder for the individual to calculate and revise the entire extensive array of forecast factors the computer would need modified to enable it to produce the same forecast results as his simple visual, manual plot. In fact, the average nonspecialist may find it impossible. The need, therefore, is for continuous simplification of the system of forecast and review until any idiot (author included) can perform the job of human forecast intervention. The author's vision of future forecast systems encompasses remarkably user-friendly simplicity, certainly not the hallmark of present forecasting software systems.

---

[14] Robert Goodell Brown, *Advanced Service Parts Inventory Control* (Norwich, VT: RGB Materials Management Systems, Inc., 1982).

Every company must decide which forecast pattern (or patterns, each with its set of formulae) is (are) suitable for its business. This decision is one of the most basic foundations of the forecasting system. The person responsible for each group of forecast items must subsequently understand which pattern to use with each item, if more than one pattern is provided. A discussion of many of the demand pattern types follows.

BUSINESS DEMAND PATTERNS: PROFILES OF THE PAST AND FUTURE

Pioneers in the academic forecasting field originally stressed the importance of three basic (but theoretical) types of demand patterns and even a combination of the three. They deemed it to be critically important to identify the actual patterns of demand as a prerequisite criterion for choosing the most suitable forecasting model (formulae) for projecting a whole business's sales of an individual item's demand. The author and others have never found more than one of these original, basic patterns (horizontal, trend, seasonal and trend/seasonal, as seen in Exhibit 5–7) in real-world businesses. This being the case, the author has simplified his early system designs by using a model suitable to any item. Although a

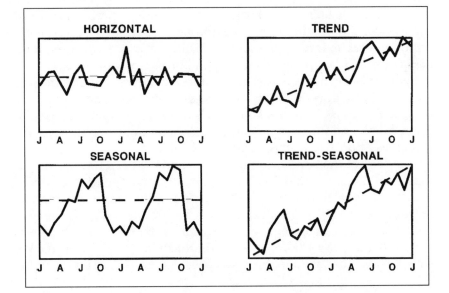

EXHIBIT 5–7

Hypothetical Demand Patterns

single model, the real-world demand pattern for which it was ideally suited was the most complex of the hypothetically simpler alternatives: the trend/seasonal model.

There are logical reasons why the three purely hypothetical demand patterns are rarely, if ever, found in the real world. For example, although the author has worked in various zones on six continents, he has found climatic and weather variations within every zone, including arctic and equatorial zones. These seasonal variations cause a host of reactions that put seasonality into the sales of all imaginable sorts of product families. Once, when working with a casket manufacturer, the author briefly imagined he might have found a product line in which there would be no seasonality. But, of course, casket sales were sharply seasonal. The reasons for seasonality, as usual, were easy to understand. In the winter people suffer greatly from influenza, colds, pneumonia, and other respiratory diseases, dropping like flies and raising the rate of casket sales well above average. Death rates also soar on the hottest days of the year, while in the delightful, temperate days of spring and fall they drop to their lowest levels. The pertinent question is not whether an item will have seasonality but how pronounced it will be. Even where there are moderate differences in temperature and rainfall from season to season, mankind has created nonclimatic conditions for sharp seasonal peaks. These include holidays (Christmas, for one, is celebrated with spending sprees in most of the world), school and work vacation periods, traditional periodic bonus dates, and traditional seasonal sales for various product families (furniture, white goods, and appliances, to name a few).

Seasonality is not the only characteristic of demand common to almost all products. Most products show long-term and short-term trends. The most basic reason for all trending demand is population growth and migration. If and when a region's population ever stabilizes or declines, all product types will trend up or down as the average age of the population increases and the need for new dwellings plummets. Further, the basic nature of competitive business ensures that sales will trend. The reason, quite simply, is that no reasonably intelligent executive could be comfortable with operating a business with a no-growth philosophy. By its nature, business demands that every company continuously strive to gain market share. Those that are successful will see upward sales trends, while the failures will see declines.

Service parts and new products also exhibit distinctive sales trends during their life cycles. In the case of products, newly introduced items tend to have rapidly increasing sales during their early life and gradual declines in their twilight. Some instantly cease when replaced by a new model. Service part sales patterns are usually the converse. They are lowest in the early useful life of the products and start to increase as accrued wear and tear cause damage that triggers the need for component replacement. Eventually, as the number of the products in use in the marketplace declines when the items are scrapped, their components' service demand also drops.

From the foregoing discussion we can safely conclude that distribution and manufacturing businesses with products of relatively insignificant trend or seasonality are rare. It follows, then, that most companies need forecast methods that consider these factors when projecting future demand. Even after replenishment lead time in the production and distribution pipeline is reduced to a bare minimum of days, these systems need to factor in all but the most insignificant trend and seasonality. However, when neither trend nor seasonality is sharply pronounced, it may be practical to use simpler systems (for the sake of operational simplicity), unless marginally improved forecast accuracy would provide a distinct competitive advantage. However, employees and executives must first master the simplest of systems before upgrading to those that are more complex.

Leading indicator data are often described as extremely meaningful in terms of their correlation to sales. For example, the number of building permits and new housing starts is almost always correlated to subsequent sales of appliances. However, although data of this type are often very useful for corporate planning, they are much more difficult to apply to forecasts for individual products. And simplicity must be the prime objective of the best systems.

In whatever form customers forecast, their forecasts, in the form of customer schedules, will be one of the most important elements of the supplier's own forecast and scheduling system. Today, however, one seldom finds customer schedules being made available to suppliers. The customer schedule will be one of the very important ingredients of twenty-first-century logistics systems.

THE MISSING INGREDIENT: CUSTOMER SCHEDULES

Virtually all statistical forecasting systems are based on the premise that all sales demand requires immediate delivery from stock. In reality, however, most businesses receive a large percentage of customer orders in the form of delivery schedules extending over one or several future demand periods. Further, customer schedules will soon be a key ingredient of superior distribution and manufacturing. Accurate, timely customer schedules can compensate for (and replace or complement) less accurate statistical forecasts and can provide a significantly better basis for planning future capacity than customer orders, limited to immediate delivery requirements.

Until such time as *all* customers are prepared to provide customer schedules (perhaps in the far distant future), the statistical forecast system must consider both demand forecasts for some customers and schedules for the other customers that provide them. Exhibit 5–8 indicates how customer schedules are used to supplement statistical forecasts to improve the accuracy of the demand plan. In the example, in period 1 the customer schedules of 1,100 are greater than the forecast, thus the "final forecast" is 1,100 (circled), the greater of the two. When reviewing period 5 the forecast analyst noted the customer schedule in period 4 (1,500), concluding that it would cause the demand in period 5 (1,000) to be 500 less. Therefore, the analyst entered 500 (circled) as a forecast override in period 5. An override supersedes both forecast and customer schedule, and becomes the final forecast for that period.

Until it is no longer deemed necessary for an analyst to review and modify forecasts and customer schedules manually, the long-term objective of forecasting by "black box" will not have been met. Nor is it desirable, prior to achieving that end, to permit too many planner overrides. For one thing, the manual planner forecast re-

LINE DESCRIPTION	BUSINESS PERIODS						
	1	2	3	4	5	6	7
FORECAST	1,000	(1,000)	(1,000)	1,000	1,000	(1,000)	(1,000)
CUSTOMER SCHEDULES	(1,100)	900	400	(1,500)	0	0	0
OVERRIDE					(500)		
FINAL FORECAST	1,100	1,000	1,100	1,500	500	1,000	1,000

EXHIBIT 5–8

Forecast/Customer Schedules

view simply cannot be allowed to delay significantly the delivery of a final forecast to the rest of the organization and to other computer systems. Even when the best computer forecasting systems are employed, the marginal forecast improvements typically made following the planner's manual review and modification are nowhere near as important to business operations as is the timeliness of the forecast's availability. Planner adjustments can be processed in real time by a "seamless" system that permits processing of forecasts, customer schedules, and planner overrides at any time.

THE SEAMLESS FORECAST: CONTINUOUS REVISION

Some of the best short-range forecasts in the world are grassroots compilations, prepared by salesmen in the field. Yet, as good as these forecasts are, they are of little value by the time they are completed. Processing and consolidating the detail forecasts of all regions and/or customers simply take too long. Therefore, the front end of the forecast has usually been shipped before the schedule becomes available to production and inventory management, and its middle and end are already woefully out of date. The stone age mentality that deems it still necessary to conduct periodically (monthly, for example) an extensive field forecast preparation, summarization, corporate review, and modification needs to be jerked into the world of modern computers. Today, both field and statistical forecast systems (and combinations thereof) can and must be designed to accept and process *continuously* (not periodically) new and revised forecast and customer schedule information. Doing so will permit the field forecaster, the salesman, to work on forecast information throughout the month as he makes customer calls. One reason that periodic forecasting takes so long is that all the effort is jammed into a few days at the end of each month. Thus the salesman needs to devote either too much time to forecasting—at the expense of making fewer customer visits or calls—or too little time to forecasting. (Customer calls and visits are almost always viewed by sales organizations as their most important function; thus field sales forecasting is usually a lower priority in their schedule).

Further, coordinating computer processing cutoff dates with *all* customers is disastrously difficult when the system depends on a common monthly cutoff for all. But, if the system is designed to permit any customer to input an updated schedule at any time, the problem evaporates. In the past, most forecasting systems and procedures entailed review and approval action for far too many products and their components. This was a serious reason for periodic (monthly) processing, since the manual review and action procedures triggered by the receipt of the monthly forecast often consumed an entire month. This being the case, it seemed impractical to forecast more frequently. Since twenty-first-century forecast systems will be virtually "black box," this reason is no longer a valid excuse. Finally, stone age systems were constrained by the tortoise-like speed of available computer hardware. There just weren't enough hours in the month to process the mind-boggling data volumes. With modern hardware, computer speed and capacity are no longer serious problems.

DISTRIBUTION NETWORK FORECASTING

To intractable proponents of decentralized operations and systems (the author included), it may come as a shock to read that the author believes centralized logistics systems (order entry, forecasting, and inventory management) must be the ultimate competitive tool. Nevertheless, that is the case. To the customer, the time required to move goods through the production and distribution pipeline is intolerably long. The slow cascade of replenishment information through the logistics network starts with the sale of end product. The retail outlet typically puts the cascade into motion by preparing and mailing a replenishment order to a regional warehouse. After the regional warehouse enters and ships the order, the depletion of its stock typically triggers another replenishment order to be sent to the supplier. And the supplier, in turn, orders materials and components from its suppliers, who then order from *their* suppliers. In the automotive industry this entire process was recently found to require up to sixteen weeks, until the earliest producer in the chain was given actual demand-driven requirements with which to work. Hence, today's distribution pipeline is usually operating with network on hand and demand information that is all too often out of date by several weeks. If, by contrast, all customers, distribution warehouses, factories, and vendors are part of a real-time network of electronic data interchange through a central computer, the entire network can share up-to-date information for planning their business operations.[15] To a very large degree, this will mean that suppliers up and down the

---

[15] The author is not alone in his conviction that these types of systems are needed. Such experts as Andre J. Martin advocate "linkages" in the network. Andre J. Martin, *DRP Distribution Resource Planning: Management's Most Powerful Tool* (Essex Junction, VT: Oliver Wight, 1990), pp. 3–4.

pipeline will no longer be working furiously to produce products that are not currently being sold while not producing others for which sales may currently be skyrocketing at the distribution pipeline terminus.

As part of every company's long-term vision, the author strongly advocates establishing company-owned production and distribution networks instead of relying on independent channels (as outlined in Chapter 2, under the heading "Independent Distributors: Siphoners of Potential Profit"). A key reason for this advocacy is the comparative ease with which a company can centralize distribution forecasting and inventory management data and data processing (as contrasted to the relative difficulty of incorporating independent distributor data systems). As long as the two systems operate independently and do not share forecast data, there will be unnecessary delay and excessive, costly safety stock inventory in the distribution pipeline. As a result, customers will suffer the penalties of poor service and higher-than-necessary prices.

KILL THE REORDER POINT CONCEPT

The time has come to bury the concept of the reorder point, which is based on the premise that an item's stock should be replenished by launching a purchase or production order when the item's balance on hand drops to or below a reorder point. The reorder point is commonly recognized as comprising two components: (1) the expected usage (forecast formally or informally) over the period between launching the order and receiving the item in stock, and (2) the amount of planned safety stock. Modern hardware and software systems and new manufacturing practices can and must consign this methodology to the intellectually interesting but arcane history of inventory management. It has little applicability to the operations of the superior distributors and manufacturers of the twenty-first century.

Single delivery purchase and production orders provide no practical, cost-effective way to keep the distribution pipeline in a state of continuous flow. Conversely, supplier schedules keep future demand in front of the supplier, permitting him to pass future demands farther back in the pipeline, so that the earliest supplier in the network can launch the *right* production into the pipeline to avoid late delivery of the final pipeline product. The continuous pipeline and other manufacturing improvements (such as setup cost elimination) will reduce lead time to remarkably lower levels. In this bright new world of supplier schedules, the use of orders and long replenishment lead time for repetitive demand items will virtually disappear.

CUSTOMER SERVICE: WILL-O'-THE-WISP?

The author has a hearty laugh any time he hears or reads a statement about a business's customer service level in terms of a percentage. Why? It is virtually impossible to describe service level as a single percentage in a universally acceptable context of a reasonable business application. A sea of mathematical theory is directed toward the notion that forecasting systems can calculate a forecasting error and use that error to define a safety stock level that will yield a predictable level of customer service. If only the eggheads would descend from their ivory towers into the real world of business, they would find a huge gulf between accepted, popular theory and actual business conditions. They need to construct new and improved theories that match reality and have practical business application! In order to calculate a projected customer service level, one must first be able to define it! Exhibit 5–9 contains four examples that begin to point out the extremely difficulty of defining a single, simple, universal system service measurement.

The first line of the exhibit shows back orders of 100 during a month in which there was a demand of 1,000. Therefore, the service level would appear to be 90 percent if one considers service level to be the quantity back-ordered as a percentage of the total period's demand. However, because the back-ordered quantity was

| -----QUANTITY----- | | | -----ORDERS----- | | |
DEMAND	BACK ORDERS	PERCENT	TOTAL	BACK ORDERED	PERCENT
1,000	100	10	100	1	1
1,000	10	1	100	10	10
1,000	1,000	100*	100	100	100*
1,000	1,000	100**	100	100	100**

* = ONE DAY ON BACK ORDER, ON AVERAGE
** = ONE WEEK ON BACK ORDER, ON AVERAGE

EXHIBIT 5–9

Customer Service Alternatives

for a single order/item, the service level achieved on the basis of order line items back-ordered appears to be 99 percent. The second line of the exhibit shows an instance in which a lower quantity, 10 (1 percent), of back orders might have caused 10 (10 percent) order line items to be back-ordered. Of these two measures of customer service, the number of order line items back-ordered would usually be better than quantity, because it is a better indicator of the number of customers that might have been inconvenienced by out-of-stock instances. However, as the third and fourth exhibit lines indicate, the mere fact that an out-of-stock condition occurred may have absolutely nothing to do with the level of service provided in the eyes of the customer. For example, on both lines every single customer order was received at an instant in time when stock levels were briefly zero. Thus customer service in these cases would appear to be zero. However, if the customer expects and receives shipment within forty-eight hours, his perception and that of warehouse management must be that the service level achieved was 100 percent! It becomes an entirely different matter if shipment of the order line items is delayed a week, and even more serious if the back order persists for several weeks. Some have advocated time-weighted back-order calculation to reflect this element of customer service. However, the author feels that is a mistake. In the first place, reporting such a statistic would require more complex systems, and any such measure would be quite difficult to understand. Second, in the twenty-first century, lengthy out-of-stock periods will no longer be a material logistics problem!

The author has reviewed numerous computer reports that depict customer service in every conceivable context: quantity, order line items, and aged back orders in quantity and in order line items, to name the most common. Sadly, as Shingo once said, in essence these reports are only "post mortem obituaries for events that have already become history."[16] Worse, they make it harder to understand the situation in a simple yet meaningful way. The author has usually found that he could best evaluate trends in customer service by reviewing trends in the simple number of *stocked items* on back order, summarized by each inventory management classification as illustrated in Exhibit 5–10 (One simple modifying provision, where practical, would be to exclude counting items that have been out of stock less than one or two days). When the inventory manager decides (after monitoring the Customer Service display or

---

[16] Shigeo Shingo, *The Sayings of Shigeo Shingo: Key Strategies for Plant Improvement* (Cambridge, MA: Productivity Press, 1987), p. 73.

CUSTOMER SERVICE

INVENTORY MANAGEMENT CLASS	NUMBER OF ITEMS	ITEMS BACK ORDERED	ACTUAL SERVICE LEVEL	TARGET SERVICE LEVEL
S	10	0	100.0	99.0
A	100	2	98.0	94.5
B	1,000	75	92.5	94.5
C	5,000	500	90.0	92.0
TOTAL	6,110	577	90.5	N/A

EXHIBIT 5–10

Service Level Monitoring

report) that unusual trending demand is the cause of unusually high or low back orders, he might choose to increase or decrease the computer factor controlling the target service level. However, it would be unwise to do so without knowledge of the potential impact on the investment in safety stock inventory. Hence, the inventory investment monitoring display or report, Exhibit 5–11, is vital to controlling the investment within reasonable limits.

In Exhibit 5–11, the actual and target inventory investments are quite close in each inventory classification and, as might be expected, extremely close in total. However, this would not usually be the case until the inventory manager has completed several cycles of adjusting the factors that control order (delivery) quantity and safety stock. In fact, the trial-and-error process of adjusting factors often requires a year or two to bring the actual and theoretical target inventory investment numbers into reasonable proximity. As Copacino and his co-authors have said, "However, because demand or use variations are expected or random, it is normally exceedingly difficult . . . to fix an absolute guarantee of availability."[17]

[17] William C. Copacino, John F. Magee, and Donald B. Rosenfield, *Modern Logistics Management: Integrating Marketing, Manufacturing, and Physical Distribution* (New York: John Wiley & Sons, 1985), p. 77.

INVENTORY INVESTMENT

INVENTORY MANAGEMENT CLASS	ACTUAL $ INVESTMENT	TARGET INVESTMENT	THEORETICAL ONE-HALF ORDER QTY	SAFETY STOCK
S	1,000,000	1,050,000	1,050,000	0
A	2,000,000	1,950,000	1,850,000	100,000
B	3,000,000	3,200,000	2,400,000	800,000
C	1,000,000	800,000	400,000	400,000
TOTAL	7,000,000	7,000,000	5,700,000	1,300,000

EXHIBIT 5–11

Inventory Investment Monitoring

Note that the safety stocks of the highest value classifications (S and A) in Exhibit 5–11 are lowest as a percentage of total theoretical investment, while the reverse is true of safety stocks of the lower value classifications (B and C). The reason is that the higher-value items are not only most closely monitored and controlled each day but also are scheduled for very frequent delivery. Thus, periods during which there would be no receipts would be of very brief duration. Frequent receipt and frequent opportunities to change scheduled receipt automatically increase the service level achieved. The higher level of safety stock for lower-value items makes it practical to control these items in as close to "black box" fashion as possible, with a lower risk of back orders. Hence, inventory planners can focus almost all their efforts on the items of highest usage value. Conversely, lower-value items are usually ordered in larger quantities that cover a longer time frame, which in itself yields higher levels of service. However, the relative infrequency of ordering usually causes the supplier's response time to be longer. Since the value of these items is quite low while the number of items stocked is very high, a company can usually afford higher safety stocks for them and therefore can expect stockouts to be rarest in the highest number of items stocked, for the least investment.

Make no mistake, the fact is that the author believes it necessary, whenever practical, to set safety stocks using computer-calculated forecast error, factored to achieve a theoretical level of service. Many companies, however, can ill afford to wait until they have gathered demand history and acquired and modified new system software before starting to control service level and inventory investment. These companies need to adopt new or improved systems and procedures using "periods of demand" (usage) to specify order quantities and safety stocks.

SAFETY STOCK: CUSHION OR CATASTROPHE?

Safety stock can be a near-ideal solution to customer service problems, even in the face of the impossibility of accurate demand forecasting. The computer-calculated forecast error, factored to provide a theoretical "service" level, is the most common form of computer-generated safety stock. The resulting safety stock is perhaps the least inaccurate way to "cover" a high percentage of future forecast errors. Extra inventory (safety stock) provides some protection against stockout resulting from unexpected demand peaks. However, somewhere between theory and practice something typically goes awry.

Although almost every warehouse inventory management textbook tends to give the impression that both individual item service levels and those of *composite inventories* are forecastable, this is rarely so. So many factors contribute to actual performance that to expect a direct link between theory and reality, especially at the individual product level, is inadvisable. Lowell Stoelting of Outboard Marine Corporation's SysteMatched Parts and Accessories Division material management group has said: "I would rarely expect to see an individual item's service level hit the pre-planned target." However, by continuously fine-tuning the system's factors, the gap between the planned and actual *composite* inventory and service levels can eventually be narrowed to a tolerable minimum.

Composite inventories (actual) are usually much higher or lower than the result of theoretical calculations based on one-half of the order quantity plus safety stock. Nevertheless, actual customer service levels are most often significantly lower or higher than the target service level percentage on which safety stock is based. The reason is the lack of *precision* in the safety stock calculations due to numerous shortcomings in conventional approaches to such calculation. (Brown has said, "Let the accountants worry about pre-

MONTH	LOWEST INVENTORY BALANCE	MONTH	LOWEST INVENTORY BALANCE
JAN	6,000	JUL	5,000
FEB	3,000	AUG	3,000
MAR	2,000	SEPT	0
APR	6,000	OCT	5,000
MAY	5,000	NOV	4,000
JUN	3,000	DEC	1,000

SAFETY STOCK = 2,000

EXHIBIT 5–12

Lowest Inventory Balance

cision. Accuracy is sufficient for inventory management.")[18] In the days of obscenely large inventories, no foreign competition, and intensely clerical inventory management systems, a higher degree of slop in inventory management may have been acceptable. In today's world of fierce international competition and "black box" inventory management, there is considerably less room for imprecision.

Exhibit 5–12 helps to demonstrate some important points concerning safety stock theory and actual practice. The author and his teams, in the process of reviewing thousands of such inventory balance records, have found that the majority of items have never had periods of zero stock and have had few in which inventory fell below the safety stock level. Even closer scrutiny has revealed another important logical set of facts related to the general economy. In the first place, the highest number of stockouts occurs during times when the economy is expanding most rapidly. At the same time, companies increase total inventories as they begin to order earlier (and schedule earlier deliveries) to get orders into vendors' hands ahead of other companies competing for suppliers' overtaxed capacities. The reverse is true in times of economic slow-

[18] Brown, Robert Goodell, *Advanced Service Parts Inventory Control* (Norwich, VT: RGB Materials Management Systems, Inc., 1982), p. 90.

down. Because suppliers begin to have excess capacity and customers are canceling and rescheduling lower-quantity deliveries at a frenetic pace, stockouts (soon) fall and inventories (belatedly) are trimmed to their lowest levels. Most inventory management systems do not respond rapidly enough to prevailing global economic conditions, and all too few executives, planners, and analysts react in time, if at all.

Most systems base safety stock solely on forecast inaccuracy. In reality, however, more shortages stem from late deliveries, engineering changes, and quality defects than from forecast errors. In the bright new world, suppliers will master fast, low-cost changeover and flexible capacity, and will reduce pipeline lead time to a degree not now imaginable. Thus, the need for safety stock to cushion late deliveries will diminish much more rapidly than anticipated in years past and will finally disappear.

As to the widely practiced safety stock calculations, most ignore some key real-world factors that, if considered, would sharply reduce the portion of inventory attributable to safety stock if only it were practical for the calculation to provide for them. Inventory management systems typically base the calculations (the author is oversimplifying for easier reading) on the absolute (unsigned plus or minus) difference between forecast and actual demand. If, for example, the average monthly demand for an item were 1,000 and the average absolute error were 100, the safety stock might be 100 or 200, based on the average error and depending on the desired level of service. These same companies usually calculate actual service level based on the quantity of the item back-ordered during the month or the number of orders (for the item) for which the item was back-ordered. As previously noted, neither of these alternatives bears much more than a coincidental relationship to the safety stock calculation.

What is the best temporary safety stock system and methodology? The starting point is to make management intervention, in early response to emerging economic changes, a systematic part of the whole methodology. Then the system must be designed to operate with rapid changes in planned safety stock based on management, not clerical, control. Finally, the real reasons for needing safety stock must be systematically attacked and permanently eliminated.

WILL THE REAL DEMAND PLEASE STAND UP?

Purist theoreticians have long bemoaned the inaccuracy of demand data by period, especially as related to the question of whether to record demand when orders are received versus when they are shipped.[19] In the theoretical model, all customer orders are due for immediate shipment as soon as the order is received. However, businesses with repetitive demand must strive to eliminate such orders and replace them with customer schedules. When they do so, the entire fabric of past demand recording must be expected to change. In the theoretically ideal environment, demand history, recorded as such when orders are received, more accurately reflects true demand than when recorded at the time of shipment. So what? There are several practical (not theoretical) reasons for purposely choosing to record shipments as demand. First, today most businesses receive two types of single-delivery customer orders: one requests immediate delivery; the other schedules delivery sometime in the future. Clearly, orders scheduled for future delivery should be counted as demand in the scheduled period rather than in the period in which the order is received. Second, although few customers today employ scheduled orders (which specify multiple deliveries over several weeks or months), this will not always be the case. Use of the multiple-delivery orders (or, better still, schedules) must become ever more prevalent as more and more customers leap aboard the just-in-time bandwagon. Again, the demand ideally should be recorded as demand in the scheduled period, not in the period in which the schedule was received. In fact, since schedules will be continuously revised, only the last schedule for a period just completed (due to new, just-in-time shipping practices actual shipments in the period should always be the same as the period's requirement) accurately represents the period demand. Third, without going into all the reasons, capturing shipments as demand is much simpler than doing so during order entry. And fourth, financial reports record sales at the point of shipment, not at the time of order entry. The author deems it desirable to synchronize forecast demand history systems and financial operating statements, using the same shipment information for each. Finally, when any single order requesting immediate shipment is considerably delayed (because the item ordered is out of stock), recording it as a demand in the period shipped will usually have minor effect on subsequent forecast projections, even though its demand was technically for an earlier period. Why? Because the forecast system must not be so sensitive to the unusual demand of a single order (or even several) that it will nervously react with huge swings in the

---

[19]Smith, for one, takes a view opposite to the author's and enumerates his reasons with conviction. Bernard T. Smith, *Focus Forecasting and DRP: Logistics Tools of the 21st Century* (New York: Vantage Press, 1991), pp. 76–77.

quantity forecast. As demand of most warehoused items always has big peaks and valleys anyway, the system just cannot afford to be very nervous. So what, indeed! Pursuit of theoretically ideal demand recording has little place in the imperfect world of free market supply and demand and the realities of actual business operations.

PERFORMANCE MEASUREMENT SYSTEMS: DON'T BASH THE TROOPS

Far too much attention has been riveted on the subject of performance reporting systems and pathetically little on the executives and managers that need to come down from their ivory towers and get out into the warehouses, offices, and factories for which their personnel are responsible. They should devote more time to seeing the performance of their organization by direct observation. Recent authors have published entire books full of various types of "performance reports." A thinking person must easily see that reviewing mountains of such reports is not only no substitute for a small handful of powerful, meaningful measures of performance. In fact, the multiplicity of such reports, if truly seriously studied, works against effective management control by stealing too many hours from the executive's busy work day. Nor is it a reasonable solution to employ an army of staff people to pore over the piles and excerpt "important issues" for executive review, or to interject performance policemen to force the line organizations to perform their jobs. If the need is for trustworthy, conscientious people in positions of responsibility, the executive's time will best be spent in recruiting and managerial training activities, not in reviewing sterile reports in the isolation of his office.[20]

Conventional operating statements, responsibility reports, and balance sheets will and always should be the backbone of business organizations' performance evaluation procedures and systems. After all, the single purpose for founding any commercial business is to make money. As long as financial reports clearly indicate that a company is profitable and that there are no unfavorable profit trends, there is little justification for executives to look for smaller problems and opportunities in organizations in which they have

---

[20] Drucker writes: "But when a company builds its organization around modern information technology it *must* ask the questions. [Who requires information, when and where?] And then management positions and management layers whose main duty it has been to report rather than to do can be scrapped." Peter F. Drucker, *The Frontiers of Management: Where Tomorrow's Decisions Are Being Shaped Today* (New York, Harper & Row, 1986), p. 204–5.

placed competent managers and supervisors. Given competent, well-trained personnel, executives should expect them to manage the successful quality and schedule performance of their own operations and to achieve favorable "bottom line" results in their own bailiwicks. However, management by walkabout is still the best way to have contact with ongoing operations.

The worst aspect of most "performance reporting" is that the data for most items virtually never show significant, enduring trends toward either improved or deteriorating performance, other than those resulting directly from sales fluctuations. Stated another way, most organizations spend enormous amounts of money to capture, process, and report all types of data, and executive and managerial staffs spend inordinate amounts of time reviewing those data.[21] But instances in which the changes made result in substantive, enduring improvements are extremely rare. Why should a company have large reporting and processing expenses for information that rarely changes significantly? Good ol' "Kentucky windage" is often the only signal an executive needs to realize that a problem requires attention.[22] For example, the warehouseman says, "There is a drawer full of back-ordered customer orders due to stock shortages, whereas there are normally only a small handful." Or the lead person on the receiving dock says, "Returns of defective goods from our customers have more than doubled, perhaps tripled, in the last few weeks." Whether there are 1,349 back orders or 659 customer returns—with detail reporting by cause codes—is unimportant. Rather than rely on such reported data, executives should easily and simply ask the persons responsible what is happening and expect them not only to rattle off the most important reasons but also to reel off the actions already under way either to eliminate or to improve the source problem.

The notion that the primary function of information systems is to provide a basis for evaluating subordinates is dreadfully wrong. Systems developed with this objective in mind almost always wind up reporting primarily on a static situation and churn out virtually

[21] "The . . . myth is that managers need and use information that is systematic and well documented. This kind of information is most often supplied by management information systems. In reality, managers prefer verbal media or information that is obtained fast, usually by telephone calls or meetings." W. Jack Duncan, *Great Ideas in Management* (San Francisco: Jossey-Bass, 1990), p. 101.

[22] Kentucky windage (for the benefit of readers not familiar with the term) is the commonsense ability to raise a wetted finger in the air to discern the direction and speed of the wind, in order to determine how to aim one's Kentucky long rifle. Executive "intuition," the basis for many business decisions, is really experience-based knowledge that permits the executive to make rapid decisions based on seemingly little evidence.

useless information in perpetuity. The executive should specify his information needs when problems and opportunities arise. Effective information systems should be servants to operating personnel—accepting, processing, and selectively reporting information of vital, current, topical interest in terms of helping businessmen quantify and solve *their* problems and capitalize on *their* opportunities of the moment. And once *their* objective has been accomplished, inputting transactions, processing, and reporting should come to a screeching halt, making computer capacity available for new, timely support of other operational problems and opportunities that have arisen. This is not to imply that the executive cannot use the information system to help gather the facts pertinent to a subordinate's performance. Rather, he should be able to mold the information-gathering process to those data which his direct observation leads him to believe are germane at the moment. Most of the best executives will find, however, that they do not need support for their own conclusions, which are based on direct, active involvement in operations.

The most valuable commodities in distribution networks are inventories, warehouses, and transportation. As such, successful management of these elements is of such vital importance that perpetual reporting of their status is a minimum system requirement. Typical balance sheet accounts usually provide an adequate basis for reporting on inventory, especially when everyone in the company is attuned to tracking inventory trend as a percentage of revenues, with the objective of continuously reducing the ratio while maintaining or improving customer service. System outputs and processes, designed to support such ongoing operations as scheduling inventory replenishment and various ABC analysis reports (required to keep classification codes up to date) will always be both necessary and desirable. But new systems geared to *changing* the status quo need to be designed to support solving the problem or opportunity of the moment. Fortunately, as time goes by more and more application software packages are becoming available, almost all of which perform the mainline tasks of *static* resource management. Numerous authors write about these systems, commonly referred to as Distribution Resource Planning (DRP) and Manufacturing Resource Planning (MRP). Few of these software packages include the features vital to twenty-first-century operations, starting with the use of supplier schedules to replace purchase orders and standard electronic data interchange formats to facilitate networks of manufacturers, distributors, and customers, interchanging schedules and forecasts with lightning speed.

Even leading-edge proponents of electronic data interchange, such as Digital Equipment Corporation, are not addressing the really big opportunities, according to Barber.[23] He reports that the cost of generating a *purchase order* was reduced from $125 to $32, a fantastic improvement when viewed from any perspective other than that of the futuristic businessman, who would ask how in the world a purchase order could be allowed to cost $125 in the first place, and why the remaining $25 was not reduced to zero by eliminating purchase orders! He also reported that Procter & Gamble reduced freight bill preparation (time lapse) from thirty-one to fourteen days, an extremely beneficial improvement in terms of the outlandish starting point but still outrageous in the eyes of countless companies who spend minutes to prepare each freight bill.

The traffic manager's budget/responsibility report should be the primary ongoing tool for tracking freight cost as a percentage of revenues. And warehouse cost reports, discussed previously, should be equally important to tracking the overall warehouse cost–revenue ratios. However, warehouse space is such a vital element of cost control that it warrants a system for ongoing monitoring. An example of space utilization systems is outlined in Chapter 6 under the heading "Utilization Systems: Empty Space Is Waste."

THE STEP-BY-STEP WAREHOUSE SYSTEM PLANNING APPROACH

The most important result of any project is the achievement of *tangible* benefits that more than offset the costs of the design and implementation and subsequent operation of revised systems and procedures. Sue Faerman and colleagues stated this point as follows: "[R]emember that a control system should be worth the resources invested in the system. If greater resources are used to measure performance than are the monetary and nonmonetary benefits received from having the system, the organization may want to reconsider establishing such a system."[24] When transport routes are changed, better deals negotiated, or transport and warehousing equipment improved, it is a fairly straightforward process to plan personnel productivity increases and to cost the improvements. When costly new computer systems are installed, they should *always* be intended to increase the business's profitability

---

[23] Norman F. Barber, "EDI: Making It Finally Happen," *P & IM Review,* June 1991, pp. 35–40, 49.

[24] Sue R. Faerman, Michael R. McGrath, Michael P. Thompson, and Robert E. Quinn, *Becoming a Master Manager: A Competency Framework* (New York: Wiley, 1990), p. 115.

(or profit maintenance, when competitive pressures force a company to pass improvement on to customers in the form of price reductions). Thus, the Cost-Benefit Analysis Planning Chart, Exhibit 5–13, describes some of the most important steps of standard system development and implementation methodology. (See the System Design Planning Chart, Exhibit 4–19 in Chapter 4, for an overview of where cost-benefit analysis fits into the overall methodology.)

However, too many companies have been far too willing to fund computer system projects without specifying exactly how tangible benefits will be achieved. The usual excuse for lack of tangible achievements stems from mismanagement by computer technicians, who are permitted to espouse the position that all the benefits of new systems are intangible or will magically begin to occur when more information is processed, stored, and reported. The fact is, unless concrete steps (supported by the output of the new system) are systematically planned and executed, benefits usually do not follow.

For example, inventory reduction is one of the biggest potential benefit areas of logistics. But in order to achieve reduction, *people* must take actions to revise (or implement) system factors that will change the quantities received, schedule them for later receipt, and also reduce safety stocks. Further, if the system allows *people* to add

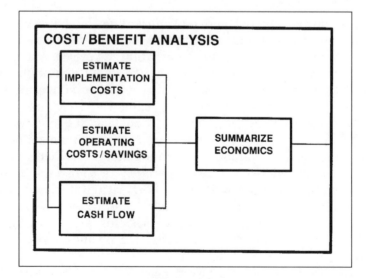

EXHIBIT 5–13

Achieve Tangible Benefits

inventory whenever problems arise (rather than solve the real problem), even if some benefits are achieved initially, they will evaporate over time. Management's most important role in system projects might well be to monitor and insist on *concrete methods* by which improvements will be effected. Management must also demand *system features* designed to help perpetuate and continuously increase the level of achievement.

SUMMARY

The most exciting systems development of the twenty-first century will be dramatic expansion of the use of electronic data interchange to link entire networks of customers and suppliers. For most companies and their logistics networks, the first step will be linkage to a single level in the chain (a supplier to its customers or a supplier to its suppliers). However, more dramatic results will accrue from future development that will link the entire production and distribution pipeline from the most basic raw material, through all production and distribution steps, and into the hands of the ultimate customer. The twin system tools for achieving linkage will be the use of supplier schedules in place of purchase orders, for all repetitive demand items, and continuous improvement of relative forecast accuracy until forecasting systems become virtual "black box" operations. Radically improved distribution inventory management and manufacturing resource planning systems, made possible by slashing order quantities, inventories, and lead times to the bone, are key subjects of the next chapter.

CHAPTER 6

Warehouse and Logistics Systems

Making It Work

Physical improvements alone are usually not enough to reap the bountiful returns of the fully reinvented warehouse. It is vital simultaneously to upgrade the paperwork and computer systems that must mesh with radically improved warehouse operations. In fact, many warehouse operations need modern modes of logical systems and procedures every bit as much as they need new storage, receiving, and shipping methods. The objectives of new systems and procedures should be simple and clear, and they must be identical to those of improved operations. The most important of these objectives are as follows.

1. Reduction of the time required to enter and ship new and changed customer requirements (improved customer service)
2. Lowering the inventory levels in the entire pipeline, thus slashing not only the required investment but also the lead time through the pipeline
3. Increasing the productivity of *all* company assets, with emphasis on reducing payroll costs by eliminating bureaucratic procedures in favor of streamlined, computer-supported white-collar operations

Distribution and manufacturing executives must know how to evaluate their warehouse operations and systems against a new standard of excellence that stretches their organization's capability to change continuously and to improve to the very limit. The following executive checklist of selected zingers presents the beginnings of the new standards for superior warehousing systems.

EXECUTIVE CHECKLIST: SELECTED ZINGERS

The handful of the most important reinvented warehouse and distribution system features that distinguish the superior company from the also-rans is not an impossibly lengthy list. Furthermore, it is not difficult to implement, at least partially, many improvements with little or no change to existing systems and procedures. This can and should be done parallel to, and without hindering the progress of, the more difficult, time-consuming, and resource-consuming *major* systems revisions and developments. The gap between the average system and that required to achieve world class status is so wide that simple patches on existing systems are not enough to propel any company into the ranks of leading-edge enterprises. Following is a list of many of the key new features.

1. Accounts receivable and payable sections of accounting organizations will virtually vanish following the establishment of long-term price agreements for use by common customer and supplier systems for electronic funds transfers between their bank accounts.
2. Laborious item-by-item check-ins at the receiving dock and the generation of a receipt transaction for every individual item will be eliminated. The multiple transactions for a partial or full truckload or a ship or land container will be replaced by a single transaction that records the receipt of every item in an entire inbound truckload of items, based on the highly reliable data entered into shared systems at the supplier loading dock.
3. Since inspection of incoming goods will no longer be required, systems and transactions to move and track receipts through inspection and into stock will also disappear.
4. Picking, sorting, packing, and shipping customer requirements still constitute a far costlier operation than it needs to be, especially when done the old fashioned way, one order at a time. New systems must provide exciting new modes of batch order picking, sorting, and shipment stag-

ing (or synchronization) to make their contribution to the spectacular improvements that physical changes in warehouse layout and operations will effect.

5. Productive utilization of warehouse space is the most important aspect of controlling all other warehouse costs. Consequently, superb space utilization reporting within each warehouse zone is a fundamental tool for monitoring progress.

6. Two vital keys to efficient warehouse space utilization are the use of standard containers for each item stocked and a standard quantity per container. Superior companies will devote more attention to capturing this item information in their databases. However, doing so will not require significant time and expenditures since modern software features will support low-cost data capture and maintenance.

7. Cubic volume and weight per stocked item, calculated by user-friendly maintenance aids and stored in the database, will enable the system to plan truckload shipments that fit the cubic trailer size and permissible load weight. The same data will be useful for "mapping" the area in which staged truckloads are assembled.

8. Warehouse replenishment inventory management systems that routinely require planners to review computer action notices add unnecessary cost to operations. Every business needs to convert to a virtual "black box" computer system of automatic supplier scheduling and rescheduling as rapidly as modern computer and communication systems capabilities make this possible.

9. The safety stock component of many companies' inventories is far too liberal to satisfy the ensuing real demand, especially in light of exciting new methods for achieving supplier delivery and quality improvements. In the short term, safety stocks can often be slashed to the bone by merely examining real historical need. In the long term, vendor programs will boost on-time, just-in-time supplier deliveries while drastically slashing vendor lead times. New systems must provide simpler data for setting safety stock and continuously reducing it, as warranted by improvements in the logistics network.

10. Traditional budgeting/responsibility reporting systems will be the nucleus of twenty-first-century management systems. But they need to be modified to include targets

and measurement of budget items as a percentage of revenues.

11. In the most perfect warehouses of the future, inventory quantity discrepancies will still occur, albeit with a fantastically lower rate of error than in the past. Lightning-fast checks to verify location accuracy in specified bays will be supported by system reports designed for that purpose. Further, the vast majority of cycle counts, conducted to detect and correct the few quantity errors that do occur, will be of the free and low-cost types that will make it practical to verify inventory record accuracy with much greater frequency and at a much lower cost.

12. Delaying shipment of an entire order (or schedule), or even an entire truckload, because one or two items are out of stock is a costly practice that reduces the service level of all delayed items, not only those in short supply. The best of the new systems must automatically dispose of back orders (of which there should be almost none). The best disposition is to add the out-of-stock items to the next scheduled shipment after their receipt.

13. Some warehouse/storage systems require deducting items picked from stock only after physically taking them from the stock location. This, in combination with large volumes of orders in process, makes it virtually impossible to predict which orders might use the available inventory when the stockkeeper discovers that there is less inventory than needed to fill all orders. It also makes accurate, efficient cycle counting very difficult, even impossible. New systems (like those used by many leading-edge companies) will meter picking documents to the warehouse as order pickers request them, just-in-time. Only orders with sufficient on-hand inventory will be issued, and the on-hand balance will be reduced as the picking documents are issued. Thus, the system's on-hand (being net of a limited amount of in-process picking requirements) will always provide an accurate basis for computer availability checking and easy physical cycle counting.

14. Kanban, in card or electronic form, will be adopted to pull deliveries of repetitive items through the network of vendors, factories, and distribution warehouses.

15. Tracking in-transit inventory between remote links in the distribution chain is a vital necessity until they can be brought into local clusters. The local clusters of suppliers

and customer warehouses will virtually eliminate the time inventory is in transit. Modern systems must therefore temporarily account for in-transit inventory.

DISTRIBUTION NETWORK INVENTORY MANAGEMENT

Effective distribution inventory management systems must achieve an array of business management objectives. First and foremost, they must support rapid fulfillment of customer requirements. Second, the systems should require the minimum practical staffing and must therefore include features that reduce manual work in both office and warehouse (new features that are *not* part and parcel of the company's competitors' systems). Third, new systems should support achieving the lowest network inventory investment practical, without jeopardizing customer service. Lastly, the systems must rapidly transmit the very latest inventory and forecast information throughout the supplier network, keeping the replenishment pipeline filled with items for which there are requirements and avoiding working on those items for which there are none. It will not be difficult for the aggressive, forward-looking company to surpass the competition in every one of these criteria, because today's state-of-the-art distribution systems are woefully out of date. Even some of the latest and best books on the subject still concentrate on describing systems of the past, suitable for companies still practicing outmoded methods of production, warehousing, and transportation. Martin, for example, has produced one of the best descriptions of what has recently become an outdated (although still apropos) distribution resource planning system,[1] based on the assumptions that there must be setup and ordering costs, hence the system must fundamentally be geared to launching replenishment orders. Realistically, few (if any) Western companies have achieved complete elimination of the need for orders somewhere in their networks. It may be another decade or two until many do so. However, companies with repetitive demand items have absolutely no excuse not to produce and supply at least some high-volume items in a manner suitable for twenty-first-century inventory management. The cornerstone of these new techniques, as previously discussed, is the supplier schedule. The following examples will be helpful in understanding the conditions under which the outdated distribution requirement planning system must continue to be used and those which permit using vastly better scheduling systems.

[1] Andre J. Martin, *DRP Distribution Resource Planning: Management's Most Powerful Tool* (Essex Junction, VT: Oliver Wight, 1990), pp. 132–33.

In both of the following examples, requirements are planned and either ordered or scheduled for an item that is stocked in both a regional distribution center and a central warehouse. The central warehouse also serves as a regional warehouse in the region in which it is located. Thus it has two types of requirements: first, for the regional warehouse that it supplies; and second, for customer demand in its own region.

Exhibit 6–1 shows how distribution resource planning for the regional distribution center is performed using outdated system techniques suitable for outdated production and distribution operations that still use orders rather than schedules. The process starts with the gross requirements for the stocked item, in this case a forecast of 100 per period. (Periods commonly used for distribution planning are weeks or even months. Such imprecise planning is inadequate in an environment in which just-in-time replenishment is the goal.) Note, in the example, that provision is made for past-due requirements. If late, unfilled past-due customer orders were extant at the planning cutoff date, the total quantity late would appear as past due. (When the author worked with Yamaha Motor Company in Iwata, Japan, the systems used for several previous years had no provision for past due. The instances of its occurrence were so rare that it did not make sense to provide for it. In the rare instances when past-due orders did occur, it made the most sense to consider them part of current demand, not past due.)

The next line of the planning example, titled "scheduled receipts,"

Regional Distribution Center

LINE DESCRIPTION	PERIODS				
	PAST DUE	1	2	3	4
GROSS REQUIREMENTS		100	100	100	100
SCHEDULED RECEIPTS		200			
PROJECTED ON HAND	200	300	400	300	400
PLANNED ORDERS		200		200	

ON HAND	SAFETY STOCK	LEAD TIME	ORDER QUANTITY
200	200	1 PERIOD	200

EXHIBIT 6–1

Outdated Distribution Resource Planning

indicates that there is a replenishment order for 200 scheduled for receipt in period one. (As can be seen in the bottom row of data in Exhibit 6–1, the order quantity for this item is 200. In the new world of zero setup/changeover and ordering cost and of daily shuttle transportation between suppliers in the cluster of company and supplier facilities, order quantities become irrelevant.[2] The reason? It will then be feasible to replenish almost every item every day or even several times a day.)

The third line on the planning report, "projected on hand," is calculated for each period as follows:

1. The gross requirements, period by period, are reduced by the beginning on hand (or previous period projected on hand). If the result is equal to or less than the safety stock quantity, an order is planned for receipt in the later period, indicated by the item's lead time. (In the continuously flowing pipeline, the concept of lead time becomes largely irrelevant).
2. "Scheduled receipts" are added to the quantity calculated in step 1.
3. Planned order receipts in the period are added, as previously calculated in step 1, to the amount in step 2. The result is the period "projected on hand." Line 4, "planned orders," are planned orders offset by lead time, from the period in which they must be received to the period in which they must be launched.

The central warehouse planning example, Exhibit 6–2, also starts with gross requirements. In the example, the gross requirements consist of the forecast of 100 per period for the central warehouse's own region plus two replenishment orders (200 in periods 1 and 3) for the regional warehouse. (One of the serious shortcomings of planning distribution order quantities is that orders equal to more than one period's need make requirements "lumpy." Combining requirements from several periods into one order puts artificial peaks and valleys into the supplier's gross requirements, making it difficult for suppliers and the central warehouse to plan manpower and equipment capacities rationally.) The steps for planning and calculation of "projected on hand" are otherwise the same for the central warehouse as for the regional warehouse.

Modern distribution resource *scheduling* is the label that should replace distribution resource *planning*, as it is descriptive of the

---

[2] See Appendix 2 for a reference to further explanation of clusters of facilities.

LINE DESCRIPTION	PERIODS				
	PAST DUE	1	2	3	4
GROSS REQUIREMENTS		300	100	300	100
SCHEDULED RECEIPTS		400			
PROJECTED ON HAND	300	400	700	400	700
PLANNED ORDERS	400		400		

ON HAND	SAFETY STOCK	LEAD TIME	ORDER QUANTITY
300	300	2 PERIODS	400

EXHIBIT 6–2

Central Warehouse Planning

process applicable to the new, twenty-first-century scheduling features explained in Exhibit 6–3. Before beginning to study the scheduling process, however, it is vitally important to understand that
the new system must perform both the old planning function and
new requirement scheduling. For many years, perhaps forever, it
will be necessary to continue to accommodate two types of items:

Regional Distribution Center

LINE DESCRIPTION	DAYS				
	1	2	3	4	5
GROSS REQUIREMENTS	20	20	20	20	20
SCHEDULED RECEIPTS	20	20	20	20	20

ON HAND	SAFETY STOCK	LEAD TIME	ORDER QUANTITY
40	40	N/A	N/A

Central Warehouse

LINE DESCRIPTION	DAYS				
	1	2	3	4	5
GROSS REQUIREMENTS	40	40	40	40	40
SCHEDULED RECEIPTS	40	40	40	40	40

ON HAND	SAFETY STOCK	LEAD TIME	ORDER QUANTITY
40	40	N/A	N/A

EXHIBIT 6–3

Modern Distribution Resource Scheduling

those for which old-fashioned order quantities are applicable and those for which scheduling is a better answer. There are two reasons why the use of order quantities will persist. First, many suppliers and customers will not yet have perfected their own or their suppliers' production, warehousing, transportation, clerical procedures, and system operations to the degree necessary for schedules to replace orders. Second, even though operations and systems may be perfected, there will always be some items and customer requirements of such low, infrequent demand that daily replenishment deliveries will be impractical. Therefore, some form of order planning will continue to be necessary (for example, an item with requirements of five a year.)

The first striking difference between planning schedules and planning orders is the remarkable new simplicity. In Exhibit 6–3, only two lines of data are required to describe the process. The top example, a schedule for an item for the regional warehouse, starts with "gross requirements" consisting of a sales forecast (or sales plan) of 20 per day. In the previous example (Exhibit 6–1), a period's requirement of 100 were one week, the equivalent of 20 per day. Thus, although the periods are different, the quantities are the same except for the degree of detail. Note that lead time and order quantities are no longer applicable in the scheduling process, because systemic improvements have reduced replenishment time to the point of insignificance. (For example, all supply sources are now in the same local cluster, so shipments from the supplier are received by the user on the same scheduled day.)

It is not entirely coincidental that the example shows gross requirements and scheduled receipts to be equal. This is feasible since the supplier and user will share the same schedule information, and suppliers will virtually always ship precisely to schedule. However, the calculation of scheduled receipts, period by period, involves the netting of on hand and the provision of safety stock. As can be seen from the example, the advantages of scheduling are, in summary:

1. The "lumpiness" of demand caused by calculating and planning orders that span multiple periods of demand is eliminated. Central warehouse and supplier schedules will thus be much more rational, better leveling requirements for personnel and transport.
2. With shorter planning periods (days), increased planning frequency (daily, if practical), and lead time reduced to a bare minimum, the need for safety stock is much lower.
3. The process is incredibly simpler.

The level-by-level sequence of processing requirements is as critical to the warehousing end of the distribution network as to the supplying (production) end. Regional warehouses must be processed before processing requirements for the central warehouse, and the central warehouse prior to its suppliers. Exhibits 6–4 and 6–5 recap the level-by-level process for planning requirements of two producers in the production network: plant number 2, supplied by plant number 4. (The process would be essentially the same if the entities were *regional* warehouse number 2, supplied by *central* warehouse number 4).

The first step in the process is to "explode," or calculate, plant 2's gross requirements of part number 11 and then to net plant 2's inventory from the gross requirements. (In superior multiple-plant networks, safety stock is not required. However, in the warehouse system it would be factored into the process. Unlike the multiple-plant environment, in which both the production schedule and its supplier delivery requirements are relatively fixed, the warehouse network depends on forecasts that differ from the actual subsequent demand and thus need to plan safety stock.) The net requirements of the using plant are the same as the gross requirements of

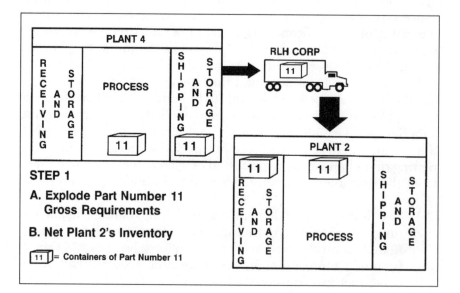

EXHIBIT 6–4

Multiple Inventory Locations

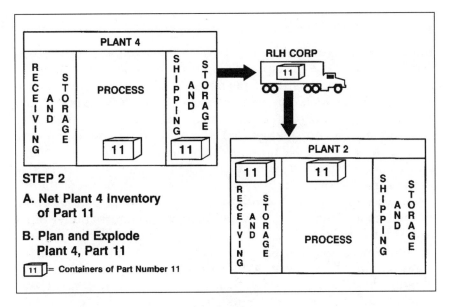

EXHIBIT 6–5

Multiple Inventory Locations (Step 2)

the supplying plant. (In this example, the supplying plant is in the immediate vicinity of the using factory, so it is unnecessary to offset the net requirements by the lead time between plants.) This is one of the simplifying advantages of the cluster of user and supplier factories.

The second step in the multiple plant (or distribution warehouse) planning process (Exhibit 6–5) for part number 11 is to net the finished inventory of the supplying factory, plant 4, from its gross requirements (which are the same as the using plant's net requirement, offset by lead time if lead time is significant). The net requirements become the schedule for the manufacturing process and are the gross requirements used to "explode" (plan) the raw material requirements from which part number 11 is made.

Incidentally, many people take some misleading overview descriptions of the famous *kanban* system far too literally. For example, some have understood that kanban is an alternative, rather than a supplement, to the type of requirement scheduling systems described here. Therefore, further examination of the kanban system is in order.

WAREHOUSE/DISTRIBUTION AND THE KANBAN SYSTEM

Initial Western reaction to Toyota's famous *kanban* system was symptomatic of the widespread plague of resistance to change.[3] In brief, the system consists of placing a kanban card with each in-process and in-stock container of parts. When a container's contents are used, the card is returned to the supplier (whether another department or an outside vendor) as a just-in-time signal that more of that item should be produced and/or shipped at once. Many scoffed at the system or, at best, described it as uniquely applicable to the Japanese or to high-volume, level demand. Some of the derision was misinformed evaluation of the kanban card-oriented systems as woefully antique. Many Western producers prefer high-tech solutions. Therefore, if the computer is not used as a key tool for problem resolution, they automatically tend to think that the approach has little merit. While these Western executives were looking down their noses at kanban, Toyota management was laughing all the way to the bank! In recent years, however, adaptations of kanban have become widespread in Western manufacturing companies and in some distribution networks.

Originally, it was commonly presumed that Toyota and its suppliers used *only* kanban and therefore had eliminated computer schedules. Nothing could be farther from the truth. Every company (and its suppliers) using kanban needs schedules from which to plan capacity in the short and long term, and kanban cards cannot meet this need. When manpower and equipment are scheduled to operate at the scheduled requirement level (determined by the computer requirement planning system), the supplier will almost automatically be able to produce enough to meet kanban replenishment needs as they are received from the user. If the stocking warehouse or using factory uses one item slower and another faster than planned, the kanban system will automatically, in real time, signal the real needs and priorities to the supplier. Thus, kanban overcomes a common shortcoming of even the best computer systems—schedules that are outdated even before they are issued.

The kanban system has superb application in distribution networks—as a signal from customer to regional warehouse, regional warehouse to central warehouse, and central warehouse to company and vendor supplier factories. However, a traveling kanban card, repeatedly carried back and forth between user and supplier, may not be as good a solution as the use of electronic kanban. One

---

[3] See Appendix 2 for reference to information on the *kanban* system.

of the most compelling reasons for the electronic alternative is the distance and time between customer and supplier. As Exhibit 6–6 illustrates, when the distance and time are very short (minutes or hours), as when a producer's factory network and distribution centers are ideally clustered), a circulating card may be entirely practical. However, when the distance is measured in days and weeks of time in transit, the card would clearly be impractical. In fact, even when the distance and time are short, electronic transmission of the kanban signal from user to supplier may pave the way for even better results than those achieved by Toyota. For example, if a supplier makes a delivery only once a day, and the delivery truck takes eight hours to complete a round trip, the circulating kanban signal may be received as much as two days later than with electronic transmission.

Some of those who have since embraced kanban were originally concerned (and justifiably so) with the massive preparation required for full use of kanban at both ends of the distribution pipeline, for all suppliers. The solution was a logical, step-by-step process. The first step entailed adopting a strictly internal kanban to train company personnel. Later the new procedures were systematically implemented, supplier by supplier, throughout the pro-

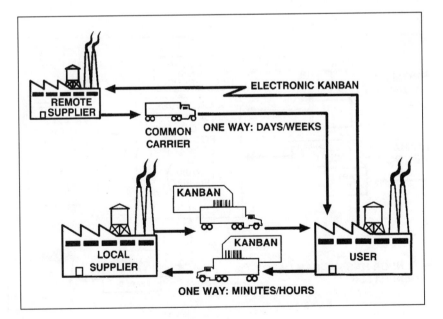

EXHIBIT 6–6

Electronic or Card?

duction and distribution pipeline. Exhibit 6–7 shows how the short-term internal kanban is first phased into operation. At the outset, the vendor receipt is matched to an internally generated, bar-coded kanban, one per container received. The kanbans and containers (each container with one kanban) are forwarded to the warehouse or focused factory storeroom. There, the kanban is read by an electronic device (wand) to update inventory records. Finally, when the receipts are used in production, the kanban cards are simply scrapped. As soon as company personnel are accustomed to this routine, one or more vendors and company factories are supplied with computer-generated kanban and henceforth send one kanban with each container shipped. Thus, the internally generated kanban is gradually replaced as vendor receipts begin to arrive from suppliers with generated cards. This process would not normally involve direct electronic (or manual) transmission of kanban cards from customer to supplier. Thus, suppliers can temporarily generate the cards on their own before taking the more complex step of linking systems through electronic data interchange.

As soon as software and communication lines and equipment are thoroughly tested, debugged, and interfaced with suppliers, the electronic kanban (Exhibit 6–8) can be implemented fully. Now,

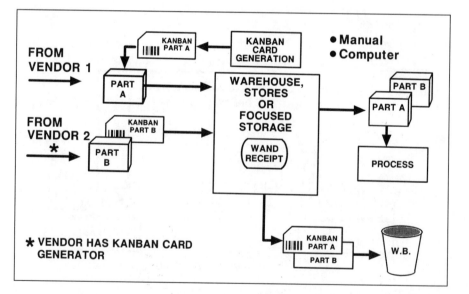

EXHIBIT 6–7

Receipt: Short Term

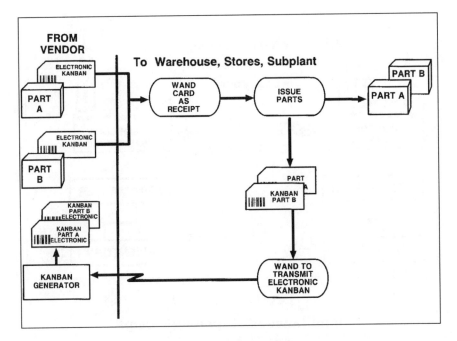

EXHIBIT 6–8

Receipt: Longer Term

instead of scrapping kanban cards as their corresponding containers are emptied, focused factories-within-the-factory close the loop by transmitting them to their vendors.

SHIPPING/RECEIVING SYSTEMS

An integrated distribution network should transmit information between supplier and user locations as instantaneously and as labor-free as possible. For example, shipment and receipt information, if accurate, must be the same at both shipping and receiving ends of the transaction. However, outdated, conventional system approaches most often require shipment/receipt transaction data to be key entered at both ends of the shipping and receiving process. Exhibit 6–9 depicts an almost ideal elimination of duplicate data entry. In the example, system inventory records for both warehouses (or plants) 4 and 2 are simultaneously updated by entry of a single transaction at the time of shipment from the supplier. As indicated, this is practical when the distance and time between the two locations are short (shipment and receipt occur almost at the same time), when issues concerning the count accuracy and quality

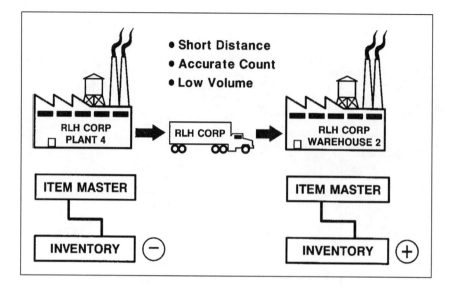

EXHIBIT 6-9

Simultaneous Shipment/Receipt

defects at the shipping location have been resolved and have become virtually perfect, and when the truckload volume of shipments is manageably small.

One of the costly paradoxes of the shipment/receiving process, a
practice widely deemed to be unavoidable, has been the counting of
items at both shipping and receiving locations to detect count errors. Costly indeed, but all too often proved necessary by the volume of count discrepancy reports prepared and transmitted to
ensure that the receiver is charged and pays for neither more nor
less than the amount received warrants. It is symptomatic of poor
management in the logistics network to let such inaccuracy continue perpetually. Superior management must pioneer new initiatives to implement foolproof counting methodology (primarily at
the supplier end of the transaction) and to develop methods for
periodic reconciliation of inventory records with actual stock when
the accumulation of unavoidable, minor count errors over time
becomes enough to warrant adjustment.[4]

In some instances, the distances and time between supplier and
user are too great and/or the volume of truckloads is too complex to
permit simultaneous inventory update for both locations. These

[4] See Appendix 2 for reference to additional information on methods for adjusting inventories in the author's prior work.

cases require tracking in-transit inventory. In Exhibit 6–10, all items on the truck's shipping manifest are deducted from the supplier's inventory and added to the inventory in transit. (Thus, the integrated distribution—or multiple plant—system does not lose track of the inventory between shipment and receipt recording.) When the using warehouse or factory enters the receipt, Exhibit 6–11, it reduces the inventory in transit and increases the user's inventory.

The bar-coded kanban card is not always the ideal, lowest-cost tool for recording receipts in the integrated distribution network when in-transit tracking is necessary or desirable. This will become clearer upon receiving a more complete description of the shipping/receiving process, starting with the steps in Exhibit 6–12.

The shipment process in the exhibit begins when the supplier's factory delivers 300 units of part number 11 to the shipping dock. The interplant shipping inquiry is used to determine the requirements of all using warehouses and factories: 200 for location 2 and 300 for location 3, in the case of part number 11. (A factory storeroom would use the same display if it issued shipments from stock rather than from the shipping dock.) Although this example uses scheduled requirements rather than order numbers, some companies with low-volume, nonrepetitive demand will still need to use order numbers for either selected part numbers or for all. Inciden-

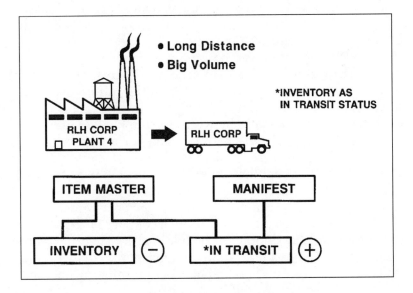

EXHIBIT 6–10

In Transit: Shipment

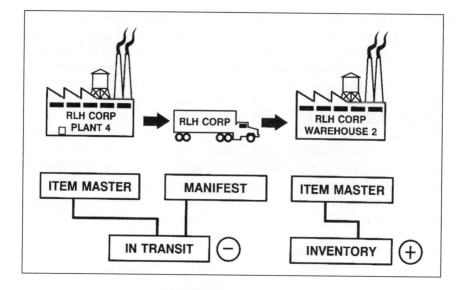

EXHIBIT 6-11

In Transit: Receipt

tally, the best systems calculate and use the weight of individual items shipped to plan and control and weight assigned to each truck and to calculate freight rates, where applicable. Note that the inquiry includes year-to-date shipment quantity, a useful tool to help user and supplier reconcile data differences in their data attributable to shipments still in transit.

By the way, the using warehouse has a virtually identical counterpart to the supplier's shipment schedule inquiry: the interplant (user's) receiving inquiry, Exhibit 6–13. The key difference is that it includes scheduled receipts of all items from *all* suppliers. (There could be a difference in dates between the supplier and user inquiry when the distance and time between supplier and user are long. However the scheduled *receipt* date is often most useful to the supplier in helping the supplier understand the shipment mode that will be required to achieve just-in-time delivery).

Continuing with the example, shipping dock personnel fairly apportion the three containers (of 100 each) of part 11 to locations 2 and 3, based on the shipping schedule inquiry. The next system screen, Exhibit 6–14, is used to update inventory balances and in-transit shipment information and to generate shipping documents, including packing tickets and kanban cards.

Next, the packing tickets are used to move the containers of part 11 to the appropriate truck staging area, where the screen illus-

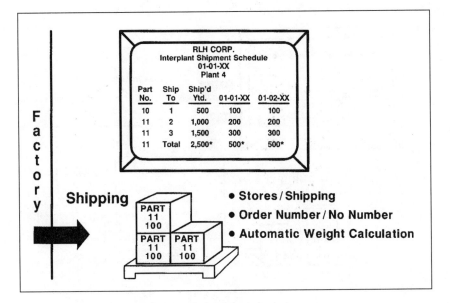

EXHIBIT 6–12

Shipment Schedule Inquiry

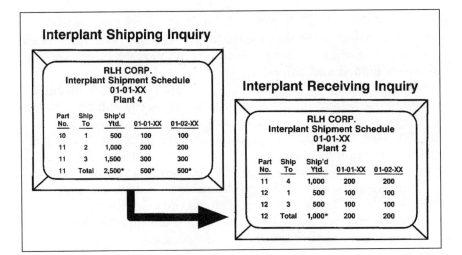

EXHIBIT 6–13

Shipment Equals Receipt

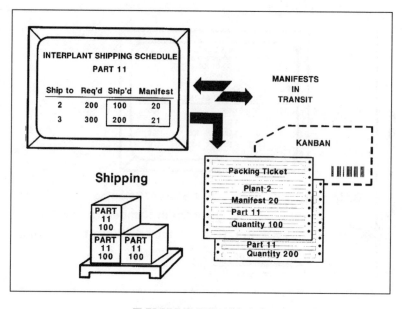

EXHIBIT 6–14

Shipment Update

trated in Exhibit 6–15 is used. The load manifest for the truck is used to verify that all items earmarked for the truck have been received, and when the load is ready, containers and their kanban cards are loaded and shipped.

In an integrated logistics or multiple-plant system, the inventory record of every item on the computer manifest file can be updated on the receiving end by a single manifest receipt recording screen, Exhibit 6–16. Entering the manifest number, 20 in this case, triggers the deletion of the manifest from in-transit status and adds every item on the manifest to the receiver's (user's) inventory. (In some situations, it might be desirable to reduce the supplier's inventory of items on the manifest records at this time rather than at the time of shipment. This would eliminate the need for an in-transit inventory record for every single part number in transit.)

In summary, this brief presentation of an integrated shipping/ receiving system merely outlines many of the key ingredients. As the opportunities for achieving superior performance are dependent on the status of improvements in the entire network, not all companies have the same needs. Warehouses and factories still operating in twentieth-century mode are already behind those pre-

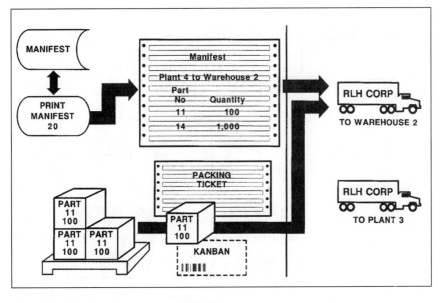

EXHIBIT 6-15

Load Manifest

paring for the twenty-first. Therefore, they must begin implementing improvements at an even faster pace just to catch up. The payoff potential in fast, low-cost operations and customer service improvements is so great that it is inexcusable that some companies are not already actively working on radical operations and systems improvements. The order entry/order picking and shipping cycle is one of the areas in which companies need improved systems to support shorter cycle time, hence better customer service.

ORDER PICKING SYSTEMS: RIDING THE WAVE-PICKING

One of the most important measures of the quality of an order picking system is how much work it requires—or, better yet, how much work can be avoided by using superior systems output and input features. When ideal electronic data interchange systems are in place, most of the initial data required to produce order picking (or schedule filling) documents can be provided by the "black box." For example, shipment schedule dates and quantities should come from the customer–dealer electronic order (schedule) entry system previously discussed, and such information as customer name and address and item price, weight, and cubic volume should come from master file data. (For more on cubic volume, see the section

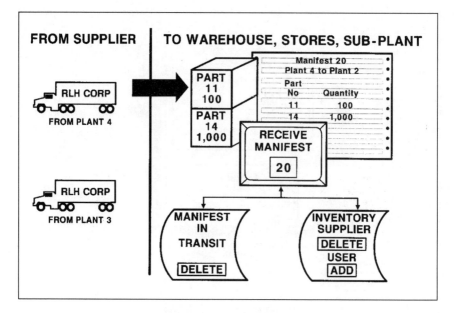

FROM SUPPLIER | **TO WAREHOUSE, STORES, SUB-PLANT**

EXHIBIT 6–16

Receive by Manifest

entitled "Item Container Maintenance: The Abacus Is Not the Answer," later in this chapter.)

Logistics systems must support the new, improved warehouse
order filling operations discussed in Chapters 3 and 4, with products that meet operational needs, in order to achieve the best results. For example, system outputs should not temporarily need to
be manually filed, awaiting action, only to be retrieved when a
warehouseman is ready for them. Nor should it be necessary to sort
documents manually or exercise such decisions as which order or
order batches to pick next. Such avoidable manual review of order
picking documents or computer screens and human analysis and
decision-making is wasteful, because it should be performed by the
computer system. These criteria lead to the selection of the following basic system performance specifications.

1. Pick documentation should be output to the warehouse, just-
in-time, when an order picker or order-picking team is ready for
another batch. The output sequence of picking batches should be
computer-controlled.

2. Systems should be able to output both wave picking batches
(for picking several orders simultaneously) and single orders. Batch
picking should be the norm, and individual order picking the ex-

ception. Individual order picking is usually used to respond rapidly to emergency orders or to prepare pick-up orders brought to the warehouse by the person who will take them to the customer.

3. Picking documentation should be geared to outputting the next batch required, just-in-time, in any one of several order-picking zones when a warehouseman completes picking a prior batch. The warehouse management objective is to have multiple individuals or teams simultaneously working on the same customer order batch, in several warehouse zones.

4. Picking documents should be computer-sequenced by stock locations within various warehouse zones, thus minimizing the warehouseman's (or automated retrieval machine's) order-picking travel distance. This requirement is as applicable to highly automated storage and retrieval systems as to manual order picking. (Considering the high capital investment in automated storage and critical capacity limitations imposed by a fixed, finite number of storage–retrieval machines, efficient retrieval travel paths are usually even more important in automated systems than in manual warehouses or storerooms.)

5. Picking documentation should never be issued for order items that are out of stock, according to the system inventory balance. Physical stock checks used to verify availability prior to picking are not only unnecessary but also costly. Thus, if frequent out-of-stock conditions are expected to persist well into the future, the system should be designed to disposition order line items automatically either for back order (to be picked and shipped when they become available) or for cancellation, with notification to the customer to place a new order for shipment on the date of the next scheduled availability.

6. Surprise shortages due to inaccurate computer inventory balances will perhaps never be completely eliminated. Order-picking systems should therefore include an exception transaction to identify order items that are out of stock, regardless of what the system inventory balance shows. The disposition of the shortage (back order, cancel, or even hold the entire order until shortages are cleared) should be automatic, as noted in the previous point.

7. Every item picked for every customer order must flow smoothly, without delay, from order picking, to order sorting, to order packing, to truck staging (or directly onto the truck), and through the customer receiving process. Accordingly, the order-picking system should provide some type of identification document (see Exhibit 6–17 for an illustration of such a document's contents) to travel through the entire process with the picked items.

PICK IDENTIFICATION

Item Number	Order Number	Customer Number & Name	Subplant	Dock
Stock Location	Quantity	Staging Location	Item Description	
Single Item Order				

EXHIBIT 6–17

Order Picking Identifier

8. Bar coding the identification document, Exhibit 6–17, is essential to eliminating ensuing key entry if reporting progress of the order item through the order-picking and shipping process is an important business need. Further, when stockkeepers take a hand-carried bar code scanner on trips around their zones, they can use it to read the identification document either to answer inquiries or to input transaction progress or status. In semi-automated warehouses like the Catalog Merchandise Centers of SLS Sears Logistics Services, the bar-coded identifier is mechanically scanned while picked items are in motion on conveyors and mechanically routed to and through order sorting, packaging, and shipment staging.

9. The computer should use master file data such as item weight and cubic volume data to calculate shipment weight and volume. For truckload shipments, the master file data should be used to preplan full truckloads' contents.

10. Identification documents, Exhibit 6–17, should contain data for controlling shipment staging locations, floor space, and cubic volumes. Those data are used to route orders to specific truckload staging areas (or conveyors) or directly to the preplanned truck dock for immediate loading. Computer power should be used to minimize warehouse space required, maximize truck capacity utilization, and minimize travel time and distance between warehouse, staging, and loading docks.

11. The system should accommodate electronic kanban, converting electronic kanban receipt transactions into order-picking kanbans. The kanbans should include some receiving location data such as warehouse receiving and storage zones (or factory subplant number and subplant receiving dock.)[5]

12. Orders for single items must not require the warehouse to sort the single item orders by order number, following order picking, or to merge them with other items on the order, because there are no other items. Therefore, the order-picking identification document, Exhibit 6–17, should have a flag that can be used to route single items directly from order picking to packing or shipping.

13. Multiple-item orders often foster a desire (though not necessarily a need) to check systematically and *report* the completion of each step in the picking, packing, and staging (and/or truckloading) process. Doing so ensures that all items on every order have been merged, packed, and staged or loaded and that none have been lost or delayed. Only when all orders planned for a truckload have been reported as loaded on the truck or in staging can the truck be loaded and/or shipped. The best-managed warehouses and storerooms would consider this progress reporting an unnecessary, wasteful step. Instead, they would use a single completion transaction transmittal for each lot of orders for which picking and packing are completed to update the status of every order in a lot.

Many order-picking systems are designed to accommodate big delays between the time picking documents are computer-generated and the time the orders are actually picked. This was necessary in the past, because systems operated on daily batches and released all order-filling documentation for one day's orders at the same time. Modern systems can process several smaller batches several times a day and can even process individual orders one at a time. Today it is no longer necessary to process daily batches. Warehouse systems should generate smaller order-picking batches immediately prior to when the warehousemen are ready to begin picking the next batch. This will dramatically slash the time between a batch release and picking completion. In the extremely rare cases in which an order item is misplaced or overlooked and not shipped with the rest of the order (or, worse, shipped to another customer), the facts will surface soon, and the items can be rushed to the customer.

---

[5] See Appendix 2 for reference to more information on subplant receiving docks.

ITEM CONTAINER MAINTENANCE: THE ABACUS IS NOT THE ANSWER

At first glance, first-time determination of every stocked item's storage volume requirement may seem to be an awesome undertaking, especially in warehouses or storerooms that stock thousands of items. However, the author has found that the warehousemen can fit one-time, basic data preparation (each item's cubic volume, for example) into their routine with barely perceptible changes in total work hours. This would not be the case if it were deemed necessary to mount a one-time special effort to measure each item stocked. That might require hundreds of thousands of overtime hours. Since a massive, one-time effort is rarely an urgent business need, the author has usually advised clients to perform the measurement during routine receiving and/or issuing of items for which cubic measurements have not yet been collected.

Converting counts of small items into pieces per cubic inch is not a task that should be performed manually, especially when there are thousands of these items to process. Exhibit 6–18 Illustrates how the warehouse initially gathers basic cubic volume basic data for small parts. A custom "measuring cup," 4 cubic inches in this example, is used to develop a quantity "per cup" for each small part. (Incidentally, most warehouses should use two or more "measuring cups," considering the extreme variability of size among the items

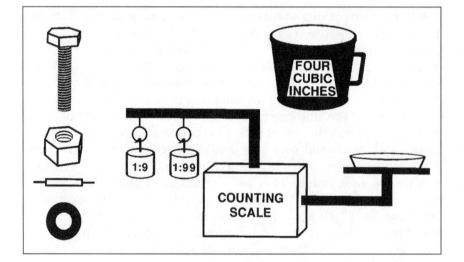

EXHIBIT 6–18

Small Item Measurement

categorized as small). The quantity thus measured is then counted on either an electronic scale or a balance scale like the one illustrated.

Exhibit 6–19 continues the process by illustrating how the computer processes the data for part numbers 8 and 9 (400 and 40 per measuring cup, respectively). The computer calculates the cubic volume for 1 cubic inch of each of the part numbers. Subsequently the cubic volume and annual sales information are used to help determine the standard container size for receiving, storing, and shipping (or issuing) each item. Far too many companies are not adequately controlling packaging and cubic volume information, as evidenced by the lack of such information in their databases.

Every superior company should be developing information like that in Exhibit 6–20, a partial display of item-related data. The exhibit, in addition to cubic volume information, includes the package codes of both an overpack and an innerpack. This permits the system to specify small containers for storage and issue. However, the supplier can deliver the small containers, and they can be received, in a larger overpack (such as skid). This would be appropriate when small containers are best for order picking but would increase receiving and storage labor because of the individual handling required.

Large items are more logically measured using a tape measure as

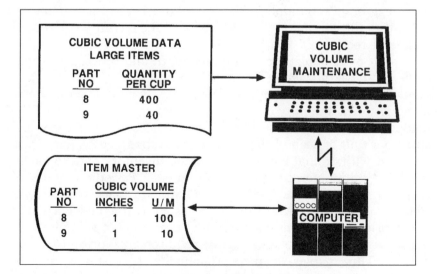

EXHIBIT 6–19

Small Item Maintenance

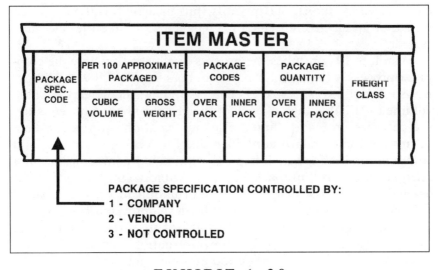

EXHIBIT 6–20

Item Container Data

depicted in Exhibit 6–21. In the case of the rear axle assembly, an item so large that each unit is stored separately, the three dimensions of the item's "imaginary box" are measured. Other items are "nested" in large containers (One example of "nesting" is the cubic-yard "egg crate" container of large transformers.) Such items require that the container be measured and the quantity per special container recorded.

Exhibit 6–22 depicts the computer input and processing applicable to the large items. The tape-measured height, width, and depth of each item's container (or imaginary container) is input, along with the quantity of the item stored in one container. The computer then uses these data to calculate and store the cubic space per unit of each of the large items. Subsequently, these data are used with annual usage and average inventory data to calculate total initial storage space requirements. Periodic updates of these data can then be used to reveal storage space requirement trends. Outboard Marine Corporation's SysteMatched Parts and Accessories Division makes additional use of cubic volume information to calculate truck staging requirements prior to order picking. This enables them to preplan the truck staging area to maximize the utilization of the staging area and truck loading productivity.

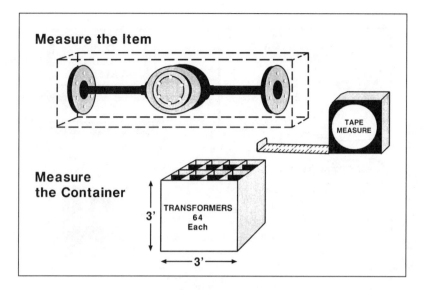

EXHIBIT 6-21

Large Item Measurement

LOCATION CONTROL SYSTEMS: FINDING THE NEEDLE IN THE HAYSTACK

The loss of a stocked item (due to inaccurate recording of its location) can have a devastating effect on customer service, even after pipeline lead time has been truncated to an optimal minimum. When a warehouse stocks hundreds or thousands of items in tens of thousands of locations, inadequate location control systems may make finding a lost item as difficult as finding a needle in a haystack. The fully automated storage-and-retrieval system solution solves almost all such inventory loss problems. Under such a solution, the storage-and-retrieval system control computer directs the storage-and-retrieval machine to specific locations and keeps track of location contents. Unfortunately, the completely automated solution is not yet one that is cost-effective for the majority of warehouses and storerooms. Therefore, superior warehouse and storeroom systems must include features to help warehousemen avoid errors in reporting locations and other features designed to help find and correct misplaced items when, despite precautions, items recorded in one location are actually placed in another.

Chapter 4 outlined several user-oriented system features that help to preclude recording erroneous locations or misplacing stock.

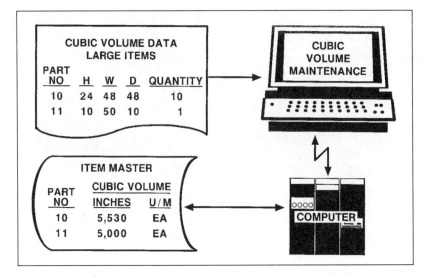

EXHIBIT 6–22

Large Item Maintenance

One such feature was a bar-coded location code label on the bin-bay that can be scanned—while stocking new receipts—to obtain and record the location information. The most powerful method for determining locations virtually eliminates the need for detailed locations codes but requires, as a prerequisite, the use of new containers, storage racks, and segregation by usage volume or issue activity. Exhibit 6–23 shows a location code–item number combination that takes advantage of the natural warehouse layout, container size, and item number to identify the area in which an item is stocked. The first digit of the "location code" consists of the ABC activity code. In the example, it is "S" (previously, the author explained that the *Super* activity code designates items stored in the fastest-moving zone of the warehouse or storeroom). The second digit identifies the type or size of shelving or storage racks, based on the size of the standard or custom container (or pallet) specified to the item's suppliers. Since the storage location scheme, within each group of shelves or racks of the same size, is in approximate item number sequence (as described in Chapter 4), no further location coding is necessary.

In the previous example, the proper warehouse location of an item is narrowed down to a very small zone, namely the activity zone, and, within the zone, to the shelving or racks that correspond to the container size for that item. In most warehouse populations,

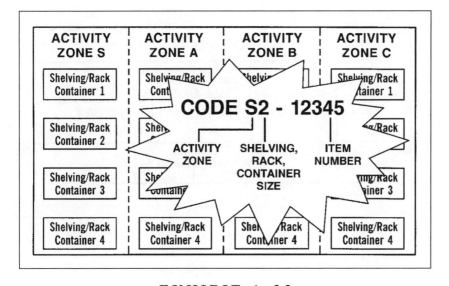

EXHIBIT 6–23

Stock Location Code

the relatively small number of items stored within a specific, limited area makes it especially easy to scan the area and locate a particular item number or an empty space in which to place a new receipt. Should a receipt be placed relatively far from where its item number would dictate, the area would usually be small enough for a warehouseman easily to locate the item and move it to its logical location. A receipt placed in the wrong sequence but in the right activity zone and container or shelving area would normally soon be found and the mistake would often be automatically corrected while stocking or issuing other items in that area. Further, it is impossible to store an item in the wrong container size area since the container would not fit the rack or shelving. Thus, special efforts to make checks to verify location accuracy will no longer be necessary in any warehouse that has achieved superior control via activity zones, container sizes, and correspondingly sized shelving and racks. However, during the interim period, before these objectives have been met, it will be desirable to be able periodically and rapidly to verify that a detailed stock location's contents match those recorded in the system.

Exhibit 6–24 is an example of a system-generated document for checking that all items recorded as being in a specified location are there, or that the quantity of each item is the same as recorded. Note that the format is very similar to the order-picking identifi-

STOCK CHECK					
Item Number 12345	Order Number NONE	Customer Number & Name LOCATION CHECK CYCLE COUNT		Subplant	Dock
Stock Location S23451	Quantity	Staging Location	Item Description WIDGET		
Single Item Order	Location OK? X	Stock Count Containers 2	Quantity Per 200		

EXHIBIT 6–24

Location/Count Checking

cation document in Exhibit 6–17, previously described. (Similar document formats are a fundamental way of simplifying systems.) These stock location checking transactions can be merged with a batch of order-picking documents to maximize stockkeepers' efficiency by enabling them to verify locations while picking orders. Interspersing the location check and order-filling transactions makes it possible for the warehouseman to process both transaction types while making a single trip to the general locations in which transactions for both types occur. Since location verification documents are normally simultaneously issued for all items stocked in one storage bay or part of a bay, an entire (small) portion of the warehouse could be checked at once. Thus, the check not only verifies the correctness of items that should be in the area but also can detect items stocked in the area that should not be there. When the document is used for location check only (in the space labeled "Customer Number and Name," a mark in either "location check" or "cycle count" indicates the document type), the warehouseman fills in only the "Location OK?" field. When the document calls for "Cycle Count," the warehouseman would fill in the three fields as shown by the manually entered data on the exhibit. Note that by recording only the number of containers and quantity per container and using the computer to perform the quantity calculation, the potential for the warehouseman to make a multiplication error is eliminated.

The simplest way for a warehouseman to check the presence of the contents of all of the items recorded in specified locations is to scan the contents in a warehouse or storeroom bay or part thereof. It is usually best to separate checking from other activities and for the computer system to supply a printed list of the contents of each designated bay, in location sequence, as illustrated in Exhibit 6–25. In the main, verification should be performed as quickly as possible, without bothering to check items with large numbers of containers on hand. To do so would take much more time. In the example, stock locations S2 001 and S2 004 were found to contain the item numbers listed on the report; the stockkeeper thus marked these locations with an "X" to indicate correct location information. According to the report, S2 002 should be empty. The warehouseman, having confirmed that it was indeed empty, entered the "X" to indicate that the location report was correct. When location S2 003 was checked, it was found to be empty, thus zeros were entered in the actual count fields. Later, during a check of location S2 006, the 23456 Poles, missing from location S2 003, were found, although the report showed that the location should have been empty. Thus, the item number and actual count in this location were entered on the report. (It would also be possible to correct the inaccuracy by physically moving the item to location S2 003.)

LOCATION CODE	ITEM NUMBER	SHORT DESCRIPTION	--- SYSTEM ON HAND ---		OK?	---- ACTUAL COUNT ----	
			CONTAINERS	QUANTITY PER		CONTAINERS	QUANTITY PER
S2 001	12345	GASKET	3	1,000	X		
S2 002							
S2 003	23456	POLE	15	50		0	0
S2 004	01234	TUBE	2	100	X		
S2 005	65432	PISTON	4	25		3	25
S2 006	23456	POLE				15	50

LOCATION CONTROL REPORT

EXHIBIT 6–25

Location Verification

WAREHOUSE ACCOUNTING SYSTEMS: COUNT BUSHELS
NOT BEANS

The author views recent accounting fads (e.g., activity-based accounting) as a continuing preoccupation of many accounting professionals (bean counters) with the picayune many versus the
powerful few.[6] Companies urgently need to understand that the
reasons for most excessive costs are well known. Increased accounting system complexity, to report on activities that should clearly be
discontinued, is simply throwing money away.[7] Distribution executives, accountants, and managers can thank their lucky stars that
they are concerned with warehouse operations, not manufacturing.
They need not be so concerned with theoretical issues concerning
whether or not overhead is fairly (accurately) allocated to parts and
products. Whoops! Perhaps they *should* be concerned that their
companies might just try to allocate warehousing costs (which are
almost always properly treated as overhead) to the products or
product lines serviced. After all, in some of their most recent writ-
ings warehouse experts advocate allocating warehouse costs to
product lines.[8] But to do so is most likely to burden them with
unnecessary reporting system complexities and would extremely
rarely be of greater value in setting product prices or any other
aspect of cost and financial management.

The key issue depends on one's perspective. Should the focus be
on determining "accurate" product, product line, or "activity" costs
(when "accurate" costs are the figment of a dreamer's imagination)? Or should the focus be on continuously reducing *all* costs
until they are reduced to the point of insignificance (eliminating
any rationale for needing greater accuracy in overhead allocation)?
The author wholeheartedly endorses the latter approach.

Conventional budgeting and responsibility reporting systems
have always been (and will always be) the basic tools that, properly

[6] See Appendix 2 for more on the author's views on cost and financial accounting.
[7] Brimson's lucid book on activity accounting would be virtually meaningless if known
avenues of waste elimination were pursued. For example, purchase order and customer
order activity should no longer be a subject of discussion. Orders *per se* should be
replaced by schedules, transmitted electronically. Thus, armies of order-processing personnel and all of their related costs should no longer be permitted and certainly no
longer need measurement. Automatic fund transfer can also be the basis for eliminating
accounts payable and receivable activities. James A. Brimson, *Activity Accounting: An
Activity Based Costing Approach* (New York, John Wiley, 1991), pp. 119, 151 (orders,
payables, and receivables).
[8] Raymond A. Nelson, *Computerizing Warehouse Operations* (Englewood Cliffs, NJ:
Prentice-Hall, 1985), pp. 217–18.

managed, serve to report actual versus budgeted expenditures continuously. However, they are effective only when reported to and controlled by operating personnel charged with the responsibility for and empowered with the authority to manage and improve costs. Indeed, many companies have admirable records of cost containment and cost reduction that are directly attributable to using budget tools and *necessary management practices.* Still, too many companies have failed to do much better than contain costs at past levels, adjusted for inflation. Ironically, the problem is only minutely related to the accounting system. Rather, it is much more a function of commitment to major, continuous improvement, coincidentally bolstered by a few new accounting system features that embody the essence of management's pledge to pursue new standards of excellence. Chief among these new accounting system features are enhancements to today's conventional, still highly valuable systems that establish dynamically reactive target costs and routinely track every cost element as a percentage of the business' revenues.

The Responsibility/Budget Report, Exhibit 6–26, is not intended to represent a complete, actual sample of an ideal report. Instead, it was devised to introduce some new wave accounting and management concepts as simply as possible. The first concept is that of the delegation of responsibility and authority to warehouse and office teams and to other executive and management individuals

EXPENDITURE	ACTUAL	% OF SALES	TARGET (T)	BUDGET (B)	T_B	YTD T	YTD B
RESPONSIBILITY / BUDGET REPORT							
ORDER PICKING TEAM 3-WAREHOUSE ZONE A							
PERSONNEL:							
PRODUCTIVE TIME	10,000	2.00	9,000	9,500			
NON-PRODUCTIVE	400	.08	800	1,200			
FRINGES	4,500	.90	4,800	4,900			
EDUCATION/TRAINING:							
TIME							
EXPENSES							
ELECTRICITY							
SPACE OCCUPIED:							
COST							
SQUARE FEET							
EQUIPMENT USED:							
LIFT TRUCK COST							
NUMBER							
TOTAL	20,000	4.00	20,000	21,000			

EXHIBIT 6–26

Targets and Limits

who can control and improve expenditure levels. The report is issued to the warehouse order-picking team responsible for the fast-
moving warehouse zone A. Giving such a report directly to the team
will be a radical departure from most companies' practices. Why?
They have a double-edged rationale for purposely withholding such
cost information. On one hand, the team members, as uneducated
louts, are incapable of understanding the report data. On the other
hand, they view the team as cunning, disloyal, and likely to take
advantage of access to cost data and to use it against the company
in union organization or contact negotiation activities or sell con-
fidential cost data to competitors.

Such foolish rationales are no longer acceptable to modern executive management. Management, after all, bears the responsibility for better, career-long education and training of *all* personnel
(not just management individuals on fast-track career paths). Thus,
if employees lack in education and training, the blame lies at the
feet of their company. Unless the company does an exceptional job
of building employees' value, management cannot expect the entire
organization to excel in every aspect of performance vis-à-vis their
service or product competitors. Nor can the company protect itself
from other local businesses interested in attracting and retaining
dedicated employees.

In the long run, openness in such matters as expenditures and
revenues will reduce, not raise, confrontation with organized labor.
It is to the advantage of company management to open the books.
By doing so, they can educate and train all employees to understand the operating statement, including the relatively meager percentage of company revenues returned to stockholders in the form
of dividends. This might put to rest, for all time, the popular myth
that those who initially financed the business and subsequently
fund new plants and equipment (thus providing continuous employment) bleed extravagant profits from the business to the det-
riment of the working people. In fact, the price–earnings ratio of
many companies' stock is often lower than the interest rates earned
by workers' savings.

The most important feature of the report in Exhibit 6–26 is target cost as a percentage of warehouse revenues. The author has
long held that the most effective way to contain expenditures and
costs and to improve them in a way that falls to the bottom line of
the profit-and-loss statement is to report on them and to track them
as a percentage of revenue or of margin. If management's express
business philosophy were that all teams and managers should hold
costs at levels no greater than past expenditures (as a percentage of

revenues), it will ensure better business management. All levels of the organization will more rapidly react to downturns of demand with logical, easy reductions of variable costs and new, imaginative cost-cutting methods for those items traditionally (but erroneously) considered semivariable or fixed. Nor do temporary or even permanent surges in demand mean that teams, managers, or executives will go hog wild in increasing expenditures. To the contrary, increasing volume must be the most obvious way to increase profitability through improved absorption of fixed and dynamically controlled, semivariable costs. Therefore, management must stress companywide responsibility for not simply containing costs (as a percentage of revenues) but continuously improving them. Thus, the percentage should be used to define a *maximum* limit of acceptability, rather than an acceptable target.

The author views the use of both target and budget expenditures, Exhibit 6–26, as a temporary solution to merging old-fashioned annual budgets with new, dynamic reduction target planning and execution in a continuous improvement program. Were this more than a temporary expedient, it might permanently impose unneeded complexity on the process. In fact, leaping directly from inflexible budgets to more germane, dynamic targets (whether termed targets or flexible budgets) would avoid going through a painful period of added complexity but would require a greater investment of time and resources in new systems.

In the author's view, setting (lower than last year's) targets should be a top-down process. Carl J. Mungenast, Executive Vice President of SLS Sears Logistics Services Distribution and Delivery Divisions and a self-styled "brown box pusher," says of their top-down (target) budgeting process that it isn't hard to get the buy-in to quantum operating improvements. Carl quickly got the message across when he introduced the customer-oriented budget process (Sears, Roebuck, of course, being the biggest customer) in which the new budget started with the projected customer revenues, less margin, as the maximum available for operations. He simply told his organization, "Welcome to the new reality." By this, he meant that continuing old ways was no longer possible. To forge ahead into and remain in the leading edge of logistics, his organization had to find ways to increase dramatically the productivity of every aspect of logistics, for he correctly defines logistics as "the optimization of all assets, both idle and in motion." This means not only the people, plant, and equipment used to operate the network of transportation, receiving, storage, and shipment, but also the information systems, office staff, and inventory investment (to date,

Carl's organization has taken more than $200 million out of their logistics operations).

Both management and labor need to understand that every element of cost can be (at least) contained or (even better) reduced. For example, most will understand that the warehouse personnel costs in Exhibit 6–26 can be reduced by working more productively, by cutting nonproductive activities, and by investing in labor-saving equipment. And although many workers work well below their capabilities, the main thrust of efforts to improve personnel productivity does not need to rely on either incentive payments or other performance monitoring techniques that tend to encourage employees to work continuously at a pace that turns work into an exhausting, mind- and body-numbing hell. Rather, companies should target achieving their most important gains in personnel productivity through the use of techniques and equipment that help people work smarter, not harder, in an environment where it is exciting and comfortable to work. This, however, does not invalidate the need for both management and labor to agree that it is necessary for all employees to give a fair day's work in return for a fair day's pay. Thus, when a team's employees have been working well below a reasonable level of output, they must be encouraged to improve their methodology. For example, considerable amounts of nonproductive time in many warehouses stem from peaks and valleys in orders received, picked, and shipped. Too few warehouses dynamically vary staffing to match workloads and tend to staff at levels closer to the peak than to the valley (perhaps more so in production operations than in distribution). Management and labor would be well advised to adopt flexible hours and a flexible workday calendar such as the one described in Chapter 5. Matching for hours and days worked to actual workloads would reduce periods of make-work, nonproductive tasks.

Exhibit 6–26 includes electricity among the expense items controllable by the order-picking team. The author will expect this to raise the hackles of those who believe electrical consumption in the warehouse to be neither controllable by the people working in a single zone nor measurable. The reasons for this superstition are twofold. First, all warehouse lights are most often controlled from a single, central control box. Second, often a single meter measures electric consumption for the entire warehouse. Neither of these too widely accepted norms should be permitted to interfere with new methods for controlling the cost of this expensive utility. Challenging the fundamental, existing parameters that lead people to limit opportunities for improvement goes directly to the heart of the erroneous assumptions for which practical solutions can be developed. In the case of electrical consumption control, for example, placing meters on the circuits in each warehouse zone can be a relatively low-cost way to obtain data on the area's consumption. The installation of switches in each warehouse bay would enable any team member to turn lights on only when working in the bay. This is especially practical when wave-picking methods reduce the time spent in some warehouse bays to a few minutes a day.

Some would say that it would be unreasonably naïve to expect employees to participate in improving *personnel* productivity. In fact, some major automotive companies have forbidden their project teams to state that personnel savings are part and parcel of their objective. The rationale is that any reference to personnel productivity might easily be equated, by union officials and the rank-and-file, with personnel reductions. This, management often rationalizes, might cause their unions to refuse to cooperate in programs to improve productivity and, hence, competitiveness. However, the author considers such an argument to be the epitome of naïveté. How dare management assume that the rank-and-file and their elected representatives are too ignorant to see that working smarter and more productively will ultimately be the means of protecting jobs! How dare they fail to recognize that the ingrained will to excel is part of the character of not just management but also the overwhelming majority of all employees. To set roadblocks purposely between improvement opportunities and the largest group of employees capable of contributing to their achievement is the most flagrant folly.

In Exhibit 6–26 the cost of space occupied is another example of new thinking. Objectors will be very quick to point out two salient points regarding common but outmoded warehouse management facts. The first is that unused space in the warehouse is scattered through every bay, so there is no way to use it. The second is that, even if available, underutilized space were to be conveniently located in a segregated portion of the warehouse, it would have no value and no potential for alternative use. Both objections are absurd! In the first place, it is imperative that warehousemen be trained to improve the organization and space utilization continuously in their areas of responsibility and to segregate the space vacated. Second, executive management must more aggressively find new customers, products, and product lines to occupy available space or must consider leasing or selling portions of the warehouse or making portions available for other company operations. Thus, the cost of unused, segregated space should normally be charged to the executive with the power to develop strategic plans for its use and to execute the necessary tactics to bring the plans to fruition. Finding productive uses for surplus space adds to business revenues and reduces costs of existing operations by cutting the unabsorbed overhead costs of otherwise unoccupied areas.

The bottom-line, total cost of all warehouse operations is the bushel-basket measurement on which the success of its operation stands or falls. The beans in the basket can be moved from one side to the other, but the number of beans will not change. Too much focus on the location of beans is like undue focus on allocation of warehouse costs to product lines. No matter how much time is spent shuffling the detail costs, the bottom-line results won't change.

UTILIZATION SYSTEMS: EMPTY SPACE IS WASTE

Most conventional warehouses are, on average, one-half empty, if compared to the maximum practical utilization of available space. Businesses worldwide are therefore wasting an investment amounting to hundreds of billions of dollars on buildings housing mostly air. Nevertheless, when one visits one of these warehouses or works in one, it is easy to overlook the wasted space, especially when even the aisles are cluttered with skids of loads for which no rack space can be found. Still, as will be shown, space is being wasted. Further, businesses must continue to capitalize on drastic inventory reduction opportunities; they will exacerbate the world's underutilized warehouses unless something is done to focus attention on the unnecessary waste. The process of shrinking inventory must never end, as long as it remains necessary to store goods in a warehouse (instead of cross-docking or producer-to-customer direct delivery from production, as previously discussed). Hence new, superior systems will need to support warehouse operations personnel with information on space utilization, cost, and trends.

The warehouse space utilization report for the order-picking team responsible for the fast-moving storage zone A, Exhibit 6–27, helps the team see quickly where, in their areas, opportunities for improvement lie. The report shows that overall the zone has 75 percent utilization. The space unused, if made available, would be equivalent to one entire storage bay. In this example, bay A-14, with the most unoccupied space, is the most suitable candidate for reorganization to isolate and make empty space available for other uses. In the portion of the warehouse where random location control is appropriate, such a report can be based on the system's

BAY	- - - - BINS - - - -			- - CUBIC YARDS - -			- - SQUARE FEET - -		
NUMBER	TOTAL	USED	%	TOTAL	USED	%	TOTAL	USED	%
A-11	200	180	90	200	180	90	720	648	90
A-12	200	160	80	200	160	80	720	576	80
A-13	200	160	80	200	160	80	720	576	80
A-14	200	100	50	200	100	50	720	360	50
TOTAL	800	600	75	800	600	75	2,880	2,160	75

WAREHOUSE SPACE UTILIZATION

ORDER PICKING TEAM - ZONE A

EXHIBIT 6–27

Space Utilization: Team

quantities of containers on hand, multiplied by the containers' cubic sizes (carefully controlling the size of containers is, therefore, an important element of achieving better space utilization). In other parts of the warehouse where items are stored in approximate item number sequence, not by the random location control method, it is necessary simply to identify the first and last item number in each bay in order to enable the system to calculate the volume stored in a bay.

The warehouse executive's space utilization report, Exhibit 6–28, lists the totals of each warehouse area. (Note that the Zone A total from Exhibit 6–27 is "rolled up" to the warehouse executive's report. The executive need not be concerned about the detail behind the total. He has delegated the authority and responsibility for managing the details to the team in that area and can be confident that they will continuously work at consolidating empty space into a single bay.) The executive's report also shows operating cost information in addition to that of space utilization. The period's expenditures and costs for each area, taken from the budget/responsibility reporting system, and the square feet occupied, taken from the space utilization system, are used to calculate the cost per square foot of space occupied (ten dollars in this example). (The cost data are not intentionally omitted from the team report. It is simply easier to show them in two different exhibits.)

The cost per square foot of storage utilized for a single period is

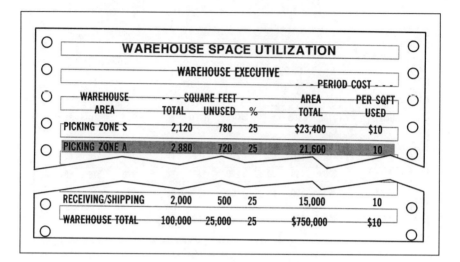

WAREHOUSE AREA	SQUARE FEET TOTAL	UNUSED	%	AREA TOTAL	PERIOD COST PER SQFT USED
WAREHOUSE SPACE UTILIZATION					
WAREHOUSE EXECUTIVE					
PICKING ZONE S	2,120	780	25	$23,400	$10
PICKING ZONE A	2,880	720	25	21,600	10
RECEIVING/SHIPPING	2,000	500	25	15,000	10
WAREHOUSE TOTAL	100,000	25,000	25	$750,000	$10

EXHIBIT 6–28

Space Utilization: Warehouse

nowhere near as valuable as a history of cost, either produced by the system or recorded manually or by computer in graph form, as in Exhibit 6–29. The gradually increasing cost per square foot of storage stems from a successful ongoing inventory reduction program. The subsequent sharp decrease has occurred as a result of the warehouse executive's having put a plan for increasing the warehouse space utilization into effect. (He might have done this by adding a new product line or by leasing part of the warehouse to a sister or an outside business.)

In summary, the ultimate vision of the ideal warehouse is one in which there is no longer a need for warehousing. Until this goal has been achieved, management must do everything possible to reduce the warehouse inventory required to provide better than expected customer service. Also, it must continuously improve the productivity of its operations by constantly inventing new practical ways to utilize warehouse space better, disposing of the surplus space or filling it with new business.

THE STEP-BY-STEP WAREHOUSE SYSTEMS APPROACH

Executive decisiveness is an automatic by-product of high-quality informal and formal information on which to base decisions. The most important facets of outstanding executive data reporting are

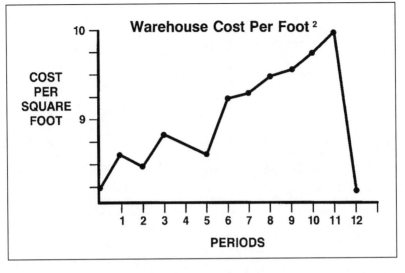

$$\text{EXHIBIT } 6-29$$

Warehouse Cost Trend

its relevance to the business's profitability from an executive perspective and the simplicity of the presentation of facts.[9]

During the various phases of a logistics project—initial design, implementation, and follow-up—a project team should routinely conduct progress meetings to keep executives and all others abreast of the latest design and implementation ideas. The importance of these interim meetings cannot be overemphasized. By keeping everyone informed and involved, people's reservations about new ideas can be addressed and put to rest long before the "final" management meeting. Because no one is surprised by new revelations at that time, there are rarely new doubts and objections. The culminating activity of *every* project phase is the preparation and conduct of a *final* management review meeting, the steps of which are the subject of the management review planning chart, Exhibit 6–30.

[9] Clear, simple, everyday language is rapidly being obsoleted, in data processing circles, and is being replaced by "Technobabble." Executives and managers who have learned to express their thoughts to their organizations completely free of technobabble find it easier to win understanding and cooperation. For those convinced they cannot escape the mind-boggling onslaught of technobabble, Barry's book will help in understanding some of the roots and misuses of its commonly used words. John A. Barry, *Technobabble* (Cambridge, MA: MIT Press, 1991). The author has also had some choice words to say concerning "technical fog" in his previous book (see Appendix 2).

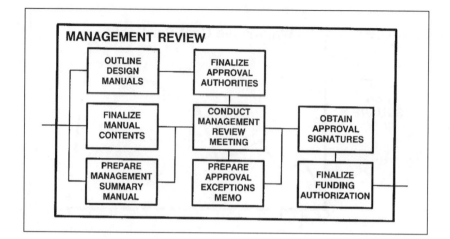

EXHIBIT 6–30

Executive Decision Support

Project teams, especially those working on computer systems, usually generate tons of various types of documentation. Of these tons, only a few pounds are worth permanent retention by executives and managers. The highly valuable exceptions—easy to understand and capturing the very essence of the purpose and construct of the system—should be permanently documented in executive summary reports. Throughout any project, each team member must give special attention to the documents that are most vital for the "final" presentation. To ensure the best possible results, one of the earliest project management tasks is to prepare a "sample deliverables" package, containing realistic examples of the various types of management presentation documentation expected from every team member.[10] Thus, when a project phase is completed, preparation of a final presentation package takes relatively little time and effort. Since the project team produced the package contents throughout the entire duration of the project, at its end the team needs simply to select and organize from the wealth of available documentation. As Exhibit 6–30 shows, the steps for doing so include outlining the various manuals that will be permanent documents. The wider the project scope, the greater the number of

---

[10] In an earlier book, the author wrote, "Project management's single most important product is a customized sample package of the deliverables that must be produced by each analyst. It should eliminate any confusion about what work must be done and what format must be used when presenting results to all levels of management." See Appendix 2 for more information on project organization activities.

manuals. (For example, one or more *detailed* manuals are often prepared for each functional organization.) While selecting and organizing the contents of the detail manuals, the team should extract an executive synopsis. (The first section of every manual should be an executive summary of the most important documents from the executive's perspective.) The management summary synopsis is therefore often a collection of the management summaries from each of the detail manuals.

Successful end-of-phase management review meetings should always be structured to produce an automatic transition from the completion of one phase to the start of the next. For, as previously noted, management commitment and involvement should be so strong and the benefits of the project so great that there should never be any doubt about continuing. Nevertheless, many managements are *not* dedicated or capable to the degree that they will understand how to give instant (almost rubber-stamp) approval. In some cases it is even difficult to understand who the decision maker or makers are. Therefore, during both the organization and administration activity at the start of the project, and again at the end, the planning charts include a step for determining the people or person who will ultimately make the decision (see Exhibit 6–30).

If executives and managers have not been adequately committed and involved during the course of a project, the inevitable result will be that they will harbor doubts and reservations even after they have participated in the management review meetings. Rather than bring the project to a halt while trying to resolve these doubts, it is better simply to record them as points needing resolution *during the next program phase*. These points should then be formally recorded in an "approval exception memo" (Exhibit 6–30) to guarantee that they will be resolved during the next program phase. Such careful contingency planning helps to keep the program on track and running at high speed.

SUMMARY

All too often, system analysts make the mistake of constructing complex systems to accommodate unnecessarily complex business practices. In the past those charged with the responsibility for the system development effort did not have the clout to change bad or overly complex operating practices. Often they did not even perceive that there were better alternatives. Executives, managers, and their brightest associates (employees) can all contribute to better future systems. Top management must use its clout, long experience, and superior qualifications to channel available resources into changing unacceptably complex practices. All involved must learn to challenge past procedures routinely and to develop new, simpler ways of achieving better results. To do so, it is not necessary to reinvent wheels that have already been invented. Keeping abreast of modern operating practices and systems is one way of short-circuiting unnecessary reinvention. With this book the author hopes to contribute to the available body of knowledge and thought. Making it all happen, however, will require the dogged determination of a superior generation of business executives and managers.

CHAPTER 7

Industry Applications

The universe of new and exciting ideas for improving warehousing and distribution logistics includes new techniques of widespread relevance to virtually every industry that stores, purchases, manufactures, distributes, or sells goods. However, a few techniques and procedures are more applicable to one industry than to others. The purpose of this chapter is to present a few examples of physical operations and systems that are particularly applicable to one industry. The subjects and their sequence within the chapter are (1) "Service Parts Warehousing and Distribution," (2) "Consumer Products Distribution," and (3) "Manufacturing Storage and Logistics."

PART 1

SERVICE PARTS WAREHOUSING AND DISTRIBUTION

The management of service parts and accessories is often one of the most complex, high-volume forms of distribution. Inventory management of service parts requires controlling inventories of most of the components of products currently in production, but also components of purchased assemblies, accessories, and products plus components of products no longer in production. Thus, whereas a

factory needs to forecast and plan only end products, service logistics systems must forecast dozens, hundreds, and even thousands
of "service products" to be able to maintain control of its customer
service level and minimize its inventory investment. Accurate forecasting of service demand presents some additional unique requirements. New *component* demand projections would ideally need to
consider the anticipated rate of failure, correlated to the sales of the
finished products (in which the component is used) and offset by
an expected pattern of failure (or useful life) over the product's life
cycle. Further, the best-engineered components have very low sales
from period to period because of their reliability over long periods.
To complicate matters further, when an end customer needs a replacement part, it often means that the product is out of commis-
sion. Thus the potential for customer loss due to slowness of
response makes it imperative that service provided for a one-dollar
component be considered every bit as important as delivery of an
entire product costing thousands.

Carrying thousands of components used to service hundreds of
products necessitates having highly efficient cataloging systems to
access the item numbers for components of a specific product rapidly and accurately. The purpose of the access is to facilitate ordering the right component. Large volumes of product engineering
changes make control of the product configuration more complex.
(It breeds confusion over which components were used on which
product serial number). Further, the theoretical approach to limiting the period over which products will be serviced, based on the
number of the products still in operation, often doesn't work as well
as one would like. Conscientious preventive and repair maintenance of almost any product should give it almost infinite life. The
customers who maintain their products best are most likely to resent it if service is discontinued and will switch their purchases to
a competitor when it happens. Therefore, service life policies must
often be ignored, in favor of keeping parts in stock well beyond the
point where sales appear to have ceased altogether.

Many service parts facilities are a combination warehouse and
factory. For example, many have a relatively high-volume packaging operation that not only packages or repackages items received
in bulk from vendors and company factories but also makes kit
"assemblies" (a gasket kit, for example, might comprise all the gas-
kets required to rebuild a product completely). Sometimes simple
out-of-production subassemblies and even machined components
are produced in the service "factory."

Finally, many service part operations will be unable to enjoy some aspects of the realized vision applicable to other types of distributed products. For example, although it may be practical to mold consumer purchase habits of truly seasonal products such as air conditioners and winter sports equipment, service parts will be needed most during the season when these products are in use.

SERVICE DISTRIBUTION VISION

The service organization of the future will be a much more complete structure, performing functions designed to provide the best possible customer service. The consumer of the future will have much larger blocks of time for leisure activities, thanks to shorter work hours and improved home shopping and delivery services that will move the showroom into the living room (as outlined in Chapter 1, under the heading "Eliminate the Middleman"). And because the average person feels compelled to fill idle hours with gratifying, productive activities, do-it-yourself projects will flourish. Do-it-yourself activities are and will be especially appealing to the consumer, because they reduce the high cost of mechanics and others who provide such services. (Mechanics' costs will probably never be completely eliminated, since some repairs will continue to require costly equipment and specialized skills.) The consumer will make money available for purchasing more luxuries and entertainment by reducing outgo for high-cost services. Thus, the demand for goods and services will ultimately rise.

The ultimate service vision might be one in which repair and maintenance would no longer be required by virtue of perpetually reliable, indestructible product designs. It might be more appropriate to label this a fantasy rather than vision, however, since it will probably never come to pass. Therefore, the best service organizations can do is to strive toward the fantasy by implementing systems and practices designed to expose a product's component design weaknesses that, corrected, will extend their useful life and reduce the amount of cost of required repair and maintenance. Service engineers, specialists in this field, will work hand-in-glove with the focused product design team during the new product development stage.[1] They will concentrate on the serviceability and reliability of the product's design, producing design features to make it simpler, faster, and easier to perform service and mainte-

[1] See Appendix 2 for reference to information on focused product design teams.

nance. During a product's life the service engineers will focus on correcting problems of greater and earlier than acceptable component failures and will continue to improve the product's serviceability.

Home delivery of service components and supplies will be one way in which the most visionary companies will help owners avoid the high cost of service. Vans carrying one producer's components will shuttle about a community, linked via computer telecommunication to a home base dynamically providing directions to the next closest customer. Customers will have entered their orders via integrated, interactive home computer and cable or telecommunications systems. These systems will help the customer identify and order the right repair components via service catalog systems like the one described later under the heading "Electronic Dealer/Customer Catalog and Order Entry." The order entry feature will record the order and process the funds transfer or credit card charge payment. The supplier's systems will then maintain the delivery van's inventory status and delivery schedule, transmitting a delivery report to the van's computer printer.

The visionary service system of the twenty-first century will not cease to serve customers when repair parts are delivered. Superior companies, searching for every possible way to increase their legion of enthusiastic, satisfied customers, will make troubleshooting and repair instruction material and systems available seven days a week, twenty-four hours a day. Vastly improved service manuals will be made simpler to understand through the use of more pictures and illustrations, while the number of hard-to-understand, confusing words will be reduced. Wherever possible, videotapes and disks will be made available to guide the do-it-yourselfer; materials of this type will be even be accessible on interactive home computer–video systems linked to the producer or distributor via telecommunication networks. Ultimately, however, the best possible service satisfaction will come from direct telephone contact with service specialists trained to work with the customer until his or her problem has been solved. The word-of-mouth advertising that such personalized dedication to customer satisfaction will generate will have far more impact than the cleverest television commercials.

Some aspects of repair and maintenance require equipment and components of a size and cost that will prohibit their availability in the average do-it-yourself person's home. Nevertheless, it will still be practical for him to do all or most of the work in do-it-yourself service centers, where he can "rent" a cubicle with the equipment, advice, and special tools required, as outlined later under the heading "Do-It-Yourself Service Centers".

EXECUTIVE CHECKLIST: SELECTED ZINGERS

A vision of the future of service distribution operations and systems differs only slightly from that of other logistics entities. Thus, service executives should use the checklists in the earlier chapters, supplemented by the following checklist, applicable to service.

1. The primary objective of every service organization should be almost to put itself out of operation by continuously working to improve service components that are subject to failure, thus requiring repair and replacement. This effort will require an organization that will receive and analyze major components that fail in the field, with the purpose of designing improvements that will reduce the incidence of failure.
2. Large percentages of future service repair work will be performed by the owner rather than by service shops and dealer repair facilities. To make this feasible, products will be designed to facilitate owner repair. The great majority of service repair is "grunt work" that could be performed by almost anyone, yet it is now necessary to have this work done by high-priced mechanics.
3. In addition to repair work, owners will also perform most routine preventive maintenance either in the home or in facilities designed for do-it-yourselfers. Such facilities and equipment will be available to the owner at a cost far less than the astronomical fees of today's service facilities and mechanics.

DO-IT-YOURSELF SERVICE: SIMPLIFYING REPAIR

Tremendous competitive advantage will accrue to the first producer able to advertise products so simple to repair that the owner can do it himself, at tremendous savings. Do-it-yourself repair features should be enormously attractive to the owner, not only because of the savings in repair bills but also because of the time savings—time usually spent taking or sending the product to a distant repair shop and waiting days or weeks until the repair has been completed. Far too many products are of a considerably less than fail-safe design, thus requiring periodic component replacement either before or following a breakdown.

The airplane is a classic example of the need for fail-safe design. Altogether the best possible design work goes into an aircraft's development (raising design costs to stratospheric heights), failures still occur both unexpectedly and at predictable stages of use. These failures are compensated for with redundant systems in the case of vital components, the failure of which would be fatally dangerous. Where deterioration due to wear is inevitable and predictable or detectable, periodic replacement or rebuilding of worn components is used. Most products are like aircraft in that it will probably never be possible to eliminate completely the need for planned and unplanned repair and replacement. Unfortunately, when this need arises, most owners have little choice but to take or send the product to a specialized service facility, because product designs rarely have owner-friendly features that make it practical for the possessor to do his own repair and preventive maintenance, thus avoiding the exorbitant repair shop cost.

The barriers to owner repair include product designs that make it virtually impossible for the average person, lacking special tools, to disassemble and reassemble them. For example, some products are encased in a body that is closed with rivets. Repairing such products requires rivet removal equipment and additional apparatus to replace the rivets when the repair is complete. The reason for such a design is that rivet closures are a few cents less expensive than screws or nuts and bolts. Further, because repair has historically been done in a few repair shops with special, costly equipment, servicing has not been viewed as a problem. However, since intelligent marketing and advertisement will most assuredly add value to the product in the eyes of the owner taught to value easy serviceability, redesigning closures at the cost of a few cents will be viewed as adding considerably to a product's value.

Virtually every aspect of most product designs makes simple repair and service impossible for the average owner. Take car stereos, for example. In almost every car the radio is enclosed by a dash panel that defies disassembly by anyone other than a contortionist mechanic. Yet, it would be a very simple design matter to make the stereo a simple plug-in device with some form of simple lock and burglar alarm features to discourage theft. Further, a modular dash design that would permit simple access to the jungles of systems behind the dash via removal of a single section would be of incredible value. Such features would add to the serviceability of the automobile for both mechanic and do-it-yourselfer.

Even routine preventive maintenance is bewilderingly complex for average owners. Oil changes are an example. The location of most oil drain plugs on the underside of the car almost forces the average owner to go to a service station for an oil change. Yet it would be a simple matter to route a tube to the front, side, or back of the car, making access readily available. The added cost of such an owner-friendly drainage system would be offset quickly by eliminating just a few high-cost service station oil changes.

The lack of timely availability of preventive maintenance and repair components to the average owner is also an area in which considerable progress is bound to occur. Today, a do-it-yourself repairman is hampered by the fact that spare parts must be obtained from either dealerships or retail outlets. The problem is compounded by the fact that the need for a specific part often first becomes apparent only after the car has been disassembled and is no longer capable of making the long trip to the replacement part location. Further, in the service garage, the mechanic should use trial and error in the replacement of components, determining which requires replacement and replacing only defective items. (Few do so, since replacing all components is more profitable). The owner–repairman can ill afford to run back and forth to the component supply source in the process of trial and error for determining which components are defective. To address the situation, speedy home delivery systems will begin to bring components to the customer, as described in the previous service vision section of this chapter.

DO-IT-YOURSELF SERVICE CENTERS

During the author's many visits to service repair centers he has been amazed at the percentage of time that highly paid service technicians spend turning tools (removing fasteners in the process of disassembling a product to remove a defective component, and reinstalling them during the reassembly process. Given the option and practicality of personally performing the "grunt work" portion of repair and maintenance versus paying for the high-priced technician, the author would choose the former. New do-it-yourself service centers, designed and often operated by producers, will feature "rental cubicles" for do-it-yourselfers. These cubicles will be stocked with the special and standard tools required for each specific repair and maintenance task, in the same way that mechanics' cubicles are supplied. As part of the service, master mechanic specialists will be on hand to provide expert assistance. But, in the main, most work can and will be done by the owner, assisted by computer-accessed videodisks that demonstrate actual service disassembly and reassembly steps for each type of repair and maintenance. The same computer systems will flash service and maintenance parts requirements to the center's storeroom, where they will be picked almost instantly and delivered to the appropriate cubicle by conveyor. The two-way conveyor will transport defective components back to the storeroom for collection and return to the producer, who may repair them and put them back into circulation and analyze their weaknesses for potential design improvement.

ELECTRONIC DEALER/CUSTOMER CATALOG AND ORDER ENTRY

The electronic dealer/customer order entry system notion was first introduced in Chapter 2. It was described as an exciting new tool for providing customers with a service that would differentiate them from competitors. Not coincidentally, such a system also tends

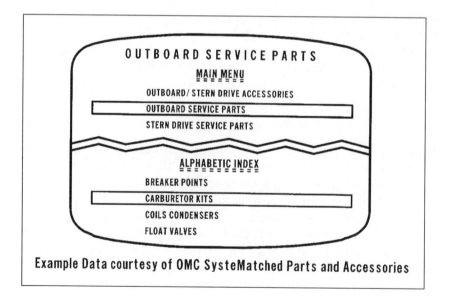

Example Data courtesy of OMC SysteMatched Parts and Accessories

EXHIBIT 7–1

Dealer/Customer Catalog—1

automatically to give the supplier a competitive advantage every time the customer works on the scheduling of time-phased stock replenishments. The customer will love the ease of scheduling replenishments and taking advantage of the latest price breaks available. The customer will be able to see, on-line, the quantity of the supplier's stock available for immediately delivery and the supplier's scheduled receipts (i.e., probable availability for future replenishment). What follows is an illustration of this type of system designed for a supplier of service parts and accessories for marine products.

Exhibit 7–1 is an example of one of two displays that could guide a dealer through the ordering process. The first screen's main menu, at the top of the display, enables the dealer to pick one of three main categories of product service items. In the example, the dealer has selected outboard motor service parts by moving his cursor to that line and keying "enter." As a result, the system returns the display at the bottom of the exhibit. It lists all major functional components in alphabetical sequence. In the example, the dealer needs a kit for repairing a 1988 75-horsepower carburetor, so he moves his cursor to "carburetor kits" and keys "enter" again.

Exhibit 7-2 is the next display, returned to help the dealer identify the appropriate carburetor kit. This display sequences all out-

OUTBOARD SERVICE PARTS
APPLICATION: CARBURETOR KITS

OUTBOARD HORSEPOWER	MODEL YEARS	PART NUMBER	REPLENISHMENT DATE QUANTITY	UNIT PRICE	DISCOUNT FLAG
75	60-63	382057			
75	64-65	382058			
75	75-88	398729			
80,85	66-68	392058			
V-4	69-79	390055			
V-4	83-84	398526-S			
V-4	91-92	434647			

Example Data courtesy of OMC SysteMatched Parts and Accessories

EXHIBIT 7-2
Dealer/Customer Catalog—2

board motors by horsepower and model year and lists the service part numbers of the applicable carburetor kit. In the example, the dealer has moved the cursor to the line on which the 1988 75-horsepower motor appears, along with the applicable kit, service part number 398729. By keying "enter" the user brings up the next screen, Exhibit 7–3. This screen assists the dealer in electronically entering an order (or schedule) with the kit's supplier. In this example, the working part of the screen is the data the dealer uses to plan replenishment. In addition, the screen displays a picture of the components of the 398729 kit. The purpose of the picture is to enable the dealer to see the kit that his confirming keystroke will cause to be delivered, to guard against errors caused by moving the cursor to the wrong line. This helps to preclude ordering a propeller instead of a carburetor kit. Having verified that the carburetor kit is the one needed, the dealer tentatively enters a requirement of 10 kits for January 1, 1993, based on an average monthly usage of 10. He then keys "enter" to see the unit price for this quantity and other price breaks available of he were to schedule additional deliveries.

The dealer uses the price break data displayed to schedule multiple deliveries as shown on Exhibit 7–4. In the example, the dealer

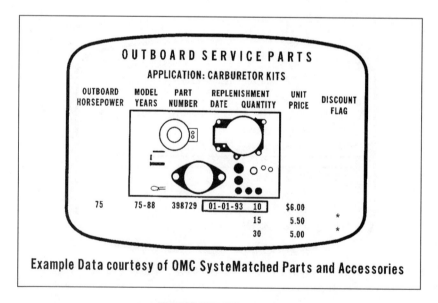

Example Data courtesy of OMC SysteMatched Parts and Accessories

EXHIBIT 7–3

Dealer/Customer Order—1

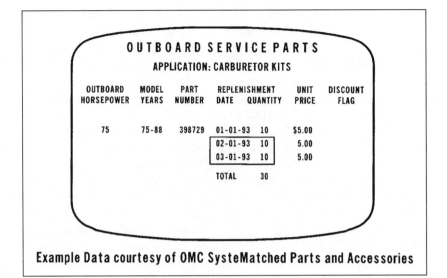

OUTBOARD SERVICE PARTS

APPLICATION: CARBURETOR KITS

OUTBOARD HORSEPOWER	MODEL YEARS	PART NUMBER	REPLENISHMENT DATE	QUANTITY	UNIT PRICE	DISCOUNT FLAG
75	75-88	398729	01-01-93	10	$5.00	
			02-01-93	10	5.00	
			03-01-93	10	5.00	
			TOTAL	30		

Example Data courtesy of OMC SysteMatched Parts and Accessories

EXHIBIT 7–4

Dealer/Customer Order—2

supplied his own judgment concerning delivery dates and quantities, and the example assumed that he had either simple, manual record cards or small computer systems from which to draw the data necessary to support decisions on when and how much to schedule. Note that a system of this type could logically include either or both purchase orders and schedules. As noted in Chapter 3, the tide of the future for most companies will be to eliminate purchase orders from their systems and replace them with schedules. However, many companies with infrequent, low-volume requirements will probably need to continue to use orders. Even those companies planning to adopt schedules will continue to use orders while they and their suppliers begin to implement all of the operating improvements required to make schedules universally applicable to all stocked items.

ABBREVIATED DISTRIBUTION CHANNELS

Service merchandise, repair parts, and maintenance materials are generally fantastically high-priced in relation to their actual production cost. For example, one analysis of the components of an automobile showed that its component parts, purchased through the service channels, cost 127 percent more than the retail price of the complete car! Considering the cost of assembling and finishing an automobile, the service price markup over cost falls in the 300–400 percent range, a range that is reasonably consistent for service components (especially those that are proprietary designs and thus available only from the end product producer). However, to keep the issue of service parts in proper perspective, one must keep in mind that most goods flowing through conventional distribution channels have factory-to-retail markups in the same range. In most cases, the seemingly ludicrous difference between factory cost and retail price is attributable, in large part, to the many-tiered distribution chain. Each link in the chain adds its cost (and its profit margin, in the case of independent distributors) to the final sales price.

Service parts distributors, therefore, have as much reason to reduce the number of distribution levels (as far as is practical) as does any distributor. Exhibit 7–5 is a schematic of typical elements of service distribution channels, starting with components shipped from a company's central parts and accessories warehouse or the vendor's warehouse. Thereafter, the flow is often through regional warehouses, to local warehouses, and, finally, to the repair shops and retail outlets (in many instances, via cross-dock facilities). Worn and defective components often have high potential for low-cost rework and rebuilding and high aftermarket sales profitability. Thus, these components are often delivered to a reclamation facility that disassembles worn component assemblies, refurbishes sal-

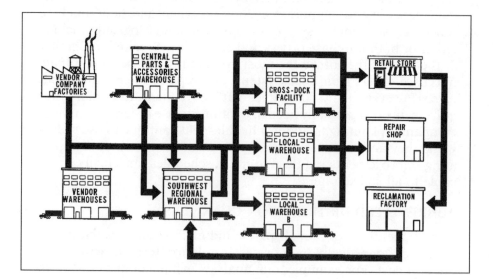

EXHIBIT 7–5

Service Distribution Channels

vageable components, and then reassembles the mixture of salvaged and new components to create products of like-new condition. The rebuilt items loop back into the channels, being delivered to and stocked by the regional and/or local warehouses.

There are several potentials for lowering logistics costs in these channels. First and foremost are the various opportunities to reduce the number of levels in the distribution network. Fast, efficient, modern delivery alternatives make cost-effective delivery from central warehouse to dealer or repair shop a one- or two-day service in most parts of the country, thus have the potential for drastic cuts in pipeline inventories, as well as in storage and handling facilities and costs. However, in the case of repair parts, fast delivery is even more important than for products, as the need for a spare part usually means a product is not functioning and the owner is unable to use it. Thus repair shop and retail outlet inventory management systems must be of superb quality and must have the lightning-fast communications features described in Chapter 5, under the headings "Dealer–Customer Inventory Management Systems" and "Electronic Data Interchange: An Electrifying Prospect." Even then, the potential delay of one or two days might be of serious concern to the customer whose product is inoperable. Delays will be almost inevitable when the service components have infrequent usage, which makes it impractical for most repair shops and retail outlets to carry stocks of the items. An alternative strategy, therefore, might be for retail and repair shop to carry inventories of the high- and medium-usage items, while either regional or local warehouses stock only the lowest-usage items. The purpose of these warehouses would be to cut the supply time for service components from one to two days (from the central warehouse) to same-day or one-day delivery from a regional or local warehouse.

Incidentally, many companies overlook the opportunity for refurbishing and rebuilding defective components, failing to recognize the low cost of salvaging components versus replacing them. Since the material value alone makes up about 70 percent of the original cost, the salvage alternative is often the lowest-cost route. Companies should always consider the viability of one or more reclamation centers for components of relatively high-value and high-service usage.

SERVICE PARTS SUMMARY

The value of imparting a sense of personal importance to customers has been far too often overlooked. Customer loyalty has been and always will be highest for those companies dedicated not only to providing the best-value products but also to rendering the highest-quality, personalized service. One of the best possible personalized services is to deliver products and services to the customer in his home or place of work with the least possible effort on the part of the buyer. New generation systems will be needed to support these new types of service.

PART 2

CONSUMER PRODUCTS DISTRIBUTION

The invention and proliferation of the automobile virtually eradicated home delivery systems and, with them, small neighborhood stores. This brought lower-cost products to the consumer by creating a boom in supermarket and chain store business, a phenomenon that would not have gained momentum without the car to carry people to large stores relatively far from their homes. However, this change came at the cost of converting customers into a self-delivery service and at the cost of traffic pollution. The recent explosive growth of catalog services, fueled by dramatically reduced delivery costs resulting from deregulation, is a likely precursor of things to come. When consumers learn to cherish hours saved by virtually eliminating shopping expeditions, they will create a new boom in home ordering services—*but only if new systems and superior logistics systems make ordering easier and delivery cheaper than self-delivery*. Companies supplying consumers need visions of ways to bring products and ordering systems into the home and office and must have fast, efficient delivery services to perform same-day delivery at nominal cost.

EXECUTIVE CHECKLIST: SELECTED ZINGERS

"Zingers" of widespread applicability to *all* warehousing and distribution logistics are listed in earlier chapters. Some of these are partially reiterated here for the benefit of the reader jumping immediately into this chapter without having read the prior chapters. As usual, the zinger checklist summarizes some of the most important topics of this section and is intended to serve as an executive checklist against which to compare the operations and systems of one's own company.

1. Retail and wholesale customers expect and deserve to know when their requirements will be shipped. In order to provide this important customer service, every customer

order/requirement, as it is placed, must reserve either on-hand stock or a future, planned warehouse replenishment receipt.

2. Vendor delivery of warehouse replenishment require-ments is of the utmost importance. Working with vendors to solve the problems that lead to upgrading their capa-bilities to just-in-time performance is a key to accurately promising customer delivery dates when stocks on hand are insufficient to meet customer needs.

3. Companies must devise better and lower-cost ways of put-ting catalogs into the hands of both retail and wholesale customers. The catalogs themselves must encourage po-tential customers to browse more frequently through their pages, thus increasing sales and market share. Some form of interactive electronic catalog display and order entry, perhaps via cable television services, is a key to future success.

4. Mammoth businesses, and many not so large, suffer from bureaucracy and inefficiencies of size. The key to being bigger without being costlier is to find ways to limit the size of the facility or ways to carve big businesses into smaller, focused businesses within the big one. Doing so in large warehouses is a special challenge.

5. Damages to warehouse and in-transit stock is not an in-evitable cost of distribution logistics. To the contrary, fail-safe warehouse and transport designed to achieve zero defects is a practical reality that must be pursued.

6. It is extremely annoying and costly for customers to re-ceive shipments in which the items and quantities re-ceived are not correct. Because some suppliers deliver erroneous goods and counts with some regularity, costly receipt-checking operations are usually an integral part of the customer's receiving procedures. Perfect deliveries are an important part of customer service that the ware-house should deliver, and should also demand of its ven-dors.

7. Retail and wholesale businesses and their distributors are almost all subject to wild fluctuations in customer de-mand, starting with peak sales days during a week (week-ends) and including seasonal sales peaks (like the extreme crest during the Christmas season). They must all operate with the workforce, facility, and equipment flexibility to match peak needs with corresponding service, without in-

curring penalties of increased cost or lowering the quality
of services provided.

8. Out-of-stock retail "slots" cause both impulse and planned
sales losses. Therefore, fast stockout replenishment response time is of vital importance and should be treated
with exceptional routines and computer systems. The first
most important line of defense against lost sales due to
stockouts is to identify customers who have looked for an
out-of-stock item, and to offer exceptional service to keep
the sale (for example, one- or two-day delivery, direct from
vendor or warehouse to the customer's home).

9. It is impossible to give customers accurate shipment dates
when the dates are based on inaccurate inventory records.
Unfortunately, inaccurate records often outnumber those
that are accurate. Outmoded systems of the past processed
daily receipts and issues in batches, making accurate cycle
counting all but impossible. They often reduced inventory
on hand either before order picking or after shipping. Both
alternatives further complicated reconciliation of record
to actual inventory. Today's real-time systems record receipts and issues into and out of detail stock locations, as
they actually occur. This makes it practical to maintain
accuracy at levels beyond imagination.

10. Bar-coding of warehouse receipts and issues (originating
way back when vendors packaged and labeled an item
with its item number, and extending through location coding in the warehouse, into shipping containers, and onto
the retail outlet floor) has been a godsend to businesses
suffering from inaccurate inventory records. Businesses
not yet taking full advantage of the power of bar-coding
and portable wands and guns must do so at once.

11. Creating or obtaining and subsequently maintaining mailing lists targeted at buyers with specific buying habits and
product interests is an expensive proposition, duplicated
in myriad businesses. Future regional mailing list "utility
companies" will increase the practicality and costs of this
expensive component of cataloging. Logistics companies
getting in on the ground floor of the mailing list utility will
steal a march on their competitors.

SMALLER IS BETTER

Of all the items on the list of executive tips for superior warehousing and distribution, the author considers the focused business-

within-a-business to be the most important. Some business units grow to such a giant size that even the hardest-working executive cannot manage them. Finding ways to subdivide large factories into focused factories-within-a-factory is relatively easy.[2] Subdividing warehouse operations is a more difficult challenge. One of the best recent examples of subdivision was that of the SLS Sears Logistics Services warehouse in Kansas City. Shortly after the wholly owned $2-billion SLS logistics business was incorporated as an enterprise separate from the retail and catalog businesses, dynamic, visionary improvements of sweeping scope began to be put into motion. As of this writing, transportation and warehousing costs have been reduced by more than $200 million, while service levels for the $20 billion of goods moved and stored have improved dramatically! Starting from a long tradition of being a cost center, the new independent business was challenged to compete with other logistics companies; it suddenly had to hone its performance to vault into a commanding position of superiority in terms of the speed, quality, and cost of its service to its biggest initial customers—Sears Roebuck retail stores and catalog businesses. Once it had achieved the necessary results, via improved operations, SLS began to put into motion steps toward becoming a supplier of logistics services to companies outside the Sears family of businesses.

One of the earliest and most dramatic changes was to move warehousing operations from single facilities servicing three customers (retail stores, home delivery, and catalog businesses) into separate warehouse facilities for each. The impetus for doing so stemmed from the three Sears customer's desires. They perceived that the combined facilities were not capable of intensely focusing attention to their individual, unique business needs. When informed by SLS Chairman Charles Reaves that all warehouse operations other than catalog merchandise would be moved out of the Kansas City facility, Dave Martin, General Manager of the Kansas City facility, told the chairman he thought it was the stupidest idea he had ever heard. He said, "Can you imagine all of the added cost of three sets of management for three different operations?" However, Dave quickly changed from a prime resister to a prime driver of change. What made the big difference? He quickly realized that, with the change, he would be able to focus all of his planning and management on his single catalog business instead of splintering service among three customer businesses. Now he and his manag-

[2] See Appendix 2 for reference to more about factories-within-a-factory.

ers are able to service the catalog business infinitely better than ever before. The bottom-line results to date have more then proved the point. Instead of increasing costs of operations, Dave's organization has reduced them by $5 million a year! Better still, the improved focus on its catalog customer has paved the way for giant strides in speedy, high-quality service.

QUALITY IN WAREHOUSING AND DISTRIBUTION

Quality in warehousing and distribution has some unique, interesting twists. Among them is the problem of damage to the product package and its contents. Every warehouse manager is keenly aware of the costs of damage to packages, and to the products within, that results from rough handling both within the warehouse and in transit to the customer. It is a great mistake to imagine that the only remedy is continuously to admonish warehousemen and truck loaders to avoid rough handling and poor truck loading that permits truck contents to shift in transit. Fail-safe devices that make it impossible for damage to occur are a far better (as well as a permanent) solution. For example, in warehouses that operate with forklift trucks that whiz up and down aisles, the drivers are clearly and properly motivated to move loads as rapidly as possible. As drivers maneuver to pick up and set down loads adjacent to stacks of unprotected pallets, accidents frequently result. When lift truck and product cartons collide, it is clear that the lift truck will not be the item damaged. General Manager Ken Clark has a quality program at the Manteno, Illinois, Retail Replenishment Center of SLS Sears Logistics Services. The quality team has invented a low-cost, fail-safe solution to this problem, which has plagued warehousemen for ages. The simple solution consisted of bolting wooden two-by-fours to the floors around the areas in which stacked and stored products could be damaged. The 2-inch border is high enough to make it a completely effective barrier against lift trucks. The scarred two-by-four barriers bear mute but eloquent witness to the fact that such protection is needed. Damage from this one source has been completely eliminated! Ken stresses that improvement in quality cannot come from routine 100 percent inspection somewhere in the process. That would only add cost and would be unlikely to solve the problem at its source. What is needed are fail-safe procedures and devices that make it impossible for poor quality (through damage or any other problem) to occur.

Nor are damaged packaging and contents the only quality-related issue in packaging. Jack De Simone, Operations Manager of the

Kansas City Catalog Merchandise Center of SLS Sears Logistics Services, pointed out another important factor: the appearance of delivered packages. In past years packaging was deemed to be solely a distribution organization issue rather than an image issue that should be of concern to the catalog business organization. Therefore, SLS shipped all catalog orders in drab brown paper bags and boxes. An invaluable new opportunity to use the package to make a bold statement to the catalog customer was available. Now the Sears catalog unit customer is the central party involved in packaging decisions. Its original initiative was to direct SLS to adopt the use of a bright, eye-catching white plastic bag, imprinted colorfully with the Sears name and design. Not only did such a package sharply enhance Sears's image, but it was also significantly less expensive than its paper predecessor. (Alternative packaging materials, while differing only by pennies, become an extremely important issue, because just a single SLS catalog warehouse ships more than 20 million packages of all varieties a year).

Unfortunately, it was later discovered that United Parcel Service's package-sorting equipment sometimes soiled the white packages, detracting from the package image. Sears found the best temporary solution to be to change to a gray package that masked the smudges. The real source of the quality problem, however, was the UPS sorting equipment, and since the white package makes a much bolder statement, UPS should eventually (as soon as possible) solve its problem. Because the soiling of packages is also bound to debase the UPS quality of service to its other customers, solving the problem will redound favorably to itself. Given the modern dog-eat-dog competition for package delivery customers, the cleanliness of delivered parcels is bound to become a differentiating factor that will give the superior delivery service a competitive advantage.

Interestingly enough, the quality of the job the warehouse does in bringing together all items on one order and all the orders slated for one truckload can be of significant importance. To fail to carry out this complex job with speed and accuracy risks losing customers whose orders are shipped partially complete, with errors in their contents, or late. For years, for example, the SLS catalog merchandise centers suffered the consequences of packages that were misdirected, delayed, and lost as a consequence of the damage and detachment of "tickets" (bar-coded labels) that were taped to each item on a customer's order. When damaged, missing, or loose, flapping-in-the-wind package tickets passed by highly automated sorter scanners that read the labels and control the package sorting, the result was missorted, unsortable, or completely unidentifiable packages. Even when the package reached the customer, usually in a banged-up condition, the shoddy-looking label subtly degraded the company in the eyes of the ultimate customer. By designing new, improved self-adhering tickets, SLS has been able virtually to eliminate label damage and detachment and the ensuing problems.

WORKFORCE FLEXIBILITY MASTERS PEAK DEMAND PERIODS

SLS Sears Logistics Services Catalog Merchandising warehouses have a unique time-of-day peak load requirement, stemming from the fact that early morning order picking requires many more workers than does order sorting and packaging. Further, catalog sales are very seasonal, with extreme peaks such as Christmas. The Kansas City warehouse meets the challenge of matching the daily order volume and time-of-day peaks by employing two basic classifications of warehouse employees. Full-time employees, who make up about 30 percent of the workforce, work a complete day every day. Part-time employees make up the second classification, about 70 percent of the workforce. They are hired as permanent (not temporary or seasonal) workers, with the understanding that their minimum work day will be approximately one-half day. However, when volume of work requires it, they would be expected to work (and be paid for) longer hours. This special provision, plus recourse to overtime, gives the warehouse a rather extreme range of capacity flexibility and results in superb customer service. It helps SLS to maintain the same delivery service regardless of the volume of orders. Essentially each day's customer orders will be shipped the next working day.

The SLS Sears Logistics Services Retail Replenishment Centers also have a unique sales peak that many centers have leveled in terms of the warehouse workload. But, as of this writing, leveling neither optimally matches the customer's peak demands nor minimizes distribution and retail inventories. The retail store's routine weekly sales peak occurs on weekends, naturally, so the ideal time to replenish stocks would be late Friday, Saturday, and Sunday, if the objective were to deliver merchandise to the stores as near to the time of the actual sale as is practical. Were this the case, the retail stores would need to master restocking the floor during the weekend, when the sales floor is most cluttered with customers and the sales force is busiest. More and more consumer product companies and grocery stores are finding that using the sales force to restock shelves during weekday days and evening hours is not the ideal way to manage inventory. Thus many have taken to employing a graveyard shift, with heaviest manning on the weekend.

In the interim, until retail stores are able to master receipts during the weekend peak (or master new peak-leveling strategies), Ken Clark's Manteno, Illinois, Retail Replenishment warehouse is delivering every customer store's replenishment needs (that stem from one weekend's sales) no later than Friday of the next week, in time to meet the next weekend peak. The store's stocks must be high enough to minimize stockouts during this period. Therefore, they typically carry inventories that are greater than would be required if deliveries more closely coincided with the weekend. The customer (Sears retail stores) has agreed to this, on the condition that every store receives a minimum of two full truckloads during the week, with the last truckload scheduled to be delivered no later than Friday.

SERVICING RETAIL OUTLETS: LIGHTNING-FAST DELIVERY

Retail customers most often base purchase decisions on the availability of merchandise, with instant availability being the best sales incentive and rapid delivery a close second. Further, a relatively high percentage of retail purchase dollars are impulse sales, triggered by the customer seeing merchandise on the sales floor. Every instance of retail store stockout results in the sales loss of not only customers' logical, planned purchases but also their impulse buying. The losses continue as long as the out-of-stock condition persists. When the retail store stock drops to zero, extraordinary steps should be taken to salvage the sale that might otherwise be lost. Two actions are vitally important to meet the stockout challenge. First, rapid, emergency action should be taken to replenish the items out of stock speedily, minimizing the period of potential lost sales. Second, every effort should be made to make the sale on the spot to customers who discover that an item they want is out of stock. For example, canny retailers put out-of-stock notices in the empty slot, advising customers to request next-day (or two-day) home delivery, and have special registers or counters at which out-of-stock home delivery service orders are processed. The provision of this extra service becomes vitally important to retailers who optimize productivity by moving personnel from the sales floor into cash register centers. While this step makes it possible to lower operating costs, it also has a downside. It severs two important aspects of repeat sales: achieving customer satisfaction by helping them find things they want, and providing special service when the item a customer wants is temporarily out of stock.

The retail replenishment systems supporting the retail outlet must be of superior, twenty-first-century caliber to provide the maximum practical customer service while minimizing the nonproductive storage space in the retail facility. Multiple-outlet retail chains can best meet the optimized service objective when supported by strategically placed warehouses in which matching world class logistics operations and systems support fast, frequent delivery to the retail outlet and directly to its customers. The logistics operations and systems not only must strive to replenish store stocks immediately *before* they are depleted, but must also perform extraordinary service to recover from stockouts that result from higher than anticipated sales. New SLS Sears Logistics Services Retail Replenishment Centers are becoming models of efficiency in delivering just such services and systems, which link outlets, their supporting warehouses, and warehouse suppliers.

The SLS computer system supporting retail outlets has been catapulted into world class status in recent years. Previously, warehouse inventory balances were not reserved for retail stores when the outlets launched orders once a day. Thus, available inventory might be overcommitted, resulting in surprise back orders when order pickers attempted to fill replenishment orders. In addition, once replenishment pick tickets were launched, their progress through the warehouse, onto trucks, and into the outlet was not tracked, so there was a vast void of status information, too much inaccuracy in inventory balance information, and a complete lack of capability to promise and deliver items after warehouse stocks were found to be depleted. All this changed when Andersen Consulting's distribution control system software (DCS) was used as a foundation for the new distribution operating system (DOS), which now speeds goods through the SLS Sears Logistics Services delivery network for not only retail outlets but also for the catalog business warehouses and those supporting direct delivery to customers, whether retail outlet or catalog customers.

Nationwide retail outlet replenishment orders are now processed overnight, every day, reserving available warehouse inventory for specific stores' orders on a first come, first served basis. The system's purchase order delivery information provides shipment promise dates for items ordered in excess of available stock. As order pickers are ready to pick a new batch (bundle) of orders, they request it at their warehouse computer terminal, and a bundle header (Exhibit 7–6) and several pick tickets (Exhibit 7–8) are instantly printed. Every pick ticket printed causes an ordered item to be picked, sorted, and packed on a truck in just two or three hours.

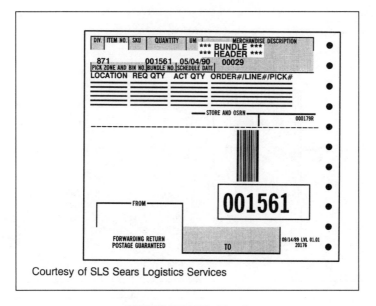

DIV.	ITEM NO.	SKU	QUANTITY	UM	MERCHANDISE DESCRIPTION

*** BUNDLE ***
*** HEADER ***

871   001561   05/04/90   00029
PICK ZONE AND BIN NO. BUNDLE NO. SCHEDULE DATE

LOCATION   REQ QTY   ACT QTY   ORDER#/LINE#/PICK#

STORE AND OSRN

000179R

001561

FROM

FORWARDING RETURN
POSTAGE GUARANTEED

TO

09/14/89 LVL 01.01
20176

Courtesy of SLS Sears Logistics Services

EXHIBIT 7–6
Retail Bundle Header

Fully loaded trucks will depart on their routes to one or more outlets no less than two times a week per outlet. Throughout this process, the system tracks the order-item's progress. Thus, any order item can be located at any time through receipt verification at the retail outlet, via computer terminals at the outlets, in warehouses, and in the office of the buyer responsible for store and warehouse replenishment.

Order pickers pick several waves of orders a day. Small items of relatively high-volume usage are picked from flow racks like the one illustrated on Exhibit 7–7. The self-adhesive, bar-coded pick ticket, Exhibit 7–8, is attached, and the picked items are placed in retail store–specific tote containers on a conveyor running parallel to the face of the flow racks. If the order picker had any problem picking any ticket, he would post the (rare) exception to the bundle header, Exhibit 7–6. After completing all items in a bundle he would report the bundle completed. In so doing he would automatically relieve both the inventory on hand and the inventory reservation of every item in the bundle. For the few exception bundles, the picker would scan the exception tickets listed on the bundle header and enter exception information prior to reporting the rest of the bundle as having been picked.

Filled tote containers are conveyed to a point at which the con-

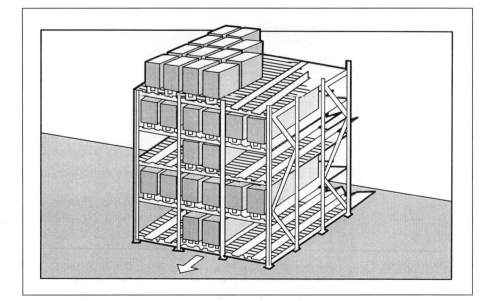

EXHIBIT 7–7

Flow Through Rack

tainer contents are wanded (or scanned by laser gun) to record the tote's items as now being in a certain container number. Each container's contents can be planned in advance, based on the items' cubic volume, a small part of the information stored on each item's computer master record. The bar-coded tote container label affixed at this point enables the automated order-sorting and conveyance system to deliver the container to the open doors of the truck, which, in very short order, will depart on its route to one or more outlets.

CATALOG BUSINESS VIABILITY: THE ELECTRONIC CATALOG

The catalog sales industry is one of the most challenging of today's businesses. In a bygone era, when a handful of catalog service giants supplied something of everything to most households, the distance and time from household to retail outlet often discouraged all but infrequent, unavoidable shopping trips. Monumental changes have since taken place, as some of the giants have abandoned their mail order businesses and other have cut back or reshaped the business to cope better with the avalanche of smaller

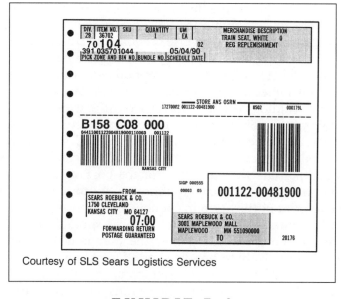

Courtesy of SLS Sears Logistics Services

EXHIBIT 7-8

Retail Pick Ticket

specialty catalog sales enterprises that have sprung into being. The plethora of competing catalog businesses, along with the drop in the amount of mail order sales due to the ever increasing number of conveniently located giant shopping malls, is a combination that makes today's catalog market one of the most fiercely competitive business arenas. The catalog firm that emerges as the victor in this race must not only master the operation of superior logistics facilities and systems but also learn to provide the highest-value products and deliver the best customer service.

The author's household is a fairly frequent customer of mail order (mostly telephone) suppliers and thus is in a position to identify the characteristics of the products and services of the enterprises that the family will probably never again patronize, versus those whose catalogs are often avidly perused. Following is a list of the business practices that sound the death knell for the companies that have fallen into the family's disfavor.

1. Comparison shopping, sometimes after the fact, has shown that numerous catalog services do not deliver satisfactory value. Although many advertise their goods as elite, high-fashion merchandise or wares of superior performance, the items they offer or comparable items are available at much lower prices elsewhere.

The lesson? Discriminating buyers might be fooled once, but in the long run they will gravitate to the supplier that delivers the best value for the money. When all else is equal, the competitor with the highest productivity and lowest operating costs can offer its customers the highest value. Thus, warehouse and distribution productivity will someday be the sole factor that will winnow out the profusion of catalog company losers from the winners.

2. A fairly high volume of purchases turn out to be not what the customer really expected and must be returned. The speed of refund or credit to the charge card used and the cataloger's willingness to compensate the customer for the cost of return shipment are of paramount importance to retaining customers. Nor is it acceptable to print notification in catalogs that return shipment costs will not be refunded. In fact, such notices should be red flags to potential customers, warning that the company taking this approach is highly likely to handle shoddy merchandise, since it apparently can ill afford to finance returns as its best competitors are likely to do. The lesson? Catalog firms must control returns better. While some returns are unavoidable (people can rarely foresee how fashion clothing and furnishings will look on the body or in the home setting), those that are due to the customer's perception that they are defective or of shoddy value must not be allowed to reach the customer or, at least, to recur.

3. Like the retail outlet shopper, the catalog browser also makes purchases based on impulse. However, once the impulse bug bites, the buyer becomes avidly and impatiently expectant, looking for as near to overnight delivery as possible. Enterprises that accept telephone orders and subsequently discover they are out of stock and thus experience delivery delays are usually an abomination in the eyes of the customer. Nor do customers look kindly on those that routinely or even occasionally have inordinately long delivery times. The lesson? Every mail order business must be prepared to inform every customer accurately of the projected delivery (not shipment) date, must maximize the instances in which same-day or next-day shipment occurs, must continuously fine-tune inventory management factors with the objective of cutting stockout occurrences to the bare bone, and must train vendors to operate factories to respond rapidly to unexpected surges in demand.

4. The folly of specialty catalog mass mailings will one day emerge as untenable. Even though a fairly frequent catalog buyer, the author's order per catalog received must fall in the range of hundredths of a percent. Who pays for these catalogs? Unrealistically low catalog mailing prices are subsidized by the homeowner

and other business mailers whose postage rates are much higher than they would otherwise need to be. The author's daily mail (by weight), for example, routinely consists of less than 2 percent mail and 98 percent catalogs and other mass mailing advertisements. As compared to the number of orders each catalog generates, the glossy catalog's costs plus the expense of obtaining and maintaining mailing lists and processing a mailing are clearly reasons that the value of the items offered is not consistent with their high prices. The lesson? To survive the inevitable, eventual rationalization of mailing prices, every catalog business must apply its best brainpower to focus on exciting, new, imaginative ways to slash drastically the costs of putting catalog information into the hands of potential customers.

As one example of new avenues for putting catalogs into customer's hands, the author envisions regional catalog service centers that will, in the near term, more efficiently maintain mailing lists. These lists will be marketed to all catalogers interested in offering their catalogs in the region. The service centers will use the lists to produce and/or merge all of their clients' catalogs into large (perhaps weekly) bundles of that week's catalogs for every homeowner in the region and deliver these bundles via extremely efficient transport services. Eventually, however, new electronic alternatives will completely replace paper catalogs. Technology such as interactive computer/cable television will present "electronically mailed catalogs" to the addressee's household, in order to capitalize on the potential impulse buying of the recipients as they "browse" electronically in the comfort of their own home. Such a system would have a huge advantage over paper catalogs, most of which the recipients put directly into the trash (sometimes after having skimmed through them, other times not even bothering to review them). New electronic services could keep current catalogs on file, permitting the homeowner to retrieve catalogs easily for specific items as the need for them arises. This would permit the customer to shop for the best values and delivery. Therefore, the catalogers offering low cost and high value would benefit tremendously by always having their catalogs accessible when a customer has the impulse to buy. Order entry features of the interactive electronic catalog system will shift the cost and workload of customer order entry out of telephone order-processing centers and into the hands of the customer, eliminating this expensive link in the mail order chain and hence permitting the cataloger to increase the value of products delivered. However, no matter what the value of the products cataloged, if an item is delivered with less-than-lightning speed it will be difficult to retain the customer's loyalty and, thus, to attain superior, world class status.

SERVICING CATALOG CUSTOMERS: NEXT-DAY SHIPMENT

The speed, accuracy, and efficiency of the catalog warehouse facility and its supporting systems are vital to selling the cataloger's service to its customers. Ideal catalog order-filling systems are remarkably like those needed for replenishing retail outlet inventories from warehouse stock. Further, catalog service centers, at which customer orders are stored for pickup by the customer, must rapidly become an ever smaller part of catalog service.[3] They simply cannot beat direct delivery to the customer in terms of convenience and service, except in problematic instances of home delivery. One such problem situation involves customers whose working hours make it impossible for them to be home during normal delivery hours, thus the potential for theft if packages are simply left on the doorstep. Further, catalogers know that direct delivery to the customer sharply cuts the volume of returns, as compared to the return rate at catalog convenience stores. The reason is simply that a relatively high percentage of all returns, 30 to 40 percent, are items customers simply have not picked up. Even prior to discontinuing its catalog service centers, Sears sharply increased the volume of Sears catalog sales delivered direct to the customer's door, in recognition of the advantages of home delivery.

Incidentally, since returns will always be a real part of catalog business, and since the customer has a right to resent the fact that he or she must go to the trouble to make them, companies that make returning merchandise easy and are quick to give credit will reap the benefits of resulting customer loyalty. Some catalog companies include return package labels and packing lists with each mail order shipment to facilitate returns. The best also include procedures for obtaining reimbursement for the cost of return or for returns by collect delivery. However, although some causes of returns are unavoidable, others (damage in transit for example) should not be tolerated. The root causes should be identified, and new, permanent, fail-safe methods of return avoidance developed.

SLS Sears Logistics Services has been able to capitalize on the

[3] Within a few months of the author's writing this, Sears, Roebuck & Co. announced discontinuance of its catalog centers, leaving only J. C. Penney as a major purveyor of this type service.

common requirements of cataloging and retail replenishment systems during the course of developing the state-of-the-art Distribution Operating System now used by all its retail and cataloging customers, thus lowering the cost as against developing different systems for each. Catalog sales, entered through nine mammoth telephone centers, come in through on-line, real-time computer systems that access inventory information by detail warehouse location and use the data to inform the customer if the ordered items can be shipped from stock. When an item is not in stock, the system identifies the next available receipt date and, from that, the earliest feasible shipment date. When the customer's regional warehouse is out of stock and the shipment date is too late for the customer, the system permits the order entry operator to access inventories in other regions. The operator interacts with the customer to determine if the order should be filled from a more remote regional warehouse, thus entailing a slightly higher delivery charge. Similar capabilities are available on the computer terminals in the retail stores. Thus, a sale need not be lost when a store is out of stock and the customer is unwilling to return to the store after the item is received. Rather than lose the sale, the salesperson can instantly enter an order for direct delivery to the customer's home.

As orders are entered, they are assigned to specific, planned truckloads. Several "waves" of order-picking batches are released to various areas within a warehouse each morning, in the sequence of the planned loading and scheduled departure of full truckloads. The SLS Sears Logistics Services Catalog distribution centers stock more than 100,000 items for Sears alone. Therefore, it should come as no surprise that a complex system of conveyors, wire-guided vehicles, automated and semi-automated sorters, and order accumulation and packaging stations process items picked through the entire process and onto the designated trucks. The typical, average elapsed time from order picking to delivery to the truck for loading is about two hours. And because the workload imbalance at various stages of the process is so great and since sales volumes include major peaks and valleys, the SLS catalog distribution centers rely heavily on permanent part-time personnel (approximately 70 percent of the workforce), who are guaranteed four hours of work a day, with the understanding that they will be expected to work flexible hours in days and weeks of peak demand, as previously noted.

Many catalog orders are for a single small item and require a quite simple bar-coded warehouse pick ticket/label. Exhibit 7–9 is

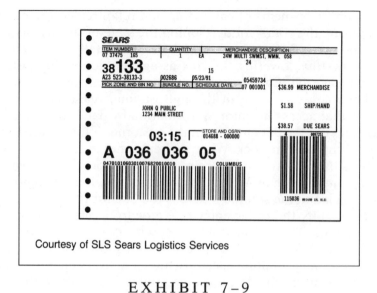

Courtesy of SLS Sears Logistics Services

EXHIBIT 7–9

Catalog Pick Ticket: Small Item to Store

the ticket SLS once used for deliveries to catalog centers.[4] Single-item orders did not need to be combined with other items ordered by the same customer. These orders needed only to be sorted, combined, and packed with other small items for the same catalog service center. The ticket/label, as illustrated, served as a label until the order was placed in the retail customer's hands. Multiple-item orders had to be sorted and directed to order accumulation work stations, where each order item was checked against the items listed on the multiple item order sales check, Exhibit 7–10.

After all items on the multiple-item order are received by the order accumulator-checker, the completed order was packaged, labeled with the overpack label, and routed to the planned truck dock. Not only does the Distribution Operating System calculate the total order value for use by the catalog store, but it also uses the latest sales price offered. This small touch is a valuable way to show the customer how important he or she is. Even though he or she may have ordered from an earlier catalog at a higher price, the ticket prepared uses the lowest price in effect at that time.

The conveyance and automated sorting systems for small catalog items, such as clothing and hardware, are different from those

---

[4] As previously mentioned, Sears discontinued the use of catalog service centers after these passages were written.

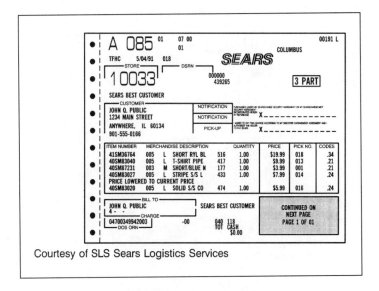

Courtesy of SLS Sears Logistics Services

EXHIBIT 7-10

Catalog Sales Check: Multiple Item Order to Store

required for larger items, such as the storage cabinet on the large item pick ticket, Exhibit 7–11. The top of the ticket is used primarily in the warehouse, whereas the lower bar-coded label is affixed to the item's container and travels with the item all the way into the hands of the customer. These large items flow through a large conveyor system that is capable of handling all but the very largest of items. Laser guns along the conveyor network read these labels and automatically route them through their own sorting systems and to the specific designated trucks, largely untouched by human hands until being loaded on the truck.

In the meantime, as small and large items picked from stock are being processed, the very largest of items (tires and appliances, for example) are cross-docked. Cross-docking means items are received at one dock, sorted and separated, and delivered directly to the outbound truck for loading. The cross-docked items fill up to 35 percent of the average outbound truck's capacity. Catalog distribution center warehouse inventory of these items is thus only a few hours at most.

As shown in Exhibit 7–12, items picked for direct shipment to a customer via United Parcel Service (UPS) are processed like any other order. However, items picked for direct shipment to customers are not always stored in suitable shipping packages. They are therefore packaged attractively for UPS shipment, and the lower

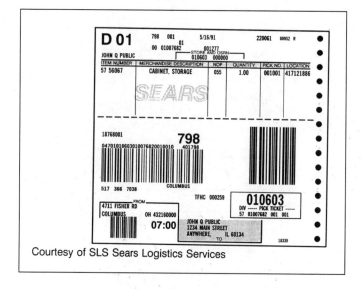

Courtesy of SLS Sears Logistics Services

EXHIBIT 7-11

Catalog Pick Ticket: Large Item to Store

part of the pick ticket/label (with UPS shipper number), Exhibit 7-13, is appended to the outer package. In every step of the order-picking, sorting, packing, and truck-loading operations, the bar-coded label information is scanned and used to update computer records. Therefore, when the last customer order item is loaded, the loading team can see that every item has been received, and the load can be shipped. In the rare event of order items that are lost or delayed somewhere in the process, the computer system supports the truck loader with information with which to make a decision as to whether to delay the dispatching of the truck until the errant items are received, or to send it on its way because of an anticipated delay.

All the modern products of the state-of-the-art computer system and its information are of little avail without the wholehearted involvement, commitment, and cooperation of everyone in the organization to high-quality service and exceptional performance. Above all, success requires that everyone take pride in the results of their efforts.

PROUD PEOPLE ARE PRODUCTIVE PEOPLE

The great significance of quality to world class logistics operations is readily apparent when most experienced warehouse executives,

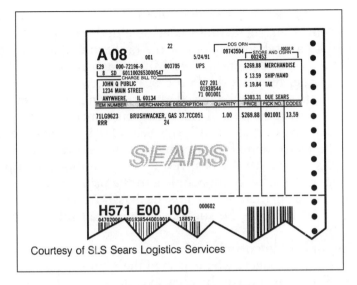

Courtesy of SLS Sears Logistics Services

EXHIBIT 7-12

**Catalog Pick Ticket: Single Item Direct to Customer
(Part 1)**

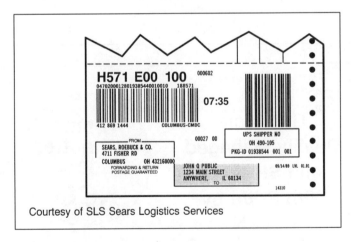

Courtesy of SLS Sears Logistics Services

EXHIBIT 7-13

**Catalog Pick Ticket: Single Item Direct to Customer
(Part 2)**

such as Ken Clark, rate it as the most important aspect of future improvement. Ken, incidentally, deems empowerment of *all* employees to be a vital component of the orchestrated attack on defective quality performance. Carl Mungenast fits quality into a somewhat larger framework of process review, in which every process and all its steps are reviewed, analyzed, and either simplified or eliminated with the goal of enhancing customer service, quality, and productivity. Carl says: "All SLS Sears Logistics Services people must be instrumental in applying the process review methodology if it is to achieve the best results." The author has supreme confidence in the value of all people and the pride they take in the way they perform their jobs; thus he has no doubt about their ability to contribute to the success of the organization's drive to excellence!

Surveys of working people have unaccountably surprised a lot of executives and managers who expected their employees to be quite blasé about their work. On the contrary, the surprising fact is that the vast majority feel pride in their work, doing their utmost to do the best job possible. Companies like SLS Sears Logistics Services give pride a boost by giving individuals recognition for their contributions. The type of sign shown on Exhibit 7–14 is used to label

Courtesy of SLS Sears Logistics Services

EXHIBIT 7–14

Entrepreneurial Pride

storage bays in Dave Martin's Kansas City Catalog Service Center. Helen, the person referred to in the exhibit, while demonstrating her merchandise-receiving procedure, did not hesitate to point out the finicky bar-code wand with which she was equipped. She fairly frequently had to make multiple wand passes before successfully reading bar-coded product labels or bin location labels. In many instances, it was necessary to key-enter the data. Clearly, better devices would speed up the process. From listening to Helen and others, Jack De Simone, the warehouse operations manager, had already initiated a search for and testing of a gun that would sharply reduce the difficulty related to reading the labels.

Further, Dave Martin, the general manager, initiated his quality program in a way designed to ignite the dormant pride of his workforce. He extolled to his people the benefits of being excited to come to work. He urged them to become committed to the company's program and honored and identified committed people by giving them the KCQ (Kansas City Quality) commitment button shown in Exhibit 7–14 if they declared a sincere commitment to the process of quality improvement. In instances where Dave has found the commitment was not deep and sincere, he has insisted that the individual relinquish the button! Nor does Dave think that the need for commitment is confined to warehouse and office *associates*. ("Associate" is a term everyone at Sears uses to describe employees other than those who are executives and managers. They coined the term as an alternative to other terms, such as subordinate and employee, words that the author has long felt erroneously imply lesser value and respect for those thus labeled. The term "associate" ascribes individual value to *every* person employed by Sears, regardless of classification.) While brainstorming the new world class attributes of managers and their assistants (i.e., capable of leading the organization into the twenty-first century), Dave concluded that the most important characteristics were an innate love and respect for people and the talent for maintaining meaningful two-way communications with all personnel.

CONSUMER PRODUCTS SUMMARY

The world of consumer product retailing and distribution will inevitably undergo massive change in the twenty-first century. Those who revered Sam Walton for the phenomenal success of his Wal-Mart chain have good reason to do so. However, they must soon realize that what Wal-Mart has been doing is making retailing better, not inventing new, better retail sales techniques. In a world in which the product sells itself by virtue of its value, the retail establishment itself clearly adds cost to a product without increasing its value. Producers and distributors of big-ticket items must soon realize this and strive to eliminate the middlemen in the distribution network, thereby reducing prices to their ultimate customers. To do so will make products more affordable, increasing the demand for them and restoring the jobs lost by eliminating levels in the logistics chain.

PART 3

MANUFACTURING STORAGE AND LOGISTICS

The master keys for unlocking the secrets of readily available, higher-value, lower-cost products are already in the hands of their vital sources, the product manufacturers. Without these improved products, available on demand, distribution networks will continue to deliver goods of unacceptable value, too late to satisfy customers' needs, and from unnecessarily large product inventories. The excess inventory in distribution channels is ultimately borne by the customer and, added to the excessive costs of transportation and storage, dampens sales by inflating prices without adding even incrementally to product value. One of the most important of manufacturing management's arsenal of weapons is virtual elimination of setup (changeover) and ordering costs. This permits a producer to switch from one product to another with ease, without significant cost, giving it the flexibility to respond rapidly to customer demand. A second key is mastery of production in smaller factories, permitting companies to establish regional factories (and clusters of supplier factories) in the midst of their most important markets. Doing so is a giant step toward reducing the excessive costs related to today's production and distribution networks, which take materials, components, and finished goods on a tour of the world at the expense of the ultimate customer.

However, although manufacturing already has the established twentieth-century keys to success, the superior companies of the twenty-first century need to forge new keys in terms of the visions uniquely applicable to their distribution and sales channels of the coming age. At a recent annual seminar of the Operations Management Association, the author was astounded to learn, during a lively roundtable discussion, that some still view "manufacturing" and "manufacturer" in the narrow context of factory operations. In fact, almost all manufacturing companies' operations include or are at least coordinated with all of the entities in the logistics networks, including vendors, transportation, distribution, and service parts and repair. Indeed, manufacturing companies are in the van of all companies attempting to integrate the entire network from raw material to consumer and sale to the end product user. As producers, they are privy to the new proven production techniques that, when fully achieved, also have the potential for revolutionizing the logistics function.

Although the keys to twentieth-century manufacturing success are well established, progress toward fully implementing change is flagging. Too many executives unrealistically expected overnight revolution. In fact, in most companies decades of dedication to continuous improvement will be required to realize the fruits of today's established, successful techniques and technology. The long time required should not deter executives from the quest for new visions, undreamed-of today. If mankind is to benefit from technology, manufacturers, the sources of all products and the generators of most real economic value, must formulate the required visions and must be the key movers in making them a reality. The new wave of visionary, revolutionary change is most likely to be founded in the way products are designed and in solving such thorny distribution and retail problems as peak and valley sales. The author's view of these visions is presented in earlier chapters. The purpose of the following manufacturing topics is to reinforce and expand upon the author's previous works dealing with established technologies, rather than present his (as yet unformed) vision of manufacturing operations. Chief among the new manufacturing concepts related to storage and warehousing is the decentralization of inventories into small subplants throughout a factory. The executive checklist is a convenient tool for comparing the characteristics of the outmoded central or remote manufacturing storeroom to that of the focused storeroom of the twenty-first-century facility.

EXECUTIVE CHECKLIST: SELECTED ZINGERS

The manufacturing storeroom of the twenty-first century will be incredibly smaller than traditional storerooms and warehouses. The most important aspect of the new highly efficient storeroom is that components and materials will be received and stored as close as practical to their point of use in production. Following are additional important operating practices that companies aspiring to be superior must adopt.

1. Containers and receiving equipment must be designed to virtually eliminate forklift trucks from the receiving and inspection process for all but the largest components and heaviest materials.

2. Inspection must be eliminated as a step in the receiving process. Supplier programs can teach vendors how to produce perfect quality and can help them to achieve it.

3. Counting and weighing components and materials received is a wasteful procedure that must he discontinued. Errors in counts, which will probably slip through forever, can best be trapped by infrequent low-cost or free physical counts.

4. The production teams in small cells and on assembly lines might incorporate receiving, storage, and issue activities into their work routine, as long as this does not disrupt the production flow or lower equipment utilization in selected instances in which high utilization is vital.

5. Bar-coded, kanban-type receiving documents should be scanned to record receipts until such time as they can be replaced by electronically transmitted load manifests. All components of an entire truckload can then be recorded via a single transaction.

6. Recording of issues must be discontinued in favor of automatic deduction from inventory of material and components based on reported production of the product. Progress to this level will require stringent control of unrecorded floor loss and quality at the level of parts-per-million defect rates.

7. Reusable containers, designed to optimize production efficiency and minimize personnel injury and fatigue, should flow directly from the supplier's last factory operation, through shipping, to receiving and storage at the customer's factory, to the production operation, and back to the supplier. Throughout this continuous flow, it should be unnecessary to repackage or to count the contents of any container.

8. Focused storage space utilization should be every bit as high as it would be in conventional storerooms. Therefore, every trick of storage space savings should be employed.

9. Most new, focused subplant storerooms will be too small to warrant a full-time employee. If it is not practical for the production team to take over the function, a full-time per-

son might be assigned all the storerooms for a cluster of subplants.[5]

MANUFACTURING STORAGE: SMALL IS BEAUTIFUL

One of the most potent messages of superior manufacturing is that small is beautiful! Giant factories are a bane, not a blessing, although giant clusters of factories and factories within giant factories are vital to the best manufacturing. The reasons that smaller factories are back in vogue and will inevitably and perpetually dominate the world of production are easy to assimilate. The traditional giant factory encourages the fragmentation of responsibility and authority among staff and line organizations that are widely separated by both walls and distance. Too few individuals who work on the administration and production of a product are able to understand more than a fraction of the workings of the massive factory and offices, let alone work cooperatively with all employees for the common good of the business. It is virtually impossible for any single individual to learn how the complex network operates, and it is especially impractical to make and implement decisions on current operations, let alone make improvements. With armies of individuals having authority within their individual fiefs, it is small wonder that winning consensus approval is at best a herculean task. Even after majority approval is obtained, any one of the czars can often torpedo a good idea by passive resistance to its implementation.

In new, smaller factories-within-a-factory, virtually all support functions are decentralized and moved into the small subplants or clusters of subplants. All resources necessary for successful operation are directly at hand, enabling relatively small production and support teams to work cooperatively and continuously to improve the efficiency and quality of operations.

FOCUSED STORAGE: A MANUFACTURING VISION

The history of manufacturing storage in most big companies has been one of avoiding real solutions to the basic problems caused by suppliers. Instead, companies have added layers of warehouse bureaucracy (count verification, inspection and tracking of incoming goods) between material receipt and its use in machining or assembly. When companies were small, the factory received a few

---

[5] See Appendix 2 for reference to more on subplant clusters.

materials and components and stocked them as close to the operation needing them as was practical. The office where the materials
and components were ordered and where inventory records were
maintained was a few steps away from operations. Inventory management personnel were often in the factory, sight-checking inventory levels and conferring with production people about the latest
schedules in order to update material priorities. As factories got
bigger, the factory's increased size and complexity started to cause
problems. It was no longer practical for the dozens of people responsible for inventory records and purchasing to maintain control
the best way possible—direct involvement in and observation of
manufacturing operations. The office was now too far from most
operations, and there were too many factory operations to make
visiting all of them a practical option. As a result, inventory errors
became rampant.

Finally, someone hit on the idea of gathering up all the materials
and components in the factory and putting them under lock and
key in a central storeroom. Since the using departments could no
longer simply use what they needed when they needed it, new formal procedures for kitting issues and replenishing line stocks were
developed, and requisitions were required to withdraw any components from stock in excess of demands (e.g., scrap and floor loss
replacements). The new central storerooms and warehouses added
days, even weeks, to the processes of stocking and issuing. In addition, new fleets of lift trucks were needed to make the long delivery trips from central stores to the places around the factory that
used centralized materials and components, as indicated on the
schematic on the left side of Exhibit 7–15.

It didn't occur to most people that the real problem was simply
that factories had become too large to be as superbly manageable
as when they were small. A much better solution to the problem
would have been to reorganize the big factory into several small
factories-within-a-factory, called subplants. Now that many companies have seen the benefits of doing so, they are subdividing their
factories into subplants and moving materials and components out
of central storage into the subplants that use them. As the small
subplants on the right side of the exhibit illustrate, one not-so-
inconsequential benefit is that forklift truck travel is slashed, because the delivery distance from focused receiving and stores is a
fraction of what it was when stored centrally.

For big companies, the worst decision was not simply to decentralize storage but to move it to an entirely separate, offsite ware-

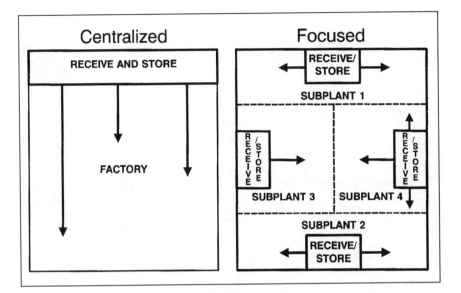

EXHIBIT 7-15

Decentralize Storage

house, as illustrated in Exhibit 7-16. In many instances, such warehouses have been located miles from the factories they were intended to service. As a result, management of the remote warehouses became an even greater abstraction. Instead of being able to see firsthand the size of piles of stored containers in the factory, inventory management relied on computer status information. On a computer screen, differentiating the investment and space occupancy resulting from an inventory of a thousand brackets and those of the same quantity of engine blocks is difficult! In big factories, all too often, warehousing, purchasing, and inventory management functions were moved out of the manufacturing executive's organization and into a central materials management organization. This fragmented the responsibilities for inventories in such a way that it became impractical for a single individual to control the investment and service level provided.

In fact, as Exhibit 7-16 illustrates, the establishment of central warehouses did not necessarily shift all inventory permanently from factory to warehouse. The factory usually continues to maintain formal and informal plant floor inventories to buffer it from delays in receiving materials and components from the storeroom or warehouse.

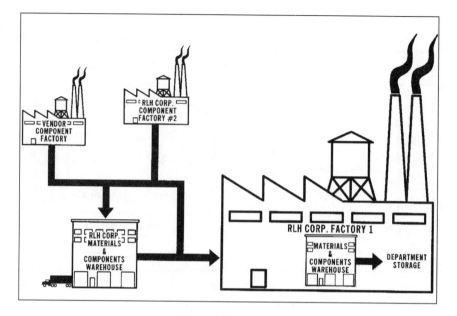

EXHIBIT 7-16

Costly Centralized Storage

The traditional storeroom of the giant (or even medium-size) factory epitomizes the worst of the centralized world. It has the following shortcomings.

1. The distances between the storeroom and the departments it serves are long, necessitating long trips between the two points.
2. Centralized storeroom employees come to feel that they are members of a business apart from the production areas they serve. It is not uncommon for them to act imposed upon when asked for an expedited delivery of parts to the factory, for example.
3. The bureaucracy of the central storeroom becomes stifling. Lines of production people often form at locked windows to obtain one or two replacement parts for lost or defective components. Each such request must be accompanied by a paperwork transaction (bureaucratic red tape).
4. A hierarchy of specialties is created within the central storeroom. The cycle-counters often become an elite group, with other warehousemen specializing in receiving, others in issuing, and still others in paperwork processing.
5. Surprise shortages and deliveries that arrive too late at the

assembly line have often caused line stoppages. As a result, the storeroom routinely schedules kit preparation far in advance of actual need, adding storeroom processing time and inventory to the manufacturing pipeline. Large sections of the warehouse are dedicated to storing kits prepared in advance but still awaiting arrival of shortage items. The advance kitting procedure doesn't only identify shortages, it causes them. A much smaller area is occupied by complete kits ready for issue but not yet required by the production department.

6. Eventually the storeroom empire builders hit upon the idea of making their business even more important! They move their operations to a separate, remote warehouse location. Separation of the factory from its storeroom exacerbates the already excessive storeroom process lead time and further complicates communication and cooperation between the "separate businesses."

The superior manufacturers of the world are hard at work breaking down the communication, distance, and physical barriers between stocks of material and components and the production workers who, through their labor, transform them into higher-value products. They recognize a revolutionary new receipt, storage, and issue concept that, when carried to its ultimate end, eliminates armies of nonproductive storeroom workers and monstrous automated storage and retrieval systems from the pipeline. The concept is simple. Receipts should be delivered to the immediate vicinity of the production operation and set down and stored there, then picked up and used at (or as near as possible to) the same spot. However, few companies, if any, have reached this ultimate goal, because to do so requires that components be produced and delivered in small, frequent lots. This requires that the supplier's setup and changeover costs be near zero, that his factories be in the local cluster of company and supplier factories, and that the transport systems between supplier and user be superbly organized, with small trucks continuously shuttling between customer and supplier throughout the day. Further, it requires receiving points (docks) adjacent to every production operation. The present state of the art in most supplier networks is not advanced enough to support the ideal. Nor is it likely that docks can ever be directly adjacent to every production operation in most factories. The required number, size, and shape of the most productive cells and lines dictates a relatively low ratio of exterior wall length (potential receiving points) to factory floor space. Therefore, the practical alternative in most cases will continue to be mini-storerooms located as close as practical (not on an exterior wall) to the cell or line, with a capacity for much smaller (but still far from optimal) amounts of inventory.

MASTER PLANNING: ROADMAP TO FOCUSED STORAGE

The author has never found a factory or a warehouse in which the layout is ideally suited to optimum productivity. In fact, when re-visiting factories for which he oversaw the layout design a few years ago, he always sees nuggets of gold—in the form of major addi-tional improvement opportunities—scattered throughout the facil-ity. The optimum will never be achieved because of continuously advancing technology of storage and factory design and changes in the business (new and discontinued products, for example) that necessitate reorganization into a changed, improved layout. There-fore, executives must always have a current master plan for revis-ing the layout and must continuously revise it to reflect both improvements and changes in the business and technology.[6] In fact, every manager and every subplant team should work contin-uously on improvements within their bailiwicks. Those who are most successful will be able to reduce constantly the area occupied by both process and storage. They must then seal off the vacated area to preclude anyone from using it wastefully and identify the space that has become available on the updated master plan. In this way they make an important contribution to the future success of the enterprise by providing islands of space which, when consoli-dated, become available for other uses, including new product man-ufacture.

In the early stages of a plantwide plan, little is known of the space requirements for the eventual cells and lines that will later be reorganized into the new sizes and shapes. The master plan's new framework of aisles, Exhibit 7–17, will ensure the achievement of high levels of productivity by providing a basis for efficient trans-port between subplants and from perimeter receiving points into the interior of the factory. The narrow, shaded bands around the perimeter of the building and adjacent to each aisle provide for focused inbound and outbound storage of not only purchased ma-terials and components but also manufactured components and

---

[6] See Appendix 2 for reference to the chapter of *Reinventing the Factory* that discusses the development of a factory master plan.

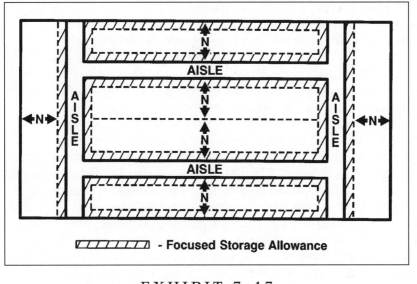

- Focused Storage Allowance

EXHIBIT 7–17
Storage Master Plan

assemblies that travel from one subplant to another during the
production process.

In the exhibit, which shows a first rough draft master plan layout, the building is well suited to receiving docks all around its
perimeter. Had some sides been inaccessible, focused storage
would not have been included on those sides. The amount of master plan space provided is determined by reducing the area and
cubic volume of current storage by the percentage of reduction
known to be achievable through better space utilization. The result
is further reduced by the company's targeted reduction in inventories of purchases and completed manufactured components and
assemblies. When the resulting space provision is doubled or even
tripled, it usually requires only a narrow band of one or two meters
around the building perimeter and along the sides of the aisles to
accommodate an even higher-than-planned inventory. The percentage of area allotted to storage is always a small portion of the total
factory and is usually substantially less than the area and cubic
volume of the existing storeroom. In a later phase, detail design and
reorganization of the physical factory and storage, more details of
the final plan emerge from the original rough plantwide plan developed in the master planning phase. Some subplants and cells
will be found to need more production or storage area, and others
less. It is then quite easy to adjust the plan by expanding some

blocks of process cells and assembly facilities and their associated storage while reducing others, sliding blocks of uniform depth but variable width back and forth along the aisles.

In the early stages of the execution of the master plan, initial preparations for reorganizing and moving the large central storeroom can be orchestrated so as to begin to yield benefits long before the actual final move. For example, one representative central warehouse for earthmoving equipment stored all components for all products in randomly assigned locations within the suitable categories. These categories, racks, shelving, and floor storage, are illustrated in Exhibit 7–18. (The size and complexity of this storeroom are simplified and stylized for ease of understanding.) The various product areas that ordered components from the central storeroom ordered only those items used on their own products. However, each production area's request for components caused one or more storekeepers to travel miles every day, all around the giant facility, gathering the items needed from scattered locations. The ratio of travel time to total issue time was therefore quite high.

Under the master plan for reorganization and movement, an approach was adopted to rearrange the storeroom, over time and within the existing storeroom, without expending extra labor (hence cost). This was accomplished by subdividing the giant storeroom into four smaller storerooms-within-a-storeroom, as illus-

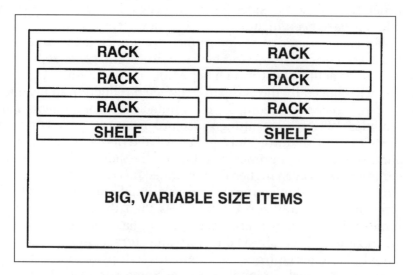

EXHIBIT 7–18

Earthmover Central Storage

trated on Exhibit 7–19. The basis for the interim organization was the longer-term plan to move stock for each product subplant cluster into the new layout. The subplant cluster products included scrapers, track-type dozer tractors, and wheeled dozer tractors, among others. However, in addition there were a substantial number of items common to one or more of the product types (mainly small, less expensive items). The longer-range master plan for these common items was to continue to receive and stock them in one storeroom and to issue them to replenish the inventories of the product subplant clusters from the central location. It was deemed necessary to continue this practice until such time as the company had systems and suppliers prepared to deliver smaller containers of the common items directly to each of the using subplants. The storeroom was almost completely rearranged, over time, by simply organizing new receiving procedures designed to direct new receipts to the *new* product-oriented storage area. Stock issues were controlled to issue oldest stock first (from an item's *old* location). As time went by, the number of items stocked in old locations (outside the product's target storage area) diminished continuously, while the number of items stocked in the product's designated storage area grew. As more and more product components' locations shifted into the new product storage zone, the time required to fill issues for each product family dropped in rough correlation to the items left outside the product zone. Thus, it was

RACK	RACK
RACK	RACK
RACK	RACK
SHELF	SHELF

BIG, VARIABLE SIZE ITEMS

| SCRAPER | TRACK TYPE TRACTOR | WHEELED VEHICLE TRACTOR | MULTIPLE USE ITEMS |

EXHIBIT 7–19

Focus Within Central Storage

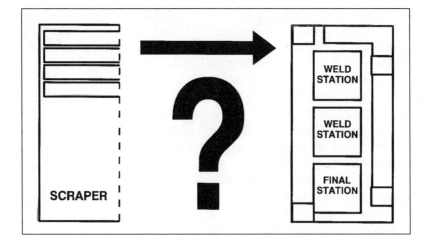

EXHIBIT 7–20

Same Space Required?

possible to achieve the initial rearrangement while simultaneously lowering the total stockkeeper manhours required to manage the facility.

Incidentally, when the reduced level of the focused storeroom inventory, further compacted by new space-saving techniques, is moved to and combined with the focused subplant cluster, a pertinent question (Exhibit 7–20) arises: Does it require the same amount of storage in the factory? The answer, not unusual in the author's experience, is that even less space is required when the production and storage areas are combined. A look at the earthmover company's scraper assembly area will help to understand why. The layout of the independently developed scraper assembly subplant has several empty areas, because it is extremely difficult to avoid having some waste space due to the unequal size requirements of different assembly stations and other constraints, such as building support columns. As Exhibit 7–21's dotted lines show, it was possible to "nest" some of the focused storage within the production area.

TO KIT OR NOT TO KIT: THAT IS THE QUESTION

Out-of-control inventory record inaccuracy, errors of omission in ordering inventory replenishment, and late deliveries from suppliers are problems that have perpetually plagued many manufacturers. The problem, as manufacturers have typically viewed it, is that

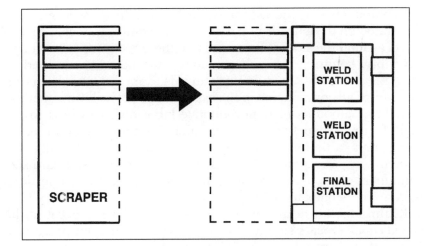

E X H I B I T   7 – 2 1

Nested Focused Storage

by the time they discover that a stockout will delay production, it is too late to take action. In many companies, this has triggered early preparation of "kits" for scheduled assembly. As Exhibit 7–22 indicates, there are basically two formal methods for delivering assem-

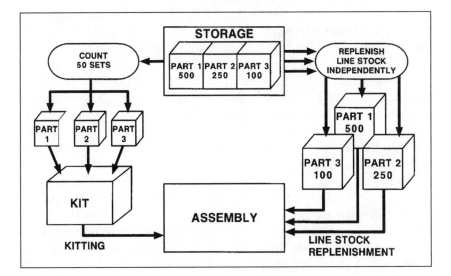

E X H I B I T   7 – 2 2

Issue Methods

bly components to the assembly line. The kitting issue method, illustrated on the left side of Exhibit 7–22, requires a stockkeeper to travel around the stockroom to retrieve the three components of an assembly, counting out and packaging the quantity required to meet the assembly schedule (fifty, in this example), and delivering the "kit" of all components to the assembly line. The kitting method adds large amounts of nonproductive labor and lead time to the manufacturing pipeline. It usually includes counting and repackaging steps (although these steps *can* be eliminated by using permanent kit equipment, designed to transport standard-size containers of each component to the line and the unused portions of containers back to stock).[7]

Kitting one kit at a time is also highly inefficient, because the stockkeeper repeats similar travel patterns for each kit processed. One better storeroom methodology would be to batch and "wave pick" multiple kits simultaneously. Wave picking is most applicable to products with small components, such as printed circuit boards and other electronic products, and components with high commonality of use on numerous products. Where each assembly's components are mainly unique to the product or a family of products, or where the components are quite large, it might be advantageous to organize storage by product or product family. This would eliminate most of the storage of wave picking batches of orders, thus simplifying the issue process.

The example on the right side of Exhibit 7–22 illustrates another method for issuing components from the storeroom to the assembly line: independent line replenishment. Independent replenishment entails restocking any item on the line shortly before the last piece is used. The kanban system of returning a permanent, plastic enclosed card and empty container to the storeroom to trigger replenishment is especially suited to independent replenishment.[8] Independent replenishment is best suited to environments in which the number of products produced on a line is low and/or components used on different products have a high degree of usage commonality.

Where the components of the many different products produced on a single assembly line have very low commonality, the kitting method of component issue is most applicable, since only the components required should be at the line while the assembly is being produced. If there are numerous products produced on the same

---

[7] See Appendix 2 for reference to information on kit issues.
[8] See Appendix 2 for reference to information on kanban.

line, and if each line has mainly unique, noncommon components, it would be impractical continuously to stock some or all components on the line, in anticipation of their use in future production runs. If the number of such components maintained in stock on the line were very high, the storage space on the line might be far larger than the assembly working area. This would cause the assembly process to have low productivity, because the assembler might be forced to walk back and forth between the containers surrounding the area and the assembly work area, as illustrated in Exhibit 7–23. If components stocked on the line were quite small and the area in which they were kept (stacked and in smaller containers like those on Exhibit 7–24) the need to walk would be eliminated. However, the larger inventory of components stored in the area would increase the time to *reach* each component, because of the need for more and larger containers. Further, twisting and turning when components are placed behind or on the side of the line adds time to the job. Such wasted motion robs time from productive work and contributes to assembler fatigue. Thus any excess walking, twisting, turning, and reaching should be squeezed out of manufacturing operations.

Where practical, assembly line and bench assembly storage in front of the assembler can eliminate unnecessary walking, twisting, turning, and even bending. The waist-high, line-edge bin storage illustrated in Exhibit 7–25 is one such valuable line storage tech-

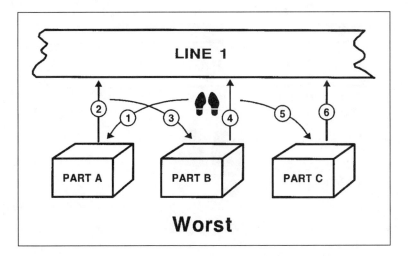

EXHIBIT 7–23

Numerous Large Containers

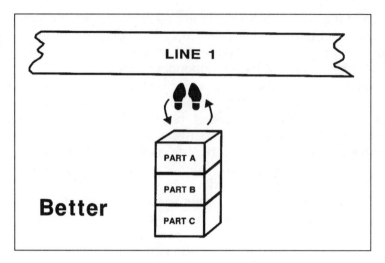

EXHIBIT 7–24
Small Containers

nique when the size of the product and its components make this
a practical option. When the space on the line occupied by the
product being assembled and its conveyor pallet is much greater,
the author even nests some components between and below two
conveyor tracks, on one or on both sides of the conveyor. This
results in increasing the number of components that can be con-

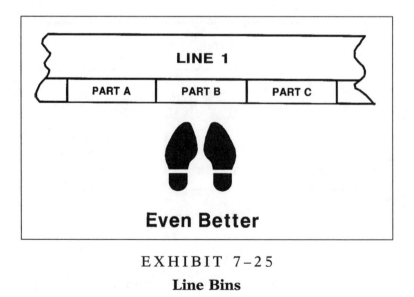

EXHIBIT 7–25
Line Bins

veniently stored in front of the operator, thus minimizing wasteful motion.

MANUFACTURING SUMMARY

Almost two decades have passed since the revolutionary improvements of the "Japanese" manufacturing model were first made known to the Western world. History may well record the simplification of processes as a second or third industrial revolution. Sadly, however, progress toward implementing the model has been far slower than desirable. Most companies are not striving to define new visions that would launch an exciting new age of industrial revolution. Fortunately, a handful of exceptional companies are unwilling to accept the status quo or settle for mere "continuous improvement." They will heed the need for fantastic visions, will produce, refine, and make them come to pass, dragging less insightful companies into the new age even as their managements continue to bemoan the impossibility of epic change. The author fervently hopes that this work will make a small contribution to the efforts of the mover-shakers who will make the future happen, *starting tomorrow!*

CHAPTER 8

Of Cabbages and Kings

The most powerful enablers of distribution and production logistics will be the enlightened executives, managers, and employees and world governments, collectively. Chapters 1 through 7 dealt with the author's industrial visions concerning relatively mundane business methods and systems. The most exciting changes, however, will be those going to the very heart of everyone's jobs and the laws that govern international business. Therefore, the purpose of this chapter is to outline a few of the author's thoughts on the subjects of executives, employee value, and international trade.[1]

EXECUTIVE, MANAGERIAL, AND EMPLOYEE ISSUES

Industry has been doing woefully little to provide the lifelong education and training necessary to enrich the lives of its executives, managers, and employees, thereby raising their skills and their value to their companies to new heights. Yesteryear's faulty promotion practices have placed some individuals in management or

---

[1] Such a potpourri! Carroll wrote: "The time has come . . . To talk of many things: Of shoes and ships and sealing wax, *Of cabbages and kings*." Lewis Carroll (Charles L. Dodgson), "The Walrus and the Carpenter," stanza 11, *Through the Looking-Glass* (1871), chap. 4. In Philip C. Blackburn and Lionel White, eds., *Logical Nonsense: The Works of Lewis Carroll* (1934), p. 188.

supervisory positions who do not have the necessary qualifications. Those individuals can often achieve noteworthy results in their own operations, while adversely effecting the operations of their companies as a whole. Some even dampen the enthusiasm of their employees, severely limiting their contributions to their companies' success. The time has come for company managements to devote markedly greater effort to developing their human resources!

EXECUTIVE CHECKLIST: SELECTED PERSONNEL ZINGERS

Following is an executive checklist of the most important personnel issues in this chapter.

1. Unqualified managers and supervisors, hampering companies' programs for employee empowerment, will be upgraded or, if necessary, weeded out.
2. Education and training programs have been more readily available for new employees than for executives and managers. New, lifelong programs will be developed for those on the upper rungs of the career ladder. Lifetime cross-training will be one of the most important tools for value improvement and job enrichment.
3. Executive jobs will finally start to get some attention and will be reengineered to improve executive productivity.
4. Video teleconferencing, one of the tides of the future, will help eliminate the waste of travel to and from meetings. It will help executives to pop into and out of meetings during the portions of the meeting that have executive importance.
5. Executives, managers, and supervisors spend disproportionate time in meetings, compared with other, more productive activities. Reengineering companies' meeting methods will be a vitally important, new program for managements that wish to increase productivity of their highest-cost human resources.
6. The scandal of unemployment will be solved through management, labor, and governmental cooperation. Although the occurrence of economic peaks and valleys will persist, albeit with moderation, unemployment will be minimized by a combination of equal sharing of available work and temporary, productive public works.
7. The fantastically wide pay gulf between low-paying jobs and high-paying ones will be narrowed. The lowest-paying jobs will be reengineered to utilize people's capabilities to the fullest.

8. Management must take bold, innovative (but humane) steps to remove change-resistant supervisors from positions in which they are able to impede progress. Pussyfooting around the issue of ill-qualified supervisors must not be permitted. Too many supervisors have been promoted from the ranks based on being among the best of warehousemen and despite never having been adept at people management skills. Now many are immovably entrenched in old ways. Management can and must remove this commonplace roadblock to progress.

PUSSYFOOTING AROUND MIDDLE MANAGEMENT QUALIFICATION ISSUES

In *Reinventing the Factory II*, the author is guilty of pussyfooting around the issues of unqualified supervisors and middle managers and the roadblocks to progress that they often impose on the entire organization.[2] After all, the main objective of the author's books is to encourage executives and their organizations boldly to throw off the shackles of outmoded practices, in favor of radically new approaches that advance the company into the ranks of superior enterprises. The fact is, there are logical ways to clear the organization's deadwood in one fell swoop, paving the way for sweeping (and humane) advances in the management of people, change, and ongoing operations.

The author's hat is off to David K. Martin, general manager of the 2-million-square-foot Catalog Merchandise Center of SLS Sears Logistics Services warehouse in Kansas City. Dave has demonstrated the practicality of eliminating an entire level of supervisors. He did so, as advocated in the author's prior work, with the type of daring and conviction that guarantees success. After only four months in charge of the facility, Dave awoke one morning with a detailed vision of an approach for sweeping out all forty-eight supervisors. His problem was the past process for selecting the best-performing warehousemen as supervisors. Superb warehousemen were promoted into supervisory positions, without regard to their lack of management skills. That left the facility with a cadre of elderly supervisors almost devoid of the talents necessary to manage people. Nor were most capable of contributing meaningfully to the mastery of radically improved operations expected to evolve from Dave's planned companywide participation in a quality improvement program. The solution was to eliminate the su-

[2] See Appendix 2 for reference to more about roadblocks to progress.

pervisor jobs (48) and to establish a new position for assistant managers (27) with an entirely new job description that ranked people skills over long warehouse experience and technical ability. Then, by defining in detail the required job qualifications of the new assistant manager and by thorough evaluation of all supervisors, Dave and his managers identified those deemed best able to qualify for the new positions. (Twelve out of the forty-eight supervisors were ultimately evaluated by their managers as having the necessary qualifications. (However, subsequently shortcomings of some new assistant managers surfaced, necessitating further reduction of the original group.) The real challenge was to effect the change humanely, and Dave did so by offering the unqualified supervisors three options: (1) take early retirement with liberal retirement benefits; (2) take other jobs for which they were qualified, at the same pay; or (3) leave with liberal separation pay. The author is pleased to report that a majority of supervisors took one of the first two options. This entire original transformation of middle management was accomplished in forty-five days! Dave's slimmed-down organization of superior managers and assistant managers was then ready to go to work on a total quality management program geared to warehousewide participation.

In the future, management will need to recognize the very special skills required to manage and develop all of an organization's people. It will no longer be possible for managers to rely on *all* or even most people to have the inborn talents and drive necessary to qualify for advancement. Career-long education and training programs are needed to identify those with the basic qualifications and to nurture continuous individual growth. Only executive management can then be held responsible for promoting individuals without adequate skills or preparation for new responsibilities.

EXECUTIVE/MANAGERIAL CAREER VISION

Excitement pulses through the author's veins as he contemplates the exhilarating roles of logistics executives in the next century. The harried, long hours of work that barely achieve adequate command of complex, far-flung logistics network operations will be transformed by reengineering executive jobs, their tools, and their skills. Twenty-first-century logistics executives will be closer to achieving the apex of productivity than ever before. The dawning of the age of executive enlightenment will come by virtue of dramatically increased breadth of career experience, lifetime education, techno-logical advances in executive work environment, and improved executive job productivity. With wide, in-depth business experience and knowledge, executives will be better equipped to address prob-lems and opportunities in every aspect of their companies' opera-tions, regardless of the discipline involved. Executives will no longer be on a single-discipline career track that forever stamps them as logistics specialists, marketeers, engineers, accountants, or whatever. Meaningful, career-long job cross-training in more than one discipline will become the norm for those on the executive career path.[3] Thus, executives' success will no longer depend solely on whether or not subordinates and other executives make the right discipline- and knowledge-based decisions. Superior execu-tives will possess their own in-depth knowledge of the same disci-plines and therefore will be readily able to participate meaningfully in the decision process. The author, like Kotter, believes that man-agement has a powerful motivation for focusing more attention on executive development: business profitability![4]

No longer will logistics executives flit from meeting to meeting, acquiring small bits of information on which to base executive direction and decisions.[5] New methods of structuring and conduct-ing meetings, coupled with state-of-the-art computer and commu-nications technology, will provide better, faster, easier-to-understand information. Further, executives will no longer be frustrated and burdened by the deluge of information supplied by today's "management information systems." Information reengi-neering and mail processing improvements hold the promise of drastically lowering the flood to manageable, executive-specified levels. Future executives so inclined, therefore, will be able to pack even more activities into their even more highly productive fourteen-hour days. Also, the few who would prefer to enjoy more leisure time will be able to do.

[3] Gardner has said it very well: "Tomorrow's leaders will, very likely, have begun life as trained specialists, but to mature as leaders they must sooner or later climb out of the trenches of specialization and rise above the boundaries that separate the various seg-ments." John W. Gardner, *On Leadership* (New York: Free Press, 1990), p. 158.

[4] "A firm that has taken the time to develop practices and programs that build strong management teams able to provide a business with effective leadership has a most powerful source of competitive advantage today." John P. Kotter, *The Leadership Factor* (New York, Free Press, 1988), p. 133.

[5] Mintzberg, in his study of executive and managerial time, found executives attend, on the average, six meetings a day, with an average meeting duration of sixty-eight minutes for scheduled meetings, and twelve minutes for those that are unscheduled. Henry Mintzberg, *The Nature of Managerial Work* (New York: Prentice-Hall, 1980), pp. 30–33.

Executives and managers should be every company's most valuable assets. However, in many instances this is not the case. One or more of three vital elements of executive development and productivity are often lacking: (1) a lifetime education and cross-training program to develop well-rounded expertise in multiple business facets and professional disciplines;[6] (2) effective personnel systems that reward executives and managers for preparing their employees for promotion and that base performance rating systems *on the specific skills that are of greatest value to the business*; and (3) executive and managerial job design that equips the executive or manager with the equipment, facilities, and techniques required to achieve highly productive use of the person's time and skills. For example, the vast majority of meetings observed by the author waste from 50 to 90 percent of the time of many executives and managers in attendance. For this very reason, some executives often leave meetings still in progress. Yet the keys to successful meetings are the simple but powerful methods of preparation and conduct outlined under the following heading: "Reengineering Executive and Managerial Jobs."

Once the science of engineering and conducting meetings has been mastered, additional state-of-the-art technology can be applied for incremental gains in executive and managerial productivity. For example, the continuous development of improved telecommunication, video, and computer technology should play a vital role in improving meeting productivity, in terms of permitting attendees to tailor their involvement according to need by electronically "popping in and out" of meetings in which they have an important role. Video teleconferencing will allow executives to be "present" at meetings of the future that are simultaneously conducted in several widely disbursed but linked conference rooms and executive offices. Involved managers and executives may cluster in the linked conference rooms or "attend" from their individual offices. Thus, even the mundane time lost in traveling to and from meeting locations can be minimized. Further, as is the case with every vision, a simple, practical, low-cost version of video teleconferencing is already available. It simply requires the use of a telephone speaker. Although audio teleconferencing does not permit attendees to catch facial nuances, it can provide many of the benefits of the conference of the future.

The marriage of video and computer technologies will permit

---

[6] See Appendix 2 for reference to more information on cross-training.

electronic video recordings of meetings to be accessed via a computer meeting agenda database, with direct access to specific subject matter. Executives and managers will thus be able to simplify maintenance of their meeting calendars. When schedule conflicts arise, they will be able to "attend" the highest-priority meeting via live video teleconference and to view lower-priority meetings later, as their schedule permits.

Since executives and managers are the captains and mates of the ship of business, designing their jobs and work environments to use their time productively must be one of the highest business priorities. Unfortunately, most business reengineering efforts neglect the executive office.

REENGINEERING EXECUTIVE AND MANAGERIAL JOBS

At the top of the career ladder, changes in executive management practice and style occur soon after an executive passes the baton to his successor. This is evidence (perhaps proof) that neither executive jobs nor any component tasks thereof have been systematically designed to achieve near optimum results, regardless of which executive is sitting in the chair at the moment. If an executive's job and environment were engineered for near-optimum performance, the job tasks would remain the same no matter how often the executives performing those tasks came and went. Many would argue that the executive should be permitted and even encouraged to alter the job to fit his own unique work experience, education, on-the-job training, and aptitudes. This argument, within reasonable limits, has great merit, *especially when the executive's career path has not been subject to uniform cross-training and education designed to equip him with well-rounded experience. The executive needs education and training in how to develop and hone the skills and aptitudes that are of greatest value in a specific company as well as those of great value to any company.*

Reengineering executive jobs, like any design undertaking, should start with an analysis of how executives spend their time. The purpose of such activities should be to focus on the few activities that occupy the biggest portion of time. The results of virtually every investigation have shown that the single greatest opportunity for reengineering executive productivity lies in the realm of meetings. One such study, by Mintzberg, is summarized in Exhibit 8–1.[7]

---

[7] Mintzberg, *Nature of Managerial Work.*

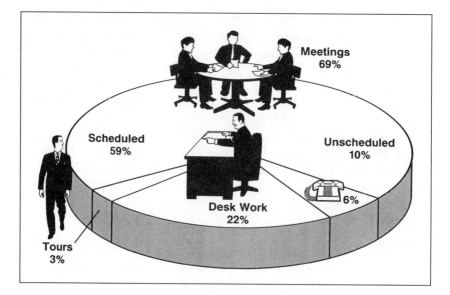

EXHIBIT 8–1

Executive Time Distribution

In this study, the three activity categories accounting for 97 percent of the executive's time were meetings (69 percent), desk work (22 percent), and telephone conversations (6 percent). The author has seen a wealth of opportunity for improving meeting conduct. Some attendees of almost every meeting, when queried, say that either their presence at the meeting was unnecessary or it was unnecessary for selected portions of the meeting.

One easy way for a company to assess the productivity of meetings is to formalize meeting time logs for recording the participant's evaluation of the applicability of the meeting to his mission. In Exhibit 8–2, an example of a meeting log, an attendee (one of several who use the form) has recorded data in the shaded areas. For example, the log (which might cover two hours per page) does not indicate the hour. Thus the attendee recorded the scheduled start time, *10*:00. (Had the meeting lasted several hours, more than one page would have been used). And because the meeting actually started late, the attendee recorded this free-form information. (Other types of free-form entries might be meeting interruptions and overrun of the scheduled time). In the example, the entry "U" and arrows from 10:15 until 10:45 indicate that the attendee thought his presence at the meeting during this period was unnecessary.

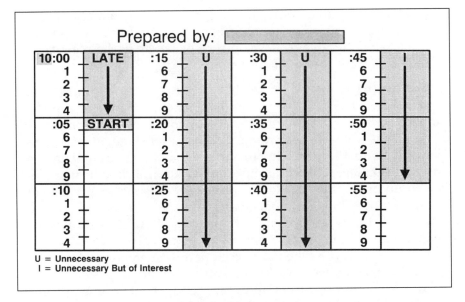

EXHIBIT 8-2

Meeting Applicability Log

From 10:45 until 10:55, the attendee thought his presence was unnecessary but deemed the subject to be interesting. Therefore, by his entry he indicated that he would have chosen to attend the meeting on this subject, had it been elective. The primary recipient of this information is the person who designed the meeting agenda and invited those in attendance. The purpose of feedback is to help teach meeting designers to tailor their subject to the audience and the audience to the subject.

Poor fit of meeting subject matter to the attendees is not the only aspect of low-productivity meetings. Following are some other problem areas.

1. Meeting agendas are not detailed. Prospective attendees might not be able to tell if they should attend any, part, or all of the meeting.
2. The time allotted each agenda item is not religiously adhered to by a meeting controller.
3. Meetings start late and overrun their schedule.
4. Meeting agendas include unnecessary subjects. (One example is rote status reporting, even though everything might be either on schedule or close enough that the difference is inconsequential.)

5. Meeting conductors try to answer every possible question during the meeting, even if unprepared to do so. It would be far preferable to develop a response after the meeting and present it at a later date.

The two basic meeting types in Exhibit 8–1 are scheduled and unscheduled. The need for an unscheduled meeting is triggered by some business emergency that calls for initiating the immediate actions that will soon restore normal operations and, at least temporarily, solve the problem. In the emergency environment, the meeting is called without advance preparation. It entails immediate group interactive problem definition, temporary or permanent solution, operation continuance approach definition, and individual responsibility assignment. The meeting is far less structured than scheduled meetings. When meetings are planned and scheduled in advance, the schedule should permit adequate preparation in rigid conformance with "best meeting practices."

All too many executives and managers permit meetings to be conducted as "brainstorming" sessions, although some studies have shown completely unstructured, free-form "brainstorming" sessions to be less productive than individuals working on the issues.[8] The author's experience is that the power of the group, in bringing alternatives and improvements to the individual's initial effort, can make a contribution of magnificent proportions. However, the group can be most productive if it can start with the work performed by an individual who formally presents it to the group. The best working group consists mainly of experienced persons with direct responsibilities in the subject area under consideration. However, to avoid meetings that deteriorate into "design by committee" or "free-form sessions" requires the meeting controller to maintain tight control of the agenda and meeting schedule. Incidentally, one of the most common mistakes is the assumption that the meeting purpose must be to make decisions. Decisions at scheduled meetings, conducted properly, are never necessary. The purpose of *every* meeting should be to agree on the ensuing steps. Although in a few instances the next logical step is to cease pursuing the subject, in most cases the only logical reason for not "buying off" on work to date is simply that not enough work has been done to prove the validity of the recommended approach beyond any *reasonable* doubt that the group may have. Accordingly, the next step is usually to do the additional work necessary. Eventually,

[8] For more information on brainstorming, see Harold Koontz and Heinz Weihrich, *Essentials of Management* (New York: McGraw-Hill, 1990).

enough work is completed to make the advantages of a recommended approach of such crystal clear validity that the group consensus will be that work should proceed to the next level of analysis,
design, or implementation.

The agenda is the most important ingredient of every meeting.
The ideal agenda ensures that the meeting will be fruitful and productive. Following are key features of the ideal agenda and subsequent meeting.

1. Agenda subjects should be broken into segments of no more
than 30–45 minutes, and schedules should be strictly followed.
Each segment's schedule allotment should include time for both
presentation by the presenter and interaction with the attendees.

2. The presentation portion of each meeting segment should
start with an executive summary that distills the subject into the
answers or conclusions reached by the presenter. Thus, executives
with multiple urgent demands can attend meetings during the brief
summaries and leave to do other things between them. If deviation
from schedule were routinely tolerated this would not be possible.
Incidentally, formal presentation should start on schedule, regardless of attendees arriving (or reentering the meeting following a
break) late. Since all meetings should be videotaped, the schedule
abusers will need to view the videotape on their own time at some
later time if they feel it necessary to see and hear the missed portion
of the meeting. After all, their own lack of schedule control caused
the problem.

3. Presentations should be primarily in visual form. Sketches
and meaningful, simple schematics are easiest to understand. Brief,
hard-hitting tables of information are also highly desirable. Many
presenters have a tendency to use business reports pages, consisting of thousands of numbers, as visuals. (The author calls these
terrible forms of visuals "universe on one page.") Word visuals are
the lowest-value presentation form, unless they contain key words
(never sentences) that succinctly describe the very essence of vitally
important messages.

4. Presenters (of each segment) should rigidly adhere to the
planned schedule, starting and completing on time.

5. Questions (except those vitally necessary to understanding
the subject) should be held until scheduled question-and-answer
sessions.

6. If the meeting leader permits more than a few questions or the
presenter's answers are too lengthy, a schedule overrun might occur. The most important order of business is (1) to surface attend-

ees' need for more detailed information and (2) to identify areas of concern, including alternative suggestions. It is highly unlikely that most presenters would be prepared to answer the queries efficiently and adequately. The best approach is to answer only those questions easily addressed within the scheduled time and to inventory all other questions. Unanswered questions should be the subject of a followup meeting, using formal presentation material to address all questions and issues in the most productive fashion, through effective visual presentation.

7. The meeting leader (not the presenter) must cut off questions, allowing time for the presenter to summarize the subject, status, and action plan. This involves:

a. Buyoff on the subject matter if there are no outstanding questions, issues, or concerns. (Buyoff does not always mean proceeding with implementation, but rather often means agreement to proceed with the next work phase. The most immediate steps of the next phase would be to answer open questions.)

b. Assignment of action responsibilities, if any, to anyone other than the presenter

c. Identification of attendees for the next meeting

Next to interpersonal skills, time management methodology is perhaps one of the most important executive productivity needs.[9] However, it bears repeating that executive development must be a lifetime process of education, training, and cross-training. A career, as Kotter wrote, must not be permitted to be "thought of as beginning with an educational program and then proceeding through a series of promotions and salary increases into bigger and better jobs." Rather, it should be "thought of as a continuous process in which people become equipped [with additional skills] to handle more and more difficult challenges."[10]

EMPLOYEE BENEFITS AND VALUE RECOGNITION

A bold new vision would be incomplete without provisions for enriching the life-styles of all of society's people, which means every stratum of public and private working people, including associ-

---

[9] For the reader interested in honing interpersonal skills, Bernstein and Rozen have written amusingly and informatively. Albert J. Bernstein and Sydney Craft Rozen, *Dinosaur Brains: Dealing with All Those Impossible People at Work* (New York: Wiley, 1989).

[10] Kotter, *Leadership Factor*, pp. 124–25.

ates.[11] Business and government have incredible opportunities to enrich the lives of everyone in society. They must value people, giving them the opportunity for rich, lifetime employment and personal value improvement by providing career-long education and training opportunities. For example, the scourge of the working man, unemployment, is an anachronism that should have no place in the world of rational thinkers! Every nation and every industrial business has mountains of work that cry out to be performed. The infrastructures of both developing and the most developed countries are never ideally maintained or developed. Thus, public works are *always* a vast source of jobs. Unfortunately, most politicians seem to be incapable of managing and eliminating unemployment through the simple expedient of efficiently diverting surplus labor, temporarily, into meaningful public works projects during periods of business downturn. It is easy to see that to do so would eliminate the ludicrous waste of nonproductive unemployment and welfare benefits, which drain the public coffers by paying people to be idle. Further, virtually any public work project involves construction, which in turn generates increased demand for materials and products of the companies that supply them. Thus, efficient use of otherwise idle people will not only give them gainful employment but also stimulate the economy by creating demand in industry.

Industry and labor unions have the potential for making great strides toward reducing unemployment far sooner than it is reasonable to expect the rascals in government to do so.[12] It is truly incredible that neither management nor labor has seen the inhumanity and inefficiency of a system that has three work alternatives: full-time employment, full-blast overtime work, and unemployment. Why, if unions are truly brotherhoods, should siblings condone throwing their brethren out of work when business slackens? One logical, humane way to adjust would be to share the

---

[11] While working with Sears, the author was first exposed to the term "associate," used by Sears (and other companies) to identify those working people who cannot be described as executives, managers, or supervisors. The author has long sought a term that would impart the proper degree of respect and dignity for working people other than those considered part of "management." Employee, worker, bottom-rung person, and many other terms do not adequately reflect the value of people who, after all, are potentially a business's most valuable asset. "Associate" is a term that seems to fit best.

[12] Unlike those who predict the demise of labor unions, the author sides with Drucker, because humans are fallible, and managers will not always automatically do what is right for their employees. Drucker writes, concerning the importance of countervailing power: "Modern society, a society of organizations each requiring strong management, needs an organ such as the labor union." Peter F. Drucker, *The Frontiers of Management: Where Tomorrow's Decisions Are Being Shaped Today* (New York: Harper & Row, 1986), p. 231.

reduced workload equitably by cutting a companies' workers' hours (and pay and benefits)[13] each day to the level of the work available. Unfortunately, human greed and potential financial disaster stand in the way of equal sharing of available work. Thus, even though most business slowdowns raise unemployment rates from a seemingly irreducible 2 percent, workers with seniority resist seeing their own paychecks reduced by the nationwide average of 8 percent that would be necessary to keep all people employed.[14] In the United States, where saving and credit purchase habits are abominable, cutbacks in pay would severely jeopardize the personal assets of large numbers of workers who commit every penny of earnings to credit payments and routine living expenses. However, the burden now falls most heavily on the associate least able to weather the downturn, the youngest employee likely to have the least savings and assets and highest amount of debt. Hence, to apportion available work fairly to all associates will require solving this dilemma.[15]

Another logical way to eradicate unemployment, long practiced in logistics companies, is to employ "part-time" people. Part-time does not need to mean either temporary or intermittent work. At SLS Sears, it means that the part-time worker is guaranteed a minimum of four hours a day and can expect to work full days and even overtime when workload peaks occur. When part-time workers enjoy circumstances in which the part-time work is preferable to full-time (high school and college students, farm operators, one of two earner-parents of small children, for example), they may be most able to absorb reductions of work hours during downturn periods. The author believes there are far fewer part-time jobs offered (although many should be made available) than there are

[13] During periods of business downturn, the author especially advocates slashing the pay and benefits of all executives, including those who receive obscenely large remuneration. In the recent past, they have shown excessive, deplorable greed in continuing and even increasing their rewards at the same time that their employees are swelling the ranks of the unemployed.
[14] The Japanese manage unemployment as well as anyone but have so far been unable to reduce it much below the 2 percent level.
[15] It is helpful to keep the nationwide benefits of eliminating unemployment in mind. One such benefit would be the drastic reduction of unemployment taxes and welfare payments. Even if tax money were used to compensate associates for reduced hours, the *total* costs to society would be less, because every person would continue to earn roughly the same amount during a business downturn and thus would be much less likely to lose a home and personal property as a result of being unable to pay bills. Better still, since the workforce would continue to earn as much as always, it would have money to spend. Recessions would not feed on themselves by reducing the population's disposable income.

potential part-time employees. Therefore, progressive companies will be more readily able to adopt the use of part-timers than might be suspected. However, business and government must learn to value every person's work contribution and to foster a lifetime enhancement of that value, through career-long education and training.

In a society that would logically place equal, universal value on every type of labor, regardless of the task performed, great gulfs should not separate the wages of the highest-paid and lowest-paid workers. The rationale for paying different wages for different types of work, after all, stems from the fact that some jobs are more complex than others and require longer periods of education and on-the-job training.[16] Businessmen and government officials must recognize and capitalize on the need for and benefits of eradicating job discrimination.[17] People and the jobs they perform can be value-enhanced by improving the design of the job, by increasing the number of jobs the individual is trained to perform, and by continuous education and training designed to increase job-related and personal skills and knowledge. Increasing the value of jobs and of personnel promises to narrow the wide range of rewards for various jobs and the snobbish discrimination associated with jobs of lesser glamour.

INTERNATIONAL SOCIAL, ECONOMIC, AND POLITICAL VISIONS

The battlefield for companies vying for supremacy in distribution and production operations is not bounded by the narrow limits of industry parameters or company operations. The final destiny of these companies, their customers, their countries, and, indeed, the world's population hinges on developments in international economics and world politics. The dog-eat-dog characteristics of current world trade must not be permitted to reign supreme in future generations. Every nation's industries can and should be developed

---

[16] The author *does* believe in the need for career progression rewards for those who climb the ladder of success into more stressful management positions, and for professionals requiring exceptional levels of preparatory education.

[17] Job discrimination, here, is intended to mean the subtle and not-so-subtle discrimination associated with the erroneous belief that people in "lower-level" jobs are inherently inferior to those in more prestigious positions. The first of two reasons this does not make sense is that the process of lifetime education and training can be of universal value, greatly expanding the number of individuals equipped to climb the promotion ladder or to work on jobs of greatly expanded value. Second, one needs only contemplate life without the workers who perform life's more distasteful, boring jobs to appreciate their true value.

to the point of national (or regional) self-sufficiency while using the most efficient methods and technology available to the world community. The author's honored colleague, Leroy Peterson, has counseled the author to present his views concerning government, politics, and economics as advice from a businessman to government leaders, especially in light of the fact that the author is neither a politician nor an economist. However, it is highly unlikely that any theory the author might espouse could possibly be any more damaging to our businesses and taxpayers than most government social and economic initiatives of the last several decades.

The author's complete visions will come to pass only if the performance of national and international governments is improved. He fervently believes that business people are among the best equipped to bring logic to the process of government. It is crystal clear that career politicians are not trained and experienced in managing a businesslike, balanced approach to supporting the economic interests of society.[18] Collectively, businesses are one entity with the altruistic values, the constituency (owners and employees), and the action-oriented knowhow needed to work for the common good. However, since the top candidates for the new roles are those least wanting to take them, their companies need to give them incentive and support. They should tailor executive workloads and leaves of absence (with supplementary pay to compensate for lower government salary) that will enable them to serve either part time or for a limited number of terms. The author hopes that most executives will see how vital it will be for business to do its part to bring sanity to global government as part of the ongoing business strategy.

EXECUTIVE CHECKLIST: SELECTED ZINGERS

The following checklist summarizes the author's key visions related to international fair trade practices and restoration of industries destroyed by free trade.

1. "Fair trade" will be established—once and for all putting to rest fantasies about "free trade." This will drastically alter the flow of exports and imports and enable *every* country to have a vibrant, vital industrial base.

---

[18] The author has semifacetiously said that, upon his retirement from business, he will found a new party. The new "Throw the Rascals Out Party" will give its support to the opponents of *any* incumbent politician. It has been a source of constant amazement, considering the incredibly inept performance of almost all governing politicians, that they are perpetually reelected.

2. Until no longer required, wage and benefit equalization duties imposed on low-wage countries will encourage their companies to increase their wages and benefits to avoid paying the same amount in tariff. This will infuse the local economy with a healthy consumer wealth, decreasing the need to export by increasing domestic demand. (Developing nations would temporarily be given enough allowance to make their necessary exports competitive).
3. New and revitalized apprentice programs and tax credits will be fundamental to restoring destroyed industries and revitalizing those damaged by free but unfair competition.

FAIR TRADE VERSUS FREE TRADE

In the shortest term, exports and imports of manufactured products and components will account for a large percentage of goods traveling through the logistics network. Therefore, the complications of long lead times, difficult communications, and excessive transportation costs will persist. However, in the long term, and perhaps much sooner than many might expect, the irrational export and import of manufactured products can be expected to come to a halt. The author has seen hundreds of proofs that given comparable production and distribution facilities, the people of any country can be just as productive as citizens of an industrialized nation.[19] Therefore, the only difference in major costs (as opposed to *productivity*) should be those of prevailing employee compensation and transportation to market. Obviously, once compensation in all countries is equalized in real terms (living standard) it will no longer make sense for import customers to pay the higher prices attributable to transportation from other countries, especially those from overseas. The author has no doubt that radical changes will come, but is not so confident about predicting when they will come. However, the changes are likely to come much sooner than anticipated. Therefore, companies would be unwise to base their long-term logistics vision and consequent shorter-term strategy on an assumption of perpetual expansion or even continuation of international trade in manufactured products and components.

Today's world of trade is totally irrational in that it fails to enrich

---

[19] It is easier to be highly productive in the factory than in disciplines where professional education and career experience are vital. Developing nations will be hard pressed to engineer products and processes equal to those designed in the highly industrialized countries. Therefore, these nations' fledgling industries will need to emphasize partnerships and license agreements with companies in advanced nations.

the lives of the world's populations. "Fair trade," not "free trade," is the author's prescription. Today's "free trade" is causing imports from countries with low living standards to lower the standards of those that are more industrialized while placing the burden of financing industrial and infrastructure development on the backs of their own poor people. Mankind has the intelligence to see the folly of massive trade imbalances and to solve the problems of regional poverty. International trade has never been free and must never be allowed to become free. International trade *law* does make sense. To prevent greedy companies and countries from destroying other countries' industries the world needs new "fair trade" rules of law that help developing nations to industrialize and developed nations to retain their hard-won life-styles.[20]

In the author's vision of the future, manufactured imports to any country or regional confederation of small countries will be impermissible unless the wages and benefits of the exporting companies and their suppliers are roughly comparable to the standard of living of the import country. The only healthy national economy is one driven by wealth-generating manufacturing.[21] Import duties must be imposed on companies in low-living-standard countries to bring their product prices up to the level of fair competition in the importing country.[22] Such universal, logical trade restrictions will drive money out of the pockets of a few exploiters in the developing countries and into those of their labor force. After all, for the exploiting company it will make more sense to increase workers' wages (thus, job satisfaction and motivation) than to burden their products with an import duty cost equal to the payroll increase. This will create internal wealth for the masses and will lead to the

---

[20] The author is not alone in holding these views. Drucker writes: "The trend toward *reciprocity as a central principle of international economic integration* has by now become well nigh irreversible.... Reciprocity can easily degenerate into protectionism of the worst kind. But it could be fashioned into a powerful tool to expand trade and investment, if—but only if—governments and businessmen act with imagination and courage." Peter F. Drucker, *Managing for the Future: The 1990s and Beyond* (New York: Truman Talley/Dutton, 1992), pp. 15–16. Emphasis in original.

[21] Drucker expressed his opinion succinctly: "[M]anufacturing is the integrator that ties everything together. It creates the economic value that pays for everything and everybody." *Ibid.*, p. 316.

[22] The author discusses standard of living rather than pay and benefits because monetary exchange rates make the latter unfit for use in determining if equalizing duties should be used. Many governments and their banks control their currencies' exchange rates at unrealistic levels compared to their purchasing power. Therefore, comparison of wages between countries does not reflect the real value of the wages. For example, recent comparisons of average labor cost in the United States versus Japan and some European countries have found that the foreign workers earn more. However, the workers' cost of living, for a standard of life comparable to the United States, is astronomically higher.

development of a vast new market: the exporting countries' own populations.

Nor do developing nations need to fear that there is no place in the sun for them. When they ask how they can develop a substantial industrial base, the answer is simply that they should study the Japanese. At the end of World War II, Japan lay in ruins. It was truly an undeveloped nation. It rebuilt its industrial strength through restrictions on imports and local ownership rules. Japan is not alone in this regard. Virtually every recently industrialized nation has done the same. Unfortunately, the industrial rebirth of Japan was borne on the backs of its people. Earnings were plowed back into products and facilities while a share in the fruits of their labors was slow in coming to the people who made it possible. Even today, Japan's living standards are far below those of most other industrialized nations—a vital necessity in terms of enabling Japanese companies to compete internationally. Were the people able to enjoy the same comforts known to the Western world, the international trade playing field would tilt in favor of others. Japanese companies would find it almost impossible to overcome the costly burden of transporting products and virtually all materials and energy across the wide oceans separating them from their customers and sources. Superb businessmen with accurate visions of the future, the Japanese are now rapidly building production facilities all around the globe. When the inevitable day arrives when "fair trade" practices make them unable to compete with local companies, those local companies will be theirs. Thus, at least the profits of these companies will be Japanese.

The United States has a long history of penetrating overseas markets by building or acquiring local factories and designing and manufacturing products in those plants that are suited to the local market. Automotive manufacturers, especially, helped many developing nations start to develop an industrial base by establishing not only local plants but also local networks of component suppliers. (The author is not sure how much of this was due to laws discouraging or prohibiting imports and imposing stiff duties but believes that high transport costs were a strong factor in persuading companies to produce locally). Companies in the United States are no less greedy than their Japanese and European counterparts, but they lack the nationalistic fervor that has served the Japanese so well. The U.S. government and producers have not adequately fought for the country's interest and, as a result, have permitted some key industries to be destroyed. The author does not in the least doubt that these industries had become lax and thus less productive than they should have been. Nevertheless, they could never have done enough to level the playing field without the full cooperation of the government and the necessary "fair trade" laws. Business and government have both had too limited a vision either to foresee the outcome or to recognize and undertake the changes necessary to reestablish the industries that have been destroyed and revitalize those in peril.

Necessity, the mother of all invention, will eventually dictate that these international trade problems be resolved. Industry movers and shakers in retail, distribution, and production, collectively, are the heads of the organizations that are probably the only force capable of launching the campaign for rational international trade laws. These laws must have the following fundamental objectives:

1. Every manufactured product and component sold in any country (or regional group of small countries with common currencies and economic unions) must be produced in that country (or regional group).
2. Countries with raw materials, energy resources, and agricultural products unavailable in other countries must maintain price levels designed to balance trade with customer countries.
3. Businesses in every country should be owned and controlled by citizens of that country. This should not exclude minority ownership by citizens and companies of other nations, especially in the transition period during which countries are developing their own industries.
4. Joint venture businesses (with majority local ownership) must originally establish assembly facilities and thereafter "nationalize" components and materials with all due speed.
5. During the transition years (on the way to full "fair trade" practices), in order to finance initial industrial development, developing nations must be permitted to have a slight advantage over competitors in wealthier countries. This should be accomplished by requiring that they and all their local suppliers pay all employees a rate comparable to a standard of living only slightly below that of the importing country. The difference would compensate for higher transportation costs. Companies not paying their employees fair wages should face equalizing tariffs that would quickly teach them the advantages of increasing standards of living for their workers instead of putting money in the coffers of foreign customer country governments.

AN ALTERNATIVE VISION (OR NIGHTMARE?)

Simple economics demands that every nation be able to generate tangible assets in order to achieve and maintain a reasonable standard of living.[23] The author disagrees with those who predict an era in which virtually all of a nation's workforce will be employed in service industries. The service industries do *not* generate tangible wealth. They are dependent on the fairly large percentage of the population that generates tangible wealth that provides the wherewithal to purchase the services rendered. Therefore, it is impossible to imagine a nation of service industries that exist only to serve the population employed by other service industries. Nor is it in any way conceivable that any nation will be capable of providing massive services for other nations as a way to acquire wealth and to maintain a standard of living equal to other nations'. Why should any nation import its services, at the cost of increasing its own unemployment and thus lowering its own standard of living? If a country's tangible wealth-generating industries decline, the inevitable result is degeneration of the nation's living standard. This phenomenon has been occurring in the United States in the closing decades of the twentieth century, as manufacturing jobs have been sacrificed on the pagan altar of "free trade."

Nor is focus on "high technology" a practical survival strategy. Although highly touted as the emerging industry of the future, it just is not so. The world will probably always need myriad products of comparatively low-technology design and process. Further, as Drucker has written, "High technology is tremendously important: as vision setter, pace setter, excitement maker, maker of the future. But as a maker of the present it is still almost marginal, accounting for no more than 10 percent of the jobs created in the past ten years. And it is reasonably certain that its job-creation rate won't increase significantly until after 1990."[24]

Tangible products fall into a limited number of categories. They

[23] Akio Morita, chairman and chief executive officer of Sony Corporation, writes: "Among the so-called 'advanced nations' of the world, any country with a strong economy possesses a dynamic manufacturing base. This is because all other industries such as service and finance are in some way dependent on the features unique to manufacturing: value added products, a large workforce, and a related network of support companies. Simply put, manufacturing is the base of the economy—any economy." Akio Morito, "Manufacturing: The Real Base of the Economy Is Subject to Erosive Tendencies," in *The World Competitiveness Report 1991* (Lausanne, Switzerland: IMD, June 1991), p. 186.

[24] Peter F. Drucker, *The Frontiers of Management: Where Tomorrow's Decisions Are Being Shaped Today* (New York, Harper & Row, 1986), p. 51.

are (1) mining and initial conversion of raw materials and fuels; (2) planting, harvesting, and initial conversion of agricultural and forestry products; (3) construction; (4) manufacturing of finished products; and (5) creation of products of the mind (books, films, works of art, etc.). The only products in the above list that a country should logically want to export are those which are replenishable. For a country to sell its nonreplenishable raw assets in exchange for other countries' labor is simply not logical for the long term, unless the country has no other wealth with which to procure the necessities of life. To do so will ultimately deplete the exporting nation's wealth, hastening the arrival of the day when the resources will be exhausted. Several oil-producing nations are in the unenviable position of having no other resources. Their recent strategy has been to extract such high prices from customer nations that their populace can have extremely high standards of living. At the same time, earnings have been massively invested in nations with bounties of replenishable wealth, especially in countries with agricultural surplus. Their ultimate goals are, first, to avoid bringing the wrath of the rest of the world down upon them, in the form of a war in retaliation for exorbitant prices (most wars have been based on economic envy and greedy craving to acquire free access to other nations' assets) and, second, to acquire such a great foreign investment as to be able to live off the investments indefinitely when the oil stops flowing. Of course, history has shown that this will never come to pass. Populous nations of industrious workers have never long tolerated financing the idle rich of other nations. Eventually they will overthrow the yoke of economic oppression either through war or through repatriation of the foreign-owned assets.

Incidentally, while debating the relative merits of company-owned fleets versus contract carriers recently, a colleague cited a recent trend that would make it difficult (if not impossible) for producer companies to achieve the same percentage of backhaul loads from the Eastern to the Western United States as the common carriers' imports from the Far East. While my colleague's argument overlooks the fact that the best producer companies could also negotiate agreements with the Japanese and others, the author believes there is a more important point. My colleague's opinion was that the volume of imports would continue to increase and would be the prevalent condition of the twenty-first century. The author holds an entirely different view: that no country can permit itself to become solely an exporter of raw materials and agricultural products and an importer of every conceivable manufactured product. On the contrary, the wisest governments restrict exports of raw materials, preferring to ship products made from them. The United States' lumber industry is currently making massive shipments of logs to the Orient and buying them back as a component of finished products. As a result of high export demand, lumber prices have soared; large future timber shortages have become a scary probability; and jobs involving the use of wood have been lost. Were the United States to ban shipment of raw logs, requiring customers to buy plywood and lumber instead, it would contribute substantially to the reduction of the balance of trade deficit and would put armies of unemployed people back to work. The destiny of the United States will not be to become a second- or third-rate power, exporting only agricultural products and raw material. Neither the United States nor any other country can permit countries with low-cost labor or unfair trade practices to drag its standard of living down (although this is *exactly* what has been happening to the United States). It cannot take forever for politicians and businessmen in the United States to wake up to these simple truths (truths that have molded the trade restrictions imposed by most other countries) and to take corrective action. When this happens, an explosion of growth will occur, as the United States rebuilds its manufacturing industry.

PREDICTIONS

That many foreign countries work in harmony (and efficiently) with their governments to ensure international competitiveness and even market dominance is clear. Equally clear is the fact that those countries see the U.S. government as incredibly naïve in this matter, ignoring or working against the survival of its own country's manufacturing strength. In the face of a global explosion of competition from newly developing nations all around the globe, the United States can ill afford to drag its standard of living down to the pitiful wage scales of the newest cheap-labor factories. However, as more and more manufacturing jobs are lost in vanishing industries, the lowering of average income is becoming ever more apparent. Survival of the nation as we know it depends on government's taking the lead in supporting industry in its fight for survival and in the revival of dead and dying industry segments. Several government programs are necessary to achieve this goal.

The first government program will be one to fund and otherwise support new "apprentice" programs to expand radically the number of people trained and working in the fields of warehousing;

storage and retrieval systems; machine, tool, and die design; and manufacturing. The most effective way to do so will be to grant tax credits to private companies and to educational and technical training schools that provide such training. Use of tax credits will rapidly heat up tax revenues, since their use will revitalize and restore industry, increase the volume of its sales, decrease imports, create new jobs, and increase the need for components and materials supplied by other companies.

Second, the government must awaken to the fact that factories being constructed in the United States by foreign companies are offered huge benefits and tax concessions by low-labor-cost states competing for the new factories and by the foreign companies' own governments and cooperating banks. Thus American manufacturers located in areas with higher labor costs and traditions of union–company adversarial relationships, and dedicated to maintaining jobs in these areas, are competing on a playing field sloped to the advantage of the newcomer whose borrowing, land, and labor force training are underwritten by local government. Obviously, leveling the field without continuing the drain of jobs from the old industrial centers and lowering the wage scales and benefits for those types of jobs requires that government at both state and federal levels more aggressively subsidize domestic industry, primarily through tax credits. American companies must and will wake up to the potential for an explosive revitalization through government help rather than government indifference and hindrance and will mount a massive campaign to alert voters and politicians to the huge benefits of nonbureaucratic government support. The end result will be a victory for workers, industry, and consumers.

Third, the American industries that have already been destroyed must be rebuilt, starting with consumer and defense electronics. Since it will continue to be impossible to compete with countries where wages are a pittance and such benefits as retirement and medical programs are virtually nonexistent, imports from such areas must be assessed import duties equivalent to bringing their product costs up to the level of reasonable wages and fringe benefits. This should be viewed as a benefit to the countries where the goods manufactured are out of the reach of all except the elite. If these export-oriented foreign companies have the option of paying decent wages or duties, they will find it much more logical to increase the worker benefits. Thus the workers in their factories will be able to afford the products they manufacture and those of other factories producing for export. The result would be to increase the countries' internal demands to the point where exporting labor and material resources to wealthier countries would no longer be necessary. In addition, reentry of American companies into industrial production of such products as cameras, bicycles, and consumer electronics will require massive new investment by companies that do not have the capital or access to low-cost borrowing in the amounts required. This requires establishment of a quasi-governmental industry reconstruction bank, to which funds would be made available from field-leveling special duties on products enjoying the benefits of having destroyed or decimated American production capacity. The massive infusion of capital to support domestic industry is the only way in which economic viability can and will be restored.

Fourth, superior personnel performance and productivity are vital to effective competition. Traditional education and training techniques, alone, are not enough to keep abreast with managing new technology, systems, and employees who are at various stages of proficiency. Andersen Consulting's Integrated Performance Support,™ a futuristic architecture, is beginning to be the structure that will integrate training, education, and skilled worker systems. The new computer will use the hands-on, actual system to simulate real-world operations as *the* primary learning tool. Other system operating features will routinely guide individuals through a network of job tasks according to their need for assistance based on their skill levels. Using artificial intelligence, the system will also tailor the assistance provided to match the unique problem being addressed. Thus, computer-based tasks (which means virtually *all* knowledge and data intensive work) that integrate skill development and systematic supervision and guidance with the routine system operation will reduce or eliminate the use of classroom instruction. Mountainous piles of written instructions that are almost impossible to understand, let alone memorize, will no longer be created. Reliance on supervision to continuously monitor and upgrade their employee's skills, on-the-job will no longer be required. Future personnel management and supervision of knowledge workers will therefore involve much less interaction as a routine part of ongoing operations. This will free the time of supervisors and managers for the more important task of continuous improvement of the business process, customer service, quality, and performance.

SUMMARY

Although companies' production and distribution logistics methods, systems, and equipment require major overhaul in the short term, the most revolutionary benefits to mankind will come by increasing people's labor value and by better coordination of government, industry, and labor on an international scale. Mover-shaker executives need to involve their companies in the quest to achieve both ends.

CHAPTER 9

Conclusion

World market dominance of some products has been achieved by some European and Asian manufacturers via certain specific, concrete characteristics of their logistics operations, processes, and products that differentiate them from competitors in other countries. As the keys to success are now widely recognized, so too are the actions our industries need to emulate.

First and foremost, survival through the next decade requires control of the massive bureaucracy of medium and large companies. The best way to do so is to reduce drastically the bureaucracy's numbers, moving as many of the remaining players as practical into smaller, more manageable warehouses within the large warehouse. The small business-within-a-business concept is one of the management organization principles that helped make the Japanese successful. The managers and work teams in new, small "focused warehouses" need to be empowered with the authority necessary to improve *continuously* everything that successful operation requires and also need to be made responsible for results.

Second, the sheer number of warehouse, machine, and tool and die designers and mechanics employed by most European and Japanese giants is dramatically higher than in counterpart industries in the United States. If industry permits the number of such specialists to continue to decline, our ability to compete will plummet

327

accordingly. American industry is not backed by either public or private technical education and training in these necessary design and mechanical skills. Further, aggressive apprenticeship programs have virtually disappeared. As the author discussed in his previous book, *Reinventing the Factory II: Managing the World Class Factory*, it is of the utmost importance that industry launch massive new programs to hire, educate, and train people in the science of designing and producing warehouses, conveyance systems, storage and retrieval systems, and custom machines and tools—to an extent unparalleled by its competitors. If the quality and quantity output of machining systems is to be noticeably superior to that of opponents, warehouse systems like factory machines (not "flexible machine centers") should be tailored to specific products, not the standard systems and machines available to every competitor. Nor is it acceptable that the machines and equipment be high technology for technology's sake. American industry must learn how to lower drastically the cost of its warehouses, storage and retrieval systems, and machines and tooling by trimming the unnecessary bells and whistles, concentrating on machines suitable for specific purposes, and forgetting the elusive goal of universal flexibility.

Third, it's time we wake up to the difference between quality and value. Most of this country's companies are working to improve the *quality* of their service and products, when what they really need is to focus on *value*. Value, simply stated, is the customer's perception of a product's worth vis-à-vis its price. In Japan department stores are filled with far more European products than products from the United States. The reason is clear to the perceptive consumer, who notices a distinct difference between these European products and the American-made products commonly found in department stores in the United States. While the prices of the European products are usually noticeably higher, the value is almost always markedly superior. This is primarily due to the use of higher-value materials and components in their manufacture. In other words *value*, not just *quality*, has been designed into the product. American consumers in the past were all too willing to purchase very low-cost products of limited value, a blessing(?) of mass production. Further, low-cost mass production of reasonably durable goods is still and will continue to be vitally important to low-income households, as long as they are a significant segment of the population. For decades, *all* consumers, not only those of low income, have focused on low cost to the exclusion of value and its all-important components: performance and durability. The time for American producers to realize that consumers have awakened and have started to appreciate value is long overdue. They must intensify their efforts to design value into their products, logistics, and processes. Practicing statistical control is no longer an acceptable approach to achieving defect-free, high-value delivery to the customer. Whether producing low-value or high-value goods, the production process and logistics network must be designed to produce and deliver perfect quality. Incredible inventions are standing in the wings, awaiting the discovery that will inevitably follow the formation of a vision. Distribution, logistics, and production executives must rise to the challenge. The Yankee Clippers of the nineteenth century spread the fame of the new North American industrialists around the globe with their unprecedented speedy, low-cost delivery. The Yankee *clusters* of producers, warehouses, and customers can once again show the world the way to extraordinary delivery service at unparalleled low cost. Let us begin.

APPENDIX 1

The Achievers

This list includes benefits achieved by a few of Andersen Consulting's more than one thousand clients who have implemented many of the superior warehouse, storeroom, and distribution hardware, systems, and management techniques described in this book. The achievers appendix in previous books[1] listed more than two hundred manufacturing clients, many of whom have implemented these same types of changes in their storerooms and warehouses. An Andersen Consulting person to contact and his office are shown in parentheses for the convenience of the reader desiring more information.

WAREHOUSE, STOREROOM, AND DISTRIBUTION ACHIEVERS

- Altos Hornos De Vizcaya, S.A.: Lesaca/Arratzubi Plant, Lesaca, Spain. Steel strips and coils. (Juan Illana, Bilbao, Spain). Customer service lead time reduction, made to order, 45%; standard strip, 75%. Inventory investment reduction, 30%.
- Altos Hornos De Vizcaya, S.A.: Lesaca/Zalain Plant, Vera De Bidasoa, Spain. Pipes and tubes. (Juan Illana, Bilbao, Spain). Customer service lead time reduction, 65%. Inventory investment reduction, 10%.
- COFAP CIA Fabricadora De Pecas: distribution center, Santo Andre, Sao Paulo, Brazil. Shock absorbers. (Aloysio Pontes,

[1] Roy L. Harmon and Leroy D. Peterson, *Reinventing the Factory: Productivity Breakthroughs in Manufacturing Today* (New York: Free Press,1990), and Roy L. Harmon, *Reinventing the Factory II: Managing the World Class Factory* (New York, Free Press, 1992).

Rio De Janeiro). Customer service lead time reduction, 50%. Space savings: warehouse/stores, 50%; receiving, packaging, shipping, 50%. Damaged or error returns reduction, 15%. Capacity increase, 93%. Payback period, 6 months.

- Epson Australia Limited: all divisions, Sydney, Australia. Personal computers and printers. (Anthony N. Holman, Sydney). Customer service lead time reduction, 66%. Space savings: warehouse/stores, 50%; office, 15%. Labor savings: warehouse, 43%; receiving, packaging, and shipping, 43%; office, 43%. Inventory investment reduction, 66%. Operating cost savings: per receipt, 25%; per stocking, 25%; per shipment/issue, 25%. Data processing cost savings per order item, 25%. Inventory inaccuracy reduction, 66%. Damaged or error returns reduction, 75%.

- IBM: Martinez plant, Argentina. Printers and tape drives. (David Stilerman, Buenos Aires, Argentina and Abel R. Evelson, Madrid, Spain). Material receipt and issue lead time, 75%.

- Metro Drug Corporation: distribution division, Manila, Philippines. Pharmaceuticals and consumer products. (Alfonso A. Aliga, Jr., Manila). Customer service lead time reduction, 66%. Labor savings: warehouse, 20%; receiving, packaging, and shipping, 20%.

- P.T. Tunggal Agathis Indah Wood Industries: Sidangoli division, Sidangoli, Indonesia. Logs. (S. Adhiwidjaja, Jakarta, Indonesia). Inventory Investment, 34%. Product cost, 20%.

- Sevel Argentina, S.A., Buenos Aires. Fiat and Peugot automobiles; Chevrolet pickup trucks. (David E. Stilerman, Buenos Aires). Space savings: warehouse-stores, 28% through compression, 15% through inventory reduction. Labor savings, 26% to date, 5–10% more anticipated when vendor program (containers and kanban) are fully implemented.

- VME Excavators AB, Eslov, Sweden. Excavator components and raw materials. (Carl A. Lilljeqvist, Stockholm, Sweden). Labor savings: warehouse, receiving, packaging and shipping, and office, 30%. Inventory investment reduction, 56%.

WAREHOUSE, STOREROOM, AND DISTRIBUTION PROJECTS IN PROCESS

As this book neared completion, a large number of Andersen Consulting's clients had warehouse and distribution projects in process but had not yet implemented all the changes designed. The following are a few of those companies and the benefits they expect to achieve.

- Alparagatas S.A.I.C., Buenos Aires, Argentina. Sport and informal shoes. (Carlos O. Schmidt, Buenos Aires). Transportation cost, 15%.
- Entertainment UK, Hayes, Middy, United Kingdom. Entertainment software: Compact disks, tapes, records, computer games, and prerecorded videos. (Tom Barry, London). Labor savings, 26%. Inventory investment reduction, 31%. Operating cost savings per transaction 19%. Damaged or error returns reduction, 26%.
- Grupo Hipervalme, S.A.: supermarket chain central warehouse (PCR), Seville, Spain. Food and other consumer products. (Javier del Barrio, Seville, Spain). Customer service lead time reduction, 50%. Inventory investment reduction, 25%. Operating cost savings per receipt, stocking, and shipment, 45%. Inventory record inaccuracy reduction, 70%. Damaged or error returns reduction, 100%.
- Harnischfeger Industries: Harnishfeger Corporation, Milwaukee, WI. Service parts, mining, and material handling equipment. (Chris Coleman, Milwaukee, WI). Customer service lead time reduction, 15%. Inventory investment reduction, 20%. Inventory inaccuracy reduction, 5%.
- Hernandez Perez Hnos, S.A.: Alguazas plant, Murcia, Spain. Canned vegetables, fruit juice, jams, and ready-to-serve dishes. (Asensio Asencio, Valencia, Spain). Customer service lead time reduction, 80%. Space savings: warehouse and stores, receiving, packaging, shipping, 50%. Labor savings: warehouse, receiving, and packaging and shipping, 37%. Inventory investment reduction, 30%. Operating cost savings per receipt, 30%; per stocking, 30%; per shipment/issue, 40%.
- La Cruz Del Campo, S.A. (Guiness Group): brewery plant, Seville, Spain. Packaging, labels, bottles, plastic film. (Javier del Barrio, Seville, Spain). Space savings, warehouse and stores, receiving, and shipping, 45%. Inventory investment reduction, 50%. Inventory record inaccuracy reduction, 75%. Damaged or error returns reduction, 100%.
- Mesquita S.A. Transportes: Alemoa/Guaruja plant, Santos, Brazil. Warehousing and distribution company. (Claudio Della Penna, Sao Paulo, Brazil). Customer service lead time reduction, 33%. Space savings: warehouse and stores, 40%;

receiving, packaging, and shipping, 40%; office, 20%. Inventory investment reduction, 10%. Operating cost savings: per receipt, 10%; per stocking, 10%; per shipment/issue, 10%. Inventory inaccuracy reduction, 60%. Damaged or error returns reduction, 50%.

NEW MANUFACTURING ACHIEVERS

This book focuses on warehouse, storeroom, and distribution topics, so the primary "Achievers" objective is to highlight success stories in that realm. However, some manufacturers may wish to see that the factories of the world are still taking important steps to move to superior manufacturing status. Following are some of the manufacturing companies joining the honor roll of achievers since the author's last book.

- Alpargatas S.A.I.C., Buenos Aires, Argentina. Textiles and dyed indigo fabrics. (Ricardo J. Backer, Buenos Aires). Labor, 20%.
- Bricard: Vimeu plant, Friville Escarbotin, France. Door locks. (Benoit Genuini, Paris, France). Manufacturing lead-time reduction, 70%. Space reduction: Machining, 30%; Storage, 30%. Inventory investment: Work in process, 60%; Finished goods, 40%. Machine downtime, 50%. Payback period, 5 months.
- Forjas Taurus S.A.: Porto Alegre plant, Porto Alegre, Brazil. Revolvers. (Rafi Tchinnosian, Sao Paulo, Brazil). Manufacturing lead-time reduction, 85%. Space reduction, machining, 20%. Labor savings, direct, 27%. Setup/changeover cost, 78%. Inventory investment, work in process, 73%. Machine downtime, 60%. Quality defects, 62%. Payback period, 16 months.
- Olin Corporation: Winchester division, East Alton, Illinois. Shell cases, bullets, loaded rounds. (Thomas E. Arenberg, Milwaukee, WI). Manufacturing lead-time reduction, 96%. Inventory investment: work in process, 96%; finished goods, 99%. Quality defects, 79%.
- Piaggio Suppliers, Pisa, Italy. Scooter components. (Raimondo Beltramo, Turin, Italy). Manufacturing lead-time reduction, 30%. Space reduction, storage, 30%. Labor savings: direct, 10%; indirect, 25%. Setup/changeover cost, 50%. Inventory investment, work in process, 30%. Quality defects, 50%. Payback period, 3 months.
- Pope & Talbot, Inc.: Consumer Products division, Newman,

Georgia. Infant and adult disposable diapers/incontinence products. (Robert L. Edwards, Portland, OR). Labor savings, direct, 40%. Setup/changeover cost, 65%.

- Taurus Ferramentas Ltda., Sao Leopoldo, RS, Brazil. Forged hardware, tools, and revolver and pistol parts. (Rafi Tchinnosian, Sao Paulo, Brazil. Manufacturing lead-time reduction, 75%. Space reduction total, 22%. Labor savings: direct, 8%; indirect, 25%. Setup/changeover cost, 78%, average. Inventory investment, total, including finished goods, 70%. Machine downtime, 73%. Quality defects, 85%. Payback period, 12 months.

As this book neared completion, a large number of Andersen Consulting's clients had factory projects in process but had not yet implemented all of the changes designed. The following are some of those companies.

- Columbus/Metal Plastic, Pisa, Italy. Plastic parts for motor scooters. (Raimondo Beltramo, Turin). Manufacturing lead-time reduction, 50%. Space reduction, storage, 30%. Labor savings, indirect, 30%. Setup/changeover cost, 60%. Inventory investment, work in process, 30%. Quality defects, 30%.
- Hernandez Perez Hnos, S.A.: Alguazas plant, Murcia, Spain. Canned vegetables, fruit juice, jams, and ready-to-serve dishes. (Asensio Asencio, Valencia, Spain). Manufacturing lead-time reduction, 80%. Space reduction: Machining and assembly, 40%; Storage, 50%. Labor savings, direct and indirect, 20%. Setup/changeover cost, 35%. Inventory investment: materials, 50%; finished goods, 40%. Machine downtime, 50%. Quality defects, 70%. Payback period, 12 months.
- VME Excavators AB: assembly, Eslov, Sweden. Excavators. (Carl A. Lilljeqvist, Stockhholm, Sweden). Manufacturing lead-time reduction, 61%. Labor savings: direct, 10%; indirect, 31%. Inventory investment, work in process, 60%. Quality defects, 17%. Payback period, 24 months.
- VME Excavators AB: chassis, Eslov, Sweden. Excavator chassis. (Carl A. Lilljeqvist, Stockholm. Sweden). Manufacturing lead-time reduction, 55%. Labor savings: direct, 10%; indirect and office, 35%. Setup/changeover cost, 60%. Inventory investment, work in process, 55%. Lift trucks, 65%. Payback period, 4 months.

APPENDIX 2

Footnote References to the Author's Previous Books

Reinventing the Factory:
Productivity Breakthroughs in Manufacturing Today
by Roy L. Harmon and Leroy D. Peterson

and

Reinventing the Factory II:
Managing the World Class Factory
by Roy L Harmon
Foreword by Leroy D. Peterson

The author's previous books are frequently footnoted sources of definitions and background information for the subject matter covered in *this* book. To help minimize the clutter that numerous footnote references to the one source would cause, this appendix was developed. Footnotes in the book, referencing *Reinventing the Factory* or *Reinventing the Factory II*, will direct the reader to this appendix. Readers interested in selected chapters of this book may wish first to read the portions of the prior books in which important background material can be found. This appendix is organized to facilitate such use. The duplication in this appendix is intentional, intended to be of help to those electing to read only selected chapters, based on their job responsibilities or interests.

Chapter/ *Footnote*	*Subject & Reinventing the Factory I or II reference*
1/8	Multiplant clusters. II, pp. 31–35.
1/9	Setup reduction. I, Chapter 7.
1/10	Strategies and tactics. II, pp. 48–54, Chapter 2.
1/17	Lead time compression. I, pp. 262–65. II, pp. 326–27.
1/20	Vendor program. I, pp. 257–65. II, Chapter 4.
1/27	Quality versus value. II, Chapter 6.
2/3	Focused factories and economies of scale. I, Chapter 2 and p. 259. II, pp. 35–36, 124, 329–31.
2/4	Setup reduction. I, Chapter 7.
2/5	General Motors shuttle run to suppliers. I, pp. 263–65.
2/8	Supplier clusters. II, pp. 31–42.
2/12	Side-loading trucks. II, pp. 132–33.
2/16	Container design. I, pp. 73–79, 151–54.
2/17	Total supplier and user inventory. II, pp. 38–42, 117–20.
2/26	Equity ownership of supplier. II, pp. 46, 112–13.
2/35	Project organization and administration methodology. I, pp. 249–50.
3/7	Product line simplification and product design standardization. II, Chapter 5.
3/8	Supplier schedules. I, pp. 222–23, 260. II, pp. 145, 228.
3/10	Open-sided trucks. II, pp. 132–33.
3/13	Perimeter docks for the factory of the future. II, p. 133.
3/14	Focused factories-within-a-factory. I, Chapter 2.
3/17	Aisle systems. I, pp. 46–53.
3/19	Fail-safe process design. II, pp. 209–14.
3/21	Project planning charts. I, Chapter 9. II, pp. 56–58, 152–53, 250–53.
4/1	Supplier schedules. I, pp. 222–23, 260. II, pp. 145, 228.
4/3	Labor standards. I, pp. 80, 94–95, 137–38, 141. II, pp. 74–76, 268, 281–84.
4/4	Vendor program. I, pp. 257–65. II, Chapter 4.
4/5	Container design. I, pp. 73–79, 151–54.

Chapter/ *Footnote*	*Subject & Reinventing the Factory I or II reference*
5/4	Future accounting. II, Chapter 7.
5/5	Kanban and electronic kanban. I, pp. 165–66, 170, 177–78, 206–15, 221. II, pp. 6–7, 147–49.
5/11	Supplier schedules. I, pp. 222–23, 260. II, pp. 145, 228.
6/2	Supplier clusters. II, pp. 31–42.
6/3	Kanban and electronic kanban. I, pp. 165–66, 170, 177–78, 206–15, 221. II, pp. 6–7, 147–49.
6/4	Inventory adjustment. II, pp. 148–49.
6/5	Receiving docks. I, pp. 48–49, 163, 170. II, pp. 132–34, 139–40, 232–33.
6/6	Future accounting. II, Chapter 7.
6/9	Technical fog: The language of technicians. II, pp. 104–5.
6/10	Project organization and administration methodology. I, pp. 249–50.
7/1	Product design teams. II Chapter 5.
7/2	Focused factories-within-a-factory. I, Chapter 2.
7/5	Supplier clusters. II, pp. 31–42.
7/6	Plantwide master plan. I, Chapter 3.
7/7	"Kit" issues. I, pp. 172–77.
7/8	Kanban and electronic kanban. I, pp. 165–66, 170, 177–78, 206–15, 221. II, pp. 6–7, 147–49.
8/2	Roadblocks to progress. II, pp, xv–xviii, 89–92.
8/6	Cross-training. II, pp. 61–62, 71–73.

Bibliography

Books of Applicability to Logistics

Aburdene, Patricia, and John Naisbitt. *Reinventing the Corporation.* New York: Warner Books, 1985.

Ackerman, Kenneth B. *Practical Handbook of Warehousing.* New York: Van Nostrand Reinhold, 1990.

Anthony, William P. *Management: Competencies and Incompetencies.* Reading, MA: Addison-Wesley, 1981.

Atkinson, Philip E. *Creating Culture Change: The Key to Successful Quality Management.* San Diego, CA: Pfeiffer, 1990.

Austin, Nancy, and Tom Peters. *A Passion for Excellence.* New York: Random House, 1985.

Bakker, Marilyn, and David Eckroth, eds. *Wiley Encyclopedia of Packaging Technology.* New York: Wiley, 1986.

Barker, Joel Arthur. *Future Edge: Discovering the New Paradigms of Success.* New York: William Morrow, 1992.

Barry, John A. *Technobabble.* Cambridge, MA: MIT Press, 1991.

Batten, Joe D. *Tough-Minded Leadership.* New York: AMACOM, 1989.

Bernstein, Albert J., and Sydney Craft Rozen. *Dinosaur Brains: Dealing With All Those Impossible People at Work.* New York: Wiley, 1989.

———. *Neanderthals at Work: How People and Politics Can Drive You Crazy . . . and What You Can Do About Them.* New York: Wiley, 1992.

Berry, William Lee; Thomas E. Vollmann; and D. Clay Whybark. *Manufacturing Planning and Control Systems.* Homewood, IL: Business One Irwin, 1988.

Blanchard, Kenneth, and Spencer Johnson. *The One Minute Manager.* New York: William Morrow, 1982.

Bowersox, Donald J.; David J. Closs; and Omar K. Helferich. *Lo-*

341

gistical Management: A Systems Integration of Physical Distribution, Manufacturing Support, and Materials Procurement. New York: Macmillan, 1986.

Briggs, Andrew J. *Warehouse Operations Planning and Management.* Malabar, Florida: Krieger, 1979.

Brown, Robert Goodell. *Advanced Service Parts Inventory Control.* Norwich, VT: RGB Materials Management Systems, Inc., 1982.

Brown, Stephen W.; Bo Edvardsson; Evert Gummesson; and Bengt-Ove Gustavsson, eds. *Service Quality: Multidisciplinary and Multinational Perspectives.* Lexington, MA: Lexington Books, 1991.

Burton, J. A. *Effective Warehousing.* London: Pitman, 1981.

Byham, William C., with Jeff Cox. *Zapp! The Lightning of Empowerment.* New York: Harmony Books, 1988.

Cahill, Gerry. *Logistics in Manufacturing.* Homewood, IL: Business One Irwin, 1992.

Cameron, Kim S., and David A. Whitten. *Developing Mangement Skills:* Second ed. New York: Harper Collins, 1991.

Castleberry, Guy A. *The AGV Handbook: A Handbook for the Selection of Automated Guided Vehicle Systems.* Ann Arbor: MI: Braun-Brumfield, 1991.

Chambers, J. C.; S. K. Mullick; and D. D. Smith. *An Executive's Guide to Forecasting.* New York: Wiley, 1974.

Charney, Cyril. *Time to Market: Reducing Product Lead Time.* Dearborn, MI: Society of Manufacturing Engineers, 1991.

Claunch, Jerry W.; Michael W. Gozzo; and Peter L. Grieco, Jr. *Just-in-Time Purchasing: In Pursuit of Excellence.* Plantsville, CT: PT Publications, 1988.

Copacino, William C.; John F. Magee; and Donald B. Rosenfield. *Modern Logistics Management: Integrating Marketing, Manufacturing, and Physical Distribution.* New York: John Wiley & Sons, 1985.

Davidson, Sidney, and Roman Weil, eds. *Handbook of Modern Accounting.* Third ed. Englewood Cliffs, NJ: Prentice Hall, 1983.

Devanna, Mary Anne, and Noel M. Tichy. *The Transformational Leader.* New York: Wiley, 1986.

Dolan, Patrick W., and Steve M. Samek, eds. *The Technology Maze in Wholesale Distribution.* Washington, DC: Distribution Research & Education Foundation, 1990.

Drucker, Peter F. *The Effective Executive.* New York: Harper & Row, 1966.

——. *The Frontiers of Management: Where Tomorrow's Decisions Are Being Shaped Today.* New York: Harper & Row, 1986.

————. *Managing for the Future: The 1990s and Beyond.* New York: Truman Talley/Dutton, 1992.

Duncan, W. Jack. *Great Ideas in Management.* San Francisco: Jossey-Bass, 1990.

Faerman, Sue R.; Michael R. McGrath; Michael P. Thompson; and Robert E. Quinn. *Becoming a Master Manager: A Competency Framework.* New York: Wiley, 1990.

Fournier, Robert, and Lorne C. Plunkett. *Participative Management: Implementing Empowerment.* New York: Wiley, 1991.

Frey, Stephen L. *Warehouse Operations: A Handbook.* Chesterland, OH: Weber Systems, 1990.

Friedman, Walter F., and Jerome J. Kipnees. *Distribution Packaging.* Malabar, FL: Krieger, 1977.

Fuchs, Jerome H. *The Prentice Hall Illustrated Handbook of Advanced Manufacturing Methods.* Englewood Cliffs, NJ: Prentice Hall, 1988.

Gardner, John W. *On Leadership.* New York: Free Press, 1990.

Gelders, L. F., and Hollier, R. H., eds. *Automation in Warehousing: Proceedings of the 9th International Conference.* New York: Springer-Verlag, 1988.

Glass, Harold E., ed. *Handbook of Business Strategy.* Boston: Warren, Gorham & Lamont, 1991.

————. *Handbook of Business Strategy: 1991–1992 Yearbook.* Boston: Warren, Gorham & Lamont, 1991.

Harmon, Roy L. *Effective Cycle Counting: A Foundation for Profitable Inventory Management.* Chicago: Andersen Consulting, Arthur Andersen & Co., 1980.

————. *Inventory Record Accuracy.* Chicago: Andersen Consulting, Arthur Andersen & Co., 1980.

Harmon, Roy L. with Foreword by Leroy D. Peterson. *Reinventing the Factory II: Managing the World Class Factory.* New York: Free Press, 1992.

Harmon, Roy L., and Leroy D. Peterson. *Reinventing the Factory: Productivity Breakthroughs in Manufacturing Today.* New York: Free Press, 1990.

————. *Une Usine Pour Gagner: Techniques Pratiques D'Organisation Industrielle.* Paris: InterEditions, 1991.

————. *Reinventar la Fabrica: Como Introducir Mejoras Sensibles en la Produccion Industrial.* Madrid: Ciencias de la Direccion, 1990.

————. *Reinventando a Fabrica: Conceitos Modernas de Produtividade Aplicadas na Pratica.* Rio de Janeiro: Editora Campus, 1991.

————. *Die Neue Fabrik: Einfacher, Flexibler, Produktiver-Hundert*

Faelle Erfolgreicher Veraenderung. Frankfurt: Campus Verlag, 1990.

———. *Reinventare La Fabrica.* Milan: ISEDI, 1991.

Hickman, Craig R. *Mind of a Manager: Soul of a Leader.* New York: Wiley, 1990.

Hickman, Thomas K., and William M. Hickman, Jr. *Global Purchasing: How to Buy Goods and Services in Foreign Markets.* Homewood, IL: Business One Irwin, 1992.

Hout, Thomas M., and George Stalk, Jr. *Competing Against Time: How Time-Based Competition Is Reshaping Global Markets.* New York: Free Press, 1990.

Iacocca, Lee, with William Novak. *Iacocca: An Autobiography.* New York: Bantam, 1984.

Jones, James V. *Integrated Logistics Support Handbook.* New York: McGraw-Hill, 1987.

Kissler, Gary D. *The Change Riders: Managing the Power of Change.* Reading, MA: Addison-Wesley, 1991.

Koontz, Harold, and Heinz Weihrich. *Essentials of Management.* New York: McGraw-Hill, 1990.

Kotter, John P. *A Force for Change: How Leadership Differs from Management.* New York: Free Press, 1990.

———. *The Leadership Factor.* New York, Free Press, 1988.

Levitt, Theodore. *Thinking About Management.* New York: Free Press, 1991.

Lupis, James R. *The Handbook of Warehouse and Distribution Forms and Reports.* Englewood Cliffs, NJ: Prentice Hall, 1991.

Martin, Andre J. *DRP Distribution Resource Planning: Management's Most Powerful Tool.* Essex Junciton, VT: Oliver Wight, 1990.

McKinnon, Alan C. *Physical Distribution Systems.* London: Routledge, 1989.

Mintzberg, Henry. *Mintzberg on Management: Inside the Strange World of Organizations.* New York: Free Press, 1989.

———. *The Nature of Managerial Work.* New York: Prentice-Hall, 1980.

Moffett, Carol G., and Rebecca Strydesky. *The Receiving-Checking-Marking-Stocking Clerk.* Second ed. New York: McGraw-Hill, 1980.

Naisbitt, J. *Megatrends: Ten New Directions Transforming Our Lives.* New York: Warner Books, 1984.

Nelson, Raymond A. *Computerizing Warehouse Operations.* Englewood Cliffs, NJ: Prentice Hall, 1985.

O'Guin, Michael. *The Complete Guide to Activity Based Costing.* Englewood Cliffs, NJ: Prentice Hall, 1991.

Peter, L. J., and R. Hall. *The Peter Principle.* New York: William Morrow, 1977.

Peters, Thomas J., and Robert H. Waterman, *In Search of Excellence: Lessons from America's Best Run Companies.* New York: Warner Books, 1984.

Robeson, James F., ed., and Robert G. House, associate ed. *The Distribution Handbook.* New York: Free Press, 1985.

Schor, Juliet B. *The Overworked American: The Unexpected Decline of Leisure.* New York: Basic Books, 1991.

Sims, E. Ralph, Jr. *Planning and Managing Industrial Logistics Systems.* Amsterdam: Elsevier, 1992.

Smith, Bernard T. *Focus Forecasting and DRP: Logistics Tools of the 21st Century.* New York: Vantage Press, 1991.

Smith, Jerry D., and James A. Tompkins. *How to Plan and Manage Warehouse Operations.* Watertown, MA: American Management Association, 1982.

————, eds. *The Warehouse Management Handbook.* New York: McGraw-Hill, 1988.

Tompkins, James A., and Jerry D. Smith. *How to Plan and Manage Warehouse Operations.* Watertown, MA: American Management Association, 1984.

Tompkins, J. A., and J. D. Smith. *The Warehouse Management Handbook.* New York: McGraw-Hill, 1988.

The World Competitiveness Report 1991. Lausanne, Switzerland: IMD, June 1991.

Zaleznik, Abraham. *The Managerial Mystique: Restoring Leadership in Business.* New York: Harper & Row, 1989.

Other Manufacturing and Engineering Books

Allen, C. Wesley, ed. *Simultaneous Engineering: Integrating Manufacturing and Design.* Dearborn, MI: Society of Manufacturing Engineers, 1990.

Avallone, Eugene A., and Theodore Baumeister, eds. *Mark's Standard Handbook for Mechanical Engineers.* Ninth ed. New York: McGraw-Hill, 1991.

Brimson, James A. *Activity Accounting: An Activity Based Costing Approach.* New York, John Wiley, 1991.

Gillespie, LaRoux K., ed. *Troubleshooting Manufacturing Processes.* Dearborn, MI: Society of Manufacturing Engineers, 1988.

Guaspari, John. *Theory Why: In Which the Boss Solves the Riddle of*

Quality. New York: American Management Association, 1986.
———. *I Know When I See It: A Modern Fable About Quality*. New York: American Management Association, 1985.

Gunn, Thomas G. *21st Century Manufacturing: Creating Winning Business Performance*. New York: Harper Business, 1992.

Horovitz, Jacques. *Winning Ways: Achieving Zero Defect Service*. Cambridge, MA: Productivity Press, 1990.

Hunt, V. Daniel. *Quality in America: How to Implement a Competitive Quality Program*. Homewood, IL: Business One Irwin, 1992.

Maskell, Brian H. *Performance Measurement for World Class Manufacturing: A Model for American Companies*. Cambridge, MA: Productivity Press, 1991.

Petro, Louis W., and Raymond F. Veilleux. eds. *Manufacturing Management: Volume 5 of Tool and Manufacturing Engineers Handbook*. Dearborn, MI: Society of Manufacturing Engineers, 1988.

Robertson, Gordon H. *Quality Through Statistical Thinking: Improving Process Control and Capability*. Dearborn, MI: ASI Press, 1989.

Winchell, William. *Continuous Quality Improvement: A Manufacturing Professional's Guide*. Dearborn, MI: Society of Manufacturing Engineers, 1991.

Articles

Barber, Norman F. "EDI: Making It Finally Happen." *P & IM Review*, June 1991, pp. 35–40, 49.

Copacino, William C. "Promoting the Logistics Function." *Traffic Management*, October 1989, pp. 35–36.

———. "Tackling Unproductive Inventories." *Traffic Management*, November 1989, pp. 35–36.

———. "Managing the Pipeline." *Traffic Management*, December 1989, pp. 31–32.

———. "Transactions vs. Relationships." *Traffic Management*, January 1990, p. 57.

———. "The Software Solution." *Traffic Management*, February 1990, p. 73.

———. "Measuring Logistics Performance." *Traffic Management*, April 1990, p. 59.

———. "Information and Logistics." *Traffic Management*, May 1990, p. 83.

———. "Do You Need a Quick Response?" *Traffic Management*, June 1990, p. 65.

———. "The Battle's Not Over Yet." *Traffic Management,* July 1990, p. 27.

———. "Future Directions in Logistics." *Traffic Management,* August 1990, p. 63.

———. "Should You Switch to Cross-dock?" *Traffic Management,* September 1990, p. 73.

———. "Purchasing Strategies for the '90s." *Traffic Management,* October 1990, p. 67.

———. "Matching Logistics to Customer Needs." *Distribution,* September 1990, p. 120.

———. "Carrier Selection in the '90s." *Traffic Management,* January 1991, p. 47.

———. "Delivering More for Less." *Traffic Management,* February 1991, p. 65.

———. "How's Your Inventory Performance?" *Traffic Management,* April 1991, p. 57–58.

———. "Re-engineering Logistics." *Traffic Management,* May 1991, p. 75.

———. "Building a Trade Franchise." *Traffic Management,* July 1991, p. 49.

Gonzalez, Jose Luis. "Gerenciando la Logistica." *El Universal,* October 2, 1990, p. 1.

———. "La Logistica de la Gerencia." *El Universal,* June 8, 1981, p. 1.

———. "Integrar Logistica y Ganar Ventajas." *El Universal,* June 22, 1991, p. 1.

———. "Beneficios de la Integracion Logistica." *El Universal,* July 6, 1991, p. 1.

———. "La Reingenieria de la Logistica." *El Universal,* January 18, 1992, p. 1.

Hall, Jim. "The Warehouse of the Future Is Still a Warehouse." *Industrial Engineering,* January 1992.

Harmon, Roy L. "Breakthroughs in Manufacturing Today." *APMS '90: International Conference on Advances in Production Management Systems Proceedings.* (International Federation for Information Processing, Helsinki), August 20–22, 1990, pp. 1–12.

———. "Tecnicas Modernas de Fabricacion." *Gestion de Calidad y Productividad como Estrategia de Desarroll: Memorias* (Republica de Columbia, Departamento Nacional de planeacion Seminario Internacional, Cartagena, Columbia), pp. 111–16.

———. "La Productividad: Tendencias Mundiales." *Gestion de Calidad y Productividad como Estradegia de Desarroll: Memorias* (Republica de Columbia, Departamento Nacional de Planeacion Seminario Internacional, Caregena, Columbia), pp. 171–83.

Harmon, Roy L., and Leroy D. Peterson. "Reinventing the Factory." *Across the Board*, March 1990, pp. 30–36.

———. "Focusing the Factory." *Robotics World*, January–February 1990, p. 2.

———. "La Fabrica Reinventada." *Oficina Eficeinte* (Cali, Columbia), October–November 1990, pp. 36–45.

Herman, William R. "Cost Effective CIM: Simplify & Automate." *Industrial Computing*, November–December 1990, pp. 50–51.

Mackey, Michael. "Achieving Inventory Reduction Through the Use of Partner-Shipping." *Industrial Engineering*, May 1992, pp. 36–37.

McClimans, Gary H. "Reinvent Your Company to Stay Competitive." *Cincinnati Business Courier*, February 4–10, 1991.

Monaghan, Michael J., and Robert W. Fouts. "Job Shop to Focused Factories: A Case Study in Productivity Improvement for the Electronics Industry." *Total Manufacturing Performance Seminar Proceedings*, American Production & Inventory Control Society, 1991, pp. 45–47.

Remmel, Ulf M. "Integration of Marketing and Logistics: A Way to Competitive Advantage in South Africa." *International Journal of Physical Distribution & Logistics Management*, 21 no. 5 (1991): 27–31.

Index